The GYMNASIUM of VIRTUE

STUDIES IN THE HISTORY OF

GREECE AND ROME

P. J. Rhodes & Richard J. A. Talbert, editors

The
GYMNASIUM
of
VIRTUE

Education & Culture in Ancient Sparta

NIGEL M. KENNELL

THE UNIVERSITY OF NORTH CAROLINA PRESS

Chapel Hill & London

The paper in this book meets the guidelines
for permanence and durability of the Committee
on Production Guidelines for Book Longevity of
the Council on Library Resources.

Excerpt from *English Music* by Peter Ackroyd,
copyright © 1992 Peter Ackroyd.
Used by permission of the author.

Library of Congress Cataloging-in-Publication Data
Kennell, Nigel M.
The gymnasium of virtue : education and culture in
ancient Sparta / Nigel M. Kennell.
    p. cm. — (Studies in the history of Greece and Rome)
Includes bibliographical references and index.
ISBN 0-8078-2219-1 (alk. paper)
    1. Education, Greek. 2. Education — Greece — Sparta
(Extinct city) I. Title. II. Series.
LA75.K46 1995
370'.938 — dc20   94-45772
                    CIP

99 98 97 96 95   5 4 3 2 1

TO MY PARENTS

CONTENTS

Preface, xi

Introduction, 3

Chapter 1.

In the Track of the Famous *Agōgē*, 5

Chapter 2.

Training Up the Youth, 28

Chapter 3.

The Contests of the Later *Agōgē*, 49

Chapter 4.

The Lycurgan Customs, 70

Chapter 5.

The Inventor of the *Agōgē*, 98

Chapter 6.

From Artemis to the Dioscuri, 115

Conclusion, 143

Appendix 1. *Testimonia on the Whipping Contest*, 149

Appendix 2. *The Status of Amyclae*, 162

Notes, 171

Bibliography, 219

Index, 235

TABLES AND PLATES

TABLES

1. Age Grades of the Later *Agōgē*, 39
2. The Roman *Agōgē*, 41

PLATES

1. Sickle dedication, 30
2. General view of the Orthia sanctuary from the east, 50
3. Foundations of the seating complex at the Orthia sanctuary, 51
4. Roman ruins northwest of the acropolis, 58
5. Theater below the acropolis, 59
6. Foundations of the Roman altar at the Orthia sanctuary, 72
7. Base for a statue of an altar-victor, 78
8. Archaizing sickle dedication, 88
9. Sickle dedication of Arexippus, 127
10. Theocles' *stēlē*, 140

PREFACE

In 1975 I saw the acropolis of Sparta for the first time, under the peerless guidance of Colin Edmonson. Three years afterward, it was my great good fortune to join the students under his aegis as a regular member of the American School of Classical Studies at Athens. Colin's knowledge and love of Greece, at all periods of its history, made as great an impression on me as it did on the other students at Athens in 1978/79. Many years later, this work now joins the growing shelf of books that trace their ultimate origins to his inspiration. I hope he would have found something of value here.

I began the manuscript for this book in the pleasant surroundings of the American School of Classical Studies at Athens and finished it at the Institute for Advanced Study in Princeton, whose research facilities and climate of scholarly fellowship are without equal. I would like to thank the staff of both institutions for making my work so much easier. Also, I thank Glen Bowersock, Bruce Frier, Christopher Jones, Sara Aleshire, and Brad Inwood, who all read portions of the manuscript, for greatly improving my argument. Paul Cartledge also read what has become Appendix 2, and I thank him for his very constructive criticisms, even though he may be surprised to see the material appearing in this form. Of course, any remaining errors or omissions are to be counted dead against me.

I gratefully acknowledge the permissions granted by the Antikensammlung, Staatliche Museen zu Berlin — Preussischer Kulturbesitz and the Ephorate of Antiquities for Laconia and Arcadia to publish photographs of material in their collections. In addition, I thank Peter Ackroyd for allowing me to use his version of a passage from Sir Thomas Browne's *Christian Morals* as the epigraph for this book.

Finally, thanks beyond words go to my wife, Stefanie, whose unflagging scrutiny of the manuscript as it haltingly developed has improved it beyond measure. *Corona meae vitae es.*

The GYMNASIUM *of* VIRTUE

To palliate the shortness of our lives, and to compensate

our brief term in this world, it is fit to have such an under-

standing of times past that we may be considered to have

dwelled in the same. In such a manner, answering the present

with the past, we may live from the beginning and in a

certain sense be as old as our country itself.

—Peter Ackroyd, *English Music*

INTRODUCTION

Magnum est alumnum virtutis nasci et Laconem.
—Sen. *Suas.* 2.3

From antiquity to the present day, the city of Sparta has been variously the model of discipline, obedience, and virtue, or of totalitarianism, conformity, and tyranny. The words "laconic" and "spartan" in English perpetuate the popular conception of ancient Sparta. Greek and Roman authors, followed by the classicists and ancient historians of today, invariably consider Sparta at the apogee of its power and prestige (ca. 550–370 B.C.) unique among Greek cities for the way the state controlled virtually every aspect of a citizen's life from cradle to grave. For modern as well as ancient observers, the government-run educational system was a cornerstone of the distinctive Spartan way of life.

Education has always been central to the long-lived image of the ancient Spartans as a people utterly atypical among Greeks, singular in their bravery and obedience to the rule of law, who were continually "training up the youth for war," in Milton's fitting words. Although attitudes to Spartan education ever since the fifth century B.C. have run the gamut from unalloyed admiration to visceral disgust, students of Classical Sparta have on the whole seen the way in which youths were brought up as a primitive relic of earlier times, characterized by practices other Greek city-states had long since abandoned but which survived in Sparta's rigidly conservative environment. The extant sources appear to bear this out, ostensibly describing a complicated system of grades for boys spanning the years from childhood to early adulthood, during which they were inculcated with the Spartan virtues of aggression and blind obedience in a number of violent contests, with the arts given short shrift except at times of festival.

Despite its prominence, Spartan education has never been the subject of an in-depth, book-length examination that marshals and evaluates the evidence—epigraphical, literary, and archaeological—in the proper historical and cultural contexts. This lack is particularly unfortunate, because much of what has come to be regarded as fact about the early development of Sparta (ca. 700–500 B.C.) is derived from pieces of evidence that, although dating from the late Hellenistic and Roman periods—over 500 years later than the institutions they are cited for—are held to be survivals. As the great bulk of these survivals is found in inscriptions or literary passages concerned with the educational system, the question of their validity as witnesses to earlier practice has implications reaching to every aspect of Spartan historiography.

In this book I take a path lying between that of K. M. T. Chrimes, who in *Ancient Sparta: A Re-examination of the Evidence* claimed for Roman Sparta an impossibly high degree of institutional continuity with the Classical city, and the one trodden by the authors of the recent *Hellenistic and Roman Sparta: A Tale of Two Cities*, whose title reflects the emphasis they place on historical discontinuity. Although Sparta under the Romans had certainly undergone massive transformations after the Classical period, by the same token it can in no way be described as a different city. I see, rather, a continuum of change, marked by periodic breaks and attempts to reforge links with the past, a process that can most easily be documented through the city's most famous public institution.

To understand how Spartan education was altered over time, we must be acutely aware of the nature of our evidence. Failure to take the historical and cultural contexts of the sources into account when reconstructing Spartan education has resulted in our present picture, a hodgepodge of elements wrenched out of their disparate environments and crudely cemented together to form an unharmonious, and often quite inconsistent, whole.

In tackling this problem, I have adopted a quasi-archaeological method. As excavators strip away later accretions to discover how a building or site developed, so this book begins with the latest, best-attested period in the history of Spartan education and then delves down through the strata of sources. This stratigraphic approach was chosen for two reasons: first, to obtain greater chronological accuracy in the grouping of sources and, second, to distinguish genuine tradition from specious continuity. The practical consequence for readers is that they will encounter the material in an order the reverse of usual.

Beyond the primary purpose of presenting what I believe is a more accurate representation of Spartan traditional education, I hope this book will move ancient historians and philologists to consider at least the possibility that the ancients were just as likely to reshape their own histories in light of their present circumstances as modern societies, and that this phenomenon may be much more widespread than has hitherto been acknowledged.

1

IN THE TRACK OF THE FAMOUS *AGŌGĒ*

At any time from the first to the third century of our era, visitors to the city of Sparta saw a prosperous provincial city of the Roman Empire, decked out with all the facilities thought necessary for civilized life — gymnasia, baths, shopping arcades, theaters, and a good range of public sculpture. A cultured tourist would not have been disappointed in his search for visible signs of Sparta's ancient heritage, first and foremost, in the renowned educational system known as the "rearing" (*agōgē*). Since the days of Spartan greatness in the fifth century B.C., the city's educational system had lain at the heart of the Spartan ideal. In the eyes of writers such as Xenophon, Plato, and their many successors over the centuries — philosophers, sophists, historians, and biographers — the *agōgē*'s harsh discipline transformed boys into soldiers who were the embodiments of courage, virtue, and obedience. Although Spartan military might had long been a matter for history books by the Roman period, as a paradigm the *agōgē* still exerted a considerable attraction in intellectual circles. None who traveled to Sparta could have failed to take in some, at least, of the sights associated with the *agōgē*. We have an instance of this in the author of the earliest extant guide book, Pausanias, who toured Greece in the middle years of the second century A.D., leaving us a priceless snapshot of the city during the last tranquil years of the Antonine age.[1] Often in his itineraries through Spartan streets, squares, and parks he notes monuments and buildings associated with the *agōgē*.[2] But the *agōgē* was not a lifeless relic of purely historical interest — it lived on.

In fact, it flourished in the fevered air of Greek city life under the Romans. Over the years, the *agōgē* had developed into an elaborate and highly successful expression of the distinct society that Spartans claimed they were. Royals and celebrities lent their support either by enrolling their sons or with large benefactions, for which they were rewarded with honorary offices in the *agōgē*'s administration. Visitors who flocked to the festivals of Spartan youth could watch the ancient dances of the Gymnopaediae performed in front of the newly restored Persian Stoa or, in the city's magnificent theater, could enjoy competitions between young ballplayers in the game Sparta claimed as its own invention.[3]

The best place, however, to experience the *agōgē*'s uniqueness and antiquity was on the grounds of the temple of Artemis Orthia, situated in a reedy hollow between the easternmost hill of the acropolis and the river Eurotas. Here was all the proof an antiquarian traveler needed that the contemporary Spartans had preserved their customs unsullied by change since the days of their legendary lawgiver Lycurgus. Here young Spartans vied with one another in competitions whose very names bore witness to their centuries-old origin.[4] The so-called contest of endurance, the renowned ritual flagellation beside Artemis' altar, even more strikingly attested to the contemporary *agōgē*'s links with the distant, uncivilized past. Moreover, all around were erected tangible manifestations of its remarkable survival in the form of dedications by victors of iron sickles mounted on stone slabs, many of which were inscribed in the ancient Laconian dialect. Faced with this profusion of material evidence, any traveler would naturally have agreed with Cicero, himself a visitor to Sparta, who described the Spartans as "the only people in the whole world who have lived now for more than seven hundred years with one and the same set of customs and unchanging laws."[5]

Today few researchers would openly endorse such a view, but it remains implicit in every modern study of the *agōgē*. For, in order to reconstruct the workings of this intriguing institution, scholars have used evidence from sources as disparate in genre and date as Xenophon's *Constitution of the Lacedaemonians*, written in the early fourth century B.C., and victory dedications from the third century A.D. The pictures of the *agōgē* that result from such a synchronic approach to the evidence are valid only if we assume, as Cicero did, that absolutely no change occurred for over half a millennium. This notion is prima facie absurd and demonstrably false. On the other hand, by recognizing that historical events had an effect on the *agōgē*, as will be shown in this chapter, the evidence can be induced to reveal a much more accurate account of its development than has hitherto been possible. Such a diachronic approach brings some losses in its wake, especially in what is now believed to have been the *agōgē* of Classical Sparta. However, in compensation, the later *agōgē* can more readily be placed in its social and cultural context.

For those ancient tourists, dazzled by its monuments and rituals, it may have seemed possible to trace the *agōgē*'s existence back along an unbroken line into the dawn of history, but for us the line must break abruptly in the second century B.C. With Roman victory in a war fought against the powerful federation of cities known as the Achaean League, ostensibly for Spartan interests, and the establishment of Roman hegemony over Greece, Sparta after 146 B.C. entered a period of relative tranquillity as a so-called free city (*civitas libera*).[6] The peace was undoubtedly welcome, for the city had just endured its most internally troubled period since the days of Lycurgus, who, according to legend, had put an end to civil strife in the ninth or eighth century by establishing the governmental and social institutions for which the city was later so admired.[7] Several decades of revolutionary reform and reaction in the third century had been followed, in the second, by forced incorporation into the Achaean League. As membership in the league was to have a devastating impact on the *agōgē*, the circumstances and chronology of this period will repay study.[8]

Sparta became a member of the Achaean League in the confusion following the assassination of the Spartan leader Nabis in 192 B.C. Nabis was the last in a series of reformers and revolutionaries who had tried to revive Sparta's faded fortunes by various radical means such as redistributing land, strengthening the city's army, and increasing the citizen body by the full enfranchisement of public agricultural slaves (*heilōtai*), noncitizen residents of Laconia (*perioikoi*), and foreigners.[9] Needless to say, these policies and Nabis' aggressive expansionism greatly disturbed the propertied classes of neighboring states, who had the ear of the Romans. In 195 the Romans defeated Nabis and subsequently stripped Argos and, more dramatically, the coastal cities of Laconia from Spartan control, placing the latter under the protection of the Achaeans.[10] This severe loss, which the city was never able to make good, precipitated Nabis' death and Sparta's entry into the Achaean League.

In 193 Nabis attempted to snatch back Gytheum, the most important of these cities. After some initial success, he was bested by the formidable Achaean general Philopoemen, and a Roman-brokered truce reestablishing the terms of 195 soon followed.[11] By showing yet again his willingness to come to terms with the Romans, Nabis' usefulness to the Aetolians in the anti-Roman coalition they were building was now at an end. On the pretext of offering military aid, an Aetolian force came to Sparta and murdered Nabis as he was holding joint maneuvers outside the city.[12]

In the anarchy that followed, Philopoemen seized his opportunity and advanced into the city. Through a combination of persuasion and compulsion, he induced the leading men (probably the members of the Gerousia, Sparta's supreme legislative body) to accept membership in the league.[13] Entering states normally signed a treaty of accession, which was later inscribed on a *stēlē* for public display. Although no such document has survived at Sparta, there is no reason to suppose that, at this time, Sparta's situation was at all unique. It did enter with all its laws intact, including those of Nabis, but member states generally were allowed a great deal of internal autonomy.[14] Even so, many Spartans mindful of the great days past must have thought that the city's fortunes had reached their nadir. They would have been mistaken.

Sparta was far from docile as an Achaean city. Almost immediately, factional strife broke out between supporters and opponents of the Achaeans. In 189, after a series of coups and countercoups, an anti-Achaean party became dominant. Still irked by the loss of their coastal towns, the Spartans could not tolerate the occupation of one of them, Las, by pro-Achaean exiles. When the Achaeans learned of the Spartan attack, they immediately voted to regard it as a violation of the treaty of 195, by which Nabis had undertaken not to interfere in any of the cities formerly under his power. Both sides, as was now the practice, dispatched embassies to plead their cases before the Senate at Rome, which declined to intervene in what it saw as a purely internal affair of the Achaean League.[15] Philopoemen, justifiably regarding this as a carte blanche, marched into Spartan territory in 188 and, after encamping at Compasium, demanded that the Spartans surrender the anti-Achaean leaders in return for a pledge to spare the city and to give his prisoners a fair trial. The depth of his sincerity became apparent when seventeen of the prisoners were killed in a melee upon their arrival, while the remainder were executed the next day after a perfunctory trial.[16]

Philopoemen then took his revenge on Sparta, since, as Polybius put it, "it was expedient for him to reduce the city of the Lacedaemonians."[17] He ordered the fortifications demolished, mercenaries and helots in the citizen body exiled, and the current set of exiles restored.[18] Most significantly, Philopoemen was responsible for a radical alteration of the Spartan constitution along Achaean lines. As might be expected, the ancient sources emphasize the demise of Sparta's most famous institution. Livy writes that Philopoemen commanded the Spartans to abrogate the laws and customs of Lycurgus and to become accustomed to Achaean laws and institutions; in a summary, he states that none of Philopoemen's actions caused as much hardship to the Spartans as the removal of the Lycurgan discipline.[19] For his part, Pausanias simply says that Philopoemen destroyed the walls of Sparta and forbade the Spartan youth to exercise according to the laws of Lycurgus but ordered them to follow the example of the Achaeans.[20] Two inscriptions from the years after 188 confirm that the constitution did not survive unscathed. No traditional Spartan offices appear in them; instead, we have offices common in cities of the Achaean League.[21] Most would now accept that all Sparta's laws and institutions, not just the *agōgē*, were overturned and replaced by others of a type more common in Hellenistic Greece.[22] Nevertheless, it can be argued on the basis of the traces Philopoemen's settlement left in the later constitution that he did not simply wipe the slate clean, but rather adjusted preexisting Spartan institutions, except for the *agōgē*, to conform to an Achaean model.[23] Such an adjustment, with the addition of a few Achaean offices, is much more plausible than the wholesale elimination of Spartan organs of government and their replacement with alien ones. Understandably, ancient writers might have been unsure of the extent of Philopoemen's constitutional revision, but they would have been certain of one thing—the Spartan *agōgē*, in which Spartans had been trained to excel in military virtue for so many centuries, was no more. For it is inconceivable that anyone in Philopoemen's position would have tolerated the continued existence of such a threat to his new order.

It is clear that the Spartans lived without their *agōgē*, under an Achaean constitution, for a considerable length of time, in spite of the modern consensus that the traditional constitution had been restored by 183–178 B.C., after a short hiatus lasting five to ten years.[24] The complex argu-

ments for one date or another ultimately depend on Livy's description of
Sparta at the time of the victorious Roman general Aemilius Paullus' visit
in 168 as "memorable not for the magnificence of its buildings, but for its
discipline and institutions."[25] From these words it is assumed that Sparta
was once again living under the old constitution, but Livy's stock phrase,
as has been recognized, cannot bear so much weight.[26] Since nothing else
remains to indicate the existence of the old constitution at the time of
Paullus' visit, the arguments for dating its reintroduction to 183–178 fail
as a consequence.

The testimony of Plutarch and Pausanias on the circumstances of the
constitution's readoption provides material for further objections to these
dates. Plutarch relates that in later times, after obtaining permission from
the Romans, the Spartans replaced the Achaean constitution with their
ancestral one, as far as was practical after their misfortunes and so much
degeneration.[27] Pausanias baldly states that the Romans later gave back
to the Spartans their ancestral constitution.[28] One thing is obvious: the
Romans were instrumental in restoring the ancestral constitution. The
Roman commission of 184/3 that attempted to reconcile the Achaeans
and the many Spartan factions did not touch upon this thorny constitutional question.[29] The subsequent agreement called for exiles to return to
Sparta and the city walls to be rebuilt, but Sparta was to remain under
league control, with the league having jurisdiction over all Spartan law
cases except those involving capital charges.[30] There was no question of
restoring the Spartan constitution. Even more significantly, the agreement
quickly became a dead letter as the Romans disavowed any interest in
Spartan affairs, and the Achaeans were confident enough to readmit the
city as a full member on their own terms.[31] In 179, when the Achaean
general Callicrates restored the final group of Spartan exiles, the Romans
went no further than encouraging the Achaeans to take this step.[32] Thus,
the extent of Roman involvement in the disputes of this period lends no
support to the supposition that the Romans were involved in anything so
drastic as the reinstatement of Sparta's traditional laws.[33]

Rome did take drastic action later in the century when it went to war in
146 with the Achaean League, nominally to protect Sparta's right to se-
cede.[34] After their victory, the Romans awarded Sparta reparations from
the Achaeans and gave it the status of *civitas libera*.[35] Now, when the
Romans were well disposed and the Achaeans in no position to object, the
time would have been ripe for the Spartans to seek permission to revive
the laws of Lycurgus. Roman belief in kinship with the Spartans and the

perceived similarity between the Spartan and Roman constitutions can only have worked to the Spartans' advantage.[36] Moreover, the *agōgē's* restoration may have provided an impetus for Jonathan, high priest of the Maccabees, to send his famous letter of friendship to the Spartans, usually dated to about 143 B.C.[37]

For over a generation Spartans lived under Achaean laws and an Achaean educational system. Not surprisingly, Achaean elements turn up in the later Spartan constitution, and we should also expect the revived *agōgē* to be somewhat different from the *agōgē* as it was before 188.[38]

This forty-two year interruption was not the only discontinuity in the *agōgē's* history; the *agōgē* Philopoemen abolished was itself the result of a revival. This revival took place during the reign of Cleomenes III (235–222 B.C.), the revolutionary king who put the Stoic philosopher Sphaerus of Borysthenes in charge of restoring the *agōgē* and the common messes.[39] Cleomenes styled his reforms as a return to the ways of Lycurgus, though many of his changes, such as the abolition of Sparta's unique dyarchy and the expansion of the citizen body to include perioeci, were radical departures from established precedent.[40] He abolished the ephorate (Sparta's ruling committee) on the flimsy pretext that it was post-Lycurgan and therefore illegitimate; he severely limited the Gerousia's power by reducing tenure from life to a single year and by creating an official called the *patronomos* (guardian of tradition).[41]

Whatever the truth in Cleomenes' claims to be returning Sparta to the Lycurgan way of life, the *agōgē* would clearly have been the centerpiece of his efforts. Accordingly, it is no surprise to find Artemis Orthia, patron deity of the *agōgē*, appearing on a series of tetradrachms minted in Cleomenes' reign, and it has been plausibly suggested that Orthia's temple was reconstructed then as another part of the "Lycurgan" revival.[42] Sphaerus' role was of some importance, then, and he was indeed the man for the job. Apart from being Cleomenes' former philosophy tutor, he shared in the widespread fascination with things Spartan, writing two books on the subject.[43] Only the titles have come down to us, a *Laconian Constitution* and *About Lycurgus and Socrates*, although a fragment of his historical work does exist, appropriately concerned with a custom in the Spartan common messes (*phiditia*). As a veritable new Lycurgus, Sphaerus had the opportunity to mold the *agōgē* in a number of ways, provided that he remained true to the spirit of the original. He would have needed to select "appropriate" traditions and reject others, guided by his philosophical and historical acumen. Although the result would not have been a complete fabrication, neither could anyone, except Cleomenes, claim that it was utterly the same as its original.[44] The full extent to which Sphaerus set his seal on the *agōgē* is an issue of the utmost importance, but its resolution is quite impossible in the present state of the evidence. I will later suggest, however, some changes that may be attributed to him.

The *agōgē* must have been restored at some time between 227, when Cleomenes launched his reforms with a coup d'etat against the ephors, and 225, when Plutarch says the Spartans had already won hegemony in the Peloponnese, "although they had only recently taken up the ancestral customs and had stepped into the track of the famous *agōgē*."[45] Cleomenes' ascendancy did not last long; in 222 he was defeated at the Battle of Sellasia by the Macedonian king Antigonus Doson and went into exile.[46] Doson occupied Sparta, reversed Cleomenes' more extreme measures and left after a few days. The *agōgē*, common messes, and other aspects of what have been called Cleomenes' social reforms were allowed to remain in place, albeit with some changes, while Doson evidently ensured that the pre-Cleomenean organs of government, with the notable exception of the kingship, were restored — the ephorate in particular — to their full vigor.[47] Thus, if we take 226 as the first year of operation, the revived *agōgē* had been functioning for thirty-nine years when Philopoemen abolished it in 188.

That Cleomenes felt it necessary to restore the *agōgē* and common messes presupposes an earlier period of discontinuity. The duration of this period is difficult to determine precisely. In his short reign (ca. 244–240), Agis IV had also tried to revive the *agōgē* in a set of reforms that foreshadowed Cleomenes', but the intense, indeed murderous opposition to his proposals brought them, and him, to nought.[48] Even so, a remark made by the Cynic Teles in a speech delivered between 240/39 and 229, to the effect that various non-Spartans were routinely accepted into the *agōgē*, has been widely believed to refer to Agis' proposed expansion of the citizen body.[49] If this were the case, then it should follow that the *agōgē* was functioning when Teles spoke. However, it has been shown that Teles is not referring to any of Agis' reforms, which, in any case, were never implemented; rather, the reference is traditional, with little or no relevance to contemporary practice.[50] Under these circumstances, we can be reasonably confident that there was no *agōgē* from the time of Agis' accession (244) until Cleomenes' coup (227).

As Agis would not have revived an already functioning *agōgē*, the hiatus must have been longer than sixteen years. Even before he came to the throne, Agis, we are told, expressed his intent to use his kingship as a means of reviving Spartan customs and the ancestral *agōgē*.[51] From this we may infer that the institutions of traditional Spartan education had ground to a halt before he was born. Since Plutarch describes Agis in language well suited for a young man in his twenties during his brief reign, we may put his birth at ca. 264 B.C. and conclude that the *agōgē* was not functioning by that period.[52] Ten years before, in contrast, King Pyrrhus of Epirus at least affected to believe in its continued existence, when in 274 he allayed Spartan fears about his intentions to invade by musing that, if nothing prevented him, he would send his younger sons to be brought up in the "Laconian customs," that is, in the *agōgē*.[53] Although we might reasonably conclude that the *agōgē* met its end at some time between 274 and ca. 264, it is perhaps prudent to extend the margin of error ten years further, because the latest person whom we know to have gone through the *agōgē* was Xanthippus, a Spartan mercenary who arrived in North Africa in 255 and enabled the Carthaginians to defeat the Romans. He was, according to Polybius, "a Spartan who had taken part in the *agōgē* and had commensurate experience in warfare."[54] Polybius derived this part of his work from Philinus of Agrigentum, who was probably contemporary with the events he narrates and may be trusted on such matters of detail.[55] Although the Carthaginians are unlikely, I suppose, to have hired a freshly minted graduate of the *agōgē* as the commander of their army, we must concede the possibility and fix the lowest possible date for the lapse of the *agōgē* at ca. 255 B.C.[56] Historically, this would make sense, since Sparta under Areus I and his immediate successors began to be transformed into something resembling a contemporary Hellenistic state. A theater was built, coinage introduced for the first time, and the kingship took on a more absolutist tinge than before.[57] Whether or not the kings had any systematic programs of reform, neglect of the *agōgē* would have been all of a piece with other trends in Spartan life.

The two periods of discontinuity just examined are the only two to leave traces in the historical record, so it will be assumed, for argument's sake, that there were no others. Two are enough, for in the 110 years 256–146 B.C., the *agōgē* functioned in a revived form for only 39 years, while during 71 years of that period the *agōgē* simply did not exist. The two hiatuses also break up the *agōgē*'s history into three distinct phases: the Classical *agōgē*, from its beginnings, perhaps early in the sixth century B.C., down to the first lapse (ca. 270–250); the Cleomenean *agōgē* as revived under the guidance of Sphaerus (226) down to its abolition (188); and the Roman *agōgē* as revived in 146 B.C. down to its last gasp in the fourth century A.D.[58]

Now that a chronological framework has been established, the sources can be assigned their proper places. This procedure will enable us to determine more effectively whether discrepancies between accounts are due to authorial ignorance, scribal error, or change in the *agōgē* itself. I do not intend an exhaustive survey: only the most important testimonia will be examined here, while those of lesser importance will be examined in the subsequent chapters.

Herodotus, at the end of his history of the Persian Wars, is the earliest author to refer explicitly to an aspect of the *agōgē*. In describing the aftermath of the Battle of Plataea, he tells us that the Spartans buried their dead in three separate tombs. As the text of most editions now stands, in the first tomb they buried the *irenes*, among whom was the impetuously brave division commander, Amompharetus; in the second, they buried the other Spartiates; in the third, the *heilōtai*.[59] The *irenes*, or *eirenes*, were about twenty years old, the eldest age grade in the *agōgē*, as later sources tell us.[60] But this reading is a modern conjecture; in both places where texts read *irenes/irenas*, the manuscripts unanimously read *hirees/hireas* (priests).[61] All scholars agree that the text of the manuscripts must be faulty, since such signal honors as separate burial in a group are un-heard of for priests in Classical Greece. Ancient priesthood did not have the same status as its modern counterpart; it was not a vocation, but simply an honorific office.[62] Neither was there a priestly caste; any man could become a priest. Even so, the "corrected" text has caused almost as much difficulty, for few credit that someone holding the rank of com-mander could possibly have been of such tender years as Amomphare-tus.[63] All in all, however, the emendation seems assured, since it rests on a definition of the word *eirēn* in an ancient glossary of unusual words found in Herodotus.[64]

Nonetheless, no reason exists to discard the manuscripts' reading. We know virtually nothing about the intricacies of Spartan society in the early fifth century beyond what Herodotus himself reports; even later, Thucydides complained about the secrecy surrounding much of Spartan life.[65] For a Spartan custom at this time to have been beyond the pale at Athens (the only city we know much about) should come as no surprise. As for the glossary, years ago it was argued, mostly to deaf ears, that many words appearing there are not to be found in Herodotus.[66] In view of such contamination, there is no proof that the *eirēn* gloss belongs with any of the words in Herodotus' *Histories*.

Positive reasons are available for preferring the manuscripts' testimony. The burial in three separate tombs of priests, warrior Spartiates, and agricultural slaves matches the *idéologie tripartie* of early Indo-European society.[67] Comparative research into the mythological and social systems of the Greeks, Romans, and other peoples who spoke languages derived from a common precursor known as proto-Indo-European has shown that their early ancestors conceived of society as divided into three distinct orders or functions: priests and kings, warriors, and herder-cultivators. Given the Spartans' conservatism, they may be expected to have preserved some customs of their early Indo-European ancestors down into the fifth century, especially in the realm of battle. Classical Spartan society did preserve some unmistakably Indo-European relics. For instance, the sign of Spartiate status was long hair, a distinct feature of Indo-European societies.[68] The red cloaks Spartiates wore in battle had been a mark of the second function in Indo-European society, the warrior.[69] The heavenly protectors of Spartan kings, Castor and Pollux, the Dioscuri, were descendants of the Indo-European Divine Twins, gods of the second and third functions.[70]

An objection might be made that, as the helots were slaves, they would have been outside the community, and, as descendants of the Messenians, they had in any case never been a part of Spartan society.[71] However, the title *heilōtai* (helots) had originally been applied to inhabitants of Laconia enslaved during the Dorian invasion.[72] Early Spartan history is at best legendary, so little credence can be given the ancient evidence on this point. Even in antiquity, the origin of the Laconian helots was a vexed question, one that modern scholarship has had no better success at solving.[73] The helots' status was ambiguous too — they were "the most enslaved" of the Greeks, yet they were able to marry, own boats, and to keep 50 percent of the fruits of their labor.[74] Moreover, the proverbial hatred and mistrust between Spartiates and helots has probably been exaggerated.[75] In the same vein, considering the controversy surrounding the identity of the men buried in the first tomb at Plataea, it is remarkable that no one has questioned why helots should have been buried in the third tomb, at public expense, in a place of honor.

The answer may be that the original helots were not the enslaved pre-Dorian population of Laconia, but the Dorian "third estate," gradually degraded and hemmed in by restrictions to the point of serfdom as Spartan society ossified in the wake of the Messenian Wars: among the ancient writers to speculate on the helots' origin, the fifth-century historian Antiochus in fact proposed precisely this solution to the problem.[76] The Messenians, who were enslaved in these wars, were assimilated to the status of the original helots, since they were also Dorian.[77] As such, they were not truly slaves in the Greek sense but neither were they free, as the Spartiates were.

Accepting the manuscripts' reading in Herodotus means that the earliest extant witness to the *agōgē* now becomes the exiled Athenian officer, Xenophon, a great admirer of Sparta (too great for his own good), who wrote a treatise in the early fourth century B.C. on Spartan society known as *The Constitution of the Lacedaemonians*.[78] Xenophon, as well as being the earliest, is also the fullest source for the Classical *agōgē*. Unfortunately, he is rather a disappointment, as his overview of the educational system (*Lac.* 2–4.6) is singularly lacking in the sort of precise information he enthusiastically provides when describing Spartan military affairs (*Lac.* 11–13). This is all the more surprising, since, according to an admittedly late source, Xenophon sent his sons to be educated at Sparta.[79] In spite of his inability or unwillingness to go into great detail, he does furnish us with a very few pegs on which to hang a modest reconstruction of the *agōgē* in the earliest recoverable phase of its development.

To argue now that one of these pegs needs to be pulled out may seem perverse. Yet, as in the case of the *irenes* in Herodotus, so Xenophon's two references to the age grade *eirēn* are modern conjectures that appear in no manuscript.[80] In their place, the manuscripts have *arrēn* (male). It is conceivable that the unusual word was corrupted, in the course of copying, into the more familiar one, but the corrections add even more confusion. As the edited text now reads, the *eirēn* appears suddenly and without warning, at the beginning of a section on ephebic communal meals: "and [Lycurgus] enjoined the *eirēn* to contribute . . . food"; only later is it made clear that some of the *eirenes* were in charge of troops of boys.[81] We never learn who or what the *eirenes* as a group were. Even with the pamphlet's obvious stylistic failings, Xenophon would not have brought in the *eirenes* without introducing them; in the two instances where he provides the titles of officials concerned with the *agōgē*, Xenophon's practice is to identify at least the essence of their duties.[82] To be sure, there are times when Xenophon does not define a specific Spartan term, but these would have been so familiar to his reader as to need no explanation—*philition* (common mess), ephors, and *gerousia*.[83] Finally, although Xenophon's description of the Spartan army has failed to impress scholarly opinion with its detail, even the most pacific of readers could appreciate from the context how the various elements of the army fitted together.[84]

The manuscripts' reading of *arrēn*, then, should be retained in spite of a perceived similarity, in the case of the second passage, with a sentence in Plutarch's *Life of Lycurgus*: "and they set in charge of each group [*agelē*] the most warlike of the so-called *eirenes*."[85] Now that the breaks between various phases of the *agōgē* have been revealed, it is clear that no assumptions about structural continuity can stand. With the lack of positive evidence for this type of continuity, the reading offered by the manuscripts is to be preferred over modern conjecture.

The production of Laconian constitutions became something of a cottage industry in the fourth century and throughout the Hellenistic period; no self-respecting academic went long before putting one under his belt.[86] All certainly touched on the *agōgē* in one way or another, but not one has survived except in the form of scattered fragments, actually quotations and references found in later works. The greatest losses among the earlier works of this type are the constitutions by Critias, Socrates' infamous pupil, and by Aristotle, who had one compiled as part of a mammoth project encompassing the constitutions of 158 cities. Although Critias' pamphlet would have been available for consultation, Xenophon followed him only in beginning his account of the Spartan discipline from conception. Otherwise, the fragments show a wealth of detail about Spartan social life that is sorely lacking in Xenophon.[87]

Aristotle's lost *Constitution of the Lacedaemonians* bulks large behind the works of later writers. Although other works that draw on it, written in the intervening centuries, have perished, Plutarch clearly used Aristotle as a source for his biography of Lycurgus.[88] From the *Constitution*'s fragments preserved there and elsewhere, it should be possible to recover the general outline of Aristotle's treatment of the *agōgē*; the harvest of information, however, is rather meager and, on the whole, surprisingly commonplace.[89] From the *Politics*, we learn that the Spartans deserve credit for the value they place on children's education; that Spartan education emphasizes brutality; that the Spartans claim a nice appreciation of music although they do not learn to play.[90] On the other hand, the *Constitution* seems to have had a significant ethnographic content, to judge from the fragments, but very little specific information on the *agōgē*.[91] A very brief résumé found in the excerpts of Heraclides covers the essential points of Aristotle's description: "They rear their children so that they are never full, in order that they become accustomed to hunger. They also accustom them to stealing, and punish whoever is caught with blows, so that as a result of this they might be able to toil and keep night vigils in wartime. Immediately from childhood on they practice speaking tersely, then good-natured bantering back and forth."[92]

Thanks to the epitomator's eye for the trifling, this is banal indeed.[93] Any more useful information has been ruthlessly excised, so that what remains could just as easily stand as a paraphrase of Xenophon's description of the *agōgē*.[94] By the end of the third century B.C., when Heraclides lived, the traditional picture of the *agōgē* had clearly been stripped to the bare essentials: scanty diet, theft of food, and punishment for those caught.[95] These same elements in the same order make up the bulk of Plutarch's description of the *agōgē* and likewise are to be found in the so-called *Laconian Institutions*.[96] That they also figure prominently in Xenophon's *Constitution* indicates that the tradition had taken shape even before his time. Unfortunately, we cannot determine whether Aristotle was able to progress beyond these chestnuts; on the whole, it seems unlikely. Even if Aristotle or a student had traveled to Sparta, the Spartans would have been unwilling to provide much help to people so obviously associated with the city's foremost enemy, Macedon.[97]

The most important body of work from the fourth century to touch upon the Classical *agōgē* is, of course, Plato's, situated chronologically between Xenophon and Aristotle. The evolution of his attitude to Sparta and the changing use he made of Spartan *exempla* have been subjects of countless studies, while Sparta's place in the Platonic conception of the ideal city-state has exercised philosophers for centuries.[98] However, I will take a more down-to-earth approach here. Plato's attitude to Sparta is of no concern except insofar as it colors the information he imparts concerning contemporary practice. Unlike his pupil Aristotle, Plato was more interested in perfecting his philosophical ideas than in collecting information on the world around him, so he cannot be expected to have concerned himself with the precise functioning of Sparta's educational system. Although much of Plato's educational theory is temptingly reminiscent of the modern picture of the *agōgē*, no information will be used unless it can be shown to be relevant to the Classical *agōgē*. For there is a likelihood that elements of the later *agōgē* which remind us of Platonic theory were in fact invented to conform to the master's ideas, since any philosopher called in to work on a city's educational system would naturally have had copies of the *Republic* and the *Laws* in his reference library.[99] Nonetheless, scattered throughout the Platonic corpus are snippets of useful information.

Of the lost works on Classical Sparta's constitution, the one with the oddest later history is the *Constitution of the Spartiates* by Aristotle's pupil Dicaearchus, who flourished in about 336 B.C.[100] Evidently, Spartan authorities were so impressed by this work that they adopted it as an official text and had it read annually to the youths assembled in the offices of the ephors: a tradition, we are told, that was observed for a long time.[101] Despite arguments that this long-standing custom belongs to the fourth century or the Hellenistic period, it must have begun after 146 B.C., as part of the Roman *agōgē*.[102] A fourth-century date is impossible, because there would not have been enough time between the work's composition, its adoption by the Spartans, and the Classical *agōgē*'s demise for the recitation to be considered an enduring tradition. The Hellenistic phase of the *agōgē*, the Cleomenean phase, lasted only thirty-nine years. Since Cleomenes would hardly have drawn attention every year to his murder of ephors by gathering the city's youth in their empty offices, it must be assumed that the custom arose after his defeat at Sellasia and subsequent exile. At the most, then, a Hellenistic recitation would have continued for thirty-four years, hardly long enough to be considered a venerable tradition. A Roman date is to be preferred: the period 146 to the fourth century A.D. allows the practice of recitation to become long-standing. The venue is suitable as well, for in the Roman age the ephors' old offices became a sort of cultural center, where dignitaries were entertained and artifacts displayed.[103] The objection that a work on the Classical constitution would have been irrelevant to an audience in the Roman period misses the point. Spartans at that time prided themselves on the ideal of their unchanging public institutions, whatever the reality. The recitation "proved" that very little had changed. Besides, it is unlikely that Dicaearchus went into any great detail; he was read for his generally edifying tone. Indeed, even Xenophon's constitution could have been read quite comfortably instead, had the final chapters been suppressed.

A fourth-century work on something called the Spartiate constitution, inevitably dealing with the *agōgē* through which all Spartiates had to pass, was read publicly in the Roman period. This implies that enough common ground existed between Dicaearchus' description and the contemporary situation for the work to have some significance for its audience. The task at hand is to identify those common elements and, at the same time, distinguish them from innovations of the second and third phases.

Due to the woeful survival rate of literature from the Hellenistic period, almost nothing has come down to us about the Cleomenean phase
of the *agōgē*. The most important exceptions are two glosses setting out
the ages and names of the Spartan age grades.[104] One concerns the passage in Herodotus just discussed, the other is a scholion in a manuscript of
the geographer Strabo. Their contents will be examined in due course; for
now, it is sufficient to note that they both are considered to be derived
from the Alexandrian scholar Aristophanes of Byzantium, who compiled
a vast and influential lexicon, some of whose entries circulated under the
title, *On the Naming of Age Groups*.[105] Starved for precise information,
students of Spartan life have seized upon these glosses as evidence for the
names of Classical age grades. Now that the corroborating literary references to age-grade names in Herodotus and Xenophon have been shown
to be unfounded modern conjectures, however, nothing compels us to
assume that the age grades in the glosses were those of the Classical
agōgē.

Aristophanes lived from about 257 until 180 B.C., with his career
reaching its peak in 195 when he became head of the Library at Alexandria.[106] His working life neatly brackets the duration of the Cleomenean
agōgē (226–188) and, as a consequence, the Spartan age grades in his
lexicon are most probably those of the *agōgē* in his own time. Taking into
account the historical evidence for the failure and revival of the *agōgē*, we
cannot blithely assume that the same names were used in the Classical
phase as well, and there is actually some epigraphical evidence from the
late fifth century B.C. for a different age-grade name.[107] The implications
for our conception of the earlier *agōgē* will become clear in later chapters.

From the Roman phase of the *agōgē*, sources both epigraphical and
literary are relatively abundant, enabling us to reconstruct the educational system as it existed during the so-called Greek renaissance of the
second century A.D. In order to do this, however, we must determine
whether a source provides historical information relevant only to one or
the other of the earlier phases, or is describing simply the last phase. The
inscriptions reflect current practice and may be used with confidence as
regards the later *agōgē*; most of Pausanias' descriptions are likewise eyewitness accounts. But in the case of some other authors, such as Plutarch,
the line is much harder to draw.

Probably the earliest of these sources are the so-called *Laconian Institutions*. These are small notices, thought to have been extracted ultimately from a book on the Spartan constitution, that form part of a

mass of improving anecdotes and sayings known as the *Laconian Apoph-thegmata*. They have come down to us as part of the Plutarchan corpus, since Plutarch had collected them as part of the research for his Spartan *Lives*.[108] The *Institutions* themselves, or the work they were taken from, are posterior to the Achaean War because the last entry mentions Roman hegemony over Greece.[109] Most scholars hold that the *Institutions* are extracts from a lengthier but ill-organized work on the Spartan constitution written sometime after 146 B.C.[110] Even so, they are of little help for the *agōgē's* last phase, as the material they contain can be shown to have come from the period before the middle of the second century B.C.

Knowing the precise nature of the *Institutions* will enable us to evaluate the evidence they do provide. First of all, we must look at the final apophthegm. It is too lengthy to quote in full here, so the less relevant passages are summarized parenthetically:

It was forbidden for them to be sailors and to fight naval battles. However, later they did fight naval battles and, upon becoming masters of the sea, stopped again, observing that the citizens' morals were being corrupted. But they changed again, just as in everything else. (*Money-making was formerly punishable by death and an oracle had foretold Sparta's ruin through greed. But Lysander introduced wealth and was honored for it.*) When the city abided by the laws of Lycurgus and kept to its oaths, it was supreme in Greece for good government and reputation for 500 years. But little by little, when these were contravened and greed and avarice crept in, the elements of their power began to weaken, and their allies were ill-disposed to them on this account. (*Even so, in the time of Philip and, later, Alexander, only the Spartans kept themselves aloof, even with all their deficiencies. Spartans were allies to no Successor, neither sending representatives to common councils nor paying tribute.*) Until the time when, having completely abandoned Lycurgus' constitution, they were tyrannized over by their own citizens and preserved nothing of the ancestral *agōgē*. And becoming just like other peoples, they gave up their earlier renown and freedom of speech and went into bondage, and now they were under the Romans just like the other Greeks.[111]

Apophthegm 42 is by far the lengthiest of all the *Institutions* and the only one even to hint that Spartans no longer followed the ways of Lycurgus. Indeed, it provides a history of Sparta in capsule form from the end of the Peloponnesian War to the middle of the second century, with allusions

to Lysander, Philip, Alexander, the Epigoni, the Spartan tyrants Machani-
das and Nabis, and Philopoemen's settlement of 188 (the Achaean bondage).[112] But most notable is that the apophthegm as a whole has only the
most tenuous of logical connections with the topic of the first sentence.
Originally, the entry must have simply recorded Lycurgus' prohibition
against seafaring. Who, then, added the mournful notice about Sparta's
decline? Its pessimistic tone and startling admission that the Spartans are
now like everybody else excludes from consideration Plutarch and other
authors from the later first and second centuries A.D. when, as I have
mentioned already, the Spartans vigorously promoted themselves as living exemplars of the Lycurgan ideal. Others have remarked on the awk-
wardness of the last sentence, especially the words translated as "and now
they were" (*kai nun . . . egenonto*).[113] They propose that it preserves some
of the original's wording imperfectly altered when the work was copied
for Plutarch's use, as he could hardly have harbored such sentiments
himself. Most probably, then, the author of the notice attached to *Laconian Institutions* 42 lived in the later second or first centuries B.C., while
the postscript itself was perhaps composed fairly soon after 146, since
there is no mention of the *agōgē*'s reestablishment. The author may well
have been a Spartan himself, if the bitterness he exhibits is that of a
disappointed patriot. Beyond this we cannot go.

That the last part of the final apophthegm was written by the epitomator means that the *Institutions*' source must have been composed before
his time, perhaps even before 146. Although it is generally agreed that the
Institutions derive from a single, fuller original, the disarray of the entries
speaks against it.[114] They start out logically enough, with the first seventeen chapters devoted to the common messes and the *agōgē*, but then
lurch from topic to topic in no apparent order.[115] Rather than coming
from a single source of astonishing carelessness, the *Institutions* should be
regarded as a compilation of Spartan material collected after 146 by
someone who then added a postscript. Thus, the *Institutions*, as we have
them, are not Plutarch's copy of an epitome of an original, but his copy of
an original compilation of apophthegmatic material of a kind very common in the Hellenistic period.[116]

When the original collection was copied for Plutarch's use, it was altered, a process apparent from a number of grammatical anomalies in the
text, one of which has already been mentioned. Two of the three evidently
resulted from changing verbs originally in the present to a suitable past
tense.[117] This pattern of alteration, together with the other six entries that

retain their verbs in the present tense, naturally leads to the conclusion that all the *Institutions* were originally written in the present tense.[118] It follows that the compiler copied his entries down verbatim without even bothering to adjust the tenses; only later was the change attempted. If the entries of the original collection were all copied unaltered, then their sources must have been composed in the present tense as well. Therefore, the sources for the *Institutions* were contemporary with the practices they recorded and, consequently, date from before 188 at the very latest. So, although the *Institutions* were compiled in the Roman period, the information they contain is relevant only to the *agōgē* in its first or second phase.

From Plutarch's notes we turn to Plutarch himself. Of the biographies he wrote at the turn of the first to the second centuries A.D., the most pertinent is his *Life of Lycurgus*, which we have already had occasion to note. The *Lycurgus* contains a sizable section on the reforms attributed to Sparta's legendary lawgiver, which effectively constitutes an overview of traditional Spartan manners and customs.[119] Several chapters in the middle are taken up by an account of the *agōgē*; Plutarch's treatment is the fullest available, affording us a wealth of picturesque detail and telling incident. Divining all the sources for this is a hopeless task, given Plutarch's breadth of reading and citation style.[120] Luckily, for the most part it is unnecessary as well, since his depiction conforms very much to the tried-and-true approach of his predecessors.

As we should expect, Plutarch begins at birth, soon proceeding to a survey of the *agōgē*'s various stages. He touches on the ephebes' meager diet, their recourse to theft, and the punishment they could expect if caught. He enumerates the reasons for treating the ephebes in this way and, after trotting out the famous story of the boy and the fox, attests to the Spartan ephebes' fortitude in his own day, for he himself has seen them expiring under the lash at the altar of Artemis Orthia.[121] Then follow notices on the questioning of ephebes after dinner and their minimal clothing and primitive sleeping arrangements. Plutarch concludes with an outline of their rhetorical and musical education.

Of the major sources, only the *Lycurgus* furnishes so many details, some of which occur nowhere else. For this reason, Plutarch has become the fundamental authority on the Spartan *agōgē* for modern scholars, even though he was writing almost four centuries after the demise of the Classical *agōgē*. The question that therefore needs to be asked is, Which phase or phases of the *agōgē* is Plutarch describing? A real answer may seem unlikely, as virtually none of the earlier literature on Sparta's educational system has survived. In some cases, we will have to admit defeat and resort, reluctantly, to speculation. But, at other times, Plutarch himself comes to our aid.

Appropriately for a narrative concerning a historical figure, Plutarch usually put his verbs into past tenses.[122] On occasion, he uses the present tense when editorializing, citing scholarly opinion, or referring to a custom or phenomenon that still occurred in his own day.[123] As expected, verbs in the present are infrequent and are scattered fairly evenly throughout the work, with one salient exception. Plutarch's description of the ephebes' stealing of food and their punishment, which concludes with his eyewitness testimony concerning the endurance contest is written completely in the present tense.[124] Since Plutarch did not slavishly copy his sources, as we know by comparing some of his raw material (*Laconian Institutions*) with the finished product, he did not here unthinkingly transfer the tense used by his sources,[125] although some of his sources were in fact written in the present tense.[126] However, Plutarch did have a reason for writing this passage in the present tense, whatever the tenses used by his sources. Dramatic vividness could hardly have been the motive, because the first present occurs in an explanation of age-grade terminology.[127] Since the words Plutarch clarifies, *eirēn* and *melleirēn*, are known from the Roman *agōgē*, his use of the present tense here and in the entire passage conforms to his practice when describing something he had reason to believe still held true in his own time.[128]

Plutarch had visited Sparta and been a spectator at the endurance contest, but he was not just another tourist: he was there to conduct research in the public archives for his Spartan biographies.[129] Given the prominence of the *agōgē* and the claims made for its authenticity, as well as Plutarch's own interests, it is more than likely that he also saw a reenactment of the ancient food-stealing ritual. Plutarch wrote this section using the present tense because he knew that this particular custom was still in existence. There is every reason to believe, therefore, that the ephebic practice of stealing food survived in some form down into the *agōgē*'s final phase, which itself is not very much, we must admit. However, the general principle behind Plutarch's use of the present tense can help somewhat to determine which customs were still vital in the Roman period. If Plutarch does not use the present, then in the absence of solid evidence to the contrary we must assume that the particular tradition described has died out.

For example, Plutarch states that the Spartans "used to cast" weak infants into the Apothetae pit, at the command of tribal elders.[130] The use of the imperfect entitles us to infer that this gruesome practice no longer took place in the Roman period. Corroboration comes in a letter of Pliny the Younger to the emperor Trajan, in which he mentions previous communications to the Spartans from Vespasian, Titus, and Domitian concerning *threptoi*.[131] Many were foundlings who had been brought up in households as slaves; complications about their status often arose.[132] That abandoned children were to be found at Sparta, as everywhere else, means that the decision to rear an infant now rested with the individual family, and that the Apothetae had ceased to be the official repository for unwanted babies.

Next to Plutarch, the most informative source on the Roman *agōgē* is Pausanias. While Plutarch supplies a plausible narrative, Pausanias excels at individual details. His descriptions of the endurance contest and the mock battle of ephebes at the Platanistas grove are invaluable for their wealth of specific information.[133] The allure of his vignettes notwithstanding, Pausanias went to Sparta when the archaistic revival was at its height, so what he has to say about the antiquity of any aspect of the *agōgē* is suspect. For instance, he says that the endurance contest came about as a result of Lycurgus' mitigation of ritual human sacrifice demanded by Artemis to stop a plague.[134] Although most historians have tried to extract a kernel of useful information about archaic Sparta from this explanation, Pausanias' story is inherently unhistorical. And it does not stand alone: two other earlier, completely different accounts of the contest's origin are also extant, one by the Augustan mythographer Hyginus, the other by Plutarch in his *Life of Aristides*.[135] Pausanias is the only one to credit Lycurgus with the ritual's invention, undoubtedly because, just as his contemporaries did, he had allowed himself to be convinced that Sparta really had preserved its cultural heritage unchanged since the earliest times.

No other surviving writers devote as much space to the *agōgē*. What references there are usually take the form of rhetorical tropes, with more library dust clinging to them than sand from the Eurotas. Many allude to the whipping contest, which enjoys a long life as a convenient image of Spartan toughness and obedience.[136]

The satirist Lucian, who lived at about the same time as Pausanias, proves an exception to the generally laudatory tone of notices about the *agōgē*.[137] In the comic dialogue *Anacharsis*, the Scythian wise man views the endurance contest in much the same way moderns would, as a ridiculous and rather distasteful waste of time.[138] After Solon, his interlocutor, delivers a panegyric on the contest, Anacharsis simply asks if Lycurgus himself had ever endured a flogging. "He was too old," is the reply. Then the Scythian asks why Athenian youths are not flogged as well, to which Solon replies that Athenians don't go in much for foreign customs. Anacharsis punctures this by acutely observing that the reason is really because they know how useless it is to be whipped for no public or private advantage. He continues, "Their city simply seems to me to need psychiatric help because of the ridiculous things it's doing to itself." To this Solon has no rejoinder except to assure him limply that someone in Sparta will explain it all.[139]

For all his mockery, Lucian may well have seen the contest himself. His account is unlike all others in conveying a sense of how the audience behaved and supplies some extra details.[140] In addition, his brief description, so similar to Pausanias' longer one, also bears the mark of autopsy, while his erroneous explanation of why statues were erected to certain participants in the contest seems to stem from an understandable misinterpretation of the inscriptions on their bases.[141]

After Lucian, little on the *agōgē* appears beyond an unappetizing array of regurgitated rhetorical scraps. In the early third century, Philostratus, in his biography of the traveling wonder-worker Apollonius of Tyana, has his hero deliver an impassioned defense of the whipping contest. The speech has little to offer save the only literary occurrence of the contest's proper title, the contest of endurance (*ho tēs karterias agōn*).[142]

Finally come the lexica put together in Byzantine times to provide readers of classical texts with keys to understanding words and expressions no longer in current use. The three most often cited today are the volumes written by Hesychius the grammarian in the fifth or sixth centuries A.D.; by Photius, a ninth-century Patriarch of Constantinople; and a work known as the *Suda* (or *Suidas*), compiled in the tenth century. These compilers lived after antiquity's end, but they had access to the multitude of classical texts still surviving in the East and could thus draw on their accumulated store of ancient literature and scholarship. Although they stood beyond the boundary of ancient literature, their own labors preserved information from all periods of antiquity. For the *agōgē*, they can be quite useful, since many glosses confirm or clarify what was known from other sources. At other times, they mystify by providing terms said to be related to the *agōgē* but which appear nowhere else and often seem to contradict what is known from other sources.[143] Tempting as it has been to emend or ignore these entries, I will endeavor to account for as many as possible with the least possible textual change.

Without a doubt, the texts most useful for a reconstruction of the *agōgē* are the inscriptions. Over 1,000 Spartan inscriptions have been found and published, the great majority from the British excavations in the first decades of this century.[144] The focus here will necessarily be on those stones that have some connection with the *agōgē* — victory dedications, statue bases, lists of ephebes, and of ephebic officials. These, like the other Spartan inscriptions, come almost exclusively from the Roman period. Nonetheless, there are a very few (they could hardly be fewer) relevant stones from the fifth and fourth centuries B.C. that can yield a modicum of information, if squeezed correctly.[145]

As the evidence — literary, epigraphical, and archaeological — has more to say about the *agōgē*'s last phase than any other and since Roman Sparta's invented tradition has shaped modern as well as ancient conceptions of the *agōgē*, we turn first to the *agōgē* in its most familiar form, the Roman phase.[146]

2

TRAINING UP THE YOUTH

It would be no exaggeration to say that only during the third phase of the *agōgē*'s development is there enough evidence to attempt a detailed reconstruction of its organization and operation: during the Roman period, the sources are relatively plentiful and parallels ready to hand. That no one has bothered to attempt one until now is indicative also of a certain bias inherent in classical scholarship. Instead, we have the irony that the literary and epigraphical evidence, virtually all dating to the period of Roman rule, is used to elucidate the *agōgē* of some five hundred years earlier. The chapters that follow are an attempt to correct this misguided approach and to present in the greatest detail possible a picture of Sparta's preeminent institution at its most brilliant stage.

Epigraphy is the most help in this task. The texts from the sanctuary of Artemis Orthia constitute an archive of documents that can be used to reveal the later *agōgē*'s inner workings to a surprising amount. The first and largest category of inscriptions to be considered comprises *stēlai* with iron sickles affixed to them, ranging in date from the fourth century B.C. to the third century A.D., with the vast preponderance of them from the first two centuries of our era. The texts, one of which actually identifies its sickle as the prize in a contest, are almost all in prose and provide the same essential information: the victor's name, the date (by Sparta's annual eponymous magistrate), and the dedication to the goddess; they often record the specific event or events won and sometimes the victor's age as well (Plate 1). A second, much smaller group comprises a few statue bases and one dedication commemorating the endurance of youths at the goddess's altar. All of the sickle dedications and most of the second class of inscriptions were found at the sanctuary of Artemis Orthia or were built into the third-century A.D. theater there. However, none of the dedications set up by teams called *sphaireis*, who had been victorious in a ball game, were found at the sanctuary; rather, they came to light at many locations in and around the city. These dedications are dated by eponymous magistrate and two other officials and contain the names of the members of the winning teams.[1]

In those inscriptions of the first category that record it, the victor's age is not expressed in terms of years, but as a name. These names were given to Spartan youths of the same age who were grouped together at the same level of the *agōgē*, much as the terms "freshman," "sophomore," "junior," and "senior" are given to undergraduate students at American universities today; in anthropological terms, such groups are called "age grades."[2] The ages of youths in each of the Spartan age grades have been renowned subjects of controversy for many years. However, progress has been seriously hampered here too by the generally accepted synchronic approach to the problem, which assumes the evidence from all periods can be reconciled to produce a single set of age-grade names.

Since the evidence has been used so indiscriminately, recovering information on the age grades of the Roman era will inevitably entail some technical discussion of the earlier age grades as well. First, though, the ancient evidence needs to be set out. The victory dedications from Orthia's sanctuary provide us with the names, but not the ages, of the grades current in the Roman period: *mikkichizomenos* (spelled various ways), *pratopampais, hatropampais, melleirēn*, and *eirēn*. Plutarch mentions the last two in his *Life of Lycurgus* and gives an indication of the ages of *melleirenes* and *eirenes* in a passage that, unfortunately, has been roundly misinterpreted by modern historians.[3]

As I mentioned in Chapter 1, the two glosses ultimately derived from Aristophanes of Byzantium provide the names of the age grades from the Hellenistic *agōgē*. The first explains the spurious reference to *eirenes* in Herodotus: "*Eirēn*. Among the Spartans, in the first year a child is called a *rhōbidas*, in the second *promikizomenos*, in the third *mikizomenos*, in the

PLATE 1. *Sickle dedication (courtesy of the Ephor of Antiquities for Laconia and Arcadia)*

fourth *propais*, in the fifth *pais*, in the sixth *meleirēn* [*sic*]. He is an ephebe among them from fourteen until twenty."[4] The other, written in the margin of a manuscript of Strabo's *Geography*, contains the following notice: "*Eirēn, melleirēn*, among the Spartans someone about to be an *eirēn*. For among the Spartans a child is an ephebe from 14 years until 20. He is called in the first year *rhōbidas*, in the second *promikizomenos*, in the third *mikizomenos*, in the 4th *propais*, in the 5th *pais*, in the 6th *melleirēn*, in the 7th *eirēn*."[5]

Evidence for age grades in the Classical *agōgē* would be nonexistent were it not for a single epigraphical reference to *trietirēs*.[6] The question of age grades in the earliest phase of the *agōgē* will be examined in a later chapter, for now our attention will be directed to the *agōgē* in its more visibly articulated form.

Before proceeding further, we can already see that the number and nomenclature of the age grades changed from the second to the third phases. The Roman *agōgē* lost the first two grades, *rhōbidas* and *promikizomenos*. The *mikizomenos* of the second phase assumed the more elaborate form *mikkichizomenos*, while the grades *propais* and *pais* underwent a similar metamorphosis into the colorful *pratopampais* and *hatropampais*. The reasons for the changes will be dealt with later, along with the *agōgē*'s place in the culture of the Roman Empire.

Over the years, discussion of the age grades has gradually attained a degree of complexity denied all but the most intractable problems in classical studies. Once excised from their historical contexts, the various chunks of information appear so fetchingly contradictory that their reconciliation has come to be regarded as a stern test of philological acumen. Details are fussed over without regard for the larger methodological issue of the relationship between sources of such widely varying date and the long-lasting institution they ostensibly describe. Moreover, even within the confines of the synchronic approach, not all types of evidence are deemed to be equal. The privileged status of literary sources in classical studies has led to a dismissal of the epigraphic evidence because it reflects only the *agōgē* in its late and debased form, whereas Plutarch, who explicitly describes the age grades of his own time (contemporary with the inscriptions), is regarded as the single most important witness to the age-grade structure in the Classical period.

The pitfalls of this selective, synchronic use of the evidence should be obvious. A sobering recent example can be found in the most densely written synchronic attempt to expose the organization of the *agōgē*'s age grades.[7] After a survey of all the evidence from Xenophon to Plutarch, it was demonstrated through rigorously logical argument that a Spartan youth must have entered the *agōgē* at seven years of age, become a *rhōbidas* at twelve, a *promikizomenos* at thirteen, and so on up to the *melleironeia* at age eighteen. Then followed a period of up to two years of service as a noncombatant in the army, which ended precisely on the twentieth birthday when the youth became an *eirēn* and was put in charge of a band of boys still in the *agōgē*.[8] As the author of the study pointed out, a consequence of this argument is that *eirenes* were "adult . . . in the legal . . . sense," that is, they had already left the *agōgē*.[9] Unfortunately, epigraphical evidence shows decisively that *eirenes* were still enrolled in the *agōgē*, at least in the Roman period.[10] The weakness of the synchronic approach is again manifest: evidence is always available to refute any single aspect of the reconstructions generated by this method because the evidence *is* contradictory. It reflects three different age-grade systems, not one. No amount of logic when applied to this evidence used synchronically will yield satisfactory results.

In fact, to tackle the contradictory nature of the sources, historians have often implicitly adopted a quasi-paleographical approach, using one source as a touchstone against which to test the others' veracity. The accepted standard is Plutarch's *Life of Lycurgus*, even though it was composed centuries after the Classical *agōgē*. And Plutarch's authority is such that the evidence provided by the glosses and by Xenophon in his *Constitution of the Lacedaemonians* is shaped to conform to the picture of the *agōgē* as presented in the *Lycurgus*.

Valid information is sometimes distorted or even abandoned in the process. Once again, the aforementioned study provides a clear example, this time as part of the discussion of the age of a *rhōbidas*, the youngest age grade according to the scholia.[11] Apart from the glosses, which say that a boy entered this grade at age fourteen, there are references to ages approximate to this in Xenophon and Plutarch. According to Xenophon, "when [Spartans] turn from boys into youths," at an age when other cities relaxed the constraints on their young considerably, Lycurgus intensified the training.[12] The lower age limit for a youth (*meirakion*) was usually fourteen or fifteen: since this depended upon local usage, greater precision is impossible.[13] Plutarch says that when the boys were twelve years old they went year round without a tunic (*chitōn*) and were only allowed a single cloak (*himation*).[14] Scholars have assumed, without explicit justification, that this clothing restriction marked a boy's entrance into the *rhōbidas* grade.[15] The rigor mentioned by Xenophon is associated with Plutarch's reference to becoming twelve. Since Plutarch is the preferred authority, Xenophon's implicit allusion to the ages fourteen or fifteen must be erroneous, and doubt has even been cast on whether Greek youths of that age were actually freed from most restraints.[16] As a consequence, Xenophon's text has been thought faulty, with the most popular solution being the deletion, first proposed by a nineteenth-century editor, of the offending words "into youths" (*eis to meirakiousthai*), which puts all to rights.[17] The Xenophon passage now describes a young Spartan's legal coming of age (*ek paidōn ekbainōsi*) as an adult and his first taste of the demands of life as a noncombatant in the army.

Of course, Xenophon and Plutarch would only be in conflict if they were describing the same *agōgē*, which they are patently not doing. Furthermore, it is wrong to doubt Xenophon's testimony that the reins were loosened appreciably on Greek teenagers. The author of the pseudo-Plutarchan treatise *On the Education of Children*, among others, bemoaned this very practice: "I have often condemned those who were responsible for introducing depraved habits—people who, it is true, put attendants and instructors in charge of their children, but allow the impulsiveness of youth [*meirakia*] free rein, even though they should on the contrary have been more watchful and careful of them as youths [*meirakia*] than as children."[18] To associate the passage in Plutarch with any change from one age grade to another is hardly a self-evident move. The restriction on clothing is not explicitly linked to any transition in status or any significant single escalation in the discipline's severity; it is cited merely as an instance of the gradually increasing strictness of the training as the boys grew older.[19]

Doubt even in the authenticity of Plutarch's reference here to a specific age is well founded. As I have mentioned, among Plutarch's sources for the *Lycurgus* was the collection of anecdotal material called the *Laconian Institutions*.[20] A comparison of one of these with the passage under discussion shows how Plutarch used and adapted his material.

Institutions	*Lycurgus*
They went without even a *chitōn*, wearing one *himation* for the year, with their bodies dirty and, for the	Upon becoming twelve, they now went without a *chitōn*, wearing one *himation* for the year, with

most part, they were kept from baths or massages.[21]

their bodies dirty; and they did not experience baths or massages, except for a few days a year when they partook of this sort of amenity.[22]

Plutarch did not merely copy his material unchanged. As a literary artist, he made it his own by sharpening and elaborating the wording. Here, for instance, "for the most part" becomes "except for a few days a year." In characterizing baths and massages, the most popular of the pleasures of the gymnasium, as a sort of amenity, Plutarch draws directly from the lexicon of civic praise: inscriptions of his time extol the provision of this and other kinds of *philanthrōpia* by generous notables.[23]

In the same way that he altered and added to the end of the passage, Plutarch reworked its beginning as well. The reference to the boys becoming twelve years old probably came from his own pen, since he is unlikely to have derived it from another source; the traditional picture of the *agōgē* is, after all, remarkably consistent in shape and emphasis.[24] Given that writers on the *agōgē* worked within an area circumscribed for us in its essentials by Xenophon, we can trace the reference's development from when it first appears in his *Constitution of the Lacedaemonians* to Plutarch's *Lycurgus*. As part of his general introduction to the *agōgē*, Xenophon states that Lycurgus, instead of indulging boys with *himatia*, thought they should wear only one for the year.[25] This part of the *Constitution* is arranged as a set of corresponding opposites: whatever all other Greeks' (bad) practices are, the Spartans' (good) practices are the polar opposites.[26] Thus, while Spartan boys have to make do with one outer garment, other parents "pamper [their children's] bodies with changes of *himatia*."[27] Xenophon was not claiming that Spartan boys were naked except for their one *himation*, only that they were not allowed a wardrobe of appropriate *himatia* for different seasons or occasions.[28] Yet the *Laconian Institutions* imply precisely this.

Either the boys of Hellenistic Sparta were a hardier breed than those of the fifth and fourth centuries or, more likely, the author of the original version of this *Institution* exaggerated the severity of the discipline for his own purposes.[29] In turn, Plutarch elaborated still further by providing the boys with an age at which to begin their ascetic life. He chose the age of twelve years because of the passage's context, which is approximately the same in both Xenophon and the *Institutions*. In the *Constitution*, it occurs just before Xenophon's reluctant concession that pederasty existed at Sparta, which itself is the last subject discussed before the section dealing with Spartans who have just become *meirakia*. Similarly, excerpts covering strictures on clothing and pederasty occur close together in the *Institutions* as well.[30]

As Plutarch had also read Xenophon, he might well have felt justified in determining a proper age.[31] The age of twelve fitted perfectly, situated near the beginning of puberty and the youngest age sanctioned by society for a pederastic relationship; in addition, twelve was the lower limit for competition, in the nude, in athletic festivals.[32] Plutarch was hardly a stranger to this sort of invention, quite often supplying missing details or even whole speeches and characters to flesh out his biographies when the situation warranted.[33] He would have had no qualms about embellishing the historical record with a conjecture that would meet with approval even today for the methods employed to obtain it.

The aim of this rather lengthy digression has been to cast substantial doubt on the notion that Plutarch's reference to boys aged twelve has any relevance whatsoever to the age grades of the *agōgē* in any phase. Consequently, the text of Xenophon can remain unchanged on this point, and there is no need to try and reconcile the two testimonia.[34]

The age and status of those in the two eldest grades, the *melleirenes* and the *eirenes*, have attracted the most debate because we have Plutarch's testimony in addition to the Herodotus and Strabo scholia.[35] One aspect of this problem, the matter of whether Plutarch and the scholiasts calculate ages in the same way, was put to rest some years ago.[36] Plutarch says that an *eirēn* was twenty, and so, apparently, do the two scholia.[37] Unfortunately, these statements are not as straightforward as they appear, because ancient methods of reckoning age, and indeed of calculating the duration of time in general, could be frustratingly inconsistent. Two methods were in general use — inclusive reckoning, which included the starting point (day, month, year) in calculating time, and the exclusive method, used today, which did not. Ages or periods of time calculated inclusively will always be, in modern terms, one unit too long. For example, a remnant of inclusive reckoning that has survived into modern times can be seen in Easter Sunday, which is counted as the third day after Good Friday. Thus, an *eirēn* who was twenty years old might be either in his twentieth year, if his age was calculated inclusively, or in his twenty-first year, according to exclusive reckoning. Luckily, it has been demonstrated conclusively that Plutarch and the scholiasts consistently express ages for the

various grades in terms of exclusive reckoning. As a result, Plutarch's *eirēn*
who "has become twenty" (*eikosin etē gegonōs*) is twenty years old in
modern as well as in ancient terms.

The crux of the problem, however, lies in the relative ages of *melleirenes* and *eirenes*. Although the inscriptions and the scholiasts let drop no
hint of any discontinuity between the two grades, Plutarch seems to be the
exception. In a passage whose syntax at a crucial point has long resisted
easy comprehension, he explicitly sets forth the relationship of the one
grade to the other. Translations of the passage commonly sacrifice ele-
gance at the altar of what is held to be accuracy: for example, "They call
eirens [*sic*] those who are not children any longer in the second year, and
the oldest of the boys/children are called *melleirens* [*sic*]" (εἰρένας δὲ
καλοῦσι τοὺς ἔτος ἤδη δεύτερον ἐκ παίδων γεγονότας, μελλείρενας δὲ τῶν
παίδων τοὺς πρεσβυτάτους).[38] The gap of one to two years between leaving the *melleirēn* grade and entering the *eirenes* that Plutarch seems to
imply in this sentence has exercised the ingenuity of many historians for
several decades.[39]

Despite its claims for accuracy, this translation and the argument
derived from it, like almost all earlier reconstructions, is nonetheless
founded upon a misconception. The crucial words in the passage from
Plutarch, ἔτος ἤδη δεύτερον ἐκ παίδων, are usually taken together and
construed as "the second year after [the class of] boys."[40] But these words
do not form a single syntactical unit: ἐκ παίδων instead qualifies the
participle γεγονότας. The phrases ἐκ παίδων (*ek paidōn*) and ἐξ ἐφήβων
(*ex ephēbōn*) appear by themselves or with the verb "to be" in both inscriptions and literary sources to denote persons who have just left these
age grades, in other words "ex-children" and "ex-ephebes."[41] Moreover,
ἔτος ἤδη δεύτερον (*etos ēdē deuteron*), as it occurs here with a perfect
participle, does not signify "the second year after" but "the second year
before"; it looks back to the end of the *melleironeia* from the *eirenes*'
point of view. The phrase is ambiguous because the same ordinal could be
used for expressing past, as well as future, time.[42] In other instances when
the temporal accusative is used in this way, the method of reckoning
includes the current day or year, and in all likelihood the same inclusive
style figures here as well.[43] In this case, the "second year before" in inclusive reckoning becomes "the year before" in exclusive reckoning. Now I
can propose a translation of the Plutarchan passage: "*Eirenes* they call
those who left the boys' class the year before and *melleirenes* the eldest of
the boys."[44]

Now that the break between the two senior grades has been elimi-
nated, the period of military service that has been posited to bridge the
gap is no longer needed.[45] Nor need we share the unusual conviction that
Spartan youths entered the *eirēn* grade precisely on their twentieth birth-
days since, without a gap in their training, *melleirenes* surely moved more
or less as a group to the next grade.[46] Most important, there is now no
doubt that the *eirenes* were twenty years old and the *melleirenes* were
nineteen.

One last point remains to be clarified. The scholia state that Spartan
youths spent the years from fourteen until twenty as ephebes and list
seven age grades for this span. The problem is that there are only six years
between the ages of fourteen and twenty. Scholars have attempted, with
scant success, to squeeze the seven names into six years by indiscriminately using inclusive and exclusive reckoning.[47] As I mentioned, the
solution now current is to argue that *eirenes* had already graduated from
the *agōgē*, thus leaving the remaining six grades listed by the scholia
(*rhōbidas* to *melleirēn*) to fit nicely into the six-year span allotted them.

The intense focus on the precise connotations of the various age references in these few sources has caused an important and relevant word to
be overlooked. It has been universally assumed that "until" (*mechri*), as
used in the two scholia to establish the duration of the *agōgē*, signifies
"up to but not including." Thus, "from fourteen years old until [*mechri*]
twenty years old" includes the age of nineteen, but not twenty. However,
the word is used much less precisely; at times *mechri* may include the
terminal word, at other times it may not.[48] Usage is so inconsistent that
mechri can be used both inclusively and exclusively even within the same
work.

Plato, for instance, uses the word in both ways in the *Laws*. When
discussing the proper time for marriage, he says that a man should marry
at any time from when he is thirty years old until (*mechri*) he is thirty-
five.[49] That Plato intends "until" to be taken exclusively is proven by his
provision that any man who is thirty-five years old and still unmarried
should pay a fine.[50] Exclusive usage also figures in his regulation that girls
might take part in racing from the age of thirteen until (*mechri*) marriage.[51] But on other occasions he clearly intends the word to have an
inclusive meaning, as when he sets the number of citizens in his city at
5,040: "quite correctly," because that number "is divisible by every number from one to [*mechri*] twelve, with the exception of eleven."[52] Plato
also uses the word inclusively when referring to ages; since games are

required to form children's characters at the ages of three, four, five, and even six, he would allow children of both sexes to play together from age three until (*mechri*) six. After the age of six, though, they would begin their separate but equal educations.[53] True to his conservative inclinations, Plato merely codified in his ideal city what was customary at Athens and elsewhere — that education commenced at the age of seven.[54] The *communis opinio* among students of Plato appears to be that, in the *Laws*, schooling began at age six.[55] Since it has been shown, however, that references to age are usually expressed exclusively, children in the Platonic city would have entered school a year later.[56]

In view of *mechri*'s inherent ambiguity, we are perfectly entitled to construe the word in its inclusive sense when it occurs in the scholia. This allows the seven age grades to be placed comfortably into the seven years from fourteen years old through twenty and shows that the scholia and Plutarch in fact concur when they overlap. Since the scholia relate to the Hellenistic *agōgē* and Plutarch's testimony reflects its Roman phase, this agreement shows the extent to which the two phases shared the same age-grade structure. The correlation demonstrated is of vital importance in that it also makes possible a reconstruction of the *agōgē*'s age schemata in the Hellenistic and Roman periods (Table 1).[57]

The result of this reconstruction is that we can now state with some confidence that Spartans during the Roman period were enrolled in the *agōgē* from sixteen through twenty years old.[58] But age was not the only criterion of organization, as the ephebes of each grade were also divided into several smaller groups called *bouai*, a word from the same semantic field as *bous/boes* (bull/cattle).[59] Pastoral imagery continues in the title of a *boua*'s leader — the *bouagos* (cattle leader) — which is tempting to regard as a vestige of the *agōgē*'s prehistoric origin.[60] Recently, though, it was pointed out that the earliest epigraphical evidence for the term *bouagos* comes from the late first century A.D., making an early date for either word highly unlikely.[61] Like so much else from the later *agōgē*, these two terms were coined to evoke a sense of antiquity.[62]

The team competitions that have left the most epigraphical evidence are the ball games. Their victory inscriptions give an inkling of the roles some officials played, as well as provide the key to the riddle of the *agōgē*'s overall structure. This utilization is only possible, however, if we start with a clear conception of the relationship of the *sphaireis* to the other participants in the *agōgē*.[63] What little is known about the *sphaireis* nevertheless contributes substantially to our understanding of them. Unlike the

TABLE I. Age Grades of the Later *Agōgē*

Age	Hellenistic Phase	Roman Phase
14	*rhobidas*	—
15	*promikizomenos*	—
16	*mikizomenos*	*mikichizomenos*
17	*propais*	*pratopampais*
18	*pais*	*hatropampais*
19	*melleirēn*	*melleirēn*
20	*eirēn*	*eirēn*

other ephebic contests, the ball games took place in the city's theater.[64] The find spots for the victory dedications maintain the contrast: whereas the sickle dedications come almost exclusively from the area around the temple of Artemis Orthia, the *sphaireis* inscriptions were discovered in many places, even as far away as the slopes of Mount Taygetus.[65] These different locations point to the ball games possessing a significance different from the other ephebic contests. Pausanias provides a clue when he describes a particular statue of Heracles as the one "to whom the *sphaireis* sacrifice; they are former ephebes [*hoi ek tōn ephēbōn*] who are beginning to be counted as adults."[66]

The *sphaireis* were not simply *eirenes* under another name; rather, they were "ex-ephebes."[67] But if the *sphaireis* were no longer ephebes enrolled in the city's educational system, why were their victory inscriptions dated by the chairman of the board of overseers (*biduoi*), who are known to have administered the ephebic contests?[68] Lucian helps confuse things further merely by including the Spartan ball games in the discussion of ephebic athletic training in his *Anacharsis*.[69] No contradiction arises, however, between the *sphaireis'* nonephebic status and the obvious ephebic associations of the ball game itself if we understand Pausanias to be referring to a sacrifice that took place after the competition, not before. The young Spartans would then have been called "ballplayers" because they had already competed in the ball game, not because they were about to compete in this annual tournament.[70]

An important gain in understanding results. The Spartan youths who were former ephebes after the ball tournament was over must have still been considered ephebes during the tournament, since it was organized under the aegis of the top ephebic officials. The *sphaireis* game was thus a type of graduation ceremony, marking the transition from ephebe to adult. In ancient terms, it was similar to the exhibitions (*apodeixeis*) held regularly in other cities to test the accomplishments of boys and ephebes.[71]

With the *sphaireis* inscriptions in their proper place as the last documents young Spartans dedicated as ephebes, we can now explore their implications for the structure of the Roman *agōgē* as a whole. First, the victorious *sphaireis* teams billed themselves as "having defeated the *ōbai*," indicating that, during the tournament, the ephebes were divided into groups called *ōbai*.[72] The *ōbai* had names that recalled the ancient constituent communities of archaic Sparta. The first four are found in inscriptions — Limnaeis, Pitanatae, Cynooureis, and Neopolitae; Pausanias provides the fifth — Mesoatae.[73] Of these, Limnaeis and Cynooureis also appear as tribes (*phulai*) in two inscriptions, prompting some to lump the tribes and the *ōbai* together as Sparta's version of the so-called civic tribes, by which citizens in Greek cities were organized.[74] If this is the case, the Spartan civic tribes were remarkably quiescent, for there is no evidence of them except in ephebic and athletic contexts.[75] Even in the inscribed careers these names only appear in conjunction with the post of *diabetēs*, the *sphaireis'* team manager.[76] And it has long been recognized that the size of the boards of Spartan magistrates can have had no connection with the number of these tribes.[77] The evidence does not allow any definite statements at present; all that can be said is that the Spartan civic tribes of the Roman period, if indeed they existed, seem to have been of significance only in terms of the *agōgē* in particular and athletic activity in general.

The *ōba*'s relationship to the tribe in terms of the *agōgē*, however, can be defined with greater precision. *Ōbai* occur only in the *sphaireis* inscriptions, which never mention *phulai*.[78] A tribe was not, accordingly, the same as an *ōba*, in spite of bearing the same name. The only other ephebic event for which these names are attested is the endurance contest. When Pausanias tells of the contest's ultimate origins in a bloody altercation among the inhabitants of Pitane, Limnae, Mesoa, and Cynooura in the years before Lycurgus, he is actually echoing the participation in the contest, in his own day, of ephebes divided into these groups.[79] His version of the origin story is an etiological fantasy, more than likely concocted in the Roman period to furnish a Lycurgan pedigree for a contest that dated only from the Hellenistic period.[80] While of no use to histo-

TABLE 2. The Roman *Agōgē*

Team Type	Tribes				
	Pitanatae	Mesoatae	Limnaeis	Cynooureis	Neopolitae
Boua	mikkichi-zomenoi	mikkichi-zomenoi	mikkichi-zomenoi	mikkichi-zomenoi	mikkichi-zomenoi
Boua	pratopam-paides	pratopam-paides	pratopam-paides	pratopam-paides	pratopam-paides
Boua	hatropam-paides	hatropam-paides	hatropam-paides	hatropam-paides	hatropam-paides
Boua	melleirenes	melleirenes	melleirenes	melleirenes	melleirenes
Boua/ōba	eirenes/sphaireis	eirenes/sphaireis	eirenes/sphaireis	eirenes/sphaireis	eirenes/sphaireis

rians of Archaic Sparta, this tale tells us that other ephebes of Pausanias' time were divided into groups with the same names as the *sphaireis*.

I suggest that these groups were the *phulai*, each of which contained a *boua* from each of the grades from *mikkichizomenos* to *eirēn*. For the ball tournament marking the end of their time in the *agōgē*, the *eirenes* of each tribe were counted as that tribe's *ōba*. The framework of the *agōgē*, as envisioned here, can best be presented in tabular form (Table 2).

The ephebes in these ranks were not, of course, left to their own devices. Close supervision had been fundamental to the Classical *agōgē*, and the situation was no different during the Roman period.[81] We have already met the Spartan equivalents of the monitors and prefects of twentieth-century schools — the *bouagoi*, who led the members of the *bouai* under them. That there were more than one *boua* for each age grade is proved by a sickle dedication erected by two *bouagoi* of the *mikkichizomenoi*, who had been victorious in the same year.[82] The age of the *bouagoi* has been controversial for many years, with one party asserting that *bouagoi* were older than their charges, the other that they were coevals.[83] Recently, an argument has been cogently advanced that the other members of a *boua* were the same age as their *bouagos*, largely on the strength of their styling themselves his fellow ephebes (*sunephēboi*), a term characterized elsewhere as "surely diagnostic" for the Roman phase.[84] Although I think that this argument is almost certainly correct, the fact remains that

Plutarch clearly and unequivocally states, in the section of the *Lycurgus* reflecting his own eyewitness experience of the *agōgē*'s ceremonies, that the *eirenes* commanded the ephebes: "So this *eirēn*, who is twenty, commands those arrayed under him in the fights and, at home, uses them as servants at dinner. He orders the big boys to bring wood and the smaller ones to bring vegetables."[85] If this *eirēn* was not a *bouagos*, then what was he?

Plutarch's words cannot be explained away, so they must be accounted for. Notable are the different tasks assigned the "big boys" (*tois hadrois*) and the "smaller ones" (*tois mikroterois*). We might perhaps be dealing with boys of the same age but at different levels of physical development, if such a division of labor among coevals were not inconceivable for the Spartan *agōgē*, especially when, in its mannered, self-consciously "Lycurgan" phase, emphasis on at least an outward display of egalitarianism would have been heavy indeed. Boys in the same age grade must have been expected to perform tasks of similar strenuousness; in the endurance contest, for instance, the priestess of Artemis ensured that all the ephebes undergoing the trial were treated equally.[86] Collecting wood and gathering vegetables can by no stretch of the imagination be thought to require the same degree of exertion; thus, the distinction in assigning the jobs to the big boys and the smaller ones was one of age, not simply size.[87] The boys were not the same age and therefore could not belong to the same age grade or *boua*.

The tribe (*phulē*) was the only ephebic grouping to span more than one age grade. Plutarch's *eirēn*, who commands boys of differing ages, is therefore not the leader of the pack (*boua*) but of the tribe (*phulē*).[88] The *eirēn* who bore this responsibility was known as the tribe's "senior" (*presbus*), a title known from a statue base and from the *sphaireis* dedications, where the senior appears as the team captain.[89] If we accept the idea that the *boua* of the *eirenes* grade in each ephebic tribe transformed itself into an *ōba* of *sphaireis* for the ball tournament, then the *ōba*'s captain would have been none other than the *bouagos* of the *boua*, who also acted, ex officio, as head of the entire ephebic tribe.[90]

We can now sketch the outlines of the *agōgē*'s structure in the Roman period. All boys belonged to one of five age grades and were also enrolled in one of five tribes, with each tribe containing members from all the grades. In each grade, the boys formed *bouai*, probably one for each tribe, under the leadership of one of their number, who served as *bouagos*. The post was, as a rule, an annual one, for we know of a boy who was the fellow ephebe of two different *bouagoi*.[91] During their years in the *agōgē*, the ephebes contended in the various competitions, festivals, and mock battles either individually or as members of a *boua* or *phulē* until, in the *eirēn* year, the *boua* turned into the tribe's team for the ball tournament, while their *bouagos* became the team's captain and the ephebic tribe's leader. After completing the game, the youths officially left the *agōgē* and performed their first public act as young adults (*sphaireis*), a sacrifice to Heracles, god of physical endurance and success in the face of adversity.

The relationships that developed among ephebes in the *agōgē* had a semiofficial character that lasted a lifetime. Returning to the fellow ephebes noted earlier, we find a large number of adult Spartan notables identifying themselves as fellow ephebes (*sunephēboi*) of particular men who had been *bouagoi*. The title *sunephēbos* appears in catalogs of magistrates as well as individual careers from the Flavian period onward and is perhaps to be associated with the first epigraphical attestation of the *bouagos* at this time. The relationship appears to have had overtones of patronage and dependency: *bouagoi* (or their parents) sometimes paid the expenses for erecting honorific *stēlai* the city had voted for their fellow ephebes, and one year a *bouagos* and four of his *sunephēboi* had the good fortune to form the board of keepers of the laws (*nomophulakes*).[92] We should perhaps envision the *bouagos* acting as a sponsor of sorts for the members of his *boua*, with duties and responsibilities loosely analogous to those of a young Athenian *sustremmatarchēs*, who was expected to help support the ephebes under his command.[93]

The other connection some of the ephebes entered into is of an altogether more mysterious nature; unfortunately, the evidence is not such that we can penetrate the surrounding fog. A large number of Spartans called themselves "*kasen* to" someone else. Much is unknown about *kasens*, including the word's meaning and etymology. The most recent opinion has it that "*kasen*-ship" was a mechanism that enabled poorer Spartans to pass through the *agōgē* by establishing a form of foster tie with wealthier contemporaries.[94] The need for such a relationship can easily be imagined. In fact, as early as the fourth century B.C., Xenophon had already recognized the financial burden such a lengthy education could impose.[95] As well, the *kasen* is first attested, along with so many other prominent elements of the Roman *agōgē*, only from the second half of the first century A.D., virtually guaranteeing that it was an archaizing creation rather than a true relic of archaic times.

The titles of several officials involved in the *agōgē*'s administration have come down to us but in virtually no instance are their duties explicitly described. In spite of this handicap, it is still possible to get a sense of their general competencies, uncommunicative though the evidence is. Foremost was the *patronomos*, who also acted as the city's eponymous magistrate, in a striking indication of the *agōgē*'s prestige. Even though we can only glimpse the duties of the *patronomos* and his junior colleagues (*sunarchoi/sumpatronomoi*), the evidence is consistent.[96] The *patronomos* was praised for his presidency of the "Lycurgan customs," as the *agōgē* was often called in the later period.[97] Such presidencies, like the post of gymnasiarch, with which the patronomate was sometimes combined, would have entailed large benefactions in cash and kind for the upkeep of facilities and ephebic training.[98] As a gymnasiarch was expected to pay for a lavish supply of oil at the city's gymnasia, so the *patronomos* probably had a similar obligation in the sphere of the *agōgē*.[99] Their jurisdictions sometimes overlapped: a certain M. Aurelius Chrysogonus was praised for his activities while gymnasiarch at the same time as for his benefactions to the *agōgē*, and another gymnasiarch had his statue erected at the expense of the assistants to the *patronomos*.[100]

Nonetheless, the post was not exclusively a financial liturgy, which required deep pockets but not a great expenditure of time. On the contrary, the *patronomos* had some actual duties to perform as the existence of deputy *patronomoi* makes evident. These came in two categories: proxies (*epimelētai*) of the god Lycurgus and men who acted as *patronomos* on a mortal incumbent's behalf when he was incapacitated. Almost all of the inscriptions mentioning such deputies are connected in some way with the *agōgē*, as either sickle dedications, *sphaireis* dedications, or inscriptions erected by officials of the *agōgē*.[101] Conversely, *patronomoi* whose deputies appear in agogic texts appear by themselves in the dating formulas of ordinary public documents, a phenomenon well exemplified by the patronomates of the god Lycurgus: texts relating to the *agōgē* refer to his mortal proxies, whereas documents emanating from other public bodies do not.[102] The appearance of these deputy *patronomoi* almost exclusively in texts connected with the *agōgē* suggests that the recording of *patronomoi* in civic inscriptions as a whole was for dating purposes only, whereas in the *agōgē* it was thought necessary to commemorate who had actually fulfilled the *patronomos*' obligations.[103] What these obligations were precisely is impossible to determine, but it is not unreasonable to speculate that the *patronomos* regularly performed some sort of public ceremony, possibly a sacrifice, to inaugurate the contests at the sanctuary of Orthia and the theater.

The *patronomos* and his colleagues may also have been required to resolve the disputes that would inevitably have arisen over such matters as victories in the contests or eligibility for the *agōgē*. At any rate, we find a committee of former *patronomoi* being called on to hear appeals of fines levied on athletes who had misbehaved in the Leonidea games, perhaps because of the expertise the ex-*patronomoi* would have gained from similar situations while in office.[104] A role above and beyond the purely ceremonial is also intimated by a fragmentary inscription containing a joint catalog of members of the patronomate and the *biduoi*, whose function, alone of all the ephebic officials at Sparta, we know something about.[105] The board of *biduoi* was charged with the organization of the mock battle at Platanistas grove and the other ephebic contests, according to Pausanias.[106] Thus, the appearance of the *patronomos* and his assistants together with the *biduoi* suggests that he, or his representative, was more involved in the day-to-day administration of the *agōgē* than at first appears.[107]

The companions of the *patronomos* in this list, the *biduoi* (overseers), are the only other public officials known to have been involved in the overall running of the *agōgē*. They were magistrates similar to the Athenian *kosmētai* or Rhodian *epistatai* of children.[108] Like other important civic magistracies of Roman Sparta, the six *biduoi* were organized into a board headed by a chairman.[109] The office had its own measure of prestige: only the Gerousia and joint committee (*sunarchia*), the city's top magistracies, are mentioned more often in careers of Spartan notables and, apart from the lists of those same offices, catalogs of *biduoi* are the most numerous in the city.[110] The organizational duties must have entailed some paperwork and record keeping, since a secretary is attested.[111] We know that on at least one occasion the secretary of Sparta's ruling council (*boulē*) sat in on the combined sessions of the *biduoi*, *patronomos*, and *sunarchoi*, from which we can infer that the chief organs of government kept a close eye on the *biduoi*'s activities.[112]

Probably the most shocking aspect of Classical Sparta's educational system, to contemporaries at least, was that girls trained and competed in contests similar to those of their brothers and cousins. A frustratingly fragmentary allusion to "the daughters of Dionysus" in a list of *biduoi* and a reference by Pausanias to a ritual race they ran shows that in this, too, the traditions of the past were still carefully cultivated.[113] Clearly, *biduoi* administered contests for girls as well as for youths, indicating that girls were considered to be just as much members of the *agōgē* as the ephebes. Regrettably, apart from this and what has justly been called "a scatter of evidence" for the physical training of girls in the Roman period, nothing survives that might enable us to venture any guesses whatsoever about the organizational framework of the female version of the *agōgē*.[114] Despite this ignorance, we can assume that Spartan girls had training that mirrored to some extent that of the ephebes during every phase of the *agōgē*'s history.

The last ephebic official whose title we know is the *diabetēs*. The *diabetēs* differed from the *patronomos* and the *biduoi* in two respects: he was of junior rank and did not exercise jurisdiction over the entire *agōgē*. *Diabetai* were, on the other hand, attached to each of the *sphaireis* teams representing the ephebic tribes in the ball tournament.[115] Some were volunteers, implying that, as with other liturgies involving considerable personal expense, a notable willingness to shoulder the burden redounded to one's credit.[116] The impulse to spend lavishly, as with similar offices in other cities, was overwhelming and led to at least one incumbent's father underwriting the expenses himself.[117] What exactly the money was spent on is impossible to tell, but it certainly would have had to do with training the teams for the tournament. How seriously people took this task and the post itself, junior though it was, is clear from the loyalty felt by Spartans for their old teams, an affection at times approaching that of American alumni for their old college football teams. One Spartan, whose distinguished career included an embassy to the emperor Hadrian, dutifully recorded his time as *diabetēs* of the Cynooureis when they won for the first time in forty years.[118]

Not only did the *agōgē* require elected magistrates and officials to function effectively, but also trained faculty and staff. A few of these functionaries appear on inscriptions: teachers concerned with the Lycurgan customs to instruct the youths in their heritage, drill instructors to teach them the martial arts, and physical trainers to keep them fit.[119] The curriculum surely had some rhetorical and philosophical content as well but, unsurprisingly, given the primacy of athletics in later Greek education generally and its overwhelming predominance in the traditions of education at Sparta, nothing explicit has survived.[120] This does not mean that Sparta was an intellectual backwater; in fact, a recent study has

shown that from the late Hellenistic age onward Sparta had an intelligentsia of its own and drew thinkers from all over the Greek world.[121]

We must also keep in mind that the ephebes, drawn up by *boua* and
tribe, commanded by their *bouagoi* and *presbeis*, disciplined by their
teachers, and guided by the senior magistrates of the *agōgē*, were merely
part of a larger picture. Greek urban culture had been dominated by the
gymnasium for centuries. As the centers of physical and literary training,
the gymnasia assumed an importance visible even today in the immensity
of their ruins.[122] Sparta did not stand apart from this trend: the city
was studded with gymnasia, which had to be maintained and staffed.[123]
Ephebes would have made up only a portion of their clientele; the rest
were professional athletes and local enthusiasts who could not bear to
forsake the camaraderie of ephebic life. Elsewhere in Greece, such people
formed organizations of young men (*neoi*) who met together and kept up
with the old exercises.[124] At Sparta, those past ephebic age belonged to an
association of *neaniskoi*, headed by a *neaniskarchēs*.[125] The *sphaireis*, as
ex-ephebes, would have formed a contingent within the *neaniskoi*, since
neoi were usually young men older than twenty, but younger than thirty
years old, the age at which they would normally assume the responsibilities and privileges of full citizenship.[126]

Attached to the *neaniskoi* were several officials, most notable of whom
was the cavalry commander (*hipparchēs*).[127] It was a junior post, held
early in a Spartan's career, with a distinctly liturgical tinge. One man
was both hipparch and games president at the same time, while another
held the title "eternal hipparch."[128] Simultaneous tenure of two offices
was usually a sign that an incumbent's money was more important than
his personal involvement, and an "eternal" magistracy was commonly
granted persons who had endowed their city with a sum of money, the
interest from which could be used in the future to defray the expenses
associated with the office.[129] Although the hipparch may have been expected to lead the *neaniskoi* in procession with the ephebes, as was the
custom elsewhere, his main duty was assuredly to supply oil and maintain
the building used by the *neaniskoi*.[130]

Lastly, there are the three *lochagoi* attested in the Roman period. What
functions they actually performed we can only guess.[131] In the Classical
period the *lochagos* had been the commander of a company (*lochos*) in the
army.[132] Since the Spartan army no longer existed, they could not have
been true army officers. On the other hand, given the militaristic cast of

Spartan and indeed Greek ephebic training even in the later period, the
lochagos might have been an ephebic official or, more likely, a subordinate
of the hipparch in command of *neoi* drawn from one of the ephebic tribes.
This explanation gains some confirmation from that group of Spartan
youths who, as the rather self-consciously named *lochos* of Pitane, accompanied the emperor Caracalla on his desultory eastern campaign.[133]

Thus far, the *agōgē* in its Roman phase has been presented only as a
static theoretical framework. To Spartans, it was, of course, far more than
that, for the Lycurgan customs were a vital source of pride and the foundation of their civic identity. Through all the cataclysmic changes the city
had suffered, the *agōgē* had been preserved as a link with Sparta's heritage. How the *agōgē*'s structures and traditions, invented or not, were
manifested and incorporated into the continually evolving dialogue Spartans conducted with their past will form the subject of the next chapter.

3

THE CONTESTS OF THE LATER *AGŌGĒ*

For centuries, Sparta had been renowned for its festivals, whose choruses and dances, especially at the Hyacinthia and Gymnopaediae, drew visitors from all over the civilized world.[1] Just as popular were the more rigorous spectacles—the battle of the ephebes, the ball tournament, and the endurance contest. Spartans and foreigners alike, the spectators at these events would have witnessed a visible, living expression of the city's culture and heritage. During the festivals, Sparta's most ancient history was articulated in the *agōgē*: ephebes grouped according to the ancestral divisions of the city's earliest inhabitants took part in competitions that, everyone knew, had been established by Lycurgus himself. The ephebes would also have attended other spectacles in organized groups, perhaps sitting in an area specially reserved for them.[2] At one particular festival, the public reading of a flattering account of the Classical Spartan constitution further strengthened the sense of civic continuity and stability. "The world may have changed, but we have remained the same" was the message relentlessly promulgated through the media of ephebic festivals and contests.[3] This chapter focuses on these contests, since the *agōgē* manifested itself through them as the preeminent instrument for asserting Spartan identity.

PLATE 2. *General view of the Orthia sanctuary from the east*

The center of ephebic activity was the sanctuary of the goddess Artemis Orthia, situated on the west bank of the river Eurotas, just below the easternmost height of a series of hills that terminates in the west with the city's acropolis (Plate 2). The area's ancient name, Limnae (Marshes) is as suitable now as in antiquity. The temple, of modest proportions, is oriented on the usual east-west axis and, to the end of the Roman period, seems to have preserved the aspect of its Hellenistic rebuilding, assigned by the excavators to 178 B.C. but probably better associated with Cleomenes III.[4] As we would expect, the edifice was built in the Doric style, lacking a surrounding colonnade but with two columns in the east porch. To the east, at an angle to the temple's facade, are the foundations of a long, low altar of Roman date, constructed over the remains of an Archaic predecessor. In the reign of Augustus, stone seats were provided for dignitaries, while in the third century A.D. the temple and altar were incorporated into a large circular complex, which accommodated the

PLATE 3. *Foundations of the seating complex at the Orthia sanctuary*

growing audience (Plate 3). The building's design and method of construction are Roman rather than Greek, giving it an amphitheatral air.[5]

The sanctuary's grounds in the Roman period were thickly forested
with *stēlai* cut from the variegated local marbles; to them were fastened
iron sickles to commemorate victories in the ephebic contests. The competitions most often mentioned are *mōa*, *keloia*, and *kaththēratorion* (or
kunagetas), all of which can more or less be identified, even allowing for
the constraints of the evidence. But the other two, the *eubalkēs* and the
deros, still remain inscrutable.[6]

The most transparent of the boys' contests, as they should be called, is
the *mōa*.[7] The name is clearly to be linked with the Laconian word for
Muse, *mōha*, and is glossed by the lexicographer Hesychius as "a kind of
song."[8] The *keloia* is more difficult to explain, although we have an allusion to the technique needed to win. In a verse inscription, Timocrates,
son of Aristoteles, claims to have "won this propitious prize for a nim-

ble tongue," indicating that the *keloia* was also a competition in vocal prowess.[9]

A nimble tongue would have been an asset in any sort of vocal competition, from singing to recitation. Even so, despite the doubts some have expressed, clues can be found to the essential nature of the contest.[10] *Keloia* fits neatly into a group of words denoting noise, song, or exhortation that have at their root *kel-*, "call, cry, clamor, sound."[11] The same root also underlies words connected with the onset of motion.[12] Some words share characteristics of both groups, such as *kelomai*, "launch a ship, invite, call upon"; *kelados*, "rushing sound, commotion"; and *keladeō*, "sound like rushing water, celebrate loudly." I take *keloia* to be the nominative feminine singular form of *keloios*, an adjective derived from a lost word, *kelos. *Keloios* was probably formed in the same way as the analogous adjective *homoios*, "similar," was from *homos*, "single," and is related to *kelados* and *keladeō* as *homoios* is to *homados*, "din of voices," and *homadeō*, "make a noise."[13] Although *keloia* always appears used substantively on the dedications, it would originally have qualified a noun such as "call" (*boē*), or "song" (*ōdē*).

Artemis herself is *keladeinē* ("rushing with cries"), "because of the shouting in the hunt," we are told, and because of "the tumult she makes throughout the countryside."[14] The human voice was a significant element in that clamor. Xenophon advises: "If [the hounds] are on the scent, let [the hunter] stand near and urge them on, going through each hound's name, producing all the tones of voice he possibly can, high, low, soft, loud."[15] Beyond Artemis' general association with the hunt, the chase had particular importance in the ideology of the *agōgē*. This was neatly summed up in the rule that only those who had just hunted might with impunity enjoy the ritual banquet at the festival of Artemis.[16] To bring all three threads together, I propose that *keloia* means "like a hunting call" and was the name given to a competition in singing hymns that invoked Artemis, which took the form of hunting cries.[17] From what Xenophon tells us, speed and clarity of enunciation would have been essential for victory in such a contest.[18]

The last of this triad of contests is the *kaththēratorion*, another contest connected with hunting. A rough-and-tumble hunting game, an actual beast fight, and a dance in imitation of hunting have all been suggested to account for the name, patently derived from *thēra*, "hunt."[19] More precisely, *kaththēratorion* has as its central element *thēratōr*, the doricized form of the unique Homeric word for "hunter," *thērētōr*.[20] This core is followed by the diminutive suffix *-ion* and introduced by the intensifying prefix *kata-*.[21] The *kaththēratorion* was therefore the "little hunter" contest, and so we are undoubtedly dealing here with a danced or mimed hunt rather than with the real thing.

The name's outlandishness should not blind us to its dubious pedigree. It was noticed some time ago that *kaththēratorion* and *kunagetas* ("the hunter"), the name of a similar contest, never appear together on the same stone and that no inscription later than the first century B.C. mentions *kunagetas*. *Kaththēratorion*, on the other hand, is not attested in any dedications earlier than the Flavian period. The economical solution is simply to assume that *kaththēratorion* was the later name for a hunting dance that had at first been called *kunagetas*, the change having taken place at some point prior to the later first century A.D.[22] Even though we unfortunately cannot establish the date of the contest's renaming as *kaththēratorion*, this deliciously archaistic coinage, with its suitably epic allusion, would certainly fit the cultural climate in late Sparta.[23] The *agōgē* shares this prominence of hunting with other late Hellenistic ephebates, where it is often portrayed as a quintessential ephebic activity.[24]

The last two contests mentioned in the sickle dedications remain almost completely mysterious. Unlike the *kunagetas*, the *eubalkēs* and *deros* cannot be associated with any other contest, nor do we know anything about them beyond their names, "the valiant one" and "the shield," although they too may have been mimetic dances or recitations.[25] Like the *kunagetas*, the two events disappear from the epigraphical record after the first century B.C., suggesting that they fell into desuetude soon after.

However imbalanced the available evidence, I believe it useful to set out what can be said about the antiquity of each contest. The *mōa* goes back as far as the late second century B.C., and the *keloia* is attested almost as early, so they seem the best contests with which to begin.[26] Of the two words, *mōa*, as I have shown, is at least consistent in its phonology with Classical Laconian, although it appears as the name of an ephebic contest only in the *agōgē*'s last phase.[27] *Keloia* is unique and unattested outside the sickle dedications; only its occurrence in an agogic document from the Classical or Hellenistic period would prove that a contest of that name existed at Sparta before the Roman period. *Kaththēratorion* had its origins in a Homeric hapax legomenon and was probably devised quite late to replace the earlier *kunagetas*.

Was the *kunagetas* itself a true survival from the earlier phases of the *agōgē*? Probably not, because the word, *kunagetas*, was a late-Hellenistic coinage. At that time, the regularization of dialectal divergences in Greek was proceeding apace. While Attic usually swept aside less robust regional dialects, in the sphere of hunting, perhaps fittingly, the Attic forms *kunēgetō*, "I hunt," and *kunēgetēs*, "hunter," lost out to the corresponding Doric forms *kunagō* and *kunagos*, which, in their atticized guises *kunēgō* and *kunēgos*, were the terms normally used in later Greek.[28] The Spartan hunting contest's name results from a reversal of this process: here, an Attic form has been doricized. The name of the hunting contest in the Doric dialect should have been *kunagos*, but the word was evidently not recondite enough. Instead, the earlier, obsolete Attic form *kunēgetēs* was adopted and made to appear properly Laconian by means of a few Doric alphas. The laconizing *kunagetas* seemed more appealingly arcane to later taste than the tediously familiar *kunagos*, even though this was the authentic Spartan term.

If the *kunagetas/kaththēratorion* was completely an invention of the *agōgē*'s final phase, then the claims to authenticity of the other boys' contests (*mōa, keloia, deros,* and *eubalkēs*) are considerably weakened. If one of these contests can be shown to have been devised after the *agōgē* had been revived for a second time, other contests might quite possibly be later products too. I have no positive proof for this hypothesis, but neither is there any evidence for the existence of these particular contests before the late second century B.C. With the repeated disruption of Sparta's civic life during the Hellenistic period, it would be surprising if the ephebic contests had escaped unscathed.[29]

Although, for Sparta, the epigraphical record of the boys' contests is rather full, it still leaves important questions unanswered. For instance, it is not at all clear that the contests even took place at the same time and the same festival, although a connection has recently been postulated with a mysterious "festival of Artemis Orthia."[30] This uncertainty means that we do not know whether the contests marked the end, the beginning, or some other point in the ephebic year. While the dedications are of no help in the larger problem of situating the competitions within the Spartan festival calendar, a few grains of information can nevertheless still be panned out from these rather barren documents.

The well-nigh invariable order in which the contests are recorded by ephebes who had won two or more events in a single year makes it clear from the start that they competed in the *kaththēratorion* first, then in the *mōa*, and finally in the *keloia*.[31] The three other contests appear so seldom that even their place in the sequence cannot be determined. Furthermore, it appears that ephebes in fact competed in these contests as individuals, not grouped into *bouai* or *phulai*, in spite of a preponderance of dedicants who were *bouagoi*.[32] The *bouagoi* did not, as once thought, make their dedications on behalf of the boys under their command, but rather to commemorate their own victories.[33] Proof comes in the form of separate dedications in the same year by M. Ulpius Aristocrates and his *bouagos*, C. Julius Eurycles, victors in the *keloia* and *kaththēratorion* respectively.[34]

The inscriptions also point to the existence of more than one level of competition in each event. The contests appearing on the stones can be classified into three groups: contests unqualified by any adjective or noun; contests qualified by the name of an age grade in the genitive plural, for example "*keloia* of the *mikichizomenoi*"; and contests described as *to paidikon*, "the children's."[35] Those contests qualified by an age-grade name make the best sense as involving competition among boys of the same age; examples survive for four of the five age grades. Since no victor of a contest in the first two categories ever appears to have won a contest in the third, we may conclude that winning a contest *to paidikon* was considerably more prestigious. Indeed, it was recognized some time ago that the phrase was meant to refer to contests between ephebes of all the age grades.[36] A similar sort of contest is known from numerous agonistic inscriptions from all over the Greek East; the *agōn dia pantōn*, "contest of champions," was a fixture of musical festivals during the Roman period.[37] In the final event of the program, victors in every event would compete for overall victory at the festival.

No single individual could achieve such prominence at Sparta as an overall champion, but he could be victorious over ephebes from all five age grades in a single event: as one young Spartan put it, "From all my fellow ephebes, I myself took the prize."[38] Because the glory of a victory in the open competition eclipsed that of merely defeating one's age mates, we should not be surprised if these victors passed over their lesser victories. Conversely, because a victor *to paidikon* would hardly have hidden his light under a bushel by failing to draw attention to this distinction in his dedication, those ephebes who did not claim to have won an event *to paidikon* must have won only in the events for each age grade and failed in the open competition.

To examine the next contest I must move away from the certainties, however slight, that the sanctuary of Artemis Orthia provides. Much remains unknown about the ephebic "battle" at the so-called Plane-Tree

Grove (Platanistas), notwithstanding picturesque accounts by Pausanias, Lucian, and Cicero.[39] We have not a scrap of epigraphical evidence, neither implicit nor explicit, on the Platanistas fight that might shed some light on its many mysteries, including, predictably, when it was held.

First, however, I want to survey what the literary evidence has to offer. On a particular night, outside the city at a shrine called the Phoebeum, two bands of ephebes who were to compete against each other the following day each sacrificed a black puppy to the war god Enyalius.[40] Afterward, the ephebes set two boars to fight each other, with the victorious boar usually belonging to the team that would win the next day.[41] A second set of rituals also occurred, presumably in the morning before the battle, when the ephebes about to fight sacrificed to the hero Achilles.[42] Pausanias describes the site of the contest, the Plane-Tree Grove, with fair precision: "There is a place, Platanistas, named from the trees, plane trees, which grow high and unbroken around it. A channel surrounds in a circle the place, where it is customary for the ephebes to fight, in the very same way as the sea does an island; entrance is by bridges. On one of the bridges is a statue of Heracles, on the other an image of Lycurgus."[43] Lucian confirms that the place was "outlined with water" and adds that, the night before, both bands had drawn lots to determine by which bridge they would enter the island and consequently under whose patronage they would fight the next day, Lycurgus' or Heracles'.[44] Once on the island, the ephebes laid into one another with a vengeance: "they fight hand to hand and with jump kicks; they bite and gouge out eyes. Man against man, they fight in the way I've described; they attack violently en masse and push one other into the water."[45] Cicero hit the nail on the head when he called it "that incredible conflict."[46] Victory came to the team that pushed all its opponents into the water, "after which there was peace and no one let fly any more."[47] The proceedings ended with choral dances and songs, both warlike and festive, to the accompaniment of a flute.[48]

What we must first ask is, Where did this contest take place? Our only guide is Pausanias, who comes upon the Platanistas just after leaving the race course (*dromos*) area where the city's main athletic facilities were located.[49] The *dromos* was located near the city's theater, perhaps slightly to the west.[50] The Platanistas was situated between there and the city wall, in a spot northwest of the acropolis.[51] Eagerness to identify features visible in modern times with the complex described by Pausanias has misled nineteenth- and twentieth-century topographers into identifying a millstream as the water system for the Platanistas' moat.[52] Even though there are no signs of any such system at all in the area today, I am still loath to postulate that Pausanias made "an unheralded leap" in his narrative eastward to the banks of the Eurotas just before he describes the Platanistas and an equally silent jump back to the west a little later, purely on the grounds that his description presupposes a natural abundance of water.[53]

In its actual details, Pausanias' account shows the Platanistas with some conspicuously man-made elements: the plane trees can only have been planted intentionally in order to grow in an unbroken circle and the circular moat itself (*euripos*) is unlikely to have formed in a natural way. The Platanistas fits the type of an artificial landscape, enhanced through a combination of shade trees and water courses, that was commonly associated with gymnasial areas in the Hellenistic period.[54] The statues marking the two bridges onto the island were probably Hellenistic creations as well, since a statue of a semihistorical figure such as Lycurgus would be most appropriate to that period, and, without it, a statue of Heracles becomes inexplicable, given the tradition of each team fighting under the protection of either divinity.[55] Moreover, these self-conscious references in the ceremonies of the contest to the Spartans' two great ancestors, to the Homeric hero Achilles, and to Apollo smack of a studied antiquarianism typical of Greek civic culture during the Hellenistic and Roman periods.[56]

Without having any tangible remains at our disposal, the extent to which the area of the Platanistas was artificially enhanced can be an object of enjoyable speculation for the foreseeable future. Working from the assumption that the locality was almost completely artificial in the Roman period, a recent proposal to identify the ruins of an Antonine bath and gymnasium complex in an area to the west of the acropolis as part of the Platanistas is quite seductive, since the remains include part of a large curved wall that may well have surrounded an island and moat (Plate 4).[57] But I would hesitate to go so far as to claim that this very fragmentary and ambiguous structure has a "perfect identity" with the so-called Teatro Marittimo of Hadrian's villa at Tivoli.[58] All the same, it is quite within the realm of possibility that the Teatro Marittimo was at least inspired by, and perhaps was even a copy of, the Spartan Platanistas complex. The similarities between the two are certainly suggestive — a circular island surrounded by a moat that can be crossed on two footbridges — and such an imitation would conform to what we are told of

PLATE 4. *Roman ruins northwest of the acropolis*

Hadrian's intentions in building the villa.[59] Unfortunately, only in the unlikely event of a resumption of full-scale excavations in the area could this intriguing hypothesis be tested.

The board of *biduoi* administered the Platanistas battle but, as usual, we have no idea of what this entailed.[60] Although Pausanias devotes even more space to the Platanistas than he does to the whipping contest, much less information about how it was organized can be wrung out of his and other accounts. However, we can embark on the modest assertion that we do know that the battle was between two groups of ephebes, most probably ephebic tribes under the command of *presbeis*.[61]

Once this general statement regarding the participants has been made, another problem arises in its turn. All accounts of the fight mention only two groups of combatants, but there were definitely five ephebic tribes at this time—Limnaeis, Cynooureis, Pitanatae, Mesoatae, and Neopolitae.[62] The anomaly may be explained in one of two ways. We may either assume that the Platanistas battle was a single annual event, in which the

PLATE 5. *Theater below the acropolis*

two contending tribes would probably have been selected by lot, or suppose that there were preliminary heats, from which the victorious teams advanced to the final match that was the violent public spectacle our sources describe. This arrangement would at least have guaranteed the participation of all ephebes in the competition even if they did not proceed to the final round. In addition, the complexities of such a system and its potential for provoking dispute would have required close supervision by the *biduoi*, who would have had experience in such matters from their administration of the one ephebic contest that undoubtedly had preliminary rounds, the ball tournament.

As the discussion has already touched on the *sphaireis* and their tournament, I should summarize what has been established before proceeding further. *Sphaireis* were *eirenes* who had just passed out of the *agōgē*, after having competed in a ball tournament at the city's theater on the southwest slope of the acropolis (Plate 5). In this tournament, each ephebic tribe was represented by the *boua* of its eldest grade, which competed as an *ōba*. The *ōba*'s *bouagos*, who was also tribal commander, acted as the team's captain.

The *biduoi* were the most important magistrates in the contest's administration; their chairman appears in the dating formulas of the victory dedications. There were also junior officials called *diabetai*, each of whom seems to have been responsible for financing his team's training. Sporadic references to "voluntary" *diabetai* (*diabetai autepangeltoi*) indicate that tenure of this office was usually by appointment or election.[63] Two volunteers are also styled *aristindēs*. But this was not an honorific title given to the *diabetēs*, from which it is distinguished in the *sphaireis* dedications. They refer to the "voluntary *diabetēs* and *aristindēs*" or to the "*aristindēs* and voluntary *diabetēs*," and the word appears by itself at the beginning of the career of one Julius Arion.[64] It was probably an office of some kind, with its name related to the adverb *aristindēn*, "according to rank, merit."[65] An obscure Hesychian gloss confirms the derivation: "*Aristindēs*: he who has been selected from the best."[66] In terms of the *sphaireis* dedications, "the best" would have been the Spartan youths who had distinguished themselves in the *agōgē*, perhaps as members of victorious *sphaireis* teams. While we can know nothing about what duties the post involved, two of the three attested *aristindai* also volunteered to be *diabetai*, which may indicate that young Spartans selected for this honor were expected to give some financial support to their successors as *sphaireis*.

The ball contest was a tournament of several rounds. Teams that had won without the advantage of sitting out a round were not coy about advertising their accomplishment and boasted of gaining their victories "without a bye" (*anephedroi*).[67] This is enough to refute the contention once advanced that only the four epigraphically attested tribes (Limnaeis, Cynooureis, Pitanatae, and Neopolitae) survived into the Roman period. An odd number is needed for byes to be necessary, and Pausanias conveniently provides a fifth name (Mesoatae) when recounting the origin of the endurance contest.[68]

From all accounts, the matches themselves were rough-and-tumble affairs, as we should expect. Lucian describes the *sphaireis* "falling on balls in the theater and striking one another."[69] Although the Spartan evidence is, as usual, uncommunicative, it is nevertheless possible to identify precisely the game played: it was called "on the lime" (*episkuros*) or "battle ball" (*sphairomachia*) and was known to have been a local tradition at Sparta, which incidentally claimed to have invented the sport of ball playing.[70] The second-century lexicographer Pollux has left us a detailed description of the game's rules:

> The names of the ball games were "on the lime," "feigning," "dribbling," and "sky high." "On the lime" is also called the "ephebic game" and the "all-in game"; it is played in a crowd which has split into two equal sides. Then with white lime they draw a line down the middle which they call "the lime," and onto which they place the ball. After drawing another two lines behind each team, preselected team members throw the ball over the other team, whose job it was to catch hold of the moving ball and throw it back until one side pushes the other over the back line.[71]

A better candidate for the game played by the *sphaireis* could not be hoped for, especially in view of its association with ephebes. *Episkuros* would have seemed to our modern eyes like a hybrid of North American football, rugby, and a sort of netless volleyball. Winning teams would have had to rely on a combination of individual agility (to catch and return the ball) and cooperative mass strength (to push the opposing team back). For spectators, the sport must have been quite gripping, which would explain the intensity of feeling some Spartans had for their old teams.[72]

The *sphaireis* tournament marked an important transition in the lives of young Spartans, as the end of their time as ephebes and the beginning of adulthood. In most communities, ancient and modern, such changes in societal status are usually expressed in symbols of remarkable consistency, which mark what are called rites of passage.[73] To a greater or lesser extent, all Greek ephebates incorporated elements of rites of passage. While in transition between the two stages, people are considered to be in what is called a liminal state, possessing neither their former nor their future status. During this time, they are taught the traditions and duties of the group to which they will belong and are excluded from society, either symbolically or physically; in general, Greek ephebes were surrounded by signs of their liminal status.[74]

This symbolism has left a few traces in Sparta's city plan. The move in social status from ephebe to adult that competition in the ball tournament represented was mirrored in a spatial movement from the literal liminality of the Orthia sanctuary, in the area called Limnae right beside the city's late Hellenistic walls, to a theater located at the city's center, built into the very side of the acropolis, where the ephebic competitors came face to face with tangible emblems of Spartan civic pride in the form of lists of magistrates and their individual careers carved into the blocks of the east retaining wall. Even with the little that is known of the city's layout, we can observe that other elements of what might be called Sparta's ephebic topography conform to this dichotomy as well. The Phoebeum and the shrine of Achilles, where combatants in the Platanistas contest performed sacrifices, were both extraurban sanctuaries, and the Platanistas itself, like the sanctuary of Orthia, was not far inside the walls.[75]

The pairing of Lycurgus and Heracles, so conspicuous at the Platanistas, may also have recurred in the ball tournament. After the tournament had concluded, the victorious teams sacrificed to Heracles and erected commemorative *stēlai*. Furthermore, it has been argued that some pilasters carved in the shape of herms of Heracles originally decorated the stage of the theater; thus, the divinity may himself have overseen the competitions.[76] As for Lycurgus, his statue was placed before the catalogs of magistrates and individual careers that had been inscribed on the theater's east *parodos* wall. Although the statue no longer exists, and Pausanias neglected to mention it in his description of the venue, there is cast-iron evidence for it in the form of an honorific statue base still in situ bearing the provision that it be erected beside Lycurgus and two other bases found in the theater, one to be erected near Lycurgus, the other styling its honorand the "new Lycurgus."[77] A statue of Lycurgus in a theater appears utterly inappropriate at first, but the presence there of the other statues and the magistrate lists indicates the theater was thought a suitable place to advertise one's involvement in local government and display one's civic pride. The reason for this intersection of politics and public entertainment is surely that, at Sparta as at many other places in the Roman age, the theater also functioned as an occasional meeting place for the city's assembly.[78]

If this hypothesis is correct, and in view of the parallels it is more than probable, then the *sphaireis* competed not only in the geographical center of the city but at its legislative and constitutional heart as well. From being ephebes whose activities seem to have been focused almost exclusively around the edges of the city, they moved to Sparta's heart to become full citizens. To symbolize their passage out of the *agōgē*, the ballplayers alone of the ephebes were permitted to erect memorials of their victories outside the ephebic precinct, in the city at large. Sparta was probably not the only city where a change in spatial location visibly manifested a movement in societal status. A similar, but less obvious, correlation between social movement and the location of ephebic rituals can be seen at Athens, where the ephebic entrance rites took place at the prytaneum, while the graduation sacrifices were performed on the Acropolis.[79]

The *sphaireis* dedications are also useful for another important purpose: their lists provide the means to determine approximately the number of youths enrolled in the *agōgē* in a year. A single dedication has enough of its team catalog preserved to show that it contained a total of fourteen names.[80] As the *sphaireis* team was essentially a *boua*, calculating the total number of ephebes is quite simple. Multiplying that number by the number of tribes (five) and by the number of age grades (five) we arrive at a total of 350.

We should bear in mind that this figure can only be considered an extremely rough estimate, since the strength of each *boua* undoubtedly fluctuated over time. Nonetheless, it does indicate that the ephebic population at Sparta was extremely large in comparison with other cities. Even at Athens, the number of ephebes in years from which we have complete lists rarely rose above two hundred.[81] With the Spartan ephebes so numerous, the cost of administration must have been enormous, which makes the praise accorded benefactors of the *agōgē* all the more understandable.[82] Still, in assessing the sizes of the *agōgē* and other ephebates, we should bear in mind that the *agōgē*, at least theoretically, lasted five years in the Roman period, whereas most other contemporary ephebates were of one year's duration.[83] A single Spartan age grade would not, in a good year, have contained much more than seventy ephebes, a number congruent with the size of late Sparta's population as a whole.

In those years when the number of boys in the *agōgē* was not large, the *bouai* might not have contained their full complement of members, which may be the reason behind a puzzling characteristic of the sickle dedications: the later dedicants who mention their age are all *mikichizomenoi*.[84] Victors were once thought more likely to record their age if they had defeated boys from all age grades when they were among the youngest than if they won in an older grade.[85] Against this supposition, I should point out that the qualifying phrase *to paidikon* does not appear on any of the dedications later than that of an unknown *sunephēbos* in the patronomate of Timomenes.[86] In accordance with the use of that phrase in the sickle dedications, it follows that the dedicants of the later inscriptions must have won in the contests among those boys of their own age grades;

in other words, all were *mikichizomenoi* who had won contests of the *mikichizomenoi*.[87] This preponderance of ephebes from the earliest class might imply that only one year was spent in ephebic training in the late second century, and it would certainly explain why none of the victories was won *to paidikon*; if the ephebes were from only one age grade, there would have been no call for another contest involving boys of different ages.[88] The *eirēn* grade must nevertheless have continued to exist in order to account for the *sphaireis* teams. If this suggestion is correct, it means that even within the final phase of the *agōgē*, the inscriptions hint at a far-reaching reorganization in the late second century A.D., reform perhaps compelled by the unwieldiness of the earlier system and the difficulty of enrolling enough boys to make it work properly.

The contests discussed in the preceding pages were restricted to ephebes and were the Spartan equivalent of the *Schulagone* or exhibitions (*apodeixeis*) put on by other cities to show off the training of their youth.[89] Apart from them, Spartan ephebes could also compete in one of the various sets of civic games Sparta held in the Roman period, such as the Urania, Euryclea, Commodea, or Leonidea.[90] Here, the limits of the *agōgē*'s influence on life and institutions outside its confines are clear. The evidence unequivocally shows that ephebes never entered any athletic festival, not even the Leonidea, which was restricted to Spartans, as members of agogic age grades.[91] Instead, the age categories are the same as those at any other Greek agonistic festival: boys (*paides*), youths (*ageneioi*), and men (*andres*).[92] An ephebe of the Pitanatae who won in the Euryclea identified his agonistic class as "of the youths" (*ageneiōn*) without mentioning his Spartan age grade.[93] Another exulted in a string of victories in the boys' wrestling at festivals of Poseidon and Athena stretching from his year as *mikichizomenos* until his *melleironeia*; although he progressed through four different age grades in terms of the *agōgē*, his agonistic age class remained the same.[94] As a nineteen-year-old *melleirēn*, he might seem rather old to be called "boy" (*pais*), but the criteria for agonistic age categories were based on bodily development rather than chronological age alone: for example, a *pais* of eighteen is attested for the Isthmian games.[95] Since many of the games at Spartan festivals were also open to foreigners, they would, of course, have had to conform to international standards for athletic age divisions to avoid confusion among the younger competitors. This must be the reason why no Spartan athletic festival shows any trace of peculiarly Spartan elements in its organization.[96]

The three most famous festivals at Sparta were dedicated to the god

Apollo—the Gymnopaediae, Hyacinthia, and Carnea. Two, the Hyacinthia and Carnea, also included games, as we know from an Augustan list containing a "victor in the Carnea" and a pair of inscriptions from the late second century A.D. referring to "the most reverend contest of the Hyacinthia."[97] The Carnean games could claim an authentic ancient foundation: Sosibius, a Spartan antiquarian of the second century B.C., wrote that they had been founded in the twenty-sixth Olympiad (676–673 B.C.), and Hellanicus attributed the first victory to the poet Terpander of Lesbos in his chronology of winners in the Carnea.[98] From this semilegendary precedent, it can be affirmed that the Carnean games comprised musical competitions, if nothing else, and were open to non-Spartans. Consequently, in the Roman period their age categories would have been the normal Hellenic triad of boys, youths, and men.[99]

Evidence for the antiquity of the Hyacinthian games at the shrine of Apollo Amyclaeus is less straightforward. A fragmentary inscription found at Amyclae, perhaps from the late fourth century B.C., may be a victory dedication, while the choral and equestrian spectacles described by a little-known late Hellenistic writer, Polycrates, might also have been agonistic.[100] We are on somewhat firmer ground with a fragment from the fifth-century historian Antiochus concerning the foundation of Taras, in which he describes the eighth-century conspiracy of the Partheniae as taking place "at the Hyacinthia in the Amyclaeum when the games were being held."[101] Although the existence of the games at such an early date can be doubted, that they were believed to have been held in that era indicates that games at the Hyacinthia were not a novelty in the Classical period.[102] Music was probably preeminent in the Roman period too, perhaps still performed by choruses, but, as a recent study has conceded, equestrian and gymnastic events cannot be ruled out, particularly since a votive discus was found at the Amyclaeum.[103] In the absence of evidence to the contrary, we should assume that, in later centuries, the Hyacinthian games' age categories were also the same three common to all other Spartan competitions in which participation was not restricted exclusively to ephebes.

The participation of Spartan ephebes, most notably in the Gymnopaediae, was and remains these festivals' most celebrated feature. But the precise nature of that participation in terms of the agōgē is a knotty problem in view of the thin sprinkling of evidence available to us.[104] At the Hyacinthia in the late Hellenistic period, boys are attested singing, accompanied by the flute and cithara, as are choruses of young men (*neaniskoi*) singing traditional songs; for the early fourth century we also have evidence for choruses of men.[105] The boys' chorus, we may infer, was drawn from those enrolled in the *agōgē*, but how or even whether it reflected the *agōgē*'s organization cannot be determined.[106] On the other hand, the word *neaniskos* has such a protean range of meanings that it might include boys from the *agōgē* or, just as likely, might not.[107]

In addition, the principles by which chorus members were selected varied from festival to festival, even in the same city: at Athens, for example, membership in some choruses depended upon tribal allegiance, while in others it was open to all.[108] In Classical Sparta, each chorus had its own director, who chose the choristers and assigned them their places, and whose moral suasion could bring a campaigning king home to sing.[109] Since similar systems existed at other cities during antiquity, festival choruses at Sparta were also probably recruited by individuals who were more concerned with finding vocal talent from as large a pool as possible than with conforming to the later *agōgē*'s elaborate age structure.[110] To see how this might have worked, we should look to a torch race at the city of Oenoanda under the Antonine emperors.[111] Two boys were appointed as leaders of teams for the boys' torch race; each was instructed to pick twenty runners, "whomever they judged suitable." As no other restrictions are placed on them, the composition of the teams they picked can in no way have been determined by the constitutional or internal ephebic organization of the city. A similar procedure must be admitted at least as a possibility for the Spartan festival choruses of the Roman period.

The Carnea, according to the well-known description by Demetrius of Scepsis preserved in Athenaeus, was celebrated for nine days in imitation of the military way of life (*mimēma . . . stratiōtikēs agōgēs*); nine tentlike structures were erected for the festival, in each of which groups of nine men representing three clans dined together.[112] It has long been recognized that this part of the festival has no link with the *agōgē* or even the traditional Lycurgan constitutional settlement of Sparta; the recurrence of the number three and its multiples has been reasonably thought to derive instead from the three original Dorian tribes.[113] Apart from this phenomenon, however, there is one event that involved the young specifically and may thus have had some connection with the *agōgē*. The "grape runners" (*staphulodromoi*) were young men (*neoi*) who pursued a man decked out in fillets; if they caught him, good fortune was supposed to come to the city, but if they did not, the opposite would come to pass.[114]

The religious significance of this rite is outside the compass of my investigation, but the identity of the *staphulodromoi* is not.[115] Knowing that they were *neoi* does not really advance our knowledge because *neos* could be applied to as broad an age range as *neaniskos*.[116] Nor can epigraphy provide much guidance, even though we have the texts of two inscriptions presumably erected by *staphulodromoi*: they read "Menestratus *staphulodromas*, Hippodamus priest" and "Aristander *staphulodromas*."[117] Their typical inscrutability is enhanced by the fact that they are known today only from the notes of an eighteenth-century scholar, the abbé Fourmont.[118]

Although the evidence for their status is ludicrously meager, some plausible suggestions about the *staphulodromoi* may still be ventured, if we make one assumption — that the inscriptions are contemporary with the *agōgē*'s final phase. This proposal is not as insupportable as it may seem, because all but one of the agogic inscriptions and the vast majority of Spartan agonistic inscriptions postdate the late second century B.C. In every extant dedication by an ephebe during the Roman period, there is always a reference either to an age grade, a rank or relationship (*bouagos*, *sunephēbos*, *kasen*), or even a tribe, when, as we have seen, a victory was won in a festival that was certainly not associated with the *agōgē*.[119] If the dedications had been erected in the Roman period, the absence of any such indication to distinguish Menestratus out as an ephebe would strongly suggest that he was instead one of the *neoi* who had recently graduated from the *agōgē*.[120] Two glosses by Hesychius, when read in tandem, are compatible with this hypothesis: in the first we learn that the *staphulodromoi* were drawn from the Carneatae, while the second explains that the Carneatae were financially responsible for the festival for a period of four years and were unmarried.[121] It follows that the *staphulodromoi* were themselves unmarried. Since Greek ephebes were, by definition, unmarried, this restriction would have been otiose if the runners had been drawn exclusively from Sparta's ephebic population.[122] The *neoi* who ran in the Carnea were consequently either a mixture of ephebes and young adults or, more likely, young adults alone. Because of this, the ceremony itself probably had no direct structural connection with the *agōgē* in the Roman period.

To a greater or lesser degree, ephebes might have been involved in the Carnea and the Hyacinthia, but those festivals were not themselves part of the *agōgē*'s institutional framework. On the other hand, the Gymnopaediae present a much better prima facie case for being associated with the Spartan ephebate. The Gymnopaediae, which we may translate as

"The Naked Games," were to all intents and purposes an agonistic festival, with choruses competing against one another.[123] Although the composition of these choruses during the earlier phases of the *agōgē* is problematic, our sources from the Roman period and beyond consistently mention only choruses of youths, called either children (*paides*) or ephebes (*ephēboi*).[124] As a festival involving only ephebes, the Gymnopaediae would naturally have been closely linked with the *agōgē* if it was not in fact an ephebic festival per se. How the Gymnopaediae were organized — whether the choruses were formed from age grades, ephebic tribes, or *bouai* — we cannot know, although it seems altogether likely that one or another of these principles was followed.[125]

We have enough evidence from most of the span of the Gymnopaediae's existence to detect some changes in the festival. The most obvious shift is in its location. Pausanias tells us that the Gymnopaediae were celebrated in a part of the *agora* called the dancing place (*choros*), whereas the choruses had previously performed in a location called the theater (*theatron*) that was probably a rudimentary precursor of the magnificent marble theater built under Augustus.[126] The other change is the more significant one, an almost textbook example of a phenomenon we will meet again in the following chapters — the codification and segregation of the "traditional" Spartan way of life in the later *agōgē*.

As I have just mentioned, the composition of the Gymnopaediae's choruses is problematic before the Roman period. In particular, a fragment from Sosibius that is our most important evidence on this matter is textually defective at the crucial point when the ages of chorus members are being discussed.[127] Despite its disarray, the passage appears to refer to one chorus of children and another of men, who sang traditional songs by Thales, Alcman, and a Spartan songwriter. Some editors add a third chorus made up of ephebes because of the passage's similarity to a description by Plutarch of the *trichoria*, a set of three choruses, one composed of old men, one of mature males (*akmazontes*), and one of boys, who each sang ritual boasts of their age group's prowess.[128]

For my part, I would prefer to keep the two sets of choruses separate and not identify the *trichoria* with the choruses of the Gymnopaediae, since Plutarch, for one, suggests that they were not associated exclusively with a single festival (*sunistamenōn en tais heortais*). On this point, Plutarch's testimony is vital because he follows closely the wording of Sosibius himself, who wrote about the *trichoria* in his book *On Customs*.[129] Sosibius' descriptions of the two choruses differ so markedly from each other that it impossible to believe that they had to do with the same thing. In any case, the *trichoria* did not survive into the Roman period, as Plutarch's use of a past tense in his description indicates.[130]

Luckily, we are not altogether dependent on Sosibius' scrambled fragment for every bit of information on the choruses at the Gymnopaediae. In the *Hellenica*, Xenophon recounts that news of the crippling defeat at Leuctra in 371 B.C. came to Sparta "on the final day of the Gymnopaediae, when the men's chorus was on," thus implying that choruses made up of other age groups also performed.[131] Since the later Gymnopaediae were celebrated by ephebes, a chorus of youths (perhaps a *paidikos choros*) must have figured in the earlier festival as well.

In the Classical period, consequently, the choruses at the original Gymnopaediae had been composed of men and youths, whereas only ephebic choruses performed in the festival during the Roman period. The process this illuminates is a significant part of the *agōgē*'s development as it was revived in the Hellenistic period and later. A ceremony that had originally been an integral part of the fabric of life at Sparta, celebrated by adult citizens and youths alike, was transformed over time into a cultural artifact preserved as if under glass in the living museum that the later *agōgē* came to be.[132]

As we shall see, the Gymnopaediae were far from unique in suffering this fate. In the next chapter, I examine how one of the most ubiquitous intellectual and cultural trends of the Greek East during the Roman Empire affected the *agōgē* and was manifested in it. Part of this inquiry will concern itself with how the Spartans of the Roman period constructed this tremendously effective vehicle for representing their distinctive self-image. Here the work of excavation will begin, and the different layers of development and change in the institutions of the *agōgē* will begin to come to light.

4

THE LYCURGAN CUSTOMS

The most famous and notorious of the spectacles held at the sanctuary of Artemis Orthia during the Roman period is undoubtedly the endurance contest (*ho tēs karterias agōn*). This sanguinary test of fortitude, at which ephebes were flogged beside the goddess's altar, remained a popular attraction all throughout the Roman period; even after the turmoil of the third century A.D., spectators were so numerous that a new, permanent seating complex was constructed to accommodate them.[1] Incorporated into its foundations were the now obsolete sickle dedications from the musical contests, which had not been hardy enough to survive the changed climate.[2] But the endurance contest apparently prospered, attracting visitors well into the fourth century. Among them was the young orator Libanius, who took time off from his studies at Athens (336–40 A.D.) to go see "the Whips," thus becoming the last eyewitness to the contest's continued existence (T34).[3]

To the intelligentsia of the Roman Empire, the contest was the quintessence of all things Spartan. An obvious relic of the primitive past, it made strikingly visible the traditional virtues of courage and obedience, and served as a touchstone against which all other claims of endurance were tested. As Cicero put it, "And you, although you have seen boys at Sparta . . . taking the harshest blows and bearing them silently, if by chance some pain should pinch you, will you cry out like a woman, and not endure it steadily and calmly?" (T2). Beyond this, the contest and the city were inseparably linked in the popular mind: for Horace, Sparta was simply "enduring Lacedaemon" (*patiens Lacedaemon*) (T4).

Naturally, the endurance contest became part of the rhetoricians' stock in trade, to be trotted out as a fitting exemplum of outstanding fortitude (T7, T8, T14, T15). From there it was only a short step to Christian apologists such as Tertullian, who compared the false prize, glory, for which Spartans and other pagans died, to the true prize that Christians should lay down their lives for (T24, T25).[4] Later Christian writers assumed a more adversarial stance: Gregory Nazianzus, for example, saw the contest as a manifestation of traditional religion's depravity (T37–40). At last, when the old gods and their rituals no longer presented an imminent threat to the new order, allusions to the endurance contest, as one among the multiplicity of elements in the classical heritage belonging to all cultivated people, served to reveal the depths of one's education. A bishop might now liken a tyrannical governor's oppression to the bloodshed at the flogging in Sparta (T42).

Before it became a literary topos, the endurance contest had a physical existence as well. During the *agōgē*'s Roman phase, the sources are so abundant, despite the surprising paucity of epigraphical evidence at the site, that a reconstruction of the ritual in its most developed form is possible.[5]

On a day in late May or June, ephebes and onlookers, women as well as men (T19), would gather at the sanctuary of Artemis Orthia.[6] The ephebes had just completed a period of seclusion in the country, the "fox time" (*phouaxir*) (T51), whose name recalls the shadowy Alopecus ("Mr. Fox"), one of the mythological codiscoverers of Orthia's cult image.[7] During the fox time, the young Spartans had to live by their wits, sleeping rough by day and venturing out only at night to steal their food.[8] Now, with one sort of ordeal behind them, they faced another.

The audience sat wherever the view was best; before the construction of the permanent seating, people would have taken their places on the ground around the altar or even on the nearby heights overlooking the sanctuary. For dignitaries, stone seats had been provided, one set at least by private dedication.[9] After preliminary rituals, prayer, and sacrifice, the ephebes presented themselves at the altar, the remains of whose foundations are visible even today (Plate 6). They were grouped according

PLATE 6. *Foundations of the Roman altar at the Orthia sanctuary*

to ephebic tribe: Limnaeis, Cynooureis, Mesoatae, Pitanatae, and Neopolitae (T22). How many ephebes entered the contest? If we assume, as I think is reasonable, that Spartan youths endured the whips only once in their ephebic years, then the number of flogged youths will be equal to the number of ephebes in a single age grade. This number can easily be calculated, making the largest number of ephebes whipped at the altar approximately seventy.[10]

One source claims that the contest lasted "the whole day" (T18). Although this is probably an exaggeration, the ephebes can quite reasonably be supposed to have entered the contest in heats. The Roman altar was, as the excavators measured it, 2.60 meters wide and more than 8.20 meters long.[11] It cannot have been longer than 10 meters because, at that size, the clearance between the altar's northeast corner and the northern part of the seating complex's foundations is already just 2 meters, which does not leave enough space at the altar, even along the east and west sides, for seventy ephebes to stand side by side, with their hands on their heads

(T19) and still be close enough to the altar for their blood to drip onto its surface.[12] That, after all, was the ostensible point of the exercise (T6, T22, T26, T32, T37, T39). The Spartan ephebes must have approached the altar in heats, most likely in groups of fourteen or fifteen, *boua* by *boua*, as representatives of their ancestral tribes.[13]

The men who actually held the whips we know only as "the floggers" (*hoi mastigountes*: T22). Unlikely to have been ephebes themselves, they were perhaps ephebic officials or members of the public deputed for the occasion. A curious piece of business was enacted during the ceremony: Pausanias (T22; cf. T46) relates that the priestess of Artemis stood by the altar holding a small image of the goddess which grew oppressively heavy, she would claim, if ever one of the floggers whipped a youth sparingly because of his attractiveness or social standing.

The ephebes themselves were supposed to maintain a Spartan silence throughout the ordeal (T1–3), but the sanctuary still resounded with clamoring. The scene must have resembled today's midget hockey or little-league baseball games, with fathers (and mothers) sitting in the stands shouting at their sons to bear up and endure the pain, threatening them if they seemed likely to weaken (T19). Astonishingly, the sources tell us that youths often died under the whips rather than fail this test in front of their parents (T1, T9, T16, T19, T22, T25, T32, T43). Even allowing for the inevitable cultural differences, the idea that mothers and fathers sat by and, with rollicking enthusiasm, watched their sons being flogged to death is repugnant to our modern sensibilities. However, upon further examination, the foundations for this oft-repeated notion are seen, in fact, to be rather shaky.

If we exclude from consideration all the obviously derivative testimonia, five firsthand accounts remain — those of Cicero (T1), Plutarch (T16), Lucian (T19), Pausanias (T22), and Philostratus (T32).[14] Of these, Pausanias says nothing about death in the endurance contest, and Lucian's information is so garbled that he plainly did not witness any deaths himself. Cicero, in a laudable display of candor, confesses he only heard that ephebes died by the altar. The two remaining accounts appear to be diametrically opposed to each other. Philostratus explicitly states that the ritual did not entail the deaths of ephebes, whereas Plutarch says he has seen many youths dying from the blows of the whips. But *apothnēskontas*, the word he uses, can sometimes denote "being on the point of perishing" rather than actually "dying."[15] Indeed, second-century Sparta could hardly have afforded to place the lives of all potential members of its governing class at such risk. Plutarch has either been misinterpreted on this point or else was himself misled by tales of Spartan courage circulating during his visit. No doubt, a few ephebes did die on rare occasions during the contest, their demises providing rich material for the Spartan legend as it was evolving in Plutarch's time. Although death was not common, its mere possibility added a tangible element of risk for the ephebes to confront.

The emphasis the ancient authors place on deaths during the flogging is due to the endurance contest's function as a ritual of initiation. For a century, the contest has been recognized as belonging to a class of these rituals known as *rites de passage*, which are enacted whenever people move from one important stage in life — birth, puberty, marriage, death, for example — to another.[16]

Initiation rituals comprise three distinct phases. First comes separation from the original group or status, which often takes the form of a literal withdrawal from society: at Sparta, the ephebes were separated from society at the commencement of the *phouaxir*. The next stage is the liminal phase, so called because the initiands are considered to be on the threshold between states, neither what they have been nor what they will become. During this interstitial existence, they are often represented as if they were among the dead: the ephebes acted like ghosts in the fox time, appearing only after dark and spiriting food away when no one was looking. The liminal phase is also a time of education, when the elders reveal the community's secrets and train the initiands in the duties attached to their new station. Of course, the *agōgē* as an institution was concerned with education, and itself represented the liminal period in a long, multifaceted transition from child to adult, which renders an educational function less necessary for the *phouaxir*, since it was a liminal period in a rite of passage contained within the *agōgē*.

In order that the transition to the next stage be irrevocable, the liminal phase often closes with the initiand's symbolic death and rebirth.[17] The nexus of symbols characteristic of this moment usually appears in the initiation rituals themselves or in the myths surrounding them. For those members of the audience unable to appreciate the underlying significance of the endurance contest's flogging, there was always the myth. Pausanias recorded the version current in the middle of the second century A.D. (T22): "On the other hand, the Spartan Limnatae and Cynosures, and those from Mesoa and Pitane, while sacrificing to Artemis, were drawn into hostilities and from there to homicide. Many were killed on the altar, and a plague wiped out the rest. After this, an oracle was conveyed to them to stain the altar with the blood of men. Though the victim was whomsoever the lottery chose, Lycurgus converted it into a flagellation for the youths, and thus the altar is satiated with the blood of men."

The myth that the contest originated in veritable human sacrifice, later "mitigated" into flagellation, was necessitated by its function in the initiatory process of representing the final transition.[18] In the eyes of the audience and of the ephebes themselves, the participants were reenacting the myth of the rite's origin, sacrificing themselves to Artemis, dying as immature boys to be reborn at a higher level. Rumors that ephebes actually did die would have served to strengthen the symbolism by blurring the distinction between ritual and reality.

Since the initiands in the liminal period do not belong to any proper category of human existence, like the dead they may not communicate with the living. During the fox time, young Spartans avoided human contact, and even under the lash were required to keep silent (T1–3).[19] Shared hardship and complete equality among those undergoing initiation are other common features of rites of passage.[20] At Sparta, such evenhandedness was encouraged by divine sanction, for, as we have seen, Artemis made her displeasure at favoritism felt by weighing down her image held by the priestess beside the altar.[21]

The third and final stage of a rite of passage involves the integration of the recently initiated individuals back into the community. Ritual clothing highlights their new status. The endurance contest ended with a "parade of Lydians," when the ephebes, arrayed in oriental finery, walked in procession around the altar.[22]

As the endurance contest was an initiation rite, our next problem is to fix the age at which the ephebes passed through it. The ancient sources are a babel of confusion on this point: according to one authority or another, Spartans of any age from children to adults endured the whips at Artemis' altar.[23] Even so, the majority of sources are split between boys (paides) and ephebes (ephēboi), two words by no means mutually exclusive in antiquity and often plainly overlapping in meaning. We have already come across a good example of this in the form of the marginal note to Strabo on the Spartan age grades, whose second sentence reads, "For among the Spartans a child [pais] is an ephebe [ephēbeuei] from 14 years until 20."[24] Likewise, the boua members who praised their leader in verse saw no contradiction in calling themselves both boys (paides) and fellow ephebes (sunephēboi) at the same time.[25]

Nonetheless, for Spartans the two words *ephēbos* and *pais* were not completely synonymous. The *agōgē* was, in effect, an *ephēbeia*, and so all those enrolled in it could legitimately be termed ephebes, but they were not all "boys." Plutarch tells us that "*Eirenes* they call those who left the boys' class the year before and *melleirenes* the eldest of the boys."[26] We have seen that the *eirenes'* most important activity, the *sphaireis* tournament, took place in the city's main theater, not at Artemis Orthia's temple, and that, unlike the bases for altar victors, the *sphaireis'* victory dedications were erected outside her sanctuary as well.[27] The *eirenes* were also distinguished in the Roman *agōgē* by being the only age grade whose preceding grade was explicitly a preparatory one: the *melleirenes* were "those about to be *eirenes*."

All these elements point to a difference in status between the *eirenes* and the younger age grades. Artemis was the patron of children for much of the Greek world.[28] The *eirenes*, however, were considered children no longer and in consequence the focus of their activity shifted from the sanctuary of Orthia at the city's edge to the theater at the city's center.[29] But the *eirenes* had not, of course, left the *agōgē* yet; they still participated in the contests at the sanctuary, and from their number were chosen the leaders of the ephebic tribes.[30] The whipping contest, it follows, took place during the *melleirēn* year. The confusion in age terminology for the participants was due to the ritual marking the theoretical transition from boyhood to the true ephebate: Spartans began the contest as boys, but ended it as ephebes.[31]

Finally, the festival concluded with a banquet (*deipnon*). Having successfully reenacted what amounted to a foundation myth for the *agōgē*, the new *eirenes*, resplendent in barbarian robes, reentered society by participating in a community's essential activity, sharing food. As the *agōgē* was traditionally concerned with a male child's development into an adult warrior-citizen, females had no place in this celebration, but males of every age were admitted, including boys (*paides*) in the younger age grades, so that all could witness the *eirenes'* assumption of their new status.

Here too hunting, which was so prevalent in the boys' contests, makes an appearance: "It is customary for [the Spartans] in the festival of Artemis that anyone who comes to the banquet without having hunted is deemed to be doing wrong and that he pay a forfeit. This is the penalty: someone brings a jug of water and pours it over the boy's head, if the culprit be a boy, while if it is a man, then the finger of his hand is subject to this punishment. And at Sparta, this water is a dishonor."[32]

On most occasions, a hunter did not incur the ritual pollution which would disqualify him from taking part in sacrifices or any other associated activity, but at the festival of Artemis, hunting was a far from neutral act: it was the prerequisite for participation.[33] Failure to hunt in this situation became a source of impurity, since everyone at the banquet was expected to have paid the goddess her due. The shedding of an animal's blood by a hunter was analogous to the blood drawn from the backs of the ephebes by the floggers' whips; men or boys who had not hunted left the sacral act incomplete.

The penalty they suffered thus represented a proceeding of the following sort. A sacrifice normally began with attendants sprinkling water on the hands of participants and on the victim's head.[34] In the transference of this action to the banquet, the boy (*pais*), who has yet to suffer his own mock sacrifice, becomes the potential victim; the man, whose representatives "sacrifice" the boys at the altar, becomes a sacrificer himself. The two roles, "victim" and "sacrificer," need not occur in conjunction for their symbols to have value; by its very nature, this "sacrifice" is incomplete, fragmentary, reflecting the imperfection of the culprit's own (in)action. The water, anomalously, does not purify, instead intensifying and emphasizing the omission that has rendered him unfit.

A close link between hunting and men's communal meals can be seen elsewhere; Athenaeus says that no young man in Macedonia might recline at table with other men until he had killed a wild boar without using nets.[35] In Classical Sparta, members of the common messes contributed either a portion of a sacrificial victim or part of their catch to the pot.[36] A famous study has established the importance of hunting in the training of young men as warriors during the Archaic and Classical periods, while Libanius and the inscriptions show unambiguously that, in the context of the *agōgē*, the chase retained its sacred, initiatory aspect throughout later antiquity.[37]

The ephebe who had held out the longest in the endurance contest won the title *bōmonikēs*, "altar-victor," which he retained for life (T6; Plate 7).[38] The city voted him permission to erect a statue in the sanctuary as a memorial of his prowess, while runners-up also received public recognition for "having endured conspicuously" (*epiphanōr karterēhanta*).[39] Successful participants thus enjoyed a measure of prestige denied the

PLATE 7. *Base for a statue of an altar-victor (courtesy of the Ephor of Antiquities for Laconia and Arcadia)*

winners in any of the other ephebic contests, even in the ball tournament. The reason for the endurance contest's prominence, even though it did not mark the passage from the *agōgē* into manhood, is interwoven with the question of the *eirenes'* anomalous position as quasi adults still in the *agōgē*, the answers to which lie in changes that transformed the *agōgē* between the Classical and Roman periods. As will be subsequently shown, the endurance contest's predecessor indeed marked a very significant change in status.[40]

The endurance contest of the Antonine period stood forth as a fully articulated ephebic ceremony, religiously and culturally meaningful, equipped with a foundation myth that furnished a link with the city's earliest days and the totemic figure of Lycurgus. Yet it was wholly an invention, so well conceived and perfected over the years that it misleads even today in one very important way.

We begin with Pausanias. As we have seen, he assigns the endurance contest's foundation to the time of Lycurgus, in other words, the Dark Ages or early Archaic period (T22). Although Pausanias certainly regarded the contest as inextricably linked to the early years of the Orthia sanctuary, we must draw a clear distinction between contest and cult. Archaeology and epigraphy have shown that Orthia was worshiped at this location at least as far back as the Archaic period; the antiquity of the endurance contest, however, is not nearly so certain.[41] The earliest reference to a ritual identifiable as the endurance contest comes in reality from the *agōgē*'s Hellenistic phase, after its first revival.[42] From then on, through the Roman period, sources consistently depict the ceremony as a test of endurance, but if we take Pausanias' account at face value, we must then assume, although the ritual had been long established and regularly performed, that no extant writer of either pro- or anti-Spartan sympathies mentioned the contest at all before the late third or early second century B.C. Considering the wealth of allusions to the endurance contest in the later authors and the *agōgē*'s lasting prominence in literature, this would at the very least have been a remarkable omission.

For the Classical period, what we have instead is Xenophon's description of a violent cheese-stealing ritual, which took place beside Orthia's altar: "And upon ordaining it a good thing that they snatch as many cheeses as possible from Orthia, [Lycurgus] ordered others to whip them, wishing to show herein too that it is possible after having suffered for a short time to rejoice in being honored for a long time."[43]

Xenophon is not the only source for this ritual; Plato has the Spartan Megillus allude to the battle in his *Laws*, and Plutarch, relying on a fifth- or fourth-century writer, mentions it in his biography of Aristides.[44] The ceremony they describe superficially resembles the endurance contest in its location and in the use of whips. However, absolutely none of the later sources mentions cheese, and what appears in Xenophon to have involved youths trying to take objects from an altar defended by other youths bearing whips cannot be reconciled with the later ritual of passive endurance alone.[45] Consequently, Xenophon's mock battle was not the endurance contest and the claims made for the contest's pristine antiquity were bogus.[46] In its familiar form, the whipping contest was a studied creation of the Hellenistic period, instituted as part of the philosophical revival of Spartan traditions under Cleomenes III.[47]

The dichotomy between the endurance contest's historical foundation and its mythical origin has important implications for the study of early Spartan history. Because there is virtually no contemporary or near contemporary source for Sparta's internal development during the Archaic period, historians are in the habit of mining the Roman *agōgē* for nuggets of relevant information, a practice currently so entrenched that the question of what effects the *agōgē*'s two revivals had on the later evidence never arises at all.[48] While regularly excoriating the endurance contest as a bloodthirsty sham, symptomatic of Sparta's later decadence, classical historians do not scruple to pluck from the unseemly assemblage a single nugget especially pertinent to the city's earliest history.[49] Ever since it was argued that the original constituent communities (*ōbai*) of archaic Sparta were the four groups Pausanias mentioned in his account of the endurance contest's origin, historians have cited that passage, endowing it in the process with the handsome patina of fact.[50] Even an argument for the existence of a community of child-sacrificing Phoenicians in the suburbs of the Dark Age city has made use of it.[51]

For historians today, as for the ancient Spartans, Lycurgus is a talisman; here, his presence guarantees the quality and antiquity of the evidence.[52] They have accepted without question that a kernel of accurate information on archaic Sparta nestles at the story's heart, a notion dependent on the essentials of Pausanias' account having survived from the earliest history of the city.[53] Their confidence is misplaced, for quite apart from the fact that the tale is manifestly an *aition* for the endurance contest as Pausanias saw it, not for the battle over cheese known from the Classical *agōgē*, the story in Pausanias forms only one among three widely differing accounts of the endurance contest's foundation and is moreover the only one to mention Lycurgus.

The earliest version appears in the *Fabulae* of Hyginus, an epitomized collection of potted myths, whose original author is probably to be identified with C. Julius Hyginus, prefect of the Palatine library under Augustus and an authority on Italian antiquities.[54] After telling of Orestes' and Iphigeneia's escape from the clutches of Thoas, king of the Taurians, Hyginus describes how Orestes first brought Artemis' cult statue to Aricia in Latium (T6): "[Orestes] made off with the image . . . and brought it to Aricia. But since the cult's cruelty subsequently displeased the Romans, although slaves were sacrificed, Diana was transferred to the Spartans, where the custom of sacrifice was maintained in the whipping of the youths, who were called Bomonicae because they contended, placed above the altar, as to who could endure more blows."

Although at first glance a rather strained instance of *interpretatio Graeca*, here employed to provide a proper Hellenic lineage for the cult of

Diana at Nemi, the story is no mere random development. Nor was its choice of Sparta as the statue's final destination fortuitous; rather, it was rooted in a debate current in the second and first centuries B.C. over Rome's debt to Sparta.[55] Ever since and probably even before Polybius' famous comparison of the Spartan and Roman constitutions, their similarities provoked interest.[56] Sparta had two kings, Rome two consuls; Sparta's Gerousia had thirty members, the Senate of Rome three hundred; there were five Spartan ephors and twice five Roman tribunes — the list continues. Beyond this were the less tangible parallels in character — piety, conservatism, militarism, and so on.[57] There were of course those proud Roman nationalists, Cato the Elder foremost among them, who denied any connection between the two systems and affirmed the Roman constitution's innate superiority.[58] Some argued that the similarities were due to deliberate borrowing on the Romans' part: Posidonius wrote that the Romans "imitated the constitution of the Lacedaemonians in every way and preserved it better than they have."[59] Others asserted Sparta had influenced Rome through the Sabines: Dionysius of Halicarnassus conjectured the existence of a colony of Spartans among the Sabines before their incorporation into the Roman people.[60] The controversy was sufficiently well known to inspire even a writer of erotic verse. In elegiac couplets, Propertius mocked the serious tone of the debate by enumerating the ways in which Rome should imitate Sparta, among other things suggesting mixed nude wrestling and freer access to married women.[61]

Hyginus' contribution seems to have been to attribute Spartan ancestry to the Sabines in his work *On the Origin and Situation of Italian Cities*, a notion soon accepted as fact and alluded to in Ovid's *Fasti*.[62] With this background, Hyginus' version of the endurance contest's origin in the *Fabulae* can easily be seen as an attempt at furthering the discussion by showing that the current of influence between Rome and Sparta did not always run in the same direction.

Plutarch gives us another version in the course of describing an incident at the Battle of Plataea involving the notorious Spartan general Pausanias (T17): "Some say that, as Pausanias was sacrificing and praying a short distance outside the barricade, some Lydians suddenly attacked, seizing and scattering the sacrificial equipment, and that Pausanias and his companions, having no weapons, struck them with staffs and whips. Therefore, even now, the blows of the ephebes around the altar at Sparta and the subsequent parade of the Lydians are performed in imitation of this assault."

No mention of Lycurgus or the Dark Ages here; instead, Plutarch prefers a historical origin, but what he describes does not jibe with any other later description of the contest. We are not dealing here with ephebes who endured a flogging in silence. Rather, we see a mock battle between two teams, one attacking, the other defending an altar — in other words, the cheese-stealing ritual of Xenophon and Plato. Plutarch confused an account of this earlier ephebic ceremony with the endurance contest he himself saw, which had enough features in common (whips, parade, location) with the ritual described in his source for him to conflate the two.[63]

Plutarch's muddle is useful for us because it reveals something of the contemporary Spartan attitude toward the question of the endurance contest's origin. The confusion would never have arisen in the first place had Plutarch already been aware that Lycurgus was supposed to be the contest's founder. Neither here, however, in this passage from the *Aristides*, nor in his earlier biography of Lycurgus, where he drew on his own personal impressions of the contest, did Plutarch betray any cognizance of a link between the ritual and the lawgiver. Considering his own researches at Sparta and his acquaintances from among the city's elite, he would certainly have mentioned Lycurgus as the founder of the whipping contest had it been part of the received tradition of his time.

The revitalization of Sparta's cultural institutions, which had languished under the dead hand of the Euryclid dynasty, the city's de facto rulers for most of the previous one hundred years, was in its initial stages during Plutarch's lifetime. For the Spartans, as for other Greeks of the period, the Persian Wars provided inspiration for this revival.[64] Under Trajan we first hear of the Leonidea, a festival commemorating the hero of Thermopylae, which featured speeches delivered at his and Pausanias' graves.[65] The Eleutheria games, held every four years at Plataea to celebrate the Greek victory, included Athenian and Spartan orators contending over which city was entitled to lead the festival procession; Pausanias' role in defeating the Persians would have undoubtedly formed a theme of the Spartan's declamation.[66] For Plutarch to credit him with the endurance contest's foundation is, as a result, far from aberrant, and indeed a view with which many Spartans may well have concurred.

The situation had changed considerably by the time Pausanias the periegete came to the city, about fifty years later, and his text reflects how the *agōgē* had come to dominate Spartan cultural life. Of the sixty-nine paragraphs devoted to the city's antiquities, he spends fifteen on the *agō-*

gē's ceremonies, buildings, and officials. Other evidence shows a similar preponderance: there are more sickle dedications, complete or fragmentary, from the second century A.D. than any other single type of inscription — decree, statue base, even funerary *stēlē* — from the entire span of Spartan history.[67]

The *agōgē*'s preeminence entailed a renewed interest in Lycurgus. His presence was ubiquitous: his altar stood in the same quarter of the city as Orthia's sanctuary and he presided over both the battle at the Platanistas and the *sphaireis*' ball tournament.[68] By the middle of the second century, the *agōgē* had become (officially, it appears) "the Lycurgan customs" (*ta Lukourgeia ethē*).[69] The change from earlier names such as "the ancestral *agōgē*" or even "the Lacedaemonian customs" was more than window dressing, and it was no coincidence that, almost simultaneously, ancient "Laconian" was being adopted as the *agōgē*'s official language.[70] The Spartans, consciously or unconsciously, were pressing their claim to be the direct heirs of a preclassical tradition embodied by Lycurgus. As Athens, with its philosophical and artistic heritage from the Classical period, formed one pole of Hellenic culture, so the people of Sparta, through the *agōgē*'s patently archaic emphasis on physical conditioning, endurance, and obedience, now represented themselves as the other.

In this atmosphere, the *karterias agōn*, centerpiece of the Lycurgan customs, could only have had Lycurgus as its founder, whatever people had formerly thought. The story Pausanias heard from his guides was no unchanged relic of an oral culture almost a millennium old, but a recent product of Sparta's archaistic cultural climate, completely lacking in relevance to the history of early Sparta.[71]

The transformations of the endurance contest's foundation myth show the tendency of later Spartans, like other peoples throughout the ages, to view their past through the lens of the present and to effect any changes required to ensure it conformed to the idealized picture they held of their early history. The endurance contest and the *agōgē* are particularly significant because, through these institutions, Roman Sparta enabled its ephebes to experience that ideal past to a greater extent than any other ancient city.

Archaism, as I have used the term here, can best be defined as a self-conscious attempt to live the present in terms of the past. Sometimes societies bring this about by reviving obsolete traditions or by adopting out-of-date modes of behavior and dress; architecture and even governmental institutions can be pressed into service as media of this phenomenon. Spartan archaism has left its greatest impression on the historical record, but it was far from unique.

More than any other societies, with the possible exception of our own, the urban populations of the cities of the Roman Empire embraced and encouraged an insistent sense of the past. Particularly in the Greek East, this phenomenon of archaism manifested itself in art, literature, religion, athletics, architecture, and other aspects of public activity. The civic elites looked to their own histories as one means of establishing their own legitimacy in a much changed world and of framing their contemporary lives. As a result, scholarship of all degrees flourished, from the itinerant sophist who praised the antique foundation and glorious deeds of his host city to the nationalist savant from the East who proved his birthplace's authentic Hellenic pedigree.[72] For their part, writers such as Pausanias and Plutarch, one illuminating the myths, traditions, and antiquities that suffused the land, the other commemorating the great men of history, contributed substantially to embellishing the common culture of all Greeks.

The Spartans were enthusiastic players in this multifarious and culturally vital game. Their city had powerful allies: raising Sparta's status was clearly of concern to the emperor Hadrian, who first tried to include it in a renovated Amphictyonic Council but later had more success with his foundation in A.D. 131/2 of the Greek cultural league known as the Panhellenion.[73] Headquartered at Athens, the Panhellenion was an interprovincial organization designed to function as a unifying force in Greek intercity relations. It made dedications, erected buildings, dispatched embassies to the emperor, even functioning at times, through its council, as a court of appeal in disputes concerning the league itself, and, in one recorded instance, adjudicating in a city's internal crisis.[74] The Panhellenion also gave a boost to the antiquarianism evident in scholarship since the Hellenistic period, for cities became eligible for membership only by proving their foundation by Greek colonists.[75] Thus, this requirement codified and regularized the claims of kinship (*sungeneia*) made by many cities, which for centuries had provided a fertile field of endeavor for interested scholars.

Sparta, of course, did not lack its own measure of these so-called "colonies," as befitted its renewed standing.[76] With their claims to Spartan lineage ranging from the almost plausible to the brazenly concocted, cities such as Cibyra, Selge, Amblada, and Synnada celebrated their ties to the metropolis on coins, on city walls, and in official civic nomenclature.[77]

From the *agōgē*'s obvious importance to the Spartan sense of identity, one would expect to find some evidence of its influence on these cities' public education systems, but that is unfortunately not the case. On the one hand, the evidence for ephebic activity in Sparta's "colonies" is meager, even speaking optimistically, while, on the other, what has survived reveals ephebates that conform to a model common in the late Hellenistic and Roman periods.[78]

A faint whisper of Sparta's effect on ephebic culture has been heard recently at Oenoanda, a city with close connections, both cultural and political, with Cibyra. In its agora is preserved the facade of a building whose inscribed architrave identifies it as the city's *boukonistērion*. The latest study to concern itself with this structure argues that it was an athletic facility for the use of Oenoanda's ephebes, deriving its ungainly name from a combination of the Spartan word, *boua*, and *konistērion*, wrestling hall.[79] The building's appellation thus reflected a laconizing sentiment among the city's leading families, one of whom did trace its genealogy back to Lacedaemonian heroes.[80]

Elsewhere in Asia Minor, at Tralles, a city whose relations with Sparta are securely attested, two inscriptions record victories in "the sacred contest of the *Spartiatai*."[81] Despite assumptions that it was a local festival, it surely belongs at Sparta.[82] A contest of sacred status with this name is inexplicable at Tralles even if part of the population did, as was once suggested, claim Spartan ancestry. A "Spartan" festival of purely local interest that these people either competed in or administered might perhaps be conceivable, but not a sacred festival, for the title, "sacred" (*hieros*) put an agonistic festival in the top rank of international events. Only the emperor could bestow it, and victors (*hieronikai*) qualified for extensive privileges and exemptions from duties in their home cities.[83] I suggest instead that the "sacred contest of the Spartiates" was, in fact, the Olympia Commodea, the only Spartan festival known to have been of sacred rank and which attracted competitors from as far away as Asia Minor.[84] Use of the anachronistic term "Spartiate" in referring to this festival may have served to evoke Tralles' link with Spartan antiquity and dignity.[85]

We are on a still sounder footing with Cyrene in North Africa. The city's primordially Spartan credentials are beyond dispute, as are its continuing relations with the metropolis in the Roman period. Hadrian, at some point in the 130s, in several communications perhaps to be associated with constitutional reform, alluded to the Cyreneans' Dorian ancestry and Spartan heritage.[86] With greater precision, as has been plausibly suggested, an unpublished fragment shows Hadrian's interest in reforming Cyrene's educational system using Sparta as a model.[87] This suggestion is certainly correct, since the third document, a compilation of extracts from a speech or edict, explicitly mentions the rearing of children and refers to "Laconian decorum and exercise" (*Lakōnikē sōphrosunē kai askēsis*), both terms intimately associated with ephebic training.[88]

Assessing the extent to which the new ephebic system at Cyrene paralleled that of Sparta, however, is quite another matter. Like Sparta, Cyrene had a proud and ancient ephebic tradition, which would have influenced any changes immensely.[89] That changes did take place is clear: an ephebic catalog from A.D. 161 shows a different institutional structure from those from the first century B.C. and earlier.[90] But the differences are indicative more of assimilation to the norms of Roman-age ephebates than a laconization of the Cyrenean system.[91] If Hadrian was serious in putting Sparta forward as a paradigm, then the influence it exerted was perhaps felt in the style of Cyrene's ephebic training, rather than in its structure.

Although Sparta's influence cannot readily be detected in the cultural institutions of other Greek cities, its attraction for cultivated travelers can. Ever since the fifth century B.C., scholars and dilettantes had come to visit despite the city's fearsome reputation for expelling foreigners.[92] A good assessment of the broad cultural crosscurrents that impelled such travel and of the personalities involved is available elsewhere.[93] Here, I would again emphasize the importance of the *agōgē* in drawing travelers of the Roman period, from Cicero to Libanius, to see its "authentic" reenactments of ancient Spartan traditions.

Foreigners could express their affinity with the Spartan way of life by enrolling their sons in the *agōgē*. The lasting effect this sometimes had can best be gauged from the case of the sophist Herodes Atticus, who, like his father before him, was brought up in the *agōgē* and whose literary style emulated that of Critias, the foremost Athenian laconizer of the late fifth century B.C.[94] A less dramatic means of expressing admiration for the *agōgē* was to hold the patronomate, whose connection with the *agōgē* has already been remarked on.[95] Apart from the emperor Hadrian, who was *patronomos* in the 120s, we know of four non-Spartan eponymous magistrates — Tiberius Claudius Atticus from Athens, D. Cascellius Aristoteles of Cyrene, C. Claudius Demostratus of Pergamum, and the Ephesian A. Claudius Charax.[96] The group has something of an academic aura about it: Atticus was the father of Herodes, while Charax was a well-known historian in his own right.[97] In a world so concerned with establishing and legitimating links with the distant past, the patronomate's attraction could not have lain in its antiquity since, unlike the eponymous archonship at Athens, whose incumbents could envision themselves as continuing a tradition that stretched back beyond recorded history, the patronomate was known to have been founded as part of Cleomenes' reforms of the third century B.C.[98] Rather, in occupying the post, a non-Spartan could display his reverence for the Spartan ideal by becoming nominally responsible for the *agōgē* for a year. As tenure of the Athenian archonship attested to an individual's participation in the culture of one of Greece's two major cities, so serving as *patronomos* showed his support for the most obviously ancient aspects of the other.[99]

I have already had occasion to remark on some ways in which the *agōgē*'s antiquity was emphasized. Now is the time for a more comprehensive examination. In the eyes of visitors to Roman Sparta, the most conspicuous testament to the age of the *agōgē* would have been the use of the ancient Laconian dialect in prominently displayed inscriptions (Plate 8). Modern scholars have certainly been impressed; many of them have seen it as evidence for a wholesale readoption of Lycurgan practices or for a revival of Laconian in daily speech under the Romans.[100] Neither contention can stand today. Studies have shown incontrovertibly that the public institutions of Roman Sparta, allowing for inevitable variations in local practice, were essentially the same as those of any other provincial city in the eastern part of the Roman Empire, and inspection of the epigraphical evidence disposes of the idea that Spartans had begun to speak like Leonidas' contemporaries again.[101]

Over a thousand published Spartan inscriptions survive from the Roman period; for our purposes, they can be divided into two basic groups. The first embraces decrees of the city, letters to and from the city, bases honoring individuals for their services to the city, inscribed careers of noble Spartans, catalogs of city magistrates, and similar texts to a total of approximately nine hundred stones: these are the civic inscriptions. The second group contains the sickle dedications and bases for the *bōmonikai* erected at the sanctuary of Artemis Orthia, as well as the *stēlai* set up by victorious *sphaireis* teams, all in all, 151 inscriptions: these constitute the agogic inscriptions. In the civic inscriptions, *koinē* forms predominate, apart from the occasional use of a Doric alpha. Distinctly Laconian dialectal forms appear in only three inscriptions.[102] But the agogic inscriptions

PLATE 8. *Archaizing sickle dedication (courtesy of the Ephor of Antiquities for Laconia and Arcadia)*

present a different picture. Archaizing forms are present on *bōmonikai* bases, on sickle dedications, and in the dedications by teams of ball-players. In fact, out of the total number of Spartan inscriptions from the Roman period, only forty-six contain archaisms, of which forty-three are agogic inscriptions.[103] In short, linguistic archaism was not particularly widespread and was confined almost exclusively to inscriptions associated with the *agōgē*.

As linguistic archaism was limited to a single type of inscription, so it was also restricted to a narrow span of time. Evidence for the use of Laconian forms begins in the 130s and peters out, to all appearances, by the middle of the third century.[104] It is highly unlikely, then, that these few inscriptions represent a reflorescence of spoken Laconian among the Spartan population as a whole.

The most noticeable deviation from standard orthography in the archaizing inscriptions is the use of the letter rho in place of final sigmas, a phenomenon known as rhotacism, which is considered to be a defining characteristic of what has come to be called "late Laconian."[105] Rhotacism is completely absent from Spartan inscriptions of the fifth and fourth centuries B.C. but is ubiquitous in the lexicographers' Laconian glosses.[106] Since Hesychius and his colleagues were ultimately dependent on Aristophanes of Byzantium's massive compendium of Greek words, which contained a section on Laconian terms, there is some justification in thinking that the Laconian spoken in the Hellenistic period was distinguished by rhotacism.[107] These factors led linguists to conclude that the "late Laconian" in inscriptions had its origins in a peasant patois that preserved with minimal change much of the dialect spoken in the Classical period.[108] The survival into the twentieth century of Tsakonian, a Greek dialect, spoken by the inhabitants of northeastern Laconia, in which rhotacism and other elements of later Laconian have been discerned, lends support to this view.[109]

If Laconian were actually spoken as a matter of course by a significant proportion of Sparta's population, however, we would expect the same to be true of the other inhabitants of Laconia. The inscriptions from the other Laconian cities, which together formed the League of Free Laconians, would then have reflected this linguistic usage as well. But they do not: all extant inscriptions from Gytheum, Geronthrae, and other member cities are in an unexceptional Doricizing *koinē* with no discernible laconizing tendencies.[110] Forty-six inscriptions out of a corpus of over two thousand are a thin thread from which to hang a linguistic revival. Even though some form of Laconian might have survived in more remote areas, the version found on stone in Roman Sparta was not an ennobled patois or a living language: the consistent use of *koinē* in other inscribed documents at Roman Sparta attests to that.[111] On the contrary, its appearance in agogic inscriptions at Sparta is obviously motivated by ideology.

Laconian forms were used on these particular stones, as I have already mentioned, in order to envelop the later *agōgē* with an aura of antiquity. Hadrian's foundation of the Panhellenion and the resulting elevation of Sparta to one of the most sought-after mother cities in Greece more than likely provided the impetus. That the earliest extant archaizing sickle dedication was erected just two years after the Panhellenion was created is scarcely coincidental.[112]

Even the idea of a revival of the Laconian dialect per se in the epigraphical documents of the *agōgē* is essentially misleading. What we have here instead is the conversion of *koinē* into laconizing forms. The influence of *koinē* orthography (if that is not an oxymoron) on archaizing inscriptions is profound; hardly a single document is free from misspellings due to *koinē*.[113] The laconizing forms are far from representing "a peasant language which . . . changed little . . . , developed less, and preserved archaisms."[114]

Beyond the usual Doric preference for alpha over eta, the rules for conversion were simple: rhotacism of final sigmas, the substitution of sigma for theta, the elimination of intervocal sigmas to represent the original Laconian aspirate, the substitution of omega for the diphthong omicron-upsilon, and the representation of zeta by double delta. In addition, Artemis' title was commonly spelled with an introductory beta, to approximate the early digamma.

These six principles are the keys to deciphering what at first seems rather odd Greek, as we can see in the following examples:

Γά(ιορ) Ἰούλιρ Φιλοχαρεῖνορ βουαγὸρ μικκ-
ιχιδδομένων ἐπὶ πατρονόμω Ἀβιδίω
Βιάδα νεικάαρ τὸ παιδικὸν κασσηρατόριν καὶ
μῶαν Ἀρτέμιδι Βωρθέᾳ
ἀνέσηκε.[115]

Gaius Julius Philocharinus, *bouagos* of the *mikkichizomenoi*, in the patronomate of Avidius Biadas, after winning *to paidikon* the *kaththēratorion* and the *mōa*, made the dedication to Artemis Orthia.

['Αγαθῇ Τύ]χῃ
Φίλητορ
Φιλήτω
ἐπὶ πατρο-
νόμω Γορ-
γίππω τῶ (Γοργίππω)
νεικάαρ κε{λ}ῦαν
'Αρτέμιτι Βωρσέᾳ
ἀνέσηκε.[116]

To Good Fortune. Philetus, son of Philetus, in the patronomate of Gorgippus, son of Gorgippus, after winning the *keloia*, made the dedication to Artemis Orthia.

The orthographical oddities not accounted for by the rules outlined here are the result of an unlikely alliance between *koinē* and Laconian: for example, νεικάαρ (*neikaar*) for νικήσας (*nikēsas*), and κελῦαν (*keluan*) for κελοῖαν (*keloian*). The most striking instances of this occur in the words 'Ιούλιρ (*Ioulir*) and κασσηρατόριν (*kassēratorin*), which represent 'Ιούλιος (*Ioulios* = Julius) and καθθηρατόριον (*kaththēratorion*) respectively. The strange appearance of these words, and others like them, is due to a combination of laconization and a tendency in *koinē* to omit the omicron in the final syllables of words ending in -ιος (*-ios*) or -ιον (*-ion*).[117] If *koinē* influenced a word after it had undergone laconization, then bizarre formations might result, such as Πόπλην (*Poplēr*) in place of Πόπλιος (*Poplios* = Publius) and the genitive singular 'Αριστοτέλην (*Aristotelēr*) for the regular form, 'Αριστοτέλους (*Aristotelous*).[118] Other peculiarities among the archaizing inscriptions can be attributed to this process as well: μικκιχιζόμενος (*mikkichizomenos*) could become μικκιχιτόμενος (*mikkichitomenos*) and the genitive αὐτοῦ (*autou*) could change to ὠτῶ (*ōtō*).[119] *Koinē* so deeply affected the orthography of these inscriptions that καθθηρατόριν/κασσηρατόριν (*kaththēratorin*/*kassēratorin*) was the preferred spelling for the *kaththēratorion* contest, while the title of an ephebic team leader is spelled either βουαγόρ (*bouagor*) or βοαγόρ (*boagor*) indiscriminately.[120] When all these elements are taken into account, the language of the archaizing inscriptions turns out to be surprisingly banal. The words themselves are merely ordinary *koinē* forms tricked out with laconizing ornament, not true dialectal variations. This is quite clear in several cases where a genuine Laconian form is known to have existed: for example, in the agogic inscriptions ἱερεύς (*hiereus*) is rendered ἱερεύρ (*hiereur*), but the proper form is ἱαρεύς (*hiareus*); and the genitive singular of θεός (*theos*), appearing as σεῶ (*seō*) in the inscriptions, was properly σιῶ (*siō*).[121]

In all forty-six archaizing documents, there occurs only a single example of a proper Laconian dialectal variant—ποδδεξαμένων (*poddexamenōn*) for προσδεξαμένων (*prosdexamenōn*).[122] All other instances result from the mere substitution of letters to create "Laconian" forms. In contrast, the author of a counterfeit decree condemning the fifth-century poet Timotheus, which also dates from the second century of our era, concocted his Laconian forms with slightly more verve and imagination.[123] The archaizing inscriptions from the sanctuary of Artemis Orthia are, then, a conundrum. The use of Laconian is clearly artificial and reflects a desire to present the *agōgē* in a particular light, while the orthography of the words themselves results from strong tendencies in contemporary oral usage. But if the archaisms do reflect actual speech, then why are the inscriptions containing them so few and so concentrated in one area? Although the problem seems circular, a solution is available that accounts for both the revival's artificiality and its oral characteristics.

One situation meets the criteria both of artificiality and of orality: the ceremonial occasion. I suggest that the laconisms on the ephebic dedications reflect the formal language used in the ceremonies of the *agōgē*. The rituals and public announcements, as well as, without a doubt, the songs of the *mōa* and *keloia*, were presented in archaizing language that was supposed to be ancient Laconian. Spectators and participants would have been profoundly impressed by this quasi-hieratic form of speaking; it is no wonder, then, that many ephebes attempted to reproduce it in their dedications, for we should remember that the sickle dedications were erected by private individuals, usually the victors, who surely composed the texts themselves. The individualized nature of this enterprise would certainly account for the startling variations in orthography the inscriptions exhibit. Although there is no means to determine when "Laconian" began to be spoken in public ceremonies of the *agōgē*, I would hazard a guess that it was more or less contemporary with the first appearance of laconizing forms on the dedications.

Spartan archaism or, more accurately, laconism, was rooted in a desire to recreate the city's famous traditions in a vision that nonetheless conformed to contemporary cultural notions. This vision encompassed all aspects of the ephebic system. The *agōgē*'s archaism was not simply a matter of the contest names and a few dedications; laconisms were embedded in its very structure, even in the age grades themselves.

We have already seen that some of the names known from the Hellenistic period were dropped and others altered at the beginning of the Roman phase.[124] The two youngest age grades of the Hellenistic *agōgē*, *rhōbidās* and *promikizomenos*, were abandoned; why, exactly, we cannot know. But their abandonment was probably one of the compromises the Spartans had to make after the Achaean War, when they attempted to restore their traditional public institutions following forty years of foreign tinkering with the constitution.[125]

The two eldest age grades, *melleirēn* and *eirēn*, retained their names in the Roman period. Of the five surviving names, only the names of the three younger grades changed, from *mikizomenos*, *propais*, and *pais* to *mikkichizomenos*, *pratopampais*, *hatropampais*, alterations amounting, in effect, to a laconization of the Hellenistic names. The colorless *propais* and *pais* were transformed into the flamboyantly Laconian *prato-* and *hatropampais* to denote the "first and second years of full boyhood."[126] Although the prefixes were coined from Laconian dialectal variants for the words "first" (*prōtos*) and "other, second" (*heteros*), *pampais* itself was not peculiarly Laconian, also occurring as the name of a subdivision of the boys' class (*paides*) at agonistic festivals in Boeotia and Euboea during the second century B.C.[127] When the *agōgē* underwent its second revival, this name was most likely drawn from a common stock of Hellenistic age-class names and made to appear more authentically Spartan by the addition of Laconian-style prefixes.

Mikkichizomenos is unparalleled, but appears to be an intensified version of the Hellenistic *mikizomenos*. The root of both words is *mikkos*, Laconian for *mikros*, ("small"). In the Roman period, a diminutive suffix, *-ichos* was added to produce a word that can be roughly translated "being very small."[128] For want of a better explanation, the change may have been intended to accentuate its new status as the *agōgē*'s youngest age grade.

In examining the *agōgē* during its last phase we have seen how every contest and ritual, even the names of the age grades themselves, were intended to engender in both spectators and participants alike the belief that the ephebes were reenacting the customs of Sparta as they had existed during Lycurgus' lifetime. Official announcements in ancient Laconian would have contributed greatly to this intended effect, lending the same air of impenetrable antiquity to the *agōgē* that Latin does to college graduation ceremonies today.

The late *agōgē* affords the researcher an unparalleled opportunity to trace the effects of cultural archaism on a critically important social institution in a major city of Roman Greece. But why did the Spartans choose the seventh and sixth centuries B.C. as the epoch to emulate, rather than the fifth and fourth?

Sparta's harking back to the Archaic period may be unusual, but is at bottom quite understandable. In the great wave of cultural archaism that crested during the second century A.D., the period from the Persian Wars to the death of Alexander was the preferred frame of reference.[129] Orators had a repertory of topics for declamations that consistently drew on famous incidents from the fifth or fourth century B.C. — "Themistocles, after persuading the Athenians to leave, proposes that they burn the city"; "Xenophon refuses to survive Socrates"; or "the Athenians wounded in Sicily beg their fellows to kill them."[130] Plots of novels might be set in an anachronistic Athens somewhat reminiscent of P. G. Wodehouse's England, frozen in time and decked out with the requisite allusions to the Peloponnesian War and the administrative machinery of democracy for a touch of historical color.[131] Reproductions and pastiches of works by such long-dead masters as Phidias, Polyclitus, and Myron competed for space in public areas and private retreats; even architecture was not immune.[132]

The Greeks' pride in their successes against the Persians in the fifth century and under Alexander could now be marshaled against the new eastern enemy, the Parthians. Once again, Greeks were united in a single pan-Hellenic league, the Panhellenion, which might also be viewed as the belated realization of the universal congress Pericles had attempted to convene after the final settlement of the Persian war.[133] Spartans did not hold themselves completely aloof from this phenomenon. They celebrated the exploits of Leonidas regularly, and refurbished the monumental Persian Stoa, built from the spoils of the wars, whose roof was supported by marble statues representing noble Persians.[134]

Antiquarianism and the real world overlapped for Sparta later on, when Spartan soldiers served in Marcus Aurelius' Parthian campaigns of A.D. 163–66, and again in the early third century, when a contingent joined Caracalla in his inconclusive eastern campaign.[135] Following a long tradition, Caracalla depicted himself as the new Alexander, rallying the Greeks to fight the heirs of the Persians. He commissioned statues of himself in the likeness of Alexander, dressed in Macedonian costume, and drafted a Macedonian phalanx whose unfortunate commanders were required to answer to the names of Alexander's generals.[136] The Spartans called up for his army served as "the Laconian and Pitanate *lochos*," at once an allusion to the famous disagreement between Herodotus and Thucydides over the existence of a "*lochos* of Pitane" in the Classical Spartan army and a posthumous snub to Alexander.[137] For that earlier expedition, despite its pan-Hellenic propaganda, had lacked Spartan participation, a historical detail the inscription over the spoils from Granicus made notorious: "Alexander, son of Philip, and the Greeks, except the Lacedaemonians, from the barbarians who dwell in Asia."[138]

Here lies the explanation for Roman Sparta's peculiar brand of non-classical archaism. Spartans simply could not use the history of the Classical period as a model, for the triumph of the Athenocentric view of the fifth and fourth centuries meant a Sparta usually relegated to the role of villain, as exemplified in declamatory rhetoric, when it was not ignored altogether.[139] And even Spartans would have conceded that, after the Persian Wars, the city had done little to promote the cause of pan-Hellenic unity, an ideal that bound together many different manifestations of cultural archaism in the second century A.D.[140]

What Spartan rhetor would have declaimed on Sparta's victory in the Peloponnesian War when he knew that his audience expected him to present it as a catastrophe? "Dismantle the war trophies! Greek should never have fought Greek" was the proper opening for that theme.[141] Sparta's conquering general, Lysander, only merited a grudging "He started out well," and that as a concession at the start of a speech of accusation.[142] Typical is Philostratus' extended invective against Critias for using Lysander to destroy Athens' walls and Pausanias' opinion that Lysander did Lacedaemon more harm than good.[143] The fourth century offered no better material. The battles of Leuctra and Mantinea had been catastrophic, and Sparta's apathy in the face of the crises besetting the Greek cities as Macedonian power grew deprived later Spartans of a share in most of the great historical themes that fueled rhetorical discourse.[144]

The period ending with the Persian Wars was a different matter. Sparta's record was without blemish, its hegemony over the Greeks uncorrupted by dealings with a foreign power, and all could agree that it had been the time when the traditional Spartan way of life was at its apogee.[145] Corroborative evidence abounded. The Battle of the Champions, for example, fought ca. 545 B.C. against Argos over possession of the Thyreatis plain, furnished Sparta with a hero in Othryadas, the last remaining champion on the field, who erected a trophy to assert Sparta's victory, inscribing it in his own blood before he died.[146] Othryadas' courage foreshadowed that of Leonidas at Thermopylae, with whom Othryadas was often paired as one of the two paramount exempla of the Laconian ethos.[147] In fact, Lucian once inadvertently included Othryadas' story in a set of hackneyed topoi from the Persian Wars, so accustomed was he to hearing Leonidas and Othryadas mentioned together.[148]

Another instance of a later revaluation of Sparta's Archaic history was the city's public seal, which bore the likeness of an early king of Sparta, Polydorus.[149] Along with his colleague Theopompus, Polydorus was reputed to have added an amendment to the famous Great Rhetra, brought by Lycurgus himself from Delphi as the foundation charter for Sparta's legislative institutions.[150] In the third century B.C., Polydorus seems to have been transformed into a forerunner of the revolutionary kings, and his likeness (assuredly fictitious) first depicted on the public seal.[151] The reinterpretation was so persuasive that even in Pausanias' day, when the radical forces that had called it into being were long forgotten, Polydorus was "in the opinion of the Spartans, extremely partial to the people, for he did violence to no one, nor spoke a haughty word but, with humanity, kept justice in his judgments."[152] The tangible artifact that was Polydorus' seal further evoked Sparta's early history by bringing later Spartans in virtual contact with Lycurgus and his reforms.

The sort of Sparta that local and visiting orators articulated in their speeches must remain unknowable in any but the broadest outlines. We may suppose, from the very few Spartan subjects that made their way into the rhetorical canon, that the approach was predominantly ethical. Othryadas and Leonidas, for instance, received praise for acting in accordance with Spartan traditional ideals, whereas Lysander was chastised for failing to uphold them.[153] Another subject, albeit taken from the Peloponnesian War, turned on a similar ethical point, that it would not be fitting for the city to receive back those Spartiates who had been so remiss as to surrender themselves to the Athenians at Sphacteria.[154] Indeed, the most popular Spartan theme best represents the tendency to treat the city as an ideal entity rather than a historically conditioned one because the situation it envisions, a debate over whether to build a wall around Sparta, derives from no specific historical incident.[155] The subject afforded the orator, who naturally opposed this pernicious proposal, an unparalleled opportunity to praise the Lycurgan system and its values — "Sparta's own soldier-citizens are its walls; the city could have none better."

In the Roman period, especially during the second century A.D., the *agōgē* purported to be the last surviving repository of Sparta's Archaic warrior traditions. That the contemporary *agōgē* was almost completely a product of the last three centuries or so did not matter, because it gave Spartans a sense of continuity within a living tradition whose antiquity surpassed even the Classical heritage of Athens. All aspects of the ephebic system, from the crude battles at the Platanistas and the harsh floggings of the endurance contest to its organizational structure and use of ancient Laconian as the ephebic language, were knit together to project a seamless and seductive vision of a Sparta that never was, when the "Lycurgan system" had functioned flawlessly and so made Sparta the dominant power in Greece.

5

THE INVENTOR OF THE *AGŌGĒ*

In the years following the Achaean War, when the Spartans had successfully petitioned the Romans for permission to restore their ancestral constitution, they looked to the most recent phase of the *agōgē* as a model for reviving their educational system. Unlike the Classical phase, which had come to an end over a century before, Cleomenes' *agōgē* had functioned within living memory. Elderly Spartans could remember their time as ephebes, forty-two or more years previously, even if many had not been able to complete their terms. Thus, a living oral tradition was available to supplement the written record, which consisted in large part of Sphaerus the Borysthenite's works on Spartan constitutional antiquities. Other relevant studies, such as those by the local scholar Sosibius, would have been among the resource materials the Spartans consulted to ensure that the new *agōgē* conformed as much as possible to the old. Even so, change was inevitable, for instance, in the number and names of the age grades. But the Roman phase of the *agōgē* rose principally upon the foundations of its Hellenistic phase.

The studies that provided the information necessary for rebuilding the *agōgē* were originally intended to describe a preexisting institution, not to serve as blueprints for a new version. Sphaerus' works, *On the Laconian Constitution* and *About Lycurgus and Socrates*, were the exceptions that proved this rule. Whatever these two books' precise chronological and conceptual relationship to Sphaerus' task at Sparta, they must have reflected the same Stoic philosophy he brought to his reform of the *agōgē*.[1]

Unfortunately, but not unsurprisingly, an evaluation of Sphaerus' own views on education, morality, and other matters relevant to his role under Cleomenes soon meets that tiresomely familiar obstacle, an almost total lack of direct evidence. Of his thirty-one treatises, only one direct quotation survives, a description of a tradition in the Spartan *sussitia* preserved by Athenaeus.[2] Nonetheless, if a mere dearth of evidence had daunted ancient historians, they would long ago have abandoned the study of Sparta, to say nothing of Sphaerus himself. Instead, they have variously dated his Spartan books before, during, or after his sojourn with Cleomenes, considering them either a manifesto for or a justification of the reform program. Although the evidence does not permit us to choose one explanation over the other, just enough material does exist to situate Sphaerus in his cultural context and to permit some suggestions as to how Stoicism shaped the institutions of the *agōgē* in the third century B.C.

Sphaerus' first teacher was the founder of Stoicism himself, Zeno of Citium.[3] Like many of his early followers, Zeno was among those from the fringes of the Greek world who were attracted to Athens, the capital of Hellenism, in the last years of the fourth century B.C. Zeno set himself up in the Painted Stoa on the north side of the marketplace and taught a radical philosophy that would eventually have a profound influence on the world through its Roman and subsequent Christian adherents.[4] Stoicism owed its longevity to the ability of its teachings to evolve from calls for the abolition of such hallowed institutions as temples, gymnasia, lawcourts, and even money to become the main philosophical prop for Roman imperialism. Not surprisingly, later, more conservative Stoics tried, with some success, to belittle or whitewash much of Zeno's and his immediate successors' less comfortable writings.

No works by Zeno are extant, except in fragments, including what may have been his first, an account of the perfect society called *The Republic* (*Hē Politeia*), which produced such arresting proposals as the sharing of wives and legalization of incest.[5] So little is known about this work beyond its Cynic orientation, a result of his early association with the Cynic Crates, that there is not even a consensus as to whether his ideal society was localized along the lines of a Greek city-state or meant to be a worldwide community of the wise.[6] The loss of *The Republic* is particularly regrettable because Zeno devoted a prominent part of it to education. The book began with a negative assessment of the cultural curriculum usually taught as a preparation for the study of philosophy.[7] This particular subject interested Zeno sufficiently for him to expand and refine his theories in a work titled *On Greek Education*, in which he no doubt also proposed a program of reform.[8]

The idea that familiarity with, if not mastery of, certain branches of learning should be the common stock of all educated people even if they did not proceed to philosophy, later embodied in the concept known as general education (*enkuklios paideia*), was perhaps the defining intellectual characteristic of the Hellenistic period.[9] Always a vague and loosely delimited concept, general education had as its essence the seven liberal arts: grammar, rhetoric, dialectic, geometry, arithmetic, astronomy, and musical theory.[10] From the set of subjects taught aspiring philosophers, Zeno would retain only those disciplines he thought conducive to an education in virtue (*aretē*), which the Stoics, along with other philosophers, held as the sole means of attaining true happiness (*eudaimonia*). His desire for reform does not mean that Zeno held the same position as Epicurus, whose infamous dictum "Hoist your sail, sir, and flee all education!" he would have found far too extreme.[11] After all, Zeno wrote one work on the meanings of words and two on literary subjects, *Problems in Homer* (in five books) and *Listening to Poetry*, although he probably took a philosophical rather than a philological approach.[12]

Any discussion of education in the Hellenistic age would inevitably have touched on the advantages and disadvantages of the Spartan system as portrayed in academic works on the city's constitution. Zeno's book would have been no exception. On a related subject, pederasty's value as a pedagogical tool, the views he expressed were congruent with the attitudes ascribed to the Spartans.[13] Moreover, although early Stoics were accused of despising respected lawgivers like Lycurgus, Zeno used Lycurgan Sparta as an approximate basis for his *Republic*, which strongly implies he devised its educational system with an eye to the *agōgē*.[14]

Although we should not press the exiguous evidence for Zeno's attitude toward Sparta too hard, a recent study has emphasized the debt Zeno's state owed to the traditional picture of Sparta and there are signs that the city was as important a societal paradigm for the philosophical school of the early Stoics as it was for the Cynics before them.[15] Zeno's student, Persaeus, wrote a *Laconian Constitution*, while another, Herillus, published *The Lawgiver* (*Nomothetēs*), in which Lycurgus is almost certain to have figured.[16] Closely allied to the Stoic reverence for Sparta was respect for Xenophon. Zeno, it was said, took up philosophy upon hearing a portion of the *Memorabilia* being read aloud, and Persaeus apparently patterned his life after that of the Athenian soldier and litterateur.[17] Courtier to Antigonus Gonatas and commander of the Macedonian garrison at Corinth, Persaeus realized the Stoic goal of political engagement as well as following in Xenophon's footsteps as a philosophic man of action and friend to princes.[18] In addition to his *Laconian Constitution*, Persaeus paid his model literary tribute in the form of a *Memorabilia* (*Apomnēmoneumata*) and a study of ideal kingship (*Peri Basileias*) recalling Xenophon's *Cyropaedia*.[19]

Sphaerus' work or, more precisely, what little we know of it can only be properly assessed in this intellectual milieu. Born in what is now the Crimea, either at Borysthenes (Olbia) or Panticapaeum, early in the third century, Sphaerus became Zeno's pupil, enjoying an outstanding academic career as one of his star students until Zeno's death in 264/3 B.C.[20] He was constant in his intellectual loyalty to the Stoics' second head, Cleanthes of Assos, as well, gaining such a reputation for subtle philosophical definition that he could be mentioned in the same breath as Stoicism's second father, Chrysippus.[21] The list of Sphaerus' books in Diogenes Laertius shows him covering his discipline's usual bases — logic, physics, and ethics, including political theory.[22] He conformed to the Stoic model in his admiration for Sparta's constitution and traditions and in his attendance on two monarchs, Cleomenes and Ptolemy.[23]

In one important respect, though, he was unusual: by accepting King Cleomenes' invitation to assist in reviving the moribund *agōgē* and *sussitia*, he made the most of an opportunity to realize his Stoic principles. Plutarch, who, however unfairly, mocked Stoicism's great lights for the contradiction between their teaching of a perfect society's tenets and their reluctance to test them in the arena of everyday politics, could not have made such a charge against Sphaerus.[24] Sphaerus stands apart from all other ancient philosophers for this single reason: the resounding success of his attempt to make a vital cultural institution in a historically significant Greek city conform to certain philosophical doctrines. Sphaerus' revamped *agōgē* functioned for thirty-seven years before Philopoemen suspended its operations and subsequently formed the core of the Roman *agōgē* for its four and a half centuries of existence. Since our picture of Sparta's educational system today is drawn almost completely from the later stages of its development, for us Sphaerus is, in a very real sense, the inventor of the *agōgē*.

Cleomenes' invitation did not come to the philosopher as a bolt from the blue. Years before, Sphaerus had lectured extensively at Sparta on education, making a great impression on the young heir apparent.[25] Sphaerus' and Stoicism's pro-Spartan, anti-Macedonian bias were compelling enough reasons for Cleomenes to choose him for the task of revitalizing Sparta's traditions, but the philosopher may have had motives of his own for accepting the offer. The Stoic school at Athens had a new head in Chrysippus, who had assumed the post not long before Cleomenes launched his coup at Sparta.[26] Chrysippus brought a new intellectual rigor to the school, which had drifted somewhat under his predecessor, Cleanthes. The new scholarch's influence on Stoicism was profound and enduring: "No Chrysippus, no Stoa" ran the popular tag.[27] What Sphaerus felt about his new leader we cannot of course know. However, the two thinkers were at variance on at least one philosophical point, the validity of Arcesilaus the Skeptic's *methodion*, which Chrysippus attacked in his *Against the Methodion of Arcesilaus, a Rejoinder to Sphaerus*.[28] Of more importance here, Chrysippus also reversed Zeno's stance on the value of normal Greek education, maintaining it was quite serviceable.[29] Sphaerus, whose attachment to Sparta has been characterized as Zenonian, may well have taken the opportunity Cleomenes presented to show the viability of Zeno's reformist approach to education as a counter to Chrysippus' acceptance of the status quo.[30]

The evidence for Sphaerus' reform activity is scanty even for Spartan history and has been unrecognized until now. First come the glosses to Herodotus and Strabo, discussed in Chapter 2, that enable us to reconstruct the essentials of the age-grade structure in Sphaerus' *agōgē*.[31] To flesh them out, we have the relevant sections of Plutarch's *Life of Lycurgus* and the *Laconian Institutions*, which, I have argued, were originally compiled in the middle of the second century B.C. from books written before the Hellenistic *agōgē*'s demise in 188.[32] The *Institutions'* value as an independent primary source has long been unrecognized. Far from being extracted from Plutarch or even deriving from nameless Hellenistic originals, the first seventeen apophthegms are fragments from a work of utmost importance in understanding the later *agōgē*.

Institutions 1–17 form a discrete thematic unit, moving logically from the *sussitia* (1–3) to education (4–13) and concluding with notices on Spartan music (14–17), but the remaining apophthegms career wildly from topic to topic with no discernible guiding principle. They differ in another way, cruder but just as significant: the first seventeen are, on average, almost twice the length of *Institutions* 18–41.[33] The two sets of apophthegms are also markedly different in quality of material and style of presentation. The first seventeen are all lucid and complete, their contents nicely reflecting characteristic peculiarities in the Spartan way of life; while some of the remaining *Institutions* meet this standard, many fall far short in their simplemindedness or obscurity.[34] All these divergences indicate that the epitomator initially used a single work as the source for his material but, in time, abandoned it to dip into several other sources on Spartan customs. A rather disorganized compiler, he simply entered into the collection what he read in the order he read it, without bothering to group his notes according to topic. Thus, notices that should properly have been put in the section on the upbringing of Spartan children occur at random throughout the last half of the *Institutions*.[35]

The logical cohesion of the first seventeen *Institutions*, their relatively greater length, and the quality of their content and analysis all distinguish them from what follows and point to a common origin in a single work. But why should the epitomator have abandoned such a sound source so early? Leaving aside the possibility that he had to return a borrowed papyrus before he had finished copying out the information he needed, a soberer conjecture would be that the compass of the work he consulted for *Institutions* 1–17 was not broad enough for his needs. He intended his epitome to cover all Spartan customs, not merely education and the *sussitia*; once his first source was exhausted, he was obliged to pad out the rest with excerpts from a range of other, inferior, accounts.

Institutions 1–17 not only reveal something about the contents of their original source but can also aid us in determining its possible title and author. Literary theory and common sense indicate that genre to a large extent determines vocabulary: prose employs a different lexicon from poetry; comedy uses words that are inappropriate in tragedy; novels and history describe the same objects or events in different ways. Beyond being specific to a genre, word use can also depend on the practical considerations of subject matter: authors must use different ranges of terms when writing about Athenian democracy, Neoplatonism, Roman law, or lyric poetry, for instance. Similarly, the Spartan educational system had its own necessary vocabulary. Because accounts of the *agōgē* tended to concentrate on the same few elements — hardship, theft of food, and discipline — we can be quite confident about the word fields they will have in common.[36] Apart from specific Spartan terms, words denoting boyhood, youth, age, food, toil, endurance, and theft will invariably appear in descriptions of the *agōgē*. On the other hand, there are words that are not required for the depiction of a given subject but reflect an author's own approach to style and result from his personality and education. This second set, once identified, is the key to determining the authorship of a book.

Although epitomization of the first seventeen apophthegms has stripped away most of their original author's stylistic quirks, enough distinctive examples survive to show that his approach to the subject was inherently philosophical. One of the longer notices concerns diet in the *agōgē*. After running through the usual reasons for not giving ephebes enough to eat, it concludes with another motive, physical development: "They think that . . . thin and spare constitutions [*ischnas kai diakenous hexeis*] are apt to be supple in articulation [*diarthrōsis*], whereas overfed ones resist due to their heaviness."[37] Much the same reasoning had been put forward earlier by Xenophon, though he phrased it quite differently: "[Lycurgus] considered that nourishing bodies to keep them slender would be more conducive to height than distending them with food."[38] His plain speaking contrasts with the jargon of the later notice, which drew upon specialized medical vocabulary for the words, "thin" (*ischnos*), "spare" (*diakenos*), "constitution" (*hexis*), and "articulation" (*diarthrōsis*).[39]

Since medicine, like philosophy, concerned itself with the precise workings of the body as well as with the means to correct its malfunctions, doctors were generally held to be philosophers, and terminology tended to drift easily from the one discipline to the other. Galen well exemplifies this phenomenon, as much of his medical writing was taken up with philosophical critique while philosophical concepts, particularly those of the Stoics, underlay his practical teachings. In the passage under consideration, the twin orbits of medicine and philosophy meet in the word *hexis*, "constitution," which Galen defined as "breath [*pneuma*] holding together and controlling bodily parts," grounding his explanation in the Stoic concept that constitution (*hexis*) was that part of the breath or soul (*pneuma*) passing through bones and sinew which was responsible for the body's form.[40] *Hexis*, in the sense of bodily constitution, had been a commonly used philosophical term since the days of Plato.[41] With its appearance here in the company of other technical terms, *hexis* points to an author who was familiar with the vocabularies of both healers and sages.

Another example of philosophical coloring comes early in the set of notices devoted to education: "Literacy they learned for its utility [*heneka tēs chreias*], but expelled the other subjects [*tōn d' allōn paideumatōn*], teachers no less than lessons."[42] The concept of "usefulness," *chreia*, introduced to philosophy by Plato and commonly used in post-Socratic circles, and the phrase *tōn d'allōn paideumatōn*, which its definite article indicates should be construed as referring to the other subjects of the *enkuklios paideia*, put the discussion squarely into the context of Hellenistic educational theory. Spartan traditional educational practice is presented as a deliberate spurning of most of the general curriculum along the lines of Zeno's similar rejection in the *Republic*. Like Zeno, Spartans were pragmatic in their approach to education. As he had denounced the *enkuklios paideia* as useless (*achrēsta*) for attaining virtue, so they learned only what was of use (*chreia*) to them as future Spartiates.

"Utility" was given a precise philosophical meaning by the Stoics, whose fundamental ethical doctrine rested on the absolute, unbridgeable chasm between moral worth, that which they defined as morally good or evil, and everything else. The wise man should only pursue morally good things such as wisdom, virtue, and courage, and should avoid only moral evils such as vice, ignorance, and cowardice. All other qualities, even those normally considered desirable (health, wealth, and fame, for example) are morally indifferent and of no consequence to a life of virtue. The staggeringly immense class of indifferent things was subdivided according to whether they helped or hindered the leading of a life in accordance with nature. The natural life stands in the same relation to the virtuous life as membership in the Freemasons does to becoming a Shriner; the two are completely separate, independent, and incomparable, but the first is a prerequisite for the second.

Indifferent things are either conducive to the natural life, "serviceable" (*euchrēsta*), or unconducive, "unserviceable" (*duschrēsta*).[43] The best serviceable things have "value" (*axia*), which the Stoics defined as "some intermediate power or utility [*chreia*] contributing to the natural life."[44] "Utility" or "usefulness" is a quality peculiar to one class of serviceable things that are preferred not because they are themselves in accord with nature, but because through them many utilities for attaining the natural life may be secured.[45]

Foremost among the providers of utilities is education, for without learning about the virtuous, or the natural, life, one can attain neither. When Zeno chastised the general curriculum of Hellenistic education as useless (*achrēsta*) for a life of virtue, he was effectively dismissing it as irrelevant, a charge familiar to most classicists. In common with his contemporaries, Zeno held usefulness to be of prime importance in his educational philosophy, as utility was the true object of learning: "[He said] that one should not exercise the mind to remember sounds and words, but should train it in disposing them for use [*peri diathesin chreias*], instead of learning them by rote as if they were something precooked or prepared."[46] From the general curriculum, in Zeno's view, the only useful preparatory subjects were those concerned in one way or another with words and their uses—grammar, dialectic, and rhetoric—and which comprised the first grouping in his famous tripartite division of philosophy into logic, physics, and ethics.[47]

The Spartans of the *Institutions* have a markedly utilitarian approach to education. Although they go well beyond Zeno in the exclusivity of their curriculum, he and they concur on what aspects are useful, "letters" in a broad or narrow sense, and on the rejection of "the other subjects" (*ta alla paideumata*) usually taught in Greek schools. The author of *Institutions* 1–17, in effect, viewed Spartan educational practice as reifying and justifying Zeno's radical pedagogical theories.

The influence of Stoicism is unmistakable in *Institution* 14, which describes the effect traditional tunes had on the well-trained ears of Spartan youth: "they had a stimulating quality, which stirred courage and pride and which created a propensity for an enthusiastic impulse to act."[48] The philosophical underpinnings for this are most apparent in the technical terms "creating a propensity for" (*parastatikos*) and "impulse to act" (*hormē praktikē*)—hardly commonplaces in accounts of the *agōgē*. The idea of "impulse" recurs in another musical context, where Spartan military marches are described as "engendering an impulse [*parormētikoi*] toward courage, boldness, and contempt for death."[49]

"Impulse" (*hormē*) was an essential link in the chain of elements needed for a rational act to occur, according to the Stoic psychology of action. First, a "presentation" or *phantasia* of an environmental stimulus comes to the mind; reason then provides assent, *sunkatathesis*, which in its turn generates an impulse or *hormē praktikē* to impel the corresponding action.[50] Music is an effective source of presentations, as a fragment from the Stoic Diogenes of Babylon illustrates, in language strikingly similar to that of the *Institutions*: "Song naturally has a moving quality that creates a propensity for action [*kinētikon ti kai parastatikon pros tas praxeis*]."[51]

Although it was by no means a philosophical tract, the source for

Institutions 1–17 presented its material from a philosophical point of view. Its author's sure command of technical terminology, indicative of a philosophical training that involved exposure to Stoic doctrines, together with his use of the word *agōgē* for Spartan traditional education, argues for a date no earlier than the third century B.C.[52] His favorable attitude to Spartan customs in general and education in particular disposes me to the belief that the author was a Stoic, probably a follower of Zeno himself. Among the early Stoics, descriptive constitutional-cum-ethnographical scholarship along Peripatetic lines was not exactly popular; the only such works on record were all written by Zeno's students.[53] Out of these authors, only Persaeus and Sphaerus are known to have written monographs on Sparta. A fragment from each work survives, unfortunately on precisely the same topic, a tradition of the *sussitia*.[54] Even so, the subject matter of *Institutions* 1–17 tips the scale in Sphaerus' favor, since his role in reviving the common messes and *agōgē* would have led him to place disproportionate emphasis on the two Spartan institutions he knew best. Furthermore, Persaeus' known Macedonian connections would have rendered his scholarship uncongenial to the *Institutions'* epitomator, keenly aware as he was of each blow fortune had ever struck against Sparta.[55]

The scraps from this *Laconian Constitution*, coming as I believe they do from Sphaerus' lost work, afford us an excellent insight into the Hellenistic *agōgē*. The greatest gain comes in the organizational sphere, since it now becomes clear that the Hellenistic *agōgē* had a framework virtually identical to its Roman successor. *Institution* 6 describes ephebic sleeping arrangements: "the youths used to sleep on straw beds, grouped by company [*ilē*] and by herd [*agelē*]."[56] Here, *ilē* and *agelē* stand for ephebic tribe (*phulē*) and *boua* respectively. The Laconian glosses in Hesychius, who like the other lexicographers depends in the last analysis on Aristophanes of Byzantium, attest to the existence of both *bouai* and *bouagoi* in the Hellenistic period.[57] As for *ilē*, Xenophon had already used it as the Attic equivalent for the official groupings of ephebes at Sparta.[58] A visitor from Roman Sparta would have been at ease with the Hellenistic *agōgē's* organization: the familiarity of the yearly age grades divided into *bouai*, commanded by *bouagoi* and grouped into ephebic tribes, each under the direction of an *eirēn*.

If this restoration of the basic framework of the *agōgē's* later phases is correct, then what is to be done with Plutarch's well-known remark in the *Lycurgus* that the *eirenes* were in charge of *agelai*?[59] Since most scholars take *agelē* to be the equivalent of *boua*, he would in effect be saying that

bouagoi were *eirenes* and older than their teammates, which would call
into question the entire relationship of *boua* to *phulē*. Plutarch's apparent
contradiction of the epigraphical evidence has long proved an intractable
problem, made the more acute by the nearly universal assumption that he
accurately reflects authentic agogic terminology. His authority alone has
caused the word *agelē* to slip into academic usage as the preferred name
for Spartan ephebic teams even though there is no epigraphic evidence for
this designation and, outside the *Lycurgus* and *Agesilaus*, it only appears
with this meaning in *Institution 6*, cited previously.[60]

When describing these ephebic teams, Plutarch did not use their proper
Spartan name, preferring instead a word he thought would be more familiar to his audience. His attempt to clarify matters for ancient readers
has had the unfortunate side effect of thoroughly misleading his modern
ones, many of whom still believe that Spartan ephebic teams were called,
at one time or another, *agelai*. But there is no evidence that the word was
ever a distinctly Spartan term. It appears in glosses of the Byzantine lexicographer Hesychius either as a Cretan term or in the definitions of the
words *boua* and *bouagos*.[61] Epigraphically, *agelē* had wide currency as
the standard term for a group of ephebes: references to ephebic "herds"
can be found in cities on Crete, where it was the traditional designation,
and throughout Asia Minor.[62] They were organized for team sports, very
often specifically to run the torch race at a civic festival, under the leadership of their "herd leader" or *agelarchēs*, a word that also appears in
Hesychius as part of his definition for the Spartan *bouagos*.[63] Plutarch
thus had every reason to expect that *agelē* would be comprehensible in
itself and that he did not have to bother explaining it as he had the
unusual Spartan terms appearing in the *Lycurgus*.[64] Many problems that
have plagued historians for years disappear when *agelē* is removed from
the lexicon of Spartan words for the *agōgē*.[65]

The substitution of Attic equivalents for the words used at Sparta to
designate the ephebic teams may be traced back to Xenophon, who, as
we have already seen, employed the military term *ilē*. The *Institutions'*
source, probably Sphaerus, had used both *ilē* and *agelē* for the two types
of grouping in his revived *agōgē*. He knew what he meant by these words,
but it is far from clear that Plutarch did. For one thing, the meanings of *ilē*
and *agelē* were so close as to be all but synonymous in everyday usage.[66]
In chapter 16 of the *Lycurgus*, Plutarch describes the selection of leaders
for the *agelai*: "they used to set above themselves as leader of the *agelē* the
one who excelled in understanding and was the most spirited in fight-

ing."[67] In the chapter immediately following, he appears to repeat himself: "and *agelē* by *agelē*, they themselves appointed as leader invariably the most sensible and warlike of the so-called *eirenes*."[68] The second sort of *agelē*, the type Plutarch saw gathering provisions under the command of an *eirēn*, comprised boys of different ages and, consequently, cannot have been a *boua*; as I have argued already, it must have been an ephebic tribe.[69] Plutarch mistakenly uses the same word to signify two different types of ephebic teams—*bouai*, whose members picked their own *bouagos*, and *phulai*, who selected their captains from among the most talented *eirenes*.

Now that Plutarch's inconsistency has been dealt with, we can proceed to a closer examination of the Hellenistic *agōgē*. There were seven age grades, spanning the years from fourteen to twenty: *rhōbidas, promikizomenos, mikizomenos, propais, pais, melleirēn,* and *eirēn*.[70] They were introduced as part of Sphaerus' reform of the *agōgē* and show by their very existence that he converted what had been a set of traditional initiatory customs into a Spartan version of a Hellenistic ephebate.[71]

The educational systems of the Hellenistic period had a marked tendency to divide students up into age grades of increasing precision. This process can be detected in agonistic festivals as well, where competitors in the Classical period were classed as either boys (*paides*) or men (*andres*). A third division was soon added, and with the third century came further subdivision of the boys' class.[72] Only the local festivals put on for members of a city's gymnasia, however, can match Sparta in the complexity of their age categories. For instance, youths in ephebates lasting more than one year, like those at Chios and Teos, were classed either as "younger" and "elder" or as "younger," "middle," and "elder," as appropriate.[73] The best-known example of this sort of subdivision is to be found at Athens, where boys entered the Thesea divided into three classes, but similar practices are attested elsewhere.[74]

Of interest in this context is the division of the boys' class at Lebadea and Chalcis into *paides* and *pampaides*, which recalls the *prato-* and *hatropampaides* of the Roman *agōgē* and shows the two cities drawing from a common linguistic stock for their age-grade names.[75] A somewhat similar process can, I think, be detected lying behind the names Sphaerus devised for the age grades of the Cleomenean *agōgē*. Their names indicate that, after the introductory *rhōbidas* year, the Spartan grades formed three pairs, each of which having the first year serve as preparation for the one to follow (for example, *promikizomenos* before *mikizomenos* and so on). The reason for this remains obscure, though there are examples elsewhere of youths in the year before their entry into the ephebate having a formal, corporate identity under a title such as the *pallēkes* at Samos or the better-known *mellephēboi* ("future ephebes") at Athens.[76] Both these words were also in general use for referring to the age between childhood and the ephebate, so it is attractive to suppose that Sphaerus coined the name for the revived *agōgē*'s final preparatory grade, *melleirēn* ("future *eirēn*"), to parallel *mellephēbos*.[77]

No great chasm separated the Spartan from other Hellenistic ephebates, except in duration, for the *agōgē* lasted more than twice as long as the three years usual elsewhere, and, as a result, Spartans attained legal maturity somewhat later than most other Greeks, who became citizens at age eighteen.[78] For the most part, though, if one looks beyond its archaizing facade, nothing about the Hellenistic *agōgē* would have appeared irregular in any other contemporary ephebate. As in other cities during the Hellenistic period, those enrolled in the ephebate could take part in Sparta's civic festivals as members of well-defined groups that corresponded to their level in the educational system.[79] Furthermore, all available evidence indicates that Spartan boys entered the *agōgē* at fourteen, the usual age for boys in other cities, with the age grades of the *agōgē* then taking up the next seven years, the third heptad of their lives in Hippocratean terms.[80] The boys' younger years were doubtless now spent under the supervision of hired tutors, a decidedly un-Spartan custom that would have infiltrated the city in the decades after the Classical *agōgē*'s demise.[81]

The Spartan curriculum was heavily weighted toward physical education and military exercises, but so were those of most other ephebic systems. Apart from the overwhelming prestige of athletics in Greek culture since the time of Homer, military preparedness was required of all ephebes everywhere because they formed the military reserve force for their cities. Music's pride of place in Spartan life and education is well known; as Sphaerus put it, "no one was more devoted to music and song."[82] Spartan devotion, however, was far from unique, as music remained central to Greek education, with cities from southern France to the Syrian desert boasting festivals and musical competitions closely akin to the Spartan boys' contests.[83]

Despite a dispiriting though ever familiar lack of evidence, we have good reason to presume the boys' contests existed in some form or another in the Hellenistic *agōgē* because of the testimony for them from the Classical and Roman periods.[84] For the same reason, a *sphaireis* tournament was also probable, though whether it was a purely ephebic event like its Roman-age successor cannot be determined.[85] The clustering of evidence in the Roman period means that we also have no confirmation that teams of ephebes fought at the Platanistas in the Hellenistic *agōgē*, even though Plato alludes to massed ephebic battles in the *Laws*.[86] As I have already pointed out, the battle's venue according to Pausanias' description shows every sign of a substantial renovation under the influence of certain Hellenistic cultural trends; the vitality of these trends, however, continued to be as strong in the second century A.D. as it had in the third century B.C., so rendering them devoid of chronological value.[87]

Cicero's eyewitness account of the flogging used to be thought the earliest testimony for the endurance contest in the fully fledged form familiar from the accounts of Plutarch, Pausanias, and other later writers.[88] But now we have evidence for the contest in the Cleomenean *agōgē*. Redating the redaction of the *Laconian Institutions* to the middle of the second century B.C. has changed the situation, because one of the later apophthegms describes a whipping ceremony in honor of Artemis Orthia. All the characteristics of the endurance contest are present: "Among them, the boys, lacerated by whips all day long at the altar of Artemis Orthia, often until death, bear it cheerfully and proudly, contending over victory with one another as to who of them will endure being beaten the most. And the one remaining wins extraordinary renown among them. The competition is called 'The Flagellation'; it happens every year."[89]

A consequence of this redating of the collection is that the transformation of the cheese-stealing ritual described by Xenophon into the whipping contest can now be securely assigned to the Hellenistic phase of the *agōgē*.[90] Furthermore, the likelihood that Sphaerus was responsible for this change, as some have already speculated, becomes much greater, even to the point of inevitability.[91]

That much is relatively straightforward. Reconstituting a precise motivation for Sphaerus' action from the evanescent shreds of second- or thirdhand evidence available to us is another matter entirely, and I shall not attempt it. Even so, the invention of the endurance contest, when linked to a Stoic philosopher, indeed seems to represent an intriguing confluence of themes from Stoic, ephebic, and Spartan ideologies. The most achingly obvious is, of course, the quality of endurance itself. Although endurance was certainly one of the qualities needed in the earlier ritual, agility and aggression were just as important. By suppressing the theft of cheese, Sphaerus changed the entire character of the contest. No longer did two teams need to battle over the altar; instead, paramount stress was placed on endurance of pain. Even apart from the literary evidence, inscriptions make it absolutely clear that the contest was nothing more than a test of endurance: participants are praised solely for their fortitude.[92]

Endurance, of course, has long been considered a characteristic of Stoics: Diogenes Laertius says of the Socratic Antisthenes that he was the forerunner of Diogenes in impassivity, of Crates in self-control, and of Zeno in endurance.[93] For their part, the Stoics assigned endurance a position subordinate to courage in their scale of virtues. The four primary virtues were wisdom, prudence, courage, and justice; attached to each of these was a number of lesser virtues that manifested aspects of their corresponding primary virtue.[94] For example, courage might be defined as "a disposition of the soul that conforms to the supreme law when undergoing suffering" or "keeping a level head in undergoing and repelling those things which appear fearsome" or even as "a knowledge of things fearsome and hostile, or altogether negligible, and one that keeps a level head concerning them."[95] Endurance (*karteria*) lies at the heart of courage, since Stoics held that it was the ability to perceive what must be endured and was the virtue that enabled people to surmount circumstances that seemed hard to withstand.[96]

The Stoic ideal of courage seems to have owed something to Sphaerus' work in ethical theory, particularly his treatise *On Terms*, an influential book in which he set out the various explanations of the Stoic virtues as a way of bringing out their common denominators and which earned him the reputation among his fellow Stoics for being first-rate at definitions (*in primis bene definientis*); ironically, the only surviving fragment from this work appears in Cicero's translation of his definitions for courage, which I used in the previous paragraph.[97] Sphaerus must therefore have defined courage's subordinate virtues as well, endurance among them, and consequently the definitions by later Stoic thinkers of that concept should also reflect Sphaerus' contributions.[98]

The inculcation of courage and endurance had been one of the primary goals of Spartan traditional education for as long as we have evidence; Xenophon clearly saw its purpose as the training of hardy, brave, and obedient soldiers.[99] Outside Sparta, the two virtues were associated with the physical prowess of athletes, usually in combat sports, and, from the Hellenistic period on, with ephebes.[100] The ideology behind ephebic training was sometimes expressed in language that derived ultimately from philosophy: at Sestos, for instance, on the Thracian Chersonese, a late Hellenistic inscription praised one Menas for causing the the city's youth to turn to exercise and diligence, "as a result of which the souls of youth, vying for courage, are well led by force of habit toward virtue."[101] The preponderant emphasis Spartans placed on physical training even in the later *agōgē* finds expression in a number of inscriptions honoring ephebes for their courage, a particular attribute of victors in the endurance contest.[102]

The triad of physical training, endurance, and courage makes a suggestive appearance in Plato's *Laws*. In discussing the factors that contributed to Spartan courage, the Athenian helps Megillus to name four: the common messes, the gymnasia, hunting, and "endurances of pain" (*kartereseis algēdonōn*). These last are manifested in hand-to-hand combat among the youths, during "certain thefts amid blows," in the hardships encountered during the *krupteia*, when the ephebes must live in the wilderness unshod and without servants, and in putting up with the blazing heat during the Gymnopaediae.[103] Then the Athenian broadens the focus by suggesting that true courage is not just an ability to withstand physical and spiritual afflictions alone, but to conquer pleasures as well.

Sphaerus was no doubt aware that Plato had characterized Spartan education in his own day as a series of endurance tests, one of which involved a ritual around Orthia's altar. Whether he actually took it into account in molding his version of the *agōgē* must remain a matter for speculation. However, the various threads I have attempted to pick out from Stoicism, the ideology of physical culture in Hellenistic ephebates and the later *agōgē*, and the Platonic view of Sparta appear to form a loose pattern that suggests the invention of the endurance contest was very much the product of a particular time and place, imbued with Hellenistic sensibilities that had taken on a distinctly Spartan form.

The *agōgē* as an institution owes another even more significant debt to the Hellenistic period—its name. Although interest in the connection between Spartan upbringing and the city's military success had a long history, the word *agōgē* is never used in extant texts to denote traditional Spartan education until the Hellenistic age. Writers of the fifth and fourth centuries B.C. rightly presented the rituals of initiation and acculturation as wholly integrated into the unique Spartan way of life, but never attached to it any particular name. The word *agōgē* first occurs applied specifically to the Spartan educational system among the Laconian apophthegms, in one whose dramatic date is 331 B.C. but which attained its final shape only in the third century.[104] In it, the ephor Eteocles angrily refuses Antipater's demand that the Spartans surrender fifty children as hostages after his defeat of King Agis III, on the grounds that they would be uneducated and disqualified from full citizenship were they denied passage through the ancestral *agōgē* (*patrios agōgē*).[105] Apart from this occurrence, the earliest author to call Spartan traditional education the *agōgē* is Teles the Cynic, whose diatribe on exile was probably delivered sometime between 240/39 and 229 B.C.[106]

"Ancestral" (*patrios*) was a popular catchword in the turbulent politics of third-century Greece. At Sparta, it was prominent in the propaganda of Agis and Cleomenes, both of whom claimed to be restoring the ancestral constitution of Lycurgus.[107] Phylarchus, the revolution's apologist, whose writings Plutarch used for his biographies of the two kings, has a young Agis vowing to have nothing to do with the throne unless he can use it to restore the laws and the ancestral *agōgē*, while the same theme, the revival of ancestral mores, runs through his depiction of Cleomenes' program.[108] Later references to an "ancestral" Spartan *agōgē* are the fading echoes of the institution's importance to Agis and Cleomenes' reforms. "Ancestral" and other similar epithets such as "Lycurgan" or "Laconian" indicate a certain self-consciousness about the *agōgē* that would certainly fit the ambience of the third century and afterward, at the same time communicating the yearning for the past that such nostalgic terminology often entails.[109]

Spartan traditional education apparently received a distinguishing name only in the period of its first decline. We cannot, of course, give Sphaerus the credit for this, since the title was in circulation several decades before his work at Sparta. But it was Sphaerus who gave that title substance by devising an elaborate version of a Hellenistic ephebate that incorporated enough of Sparta's ancient practices, in however changed a form, for his (re-)invented *agōgē* to survive the downfall of its sponsor and to serve as the model for its Roman-age successor, which, through Plutarch's vivid description, has shaped the attitude of countless later generations towards ancient Sparta.

6

FROM ARTEMIS TO THE DIOSCURI

Anyone who has ever stood at the edge of an excavation, guide-book in hand, gazing down at a maze of superimposed walls and floors, will appreciate how difficult it is to distinguish the earliest, deepest levels of occupation. Often only a few roughly aligned stones remain as testimony to human activity. Later constructions mostly obscure, with dimensions that recall but do not precisely match their predecessors. So it is with Spartan education; the later *agōgē*, particularly during the Roman ascendancy, was so well designed to imitate the original that its outlines have long been mistaken for the real thing, rather than recognized as the elaborate reconstruction they actually were. To uncover even a partial picture of the Spartan upbringing during the fifth and fourth centuries B.C., we must disregard developments in the Hellenistic and Roman *agōgē* that are not solidly attested earlier, just as one blocks out the later accretions on an archaeological site to see, in the mind's eye, the thin tracery of rubble marking its first phase.

Among the many assumptions that have to be jettisoned, perhaps the most wrenching loss will be that of the educational system's familiar name. In fact, the Spartan *agōgē* per se did not exist in the Classical period. To forestall the sharpening of pencils for indignant marginalia, I should explain precisely what I mean. The word *agōgē* itself was not particularly Laconian. Commonly used to signify "education," its basic meaning is "a leading," and it can be used just as easily in connection with horses, ships, or water as with children. Since, as I have already mentioned, no author earlier than the third century B.C., not even Xenophon himself, ever uses *agōgē* to denote the Spartan educational system, there is no solid evidence from the Classical period that the Spartans, or anyone else, had a particular name for the round of initiatory rituals and contests that later became known as the *agōgē*. When people thought of it at all, it was as an indispensable aspect of the Spartan way of life (*diaita*). Only after its demise in the early years of the third century did Spartan education come to be viewed as a single, discrete institution and receive a name. Once this happened, as I have noted, references to the Spartan *agōgē* appear with relative frequency.

Naming the *agōgē* made it a thing apart, to be added or taken away as circumstances demanded. In the Classical period, the upbringing of the youth could not have functioned without the rest of the Spartan way of life to support it, any more than the *diaita* itself was possible without the traditional rites of education. By the Roman period this fruitful link had long been severed, and the *agōgē* served as a sort of tableau vivant of Spartan culture in the midst of a society little different from those of its neighbors.

That we cannot date this use of *agōgē* earlier than the third century has serious implications for our view of this earliest phase of traditional education at Sparta. The delineation between ephebate and adult life was not as sharp, nor were the transitions within the ephebate as abrupt as in the mannered, somewhat artificial creations of Sphaerus and his Spartan successors. Unlike the later *agōgē*, which alone carried the cultural baggage of the city's collective identity, the traditional educational system of the Classical age formed an organic part of the web of life at Sparta.

Xenophon presents it as such in a sketchy but useful description of Spartan education that has not received the attention it deserves from scholars dazzled by Plutarch's more plausible account.[1] Avoiding any reference to precise ages, Xenophon provides a cogent and consistent sequence of grades covering the interval during which Spartan boys were educated together. He briefly notes the activities of each age group, taking care to emphasize, often without any justification, that Spartan habits were antithetical and, of course, superior to those of his fellow Athenians and other Greeks. His reluctance to be explicit about the age of transition from one stage to another probably reflects an imprecision inherent in the age-group succession itself, which was so familiar to Xenophon from his own experience that even in his utopian novel, the *Cyropaedia*, he prescribed no hard-and-fast rules for the ages of graduation through the stages of education in Persia.[2]

According to his scheme, Spartans passed through three stages in their education: children (*paides*), teenagers (*paidiskoi*), and young men (*hēbontes*).[3] He mentions the same three stages in his book on contemporary Greek history, but he did not devise the names himself.[4] Thucydides, for example, refers to Spartan *hēbontes*, and the famous Laconian inscription erected by Damonon in the fifth century probably contained a reference to his son winning an athletic event while still in the *hēbon* class.[5] Nor did these names in any way represent officially sanctioned nomenclature: *paidiskoi* could also be called *sideunai*, and *hēbontes* might be *kursanioi*.[6]

Maddeningly, Xenophon obscures the age at which education began. To compound the confusion, he exaggerates the haste with which Greek parents normally divested themselves of their children by packing them off to tutor and palaestra. He gives the impression that the poor things were barely out of swaddling clothes, rather than seven years old, the usual age at which education began.[7] That Xenophon avoided drawing any attention to this point, which would have been the first example of Lacedaemonian uniqueness, strongly indicates that young Spartans began their education at the same age as children of other cities — a surmise supported by Plutarch's later testimony.[8]

He is just as allusive about the transition to the *paidiskos* stage. Even so, from his remarks about youngsters of the same age in other cities running wild with no teachers to control them, we may suppose that the change occurred at about fourteen or fifteen years of age.[9] There was, then, a rough equivalency between the age of entry into the Classical *paidiskoi* and the youngest grade of the later *agōgē*, the *rhōbidai*.

Xenophon manages to skip nimbly over the detail of when boys entered the *hēbontes* class, but other evidence comes to our aid. The *hēbontes* were anomalous because they were adult enough to fight in the army yet still considered junior to the extent that the magistrate in charge of education, the *paidonomos*, retained coercive power over them.[10] We know that Spartans were obligated to serve in the military for a span of forty years, after which they were eligible for election to the Gerousia, the city's ruling council, at the age of sixty.[11] Accordingly, the youngest *hē-*

bōntes were about twenty years old. They apparently became full citizens, or "in their prime" (*akmazontes*) as Xenophon says, at about thirty, when they might wear their hair long in the time-honored fashion, engage in economic and political activity, hold office, and marry.[12]

Anomalous as the *hēbōntes'* status may have been at Sparta, they were certainly not unique in Greek society. Even in democratic Athens, young men who had left the ephebate but not yet reached the age of thirty were expected to be the very model of soldierly punctilio, while having yet to enjoy untrammeled rights of citizenship.[13] Teles the Cynic pithily summed up how these years were spent and what waited on the horizon: "He is an ex-ephebe and already twenty. Still he fearfully awaits orders from the gymnasiarch and the general: if a watch must be kept, they keep it; if a night vigil, they stand guard at night; if an embarkation is needed, they board ship. He has become a man in his prime [*akmazei*]: he campaigns and serves on embassies for his city; he holds offices, generalships, and pays for choruses and games."[14] The rhythm of such a life would have been as familiar to a Spartan as to any other Greek.

We meet here a second correspondence, this time between the *eirenes* age grade of the later *agōgē* and the first year spent as a *hēbōn*. This equation, along with evidence for another alternative name for the *hē-bōntes*, is suggestive of the method Sphaerus used to codify the age-grade names for his restored ephebate. The evidence is unique — a single stone of fifth-century date found southeast of Sparta at Geronthrae (modern Geraki) preserving a fragmentary list of athletic victories at various local Laconian festivals, one of which the dedicant won when he was a *trie-tirēs*.[15] The editor of the inscription's best text considered this form as the singular of *tritirenes*, an age-grade name in an ephebic list from Messenian Thuria dating from the second century B.C.[16] He supported this with lexicographical glosses on the word *prōteirai*, which is usually emended to *prōteirenes*.[17] In an interpretation that has stood for over thirty years, he considered a *trietirēs* to be a third-year *eirēn*, just as a *prōteirēn* was in his first year.

Due to the disarray of scholarship on Spartan education, no challenge to this reconstruction has been mounted because it caters to the widely held belief in the antiquity of yearly age grades. I, however, am not so confident in the association of *tritirēn* with *trietirēs*. Although the simplex forms *irēs* and *irenes* are parts of the same word, and are almost certainly precursors of the word *eirēn*, the suffix *trit-* cannot be a syncopated variant of *triet-*. The ordinal *tritos*, "third," has no dialectal forms remotely similar to the *trietos needed here. On the other hand, the adjective *trietēs*, "for three years," fits comfortably, making a *trietirēs* "an *irēs* for three years." The distinction is an important one, for it shows we are not dealing with a year-by-year subdivision of a longer period along the lines of Sphaerus' later restructuring of the *paidiskos* stage. Rather, as used in this inscription, *trietirēs* refers to the three years since an individual had begun to be an *irēs*.

The ordinals in *tritirenes* and *prōteirenes*, "third" and "first," would invalidate this hypothesis only if all three terms were products of exactly the same cultural and historical circumstances, which, however, is far from being the case. Thuria, the source of *tritirenes*, had been a community of perioeci under Spartan control during the Classical period, but was politically part of Messenia in the second century B.C. Although the city undoubtedly still felt the cultural influence of its old ruling power, it requires a big leap to assume that Thuria's educational system reflected the Spartan system of some two centuries earlier without any change or distortion. But if the focus is widened to take in evidence from beyond the Thuria-Sparta axis, parallels for Thurian practice come readily into view. In the previous chapter, we noted the Hellenistic phenomenon of youths in ephebates that lasted two or three years being divided up into categories according to their ephebic year.[18] Thuria's ephebate was more than likely of this type — a three-year *ephēbeia* whose incumbents were collectively called *(e)irenes*, subdivided into groups recalling the younger, middle, and elder ephebes or the children of the first, second, and third age classes known from other Greek cities. The cumbersome Spartan system's influence can only be detected in, and was probably confined to, the name of Thuria's ephebes.

As for *prōteirēn*, properly *prōtirēs*, its closest parallel is the poetical word *prōthēbēs*, "at the height of youth," which suggests that it too was applied to young men in early adulthood rather than being the title of a specific annual age grade.[19] In their glosses, Hesychius calls *prōtirēs* "the name of an age group [*hēlikia*] among the Lacedaemonians," and Photius says they were "about twenty years old."[20] Neither scholar is more specific. A *prōtirēs* was just a young man who had recently become liable for military service.

Like *ephēbos* at Athens, the word *eirēn/irēs* originally had no institutional significance for Spartans. In the earliest securely attested literary reference to *eirēn*, Callimachus treats it as merely one among several words indicating a time of life, no different from "infant" or "old man."[21]

In the Classical period, a young Spartan who had begun to serve as a soldier, but who had yet to enjoy the full rights and privileges of a Spartiate, was known as an *irēs* (genitive *irenos*), a Laconian variant of *arsēs* (genitive *arsenos*), "male."[22] The word, more or less synonymous with *kouros*, "youth," was not the name of a specific age grade.[23] Only later, when Sphaerus sought suitably Spartan appellations for the yearly grades of his reconstituted *agōgē*, did it become the collective designation for those enrolled in the last year of the ephebate. Such sensitivity to Spartan tradition as Sphaerus showed here in recasting the ancient educational system was surely a major factor in its longevity.

Before going on to an examination of each age group's activities, a few scraps of information concerning the organization and administration, such as there was, of the entire system can be extracted from Xenophon. The boys were organized into companies, *ilai*.[24] He mentions no other grouping, smaller or larger than this, so the temptation to identify these bands with the later *ilai* found in Plutarch and the *Laconian Institutions* and, on this basis, to postulate the existence of *agelai/bouai* in the Classical period, overwhelming though many historians have found it, must be resisted. While the earlier and later *ilai* were not identical, they were similar enough for us to think that, in this instance as well, Sphaerus later adapted an institution that was already in existence. There were probably four *ilai*, one for each of the four constituent communities (*ōbai*) of Classical Sparta, each under the command of "the sharpest of the males."[25] Xenophon stresses their disciplinary function above all else: in the absence of adults, they were to maintain good order.[26]

The boys were also in the charge of a magistrate known as the *paidonomos*, a Spartiate who had to be older than thirty to qualify for this and the other highest offices.[27] Endowed with wide disciplinary powers, the *paidonomos'* main duties, the only ones Xenophon actually sees fit to mention, were to muster boys for exercise and to chastise them vigorously for any transgression. The punishments he decreed were effected by the whips of his assistants, the *mastigophoroi*, who were drawn from the *hēbōntes* and acted as prefects or trustees over the younger boys.[28] With his entourage of whip bearers, the *paidonomos* would have cut an imposing public figure, much like the *Hellanodikai*, who presided over the Olympic games, or the *agōnothetai* in charge of games in other cities. The similarities were not merely superficial, for all three sorts of official were concerned with athletics, maintaining discipline and good conduct among their charges with the assistance of men carrying whips (*mastigophoroi*) or rods (*rhabdouchoi*).[29] However, the Spartan *paidonomos'* powers were much wider ranging. His authority was not restricted to a particular festival or to any one place; all immature Spartans were under his authority, in varying degrees, at all times, everywhere. The single most unusual aspect of the Classical educational system at Sparta was the state's direct involvement in the daily activities of the young. No other Classical city had a magistrate like the *paidonomos*, which is probably the reason why Aristotle commended the Spartans for taking the education of their children so seriously that it was a communal concern.[30]

As I hinted just now, the authority of the *paidonomos* was not absolute over all young Spartans. Because *hēbōntes* were now on probation serving in the army, he shared jurisdiction over them with the board of ephors. The *paidonomos* had the power to arrest disorderly *hēbōntes*, but only the ephors might judge and punish them.[31] The ephors also carried out daily examinations of the new soldiers' clothes and bedding, periodically supplemented by inspection parades.[32] They appointed three adults as *hippagretai*, who picked three hundred *hēbōntes* to serve as *hippeis*, the crack royal bodyguard.[33] But their authority did not extend to those in the younger age groups; if a *paidiskos* misbehaved, the ephors penalized his adult lover, not the boy himself.[34] Any punishment inflicted on the boy would have come from his *erastēs*, his father, the leader of his *ila*, or the *paidonomos*. The ephors regulated the lives of adult Spartiates and their relations with the young, while the *paidonomos* had the same responsibility for those who had not yet reached maturity. His role in determining blame and administering punishment may be behind the revival of an obsolete word for "judges," *biduoi*, as the title of the board of magistrates who supplanted the *paidonomos* in the later phases of the *agōgē*.[35]

We first meet the *paidonomos* in Xenophon's account of the activities of the *paides*, but this does not mean that he thought the magistrate's powers were restricted to the youngest age group. Most of the information on the organization and administration of the boys that Xenophon presents under this rubric would have applied to those in the next stage as well. Here we come upon the earliest extant traces of those elements no later account of Spartan education could do without: scanty clothing, communal meals, and theft of food.

Unlike their mollycoddled coevals elsewhere in Greece, Spartan boys went barefoot and wore only one outer garment all year round. They worked and slept together in groups, learning to feel comfortable as small cogs in a big machine. In a much-garbled passage, but one whose general meaning is clear enough, Xenophon informs us that Lycurgus established that each boy contribute only so much food as he had so that he would never be oppressed by overindulgence and would know what it was like to go hungry.[36] Their frugal communal rations could be supplemented, but only by theft, so that the boys learned to cooperate with one another and gained the skills essential for survival as Spartan warriors.[37]

This custom gave rise to what is still probably the best known anecdote about Spartan education, the story of the boy and the fox, found in the Laconian *Apophthegmata*. So familiar is the tale to everyone, classicist and nonclassicist alike, that what it actually has to tell us is resolutely ignored:[38]

> When the time came for free children, according to custom, to steal whatever they could and being caught was considered disgraceful, another young boy was guarding a live fox cub his companions had stolen and given to him, when the owners appeared looking for it. Just then, he thrust it under his *himation* and, even though the animal was devouring his side through to his entrails, kept quiet so that he would not be discovered. Later, when they had gone away, the boys saw what had happened and criticized him, saying that it was better to show the fox cub than to hide it until death. "No way!" he said, "It's better to die without giving in to pain than to be caught out because I was soft and put a shamefully high value on living."

Doubt has been cast on the anecdote's originality, mainly because fox could not possibly have figured in the Spartan diet.[39] This observation is undoubtedly correct but is no warrant for rejecting the anecdote out of hand. In fact, the fox cub is its best guarantor of authenticity. Fox imagery popped up at several points in Spartan education: the hero Alopecus, "Mr. Fox," had discovered the cult image of Artemis Orthia; the ephebes' sojourn in the wilds was called *phouaxir*, "the fox time"; and the word used to describe training was *phouaddei*, "he plays the fox."[40] Youngsters were supposed to emulate the fox's cunning and become tricksters (*plagiaddonter*), while their parents' admiration for the animal's qualities was so well known that Aristophanes twice calls attention to Spartan foxiness.[41] In short, the appearance of a fox cub in this situation is too unusual to have come from a non-Spartan source, but is completely consistent with the symbolic representation of Spartan youths. The story's origins must remain shrouded in mystery; I wonder, however, whether it did not start out as an exemplary tale that used to be told to ephebes at Sparta.[42]

Whatever its precise nature, the passage contains a valuable drop of information. We are told that, on a specific occasion (*kairos*), it was the custom (*nenomisto*) for ephebes to steal whatever they could without getting caught. The implication could not be clearer; contrary to the canonical interpretation, Spartan boys only stole at particular times established by custom. In his account, Xenophon rationalized this ritual theft into a regular activity intended to augment the ephebes' provisions. Other commentators, ancient and modern, have understood him to mean that the ephebes stole food daily, without taking into account the consequences such continual thievery by all the younger male population would have had on a rigidly structured society such as Sparta.[43] Either the city would have degenerated into anarchy or the act of stealing would have become a counterfeit, with food set aside especially for boys to filch. Instead of an everyday occurrence, then, theft was only sanctioned in particular circumstances, as part of larger religious festivals during which the conventional norms of society were periodically overturned.[44] Xenophon himself alludes to one form of ritual theft at Sparta when he ends his discussion of larceny's pedagogical value with the cheese-stealing contest at Artemis' altar.[45]

If the ephebes' stealing was essentially a ritual activity, we should next question how much other religiously motivated action Xenophon's exceedingly rationalistic, down-to-earth account of Spartan education has disguised. For instance, he claims that the boys were required to go without sandals so that they would become surer-footed in climbing and able to run and jump more swiftly.[46] But, as was long ago recognized, bare feet have a religious, not a military, significance, and the closest parallels are to be found in festivals and rites of passage; participants in the Andanian mysteries and worshipers at the sanctuary of Despoina at Lycosura were unshod.[47]

Seen in this light, the meager rations allowed the youths have little to do with training for the harsh life of a soldier and everything in common with periods of fasting endured by those undergoing rites of passage.[48] The single *himation* worn year-round set its owner apart from the rest of society, identifying him as one of a group whose transitory status lent it an air of sanctity much as the black cloak served as the uniform of an Athenian ephebe or, at a further remove, pure white robes often distinguished initiates from the masses.[49] Unlike Spartan boys, Greek youths on the whole lived their lives as individuals except on special occasions like civic festivals, when they participated en masse. At such times, even democratic Athens presented itself as a composite of blocs defined by status, kinship, or age, rather than as a community of individual people. One of the purposes of the Parthenon's Panathenaic frieze is to show all the corporate entities of Athenian society jointly worshiping the city's patron, but when the celebration was over, these bodies dissolved back into the welter of daily life. At Sparta, in contrast, the youths displayed and emphasized their collective identity and separateness from the community not just during religious festivals, but at every moment of the day, waking or sleeping.

Indeed, the primitive beds (*stibades*) they slept on had to be made from rushes they themselves collected, without knives, from the banks of the Eurotas.[50] *Stibades* made of twigs or sticks were a common feature of ceremonies involving withdrawal to suburban sanctuaries for banquets and celebrations, such as when Athenian women abandoned their households to gather on the Anodos slope for the Thesmophoria.[51] This form of sleeping arrangement, like much else associated with Greek ritual activity, recalls a prehistoric way of life; for the same reason, household fires were sometimes extinguished, a potent symbol of reversion to a time before civilization, or stone axes used for sacrifice instead of metal ones. In a like manner, the Spartan ephebes who tore the reeds up with their bare hands were reliving the brutish life of long ago, before the gods brought civilization and technology. The other sacrifices, banquets, or withdrawals were soon over; the Spartan ephebes, however, remained beyond the pale, living neither with their families nor participating in the world of adults for many years. Their separateness may explain why, as I have noted, Spartan civil authorities, in the form of the ephors, had no jurisdiction over them: they were literally outside society.

Their segregation was for the most part symbolic, not physical, and was reinforced by the heavy emphasis Sparta placed on their identity as a group. But there were other societal currents flowing in the opposite direction for, as they grew up, the boys entered into relationships as individuals with older men who introduced them into the world of adults. Xenophon's squeamishness about this aspect of Spartan education led him to deny categorically that it had a sexual component.[52] No one believes him. On the contrary, homosexual connections of this sort had a pronounced initiatory element and can be found in other warrior societies, most notably in the cities of Crete, whose customs so resembled Sparta's that Lycurgus was supposed to have used them as a model.[53]

A boy was ready to become a man's *erōmenos* just as he outgrew the *paides* and entered the *paidiskoi*.[54] Xenophon does not spend much time on this second age group, no doubt because there was little to differentiate the activities of *paidiskoi* from those of *paides*: apart from the intensification of drills and exercises Xenophon briefly mentions, I assume that life for a *paidiskos* hardly changed from the one he already knew.[55] But there was an important exception to this continuity; his relationship with an adult meant that the boy could now enter the male world of the common messes (*phiditia*), where, in a sort of catechism, he answered questions put to him.[56] Here there arises a tension between the youths' liminal status outside society and their gradual acculturation to the communal life of adult Spartiates. A boy's guide and teacher in this whole process was surely his *erastēs*, who introduced him to the ways of a young Spartan gentleman: to keep his hands inside his robe while in public, to walk without talking, to keep his eyes always on the ground, and never to stare.[57] The ferocity that life with his age mates had inculcated in the youth was reined in and contained by the standards of civil behavior he learned as a *paidiskos*. While still outside the mainstream, Spartan teenagers were observing the life they would enter and learning its rules.

Apart from these lessons in etiquette, a young Spartan would have assimilated the general moral and ethical instruction his *erastēs* provided alone or through visits to the *phidition*. We are completely in the dark, however, about the acquisition of practical skills such as literacy. Spartans were, of course, notoriously ignorant of letters in Athenian eyes, but that picture must be modified in light of the evidence, epigraphical and literary, for a certain degree of literacy in Classical Sparta.[58] Most, if not all, of the Equals must have been able to read military dispatches, at the very least, and someone had to have composed the texts for official inscriptions, few as they were. But who taught them?

That Sparta had anything like a state system of schools seems highly unlikely. Such a regime would run counter to the entire tenor of Xenophon's description of childrearing at Sparta and would undercut Aristotle's famous criticism that the Spartans emphasized courage in training their young to the exclusion of all other virtues.[59] Fifth-century Athens cannot provide a model for Spartan practice. In the Archaic period, on the other hand, we do find parallels for the sort of aristocratic education that had been institutionalized in Classical Sparta. At that time, instruction was an individual affair, with youths getting their educations from older men, fathers or lovers, who taught their charges practical skills as well as ethical conduct.[60] At Sparta, this duty would have fallen on the *erastai*, who were also known, appropriately, as "inspirers" (*eispnēleis*).

At the end of their period as *paidiskoi*, boys participated in the ritual theft of cheeses that would become the whipping contest, but Xenophon, having a different notion of how to organize his material, alludes to this problematic ceremonial battle about halfway through his general description of the highlights of Spartan education with which he begins his account.[61] As I mentioned previously, the fight described by Xenophon and Plutarch was between two bands, one trying to take cheeses placed on Orthia's altar, the other warding them off.[62] We can know nothing of the particulars. Did the ephebes fight by *ila*? If so, were there heats? Or were they all divided into two groups, regardless of their usual affiliation? None of these questions can be answered.

It is possible, however, to solve the question of when Spartan youths took part in the ritual, even though our single piece of evidence for this particular ceremony pales beside the richness of testimony for its later avatar, the endurance contest. To do this involves drawing on a combination of parallels with other cults of Artemis and cautious extrapolation backward from what is known about the place of the whipping contest in the Roman *agōgē*.

The centrality of Artemis Orthia to the youngsters in the Spartan ephebate can hardly be denied; the epigraphical and archaeological records show that her sanctuary was not simply the site for a single odd ceremony but a focus of their activity. The existence of ephebic contests in the Classical period, happily, does not need to be inferred or supposed. There is epigraphical evidence for them — a single dedication of five sickles bearing the verse inscription, "Victorious Arexippus dedicated these to Orthia, manifest for all to see in the gatherings of boys" (Plate 9).[63] Arexippus' gatherings of boys (*sunodoi paidōn*) do not mean that the contests were restricted to members of the youngest age group. Rather, the term *paides* could be applied to all youths below the age of *irēs*, as the following observations indicate. I have already explained that *paides* proper and *paidiskoi* were both organized into *ilai* and were both under the jurisdiction of the *paidonomos*.[64] In the *agōgē* of Plutarch's time, all the age grades, up to and including the *melleirenes*, were considered to be *paides*.[65] We have noted the difference in status between the *eirenes* of the later *agōgē* and the younger grades and that the endurance contest marked the transition to the senior grade.[66] All of this fits what is known of

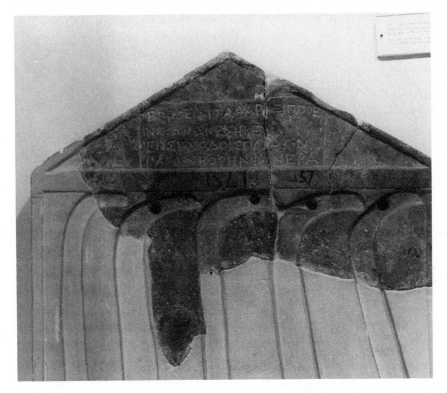

PLATE 9. *Sickle dedication of Arexippus (courtesy of the Ephor of Antiquities for Laconia and Arcadia)*

Artemis' role as protectress of the young: when her charges grew up, the girls getting married and the boys enrolling in the army, they passed out of her protection.[67]

In spite of the fact that, as I have repeatedly stressed, such later evidence often has no relation at all to the situation in Classical Sparta, a slender thread of continuity does run through the history of Artemis Orthia's relationship to the educational system. For their later versions of the *agōgē*, Sphaerus and his successors reused and adapted materials already in place: Artemis remained the younger boys' patron goddess, while the eldest youths, the *eirenes*, straddled the world of child and adult much like their forebears the *irenes*.[68] That the age grades from *mikkichizomenoi* to *melleirenes* were considered to be *paides* is, consequently, a remnant from the Classical period, when the two groups below military age were also lumped together as "children."

In the Classical period, as in later ages, a ritual at Artemis' altar marked the children's transition to the threshold of manhood at the conclusion of their years as *paidiskoi* just before they became young warriors (*irenes*). Plato alludes to the battle as "certain snatchings among many blows" (*harpagais tisin dia pollōn plēgōn*) and has his Spartan interlocutor include it among the tests of endurance youngsters must undergo to prove their worth.[69] A religious ceremony involving cheese may seem rather risible to modern sensibilities, but dairy products were quite often offered to the gods, and in this instance the cheese the youths fought over may have represented in some way the cheese Artemis made from lionesses' milk on Mount Taygetus.[70] Shocking rather than laughable is that some participants in the ritual forcibly diverted these offerings from their intended purpose as sacrificial offerings. Other rites of stealing are known, but none seem to have been as violent as the Spartan.[71]

Although the later endurance contest can quite readily be explained as a straightforward ritual of initiation into an all-male society (by the Roman period more ideal than real), a sacralized version of today's fraternity hazing or the devilment of West Point plebes in the nineteenth century, its predecessor, while clearly a rite of passage as well, presents more complex and disturbing features. Sacred precincts were havens of peace and quiet where violence was expressly forbidden.[72] The only blood normally shed belonged to sacrificial victims, and even then everything was done to conceal and mitigate the killing act.[73] The blade used to slit the victim's throat lay doubly concealed in a covered basket beneath a layer of barley, while water sprinkled on the animal's head caused it to shake and thus nod assent to its own death; at the culminating moment, the women's cry of triumph drowned out the victim's cries of pain and terror.[74]

Such lace-curtain gentility is completely absent from the Spartan ritual. The battle's violence is not hidden or redirected, as it would later be, but instead celebrated, which creates a paradox, for no participant or spectator could have been unaware that in any other sanctuary or at any other time such behavior would have been considered sacrilegious. But here the crime itself becomes sacred; by virtue of its origin, as an act of worship within the sanctuary, the violence is holy, completely different in nature from a street brawl. Even so, the battle overturns the right order of things; offerings are not made to the gods, but snatched by mortals, and action that is usually the antithesis of piety becomes its expression. Thus, the ephebes fighting over the cheeses precipitate and participate in the dissolution of Greek civilization's fundamental tenets: respect and veneration for the gods.

The final dissolution came upon the youths at the end of years spent outside society during which they had been surrounded by images of precivilized life. Now for some, if not to a certain extent for all, their very Greekness was forfeit, and they became no better than the barbarous Lydians who disrupted the sacrifice in Plutarch's story and whose robes they did indeed wear after the ritual concluded. The ephebes' temporary loss of status was intensified by the whips wielded by the defenders of the altar, for flogging was the punishment of slaves, not free men.[75] Dissolution of this kind, often expressed in images of violence and death, commonly preceded renewal and rebirth in rites of passage for individuals as well as in civic festivals marking the new year.[76] At Sparta, after they had passed through a period of utter, yet contained, depravity, the boys became young men and could begin to take their place among other members of their society.

Xenophon concludes his overview of Spartan education with a brief discussion of the *hēbōntes*, whose choruses and gymnastic competitions he thought were really worth hearing and seeing (*axiakroatotatous . . . kai . . . axiotheatotatous*).[77] The competitiveness drilled into them over the years was now given free rein. The three hundred *hēbōntes* with the best records were chosen to become *hippeis*, while the unlucky majority were encouraged to extremes of jealous surveillance over their every move, in eager anticipation of catching them acting in ways unbefitting Spartan gentlemen. If Xenophon is to be credited, the two sets of *hēbōntes* could barely stand the sight of each other and came to blows "wherever they met" (*hopou an sumbalōsi*).[78] With no lack of eager aspirants to fill vacancies from death, disgrace, or aging, the corps of *hippeis* would have been kept at full strength quite easily.[79]

Without becoming entangled in the obdurate organizational complexities of the Spartan army during the years of its slow decline, I can state that a few details of the *hippeis'* military life are relatively straightforward and can be summed up briefly. For one, the *hippeis* actually fought on foot in the Classical period in spite of being called "horsemen."[80] And it appears that ordinary *hēbōntes* were brigaded indiscriminately into the normal army units, whereas the *hippeis* had the extraordinary privilege of forming a separate corps outside the army's command structure.[81] Because the ephors directly chose the commanders assigned them, the *hippagretai*, they could count on the *hippeis'* absolute loyalty and discretion in carrying out such sensitive assignments as the apprehension of the dangerously disgruntled would-be Spartiate, Cinadon, whose attempted insurrection shook the authorities out of any complacency they might have felt after the defeat of Athens.[82] The five eldest men passing out of this elite corps each year served as special agents (*agathoergoi*) for the state, liable to be sent anywhere on government business.[83]

In becoming *hēbōntes*, young Spartans took their most significant step toward attaining the exalted status of Equals. Along with being afforded the opportunity to fight with honor for their city, they could now join the common messes, called *phiditia*, membership in which was essential for all Spartiates.[84] Dining clubs had been a common phenomenon in aristocratic circles throughout Greece during the Archaic period, when they had played important roles in politics and culture. However, only in Sparta and on the island of Crete were they officially incorporated into the machinery of the state, becoming at Sparta the preeminent medium for reinforcement of Sparta's aristocratic warrior ethic.[85]

Each new *hēbōn* applied for membership in a common mess himself, and it is not hard to imagine that family and social ties were significant factors in his choice of a mess to join and in the mess members' decision to accept or reject his application.[86] The voting procedure was extremely strict, as even a single negative vote was sufficient to cause a candidature to fail, virtually assuring that there was a good deal of canvassing among the approximately fifteen members before a vote to ensure a favorable outcome.[87]

In the *phidition*, where he was expected to eat daily while in the city, a young Spartan began his final journey toward integration.[88] No longer segregated with his coevals, he dined among men of all ages, drawing on the experiences of his elders to mold himself into an exemplary Spartiate who was ready to die rather than live ignobly.[89] Even the food carried a message: all members of the *phidition* were equal in every way. Each was obliged to contribute the same amount of unprepared food to the common larder, which the kitchen staff then transformed into the notoriously unappetizing black broth (*zōmos*) and barley bread served at each meal.[90]

Despite this emphasis on uniformity, an unusually perceptive young Spartan might have seen that his *phidition* also provided a forum for the typically Greek propensity for competitive displays of generosity. For, once the prescribed rations had been consumed, members were allowed, or more probably expected, to treat their messmates to tidbits they had brought with them. These ranged from humble concoctions of barley fried in olive oil, called "after-dinner cakes" (*epaikla*), to game or even that delightful extravagance, wheat bread.[91] Nothing could be brought in from a stand in the market; the only suitable gifts were products of the hunt or one's own estates, with magnificence, not taste, the motivating factor. Before serving, the cooks announced the name of the day's donor to his grateful companions so that they might appreciate his hunting prowess and diligence for them.[92]

Beyond what little is known of the *hēbōntes*' military life and what can be surmised about their membership in the *phiditia* lurks a mass of assumptions about their place in Spartan society as a whole. An unknown, but surely small, number of *hēbōntes* maintained a close association with boys in the younger age groups by serving as the *paidonomos*' assistants, the *mastigophoroi*.[93] Xenophon, as I have mentioned, praises the *hēbōntes*' contests and choruses, probably at festivals like the Carnea, where they would have provided the ceremonial runners called *staphulodromoi*; the Hyacinthia, at which a chorus of young men performed; or, less certainly, the Gymnopaediae.[94]

I assume that *hēbōntes* might also join the teams picked to compete in ball games. The prominence of the *sphaireis* teams in the *agōgē* of the Roman period has tended to overwhelm the evidence, slight as it is, for the existence of ball games in the Classical period. Xenophon clearly alludes to them, however, when describing the treatment meted out to cowards (*tresantes*, literally, "tremblers"): "Often this sort of man does not get a place when they are choosing ball teams."[95] Although only graduating ephebes formed teams in the later *agōgē*, Xenophon does not even hint that only *hēbōntes* played ball in his time; in fact, he mentions the teams in the part of the *Constitution* where he sets out to describe the way of life of all Spartans.[96] The transformation of these ball games from an activity open to all adult male Spartans into a solely ephebic institution is a familiar one and should be viewed as yet another consequence of the later *agōgē*'s role as the preeminent repository of Spartan culture.

The marginal status of young Spartans diminished significantly on entering the *hēbōntes*, but it still remained. In fact, the symbolic isolation of previous years became a reality.[97] For one year they were required to live in the mountains unarmed, without servants, to keep themselves hidden from view, and live off the land without being caught. Many societies have a tradition of sending their young men off into the wilderness for periods of time as part of the initiatory process, and ancient historians have profitably adduced ethnographic parallels. Unfortunately, as a perspicacious recent article has made clear, they have also confused two quite separate practices — a traditional withdrawal from society that all youths underwent and a period of police duty that was open only to the best of them.[98] In contrast to the solitude of those undergoing the *krupteia*, the name properly applied only to the period of isolation, groups of *hēbōntes* with the most nous also went out into the countryside, this time to terrorize the subject helot population, armed with daggers and a license to kill potential troublemakers.[99] While not so prestigious as the *hippeis*, these commando units were another expression of the striving for status and honor that formed the basis of Spartan education and society as a whole.

Young men in the last stage before full citizenship may have been expected to become lovers (*erastai*) of boys just leaving the *paides* phase, although that is far from definite, given that *hēbōntes* themselves had older lovers who were expected to carry out financial dealings for them until they were thirty years old.[100] *Hēbōntes* certainly could not marry. Early on, Xenophon takes pains to distinguish Spartan marriage custom from what other Greeks thought acceptable: "In addition, [Lycurgus] even stopped everyone from taking a wife whenever he wanted, laying down the rule that marriages be undertaken in the prime of bodily vigor [*en akmais sōmatōn*], because he thought this was advantageous for healthy offspring."[101] The phrase *en akmais sōmatōn* foreshadows Xenophon's use of "those in their prime" (*hoi akmazontes*) for adult male citizens who had completed their terms as *hēbōntes* (*hē hēbētikē hēlikia*) and who were then eligible for the city's highest offices, including the post of *paidonomos*.[102] However, Sparta brought enormous social and legal pressures on young men to marry as soon as they were of eligible age. Later sources describe a series of humiliating penalties confirmed bachelors suffered: in winter they had to traipse naked around the agora in a circle singing that they were getting their just deserts for breaking the law; they were barred from participating in the Gymnopaediae; and younger men did not feel obliged to pay them the respect usually due their elders.[103]

The final assimilation of a Spartan to his new status as a Spartiate Equal with no legal or social disabilities began with his becoming a full citizen at about thirty. Although marriage was expected to follow promptly, he did not yet leave behind the barracks in which he had lived for most of his life. A Spartan groom was expected to return every night to his barracks and often did not live at home until the birth of a child.[104] Only then, I believe, did a Spartan male finally shed the last vestige of his marginal status.

Not all who began this long journey were able to complete it. The risk of failure was ever present and had a disastrous consequence — exclusion from the ranks of the Spartiate elite, the *Homoioi* (Equals).[105] Of the forms failure might take for young Spartans we are ignorant except on two counts, homicide and financial embarrassment. Among the motley band of mercenaries Xenophon assembled for his expedition in support of Cyrus, pretender to the Persian throne, was one Dracontius, a Spartan from a good family who had been exiled as a boy for accidentally killing another boy with his sickle.[106] Sophisticated Greeks of Xenophon's time might have thought the punishment a trifle Homeric for their taste, but they would have understood that the Spartans' motivation for excluding Dracontius from the ranks of the Equals and banishing him lay in their fear of pollution.[107] The other reason for failure might likewise be viewed as a typically unforgiving Spartan version of a property qualification. Boys were required, like their elders, to make regular contributions of food to their bands' common messes; of adult mess contributions, Aristotle says, "This is their traditional definition of citizenship: that he who cannot make this contribution does not share in it."[108] We can assume the same was true for boys as well.

One might easily get the impression from Xenophon's *Constitution of the Lacedaemonians* that all Spartans began their schooling at seven and virtually all of them completed it successfully. Neither was exactly the case. Xenophon hurriedly alludes to the possibility of failure and its consequences — disqualification from all the rights and privileges of Spartiate status — but stresses the incentive for success it provided.[109] And although all boys of Spartiate parents, that is, from the top echelons of society, were theoretically eligible to join their fathers as Equals after passing through the rigors of the initiation process, most of the nonservile population was barred from enrolling in the *ilai* because of their status as Inferiors (*hupomeiones*).[110] Like Orwell's pigs, the Equals were quite a bit more equal than other Spartans, with one admittedly tendentious account giving a ratio of one Spartiate for every one hundred Inferiors.[111]

Ironically, in the aristocratic educational system Xenophon devised as part of his utopian fantasy on the life of Cyrus the Great of Persia, he unflinchingly confronts harsh realities downplayed in his account of the real situation at Sparta. The two institutions, as he describes them, share so many similarities in structure and philosophy that it is generally, and correctly, held that Xenophon must have based his version of Persian education upon what he knew of Spartan practice.[112] Thus, what Xenophon has to say about eligibility for his Persian system can apply also, mutatis mutandis, to the Spartan:

All Persians may send their children to the community schools of justice. But only those who can afford to raise nonproducing children send them; those who cannot afford to do not. Children who have been taught by the public teachers can join the ephebes, but it is not possible for those who do not have this sort of education. Furthermore, those who complete their time in the ephebes by carrying out their traditional duties may be counted as full citizens and partake of their offices and honors, but those who do not complete the period as ephebes may not enter the full-citizen class.[113]

Essential for this system, as for the Spartan, was wealth. A regular, and quite substantial, source of income was needed to free young men from all financial encumbrances so they might learn justice, archery, and the hunt. At Sparta, real wealth naturally took the form of land, with only the propertied families having the resources to allow their sons to join the *ilai* and contribute food.[114] But ability was severely tested too, and at every stage the numbers were thinned out so that only the best of the best could attain the reward of honor and privilege that was their due as full citizens.

We have no idea what the rate of failure at Sparta was, although scholars have pondered the deleterious effects on Spartan society of a growing number of disenfranchised Spartiates.[115] It certainly would not have alleviated the city's chronic manpower shortage (*oliganthrōpia*), which reached dire proportions in the fourth century B.C.[116] The ruthless and ultimately self-defeating ethos of Spartan education allowed for no deficiencies and would have inevitably grown more and more exclusionary as time passed had the tendency not been mitigated in several ways. Foreigners, for instance, who wished to taste the delights of ephebic life at Sparta could enroll in the *ilai* as "foster sons" (*trophimoi*), with the chance of eventually having a limited form of citizenship.[117] Boys from Spartiate families who could not, for some reason, qualify financially were sponsored by more fortunate families, it appears, becoming what the Spartans called *mothakes* to their sons.[118] No permanent stigma seems to have attached to the label, since the great Lysander, victor of Aegispotami, spent his youth as a *mothax*.[119]

As far as we can tell, the custom of allowing impoverished Spartans to be educated as *mothakes* was revived in the later phases of the *agōgē*, when they were called *kasens* instead.[120] The *suntrophoi* of Cleomenes III who helped in his coup against the ephors were not, of course, *mothakes*, despite Plutarch's (or even Phylarchus') testimony to the contrary.[121] Traditional education had collapsed before Cleomenes was even born, and the heir to the throne was traditionally exempt from it anyway.[122] Rather, they were true *suntrophoi*, noble children raised at Hellenistic courts with the royal heir, who would usually go on to great power and influence with him as king and were thus yet another example of the degree to which the third-century Spartan kings adopted the customs of Hellenistic monarchs.[123]

I have relied on Xenophon to provide a sound framework for the preceding sketch of the young Spartan age groups and their activities, but his view of Spartan education was inevitably conditioned by his own experiences on the fringes of the intellectual avant-garde at Athens. This limitation needs to be addressed, due to the marked influence his work had on the shape and tenor of later descriptions; even today, his rationalistic interpretation has found almost universal favor among historians.[124] Although scholars of ancient religion have justly noted the ritual and ceremonial aspects of Spartan education, the view prevails that it was "a mainly secular educational cycle with important religious elements."[125] This does justice to the *agōgē* of the later phases, which had been devised under the influence of Hellenistic educational practice, but it denies what I believe was the fundamentally religious, initiatory character of the Classical phase, as well as drawing an anachronistic division between the sacred and the profane.

Unfortunately, no authentic Spartan voices have survived to tell us how they themselves viewed what we call their educational system, and Xenophon's *Constitution*, our only testament, has a palpably nostalgic, utopian air about it. Despite this, there is no reason to think that any of these practices had lost their sacred significance for the Spartans of Xenophon's age. Indeed, from what we are repeatedly told of Spartans' piety, they are unlikely to have regarded the round of ephebic festivals and ritual actions as a system whose sole purpose was to produce adult male warriors. Notwithstanding the interpretations of Xenophon and his successors, everything we know about the upbringing in its early phase shows that it was an agglomeration of activities with fundamentally religious foundations, not merely a Lacedaemonian Sandhurst or West Point.

I have already called attention to the initiatory motifs ubiquitous in Xenophon's account. But there are also the gods of Spartan youth to consider, whose importance was far greater than either Xenophon or Plutarch intimates. Naturally, Artemis Orthia was paramount. Although she was the patron of Spartan youth from the earliest period for which there is evidence, her identification with Artemis is often argued to have come very late indeed.[126] The argument appears clear-cut, since the first dedication to Artemis Orthia rather than to Orthia alone comes from the late first century A.D.[127] Other evidence, however, suggests that the two deities were assimilated long before then. Tetradrachms issued by Cleomenes III bear a picture of Orthia's cult statue, a pillarlike image of the goddess wearing a helmet and carrying a bow and lance.[128] Iconographically speaking, a deity with such attributes could only have been Artemis.[129] This is, in fact, the name of the goddess of the endurance contest as recorded in the *Laconian Institutions*, whose original sources were written no later than the beginning of the second century B.C.[130] The identification of Orthia with Artemis probably happened much earlier, since sixth-century lead figurines from her sanctuary depict a goddess with a bow or a deer, which a recent study has pointed out were attributes of Artemis, not Orthia.[131]

The sixth century B.C. was a watershed in the history of Orthia's sanctuary as it was of Sparta as a whole. For it was then that the so-called Spartan revolution took place, which transformed Sparta from a ordinary Greek state, not really any different in its customs from any other city of the time, into an armed camp, with a supposedly totalitarian way of life that ordered a citizen's life from cradle to grave.[132] Early in the century, the area of the sanctuary was completely remodeled and a new temple constructed; the precise date is an object of lively debate among archaeologists but need not concern us.[133] Following the renovation, the cult's popularity, as reflected in the artifactual evidence, soared. Of the staggering number of votive lead figurines unearthed, some 100,000, the overwhelming majority comes from the sixth century; the number drops significantly in the following years, reflecting a general decline in the quantity and quality of archaeological evidence in Laconia as a whole during the Classical period.[134] A similar preponderance is evident in the number of terra-cotta masks found in the sanctuary.[135]

The sixth-century votive offerings, particularly the lead figurines, are not only far more numerous than the earlier ones but also show a marked shift in subject matter. Most suggestive is the great increase in the number of lead figurines depicting hoplites.[136] Hoplite figurines would have made appropriate dedications for those who had endured or were about to endure the rites of passage that would transform them into warriors and, in a general sense, can be taken to reflect a desire on the part of Spartans to be represented in this manner.[137] The votive masks, by turns grotesque or alluring, were the Spartan version of the terrifying and dreadful things shown to initiates into mystery cults.[138] Masks with the features of handsome young men represented the ideals for which the ephebes should strive, while monstrous gorgons and ugly, wrinkled, skull-like visages were images of what lurks, incomplete and ill-matched, beyond the bounds of society. The ephebes probably wore linen or wooden versions during the dances and other events that foreshadowed the boys' contests known from Roman times.[139]

Although the sort of archaeological evidence found at Artemis Orthia's shrine allows only tentative interpretation, her increased prosperity in the sixth century was surely a result of the changes being wrought on Spartan society. The cult practices that later came to be called the *agōgē* may possibly have been, if not instituted, at least adapted and rearranged at the same time that Orthia was transformed into a significant state deity.[140] While the Sparta of a century later was a highly regimented, backward-looking society, recent studies have tended to the opinion that, in spite of itself ushering in an age of austerity and militarism, the sixth century was a time of prosperity, with Spartan living standards, as far as we can tell, not significantly inferior to anywhere else.[141] Whatever was happening to Spartan society seems to have been beneficial, at least in the short run. With the final subjugation of the fertile lands of neighboring Messenia, Sparta embarked on an aggressively interventionist foreign policy in support of governments sympathetic to Spartan interests and against those whom it found uncongenial.[142] Sparta's success in pursuing this drive toward hegemony was surely due in part to the incessant training of the young to become citizen-soldiers. But military exercises are only part of the story and, as we have seen, not one that has left many traces in the literary or archaeological record.

Instead, ritual and cult dominate the evidence, which is as it should be, because training a boy to fight is useless without inculcating in him the desire to fight for his city. The initiatory ceremonies of Artemis Orthia cemented a bond between the youths that underwent them and Spartan society as a whole, while the use of certain Spartan mythical exempla, as I will argue next, provided these aspiring warriors with models for their own behavior.

At the edge of town, Artemis presided over the border dividing the life of the city, with its familiar institutions and rituals, from the untamed savagery of the world outside; in the decade and a half they spent under her protection, ephebes crossed and recrossed this line many times as they learned what civic virtues to emulate and which antisocial vices to avoid.[143] The terrors and obscene parodies horrifyingly represented at her sanctuary remain nameless, but the values of courage, obedience, and self-sacrifice exemplified by the masks of the handsome youth and the warrior were embodied in figures whose links to Spartan education have only just begun to be appreciated — the Dioscuri.[144]

Hometown heroes, with their birthplace just outside the city at Therapne, Castor and Pollux were major Spartan divinities. The Dioscuri, or their symbols, appear on a number of well-known Archaic reliefs and, much later, on coins.[145] Pindar calls them "stewards of spacious Sparta," grouping them with Heracles and Hermes as gods of the games.[146] At Sparta there were statues of the Dioscuri as Starters of the Race (*Aphetērioi*) at the entrance to the ephebic exercise ground, the *dromos*, while nearby stood a trophy commemorating Pollux's defeat of Lynceus and further away was an altar to the Dioscuri as *Amboulioi*.[147] In Pausanias' time, ephebes would sacrifice a puppy to the war god Enyalius at the temple of the Dioscuri on the night before the Platanistas battle.[148]

Appropriately for divinities who were usually depicted as young men, the Dioscuri were also great hunters, especially Castor, who was reputed to have originated one of the two great Spartan breeds of hound, the Castorian.[149] They invented the armed dances for which Spartan ephebes were renowned and, according to Theognis, they enforced fairness between friends.[150] In contrast to Artemis' place on the edges of civilization, where the wilderness abutted the orderly fields of culture, they were gods of the community, epitomizing the place and activities of young men as a group within society. The Dioscuri were, above all, warriors, protecting and encouraging their mortal counterparts in the din of battle; Spartan soldiers, for instance, marched to war to the strains of Castor's air (*kastoreion melos*).[151] In sum, they represented all the qualities Spartans would have found congenial: piety, justice, military prowess, and courage.[152]

Their relationship with Sparta encompassed more than just a congruence of values. Castor and Pollux were the divine counterparts and guarantors of the city's double kingship.[153] Until a dispute between kings Cleomenes and Demaratus in the late sixth century, both divine brothers used to accompany the two monarchs on campaign; afterward, when only one king at a time was permitted to lead an army out of the country, the twins took turns.[154] Indeed, Spartan kings could count themselves distant successors of their fellow citizens Castor and Pollux through Menelaus, husband of Helen.[155]

The Dioscuri thus stood at the very center of the Spartan polity, at once the legitimators of its royal houses and the embodiments of the ideal ephebe. From his first year as a *pais* until he left the *hēbōntes*, a young Spartan was led to shun the monstrous and uncivilized that lurked outside and to model himself after the Dioscuri so that he might incarnate the virtues they represented. This is no rhetorical exaggeration because, in a very real sense, the best young Spartans were in fact associated with the Tyndaridae.

The best young Spartans were, without a doubt, the three hundred *hippeis*, also known as the *koroi* (youths).[156] This alternative title appears on one of the so-called Spartan hero reliefs, whose dedicatory inscription reads "[The] *koroi* [dedicate this image of] Theocles son of Nam[——]" (Plate 10).[157] The relief is from a group that was probably erected sometime between 556 and 520 B.C.[158] Snakes and other chthonic symbols appear on the reliefs along with representations of the dead themselves, all of which points to the effective existence of a cult of the dead at Sparta.[159] The great honors given those who died in battle included veneration as a hero; as one scholar put it, "In Laconia every dead man turned into a hero."[160] The heroes on the reliefs are shown either singly or in pairs, standing or seated on chairs, but always making an offering.

The Theocles relief is one of several that show single standing figures, but is otherwise unique.[161] The relief, the bottom half of which is missing, shows a beardless youth with short hair in profile facing right, nude except for a folded traveling cloak (*chlamus*) on his right shoulder. In his right hand, which is slightly extended from his body, he holds a round offering, either a cake or a fruit, perhaps a pomegranate; to his right, a snake sinuously rises to the height of his chest. Cradled in the youth's left arm (invisible to the viewer) is a long, sticklike object that is undoubtedly a spear. It rises at a sharp angle from the middle of his back and breaks through the field of the dedicatory inscription, which runs vertically behind him. The visible portion of the spear lacks a blade, indicating it was held point downward even though the rest of the object has been lost.

The relief is incongruous. The *koroi/hippeis* fought as hoplites, but the figure on this relief does not have the characteristic equipment of this type of soldier.[162] Enough examples survive to indicate that Spartan art followed Greek iconographic conventions in depicting hoplites, who are

PLATE 10. *Theocles' stēlē (courtesy of the Antikensammlung, Staatliche Museen zu Berlin, Preussischer Kulturbesitz)*

shown, at the very least, with either a helmet or the huge shield (*hoplon*) that gave hoplites their name.[163] In fact, one of the hero reliefs shows a young hoplite standing in front of his shield, with his helmet on the ground before him.[164] His short hair and beardless state indicate that, like Theocles, he did not live to maturity. But, although both young men were *hēbōntes*, the Theocles relief does not show its subject as a hoplite because, in iconographic and symbolic terms, Theocles and his grieving friends were not hoplites, but horsemen (*hippeis*).

The Dioscuri were horsemen par excellence: "breakers of swift colts, wise riders," in Alcman's words.[165] Images of them on horseback abound, from the frieze around the Sicyonian Treasury at Delphi to pots from workshops in the Athenian Ceramicus.[166] Their association with horses was close and ancient, stretching back to their origins in the Indo-European pantheon and linking them to the Divine Twins of Vedic myth, the *aśvins*.[167] The two sets of brothers were saviors of men, bright deities whose epiphanies brought hope in the midst of despair; as Theocritus put it when addressing Castor and Pollux, "Aidbringers to mortals both of you, friends, horsemen, harpers, athletes, bards."[168]

On their horses or off, the brothers wore the same conical felt caps (*piloi*) as Spartan warriors; over their shoulders were traveling cloaks (*chlamudes*), and in their hands one or two spears.[169] Every Spartan knew how to identify the Dioscuri from these accoutrements, but even this sometimes failed to help. Pausanias relates the tale of Panormus and Gonippus, two likely lads from Andania in Messenia who, dressed up in white chitons and purple *chlamudes*, astride two white horses and clutching spears, rode into the Spartan camp in the middle of a festival to the Dioscuri. Completely flummoxing their enemies, who thought they were witnessing a divine epiphany, the Messenian youths tore through the camp, slaughtering everyone they met.[170]

The heroized Theocles also wears a prominent *chlamus* and carries a spear. On his head is a tight-fitting cap that covers the back of his neck; it is not an exact copy of a *pilos*, but neither is it the crested helmet of a hoplite. Within the bounds of propriety, he is attired as one of the Dioscuri. His pose is almost precisely paralleled by a Roman relief that shows Castor and Pollux standing on either side of Helen, their spears pointing to the ground.[171] The *koroi* were, to all appearances, the mortal counterparts of the *Dioskoroi*.[172] Before Sparta devoted its resources to the infantry, they might have ridden horses, making their identification with the Tyndaridae all the closer. The association with the divine horsemen also explains why the corps retained the title *hippeis* into the Classical period even though it fought on foot. Like Castor and his brother, who were the immortal protectors of Spartan royalty, the *koroi* accompanied the kings into battle.[173]

The Dioscuri were not just vaguely related to the rites of initiation that a young Spartan went through, but were the very focus of his aspirations. For the most capable graduates from the *paidiskoi*, there was an opportunity to become, in a sense, visible reflections of the Dioscuri. As the mythical hero Theseus was the quintessential youthful warrior for Athenians and the archetype of aristocratic education in that city, so Castor and Pollux epitomized young manhood in Spartan eyes.[174] The analogy also has a mythological resonance, which some surely felt during the Peloponnesian War: the first conflict between Spartans and Athenians was supposed to have resulted from Theseus' capture of Helen and her subsequent rescue at the hands of her brothers, the Dioscuri.[175]

Through their function as horsemen, the Dioscuri had a connection with Artemis Orthia. The representations of horses and horsemen found at her sanctuary are more numerous than those of all other animals put together, suggesting that they were considered particularly appropriate dedications to the Spartan goddess.[176] A fragmentary vessel also found there provides a tantalizing hint of a ritual function for mounted riders, as it shows a priestess figure holding a floral emblem, flanked by two nude young men on horseback who are clutching spears.[177] The involvement of young horsemen in Orthia's cult can certainly be entertained, since this would indicate that the *hēbōntes*, like their successors, the *eirenes*, still enjoyed her protection to a certain extent. Furthermore, we may have here the key to understanding an enigmatic series of pots from the middle of the sixth century B.C. painted with what is known as the "Laconian rider motif," a single mounted youth, naked and armed with a spear.[178] A recent study has suggested an iconographical link with Artemis Orthia, which would be all the closer if the rider is to be seen as a literal horseman (*hippeus*), one of the elite products of her tutelage.[179]

In conceptual terms, the ephebes moved from the periphery of Spartan society to its center, with the most able of them becoming living reminders of their most important deities. From being "antihoplites" armed with sickles, the weaponry of barbarians and criminals, as emblems of their marginality, they were transformed into true hoplites and citizens, trained to fight in a body, shield pressed on shield, for the glory of Sparta.[180]

The agglomeration of initiatory rituals and contests that produced citizen-warriors was, fundamentally, no less religious than the retreats of upper-class Athenian girls to the sanctuary of Artemis at Brauron.[181] The Attic bears and Spartan foxes were, in fact, cognate; in the same way that Athenian girls assumed the title of Artemis' *arktoi* (bears) in preparation for their future as wives and mothers, so Spartan youths were readied under Artemis Orthia for the military life awaiting them. Warrior initiation at Classical Sparta, besides producing first-class soldiers for the state, was fully as divine an institution as the *polis* itself and the *diaita*, with which it was intimately associated.[182]

CONCLUSION

The story of Spartan education is far more complex than has hitherto been appreciated. Its single constant was change, as the system adapted to meet different historical situations. We must abandon the simplistic view that has the Spartan discipline at its height during the Classical period and in gradual but inexorable decline thereafter. Rather, boys' training was transformed, revived, revised, and reinvented as circumstances demanded. As revealed here, the complexities of this process render it impossible to use the extant evidence as a basis for reconstructing Spartan educational rituals in the Archaic period, since changing historical circumstances must inevitably have had their impact on the system well before Xenophon's time.[1]

Nonetheless, ancient historians have rushed into other fields in their quest for useful information to fill the gaps in the Greek evidence. They carry with them on these treks abroad those elements of Spartan boys' initiation that have been deemed "primitive survivals"—the age grades with their archaic-sounding names, the theriomorphic titles for ephebic groups, the mock battles, and so on. A favorite destination is anthropology, which bulks large in the modern scholarship on Sparta and Spartan education. Early in this century, an influential book drew attention to quite intriguing similarities between certain Spartan initiatory practices and those of African tribes.[2] Government officials, missionaries, and academics in the late nineteenth and early twentieth centuries observed African tribes practicing lengthy initiations of boys divided among age grades with theriomorphic names, ritual battles between bands of youths, militaristic training, and other customs that uncannily recall ancient accounts of the Spartan way of life. Here were detailed reliable eyewitness accounts of age-old living traditions from cultures at a primitive level long since surpassed in Europe. Their usefulness in elucidating the arcana of Spartan life was inestimable. The pioneer in deploying this material put it in the following way: "in regard to the backward cultures of Southern Africa, we have spoken of fossilized cultures and, concerning the entire African continent, we could say that it stands as the most remarkable collection of fossils of ancient historical civilizations that it is possible to study."[3] These fossilized societies therefore afforded scholars a glimpse into the past that the pitiful scraps of ancient learning denied them.

In the years since the first flush of excitement about the utility of such ethnographic data for the study of Spartan traditions, our understanding of the relationship between the two types of material has grown more subtle. Rather than providing a guide to the traditional ritual institutions of fifth- and fourth-century Sparta, the African customs are now regarded as belonging to cultures in earlier stages of development than the *poleis* of Classical Greece.[4] Thus, historians may use the ethnological evidence, tentatively, to illuminate "the hypothetical or hidden origins of certain historical Spartan customs," but the difference between Sparta and African tribal societies "in evolutionary perspective" precludes anything more.[5]

Such reasoning can most kindly be described as Eurocentric. Other disciplines long ago abandoned the evolutionary paradigm as a means of understanding cultural development because the scales derived from it always seemed to end with modern Western civilization at their summit. Moreover, classicists' attitudes to the African evidence are founded on the assumption, explicit in earlier studies but still implicit in more recent ones, that the ceremonies recorded by European observers were archaic products of completely static, unchanging societies.[6] As historians of Africa have shown in recent decades, the reality is far different — one of constant, often deeply jarring change and discontinuity marked by desperate attempts to assert or invent cultural identities in the face of encroaching colonial and postcolonial powers.

Long-cherished notions about the characteristics of African cultures, such as the predominance of "tribes," have been shown to lack foundation. In much of southern Africa tribalism was a colonial construct, invented and fostered by European administrators in the first decades of this century as a means of indirect government.[7] Group identity seems to have been much more complex and fluid in the precolonial period, with people employing a range of allegiances (as members of clans, cults, professional guilds, or kingdoms) to identify themselves.[8] In the twentieth century, however, the colonial powers introduced indirect government, whereby the local population was divided into groups identified as "tribes" and ruled by means of proxies, who were appointed as "chiefs."[9] Even more dismaying is the opinion voiced by one scholar of African history that the creation of tribes "doubtless owed much to the Old Testament, to Tacitus and Caesar."[10] The pool of evidence is muddied indeed.

Granted that African political institutions did experience change over time, we might still expect ritual practices to remain relatively static, given religion's natural conservatism. But this notion is as fallacious in terms of African traditions as it is for Spartan, and even Greek, customs generally. Just as Plutarch was taken in by the spectacle of youths enacting what appeared to be customs dating from the dawn of Sparta's history, so also European witnesses of African ceremonies often failed to comprehend the extent to which traditions could be manipulated or invented by the Africans themselves, seeing in them instead manifestations of an eternal and unchanging African "world view."[11] The consequences of this realization are profound for the study of African traditional religion and have no little relevance for ancient historians, dependent as we are on late sources for so much of our information about cult and ritual. What has recently been said about a well-documented ceremony marking the passing of seniority from one corporate generation among the Embu people of East Africa to another could apply, with very few alterations, to the situation at Sparta: "All of the surviving accounts—written and oral, local and alien—betray an assumption that the rituals of the 1932 *nduiko* represented archaic relics of 'traditional' Embu society. In fact these ceremonies, with all their seemingly anachronistic elements, could scarcely have been more contemporary."[12]

Far from being fossils from a past stage in the evolution of society, African rituals and ceremonies were outgrowths of mutable, living traditions that were just as affected by the universal desire to construct a past that answers the needs of the present as those of any other culture.[13] These practices simply cannot be wrenched out of their own historical contexts and fashioned into instruments for exposing the prehistoric underpinnings of Classical Greek society because they are by no means products of inert "prehistoric" or "primitive" societies. While I do not deny that Spartan and African initiation rituals are analogous cultural phenomena, the analogy cannot be extended to yield any historical points about Spartan or African society. In other words, ancient historians have no warrant for reconstructing early Greek initiation rites from African "parallels" that grew out of historical situations utterly dissimilar to those of prehistoric Greece.

Once we resist the temptation to view certain elements in Spartan education as anachronistic relics merely because they bear a superficial resemblance to rituals anthropologists once dubbed "primitive," it becomes evident that nothing in the way that youths were brought up at Sparta is of demonstrably greater antiquity than anywhere else in Greece. With this in mind, I have tried to show that the cycle of initiation ceremonies that came to be the Spartan *agōgē* was not so very unusual. Other

Greek cities had similar rituals of acculturation and appear to have divided their youth up into age divisions of varying precision as well. In fact, the grading of a population by relative age has been called probably one of the basic modes of social categorization.[14] Moreover, there is nothing at all "prehistoric" about the names devised for the Spartan age grades in the Hellenistic period; American street gangs (whose most active members are approximately the same ages as Spartan ephebes) divide their membership into age grades whose names sometimes uncannily recall those of the Spartans: for example, Seniors (eighteen years old or older), Juniors (sixteen to seventeen years old), Midgets (twelve to fifteen), and Pee Wees (younger than twelve).[15] Of course, Spartan ephebes were not just undisciplined, lawless young thugs; their activities had been under the control of the civic authorities for as long as we have evidence.

Here indeed may lie the key to appreciating Sparta's unique contribution to the development of public education in Greece. I believe that the foundation of what became the *agōgē* should be linked to the renovation of Orthia's sanctuary in the early sixth century, when preexisting rites of passage held there and at other spots in the region came under the control of the Spartan authorities. This was a period in Greek history characterized by innovation and reform at several important festival sites, Delphi, Isthmia, Nemea, and Olympia among them. If this hypothesis is correct, then Sparta was by far the earliest city to make this form of education a community concern, a quality that to Aristotle was the system's one distinction.[16] But we must be careful not to make the mistake of seeing in Spartan initiatory practice the forerunner of the Athenian system of compulsory military service for the young (*ephēbeia*) that is first solidly attested in the fourth century B.C.[17] The Athenian institution has long been recognized as originating in a set of traditional rites of passage marking the transition from childhood to adulthood similar to those at Sparta, and which existed in most, if not all, Greek communities. Sparta was first to bring the rituals under government control, but the Athenians, typically, transformed their rites of passage into a "secular" military and educational institution long before the Spartans. In Lacedaemon, this metamorphosis had to wait until the restoration work of Sphaerus in the third century.

From this perspective we can see that Spartan education was just as affected by political and cultural currents throughout its history as were similar institutions in other cities for which more evidence is available. In the first stage, Spartan youths underwent a lengthy initiatory process that began at age seven and ended with marriage at approximately thirty. Within these limits, the boys were divided into three large age groups in accordance with the traditional age divisions of childhood, puberty, and youth. During this time they played cult games and fought battles among themselves while under the protection of Artemis Orthia, whose temple was and always remained central to Spartan education. Their liminal status, emphasized through their dress and sleeping arrangements, had constitutional implications as well, in that they were exempt from the jurisdiction of most civic magistrates.

The fourth century took its toll on Sparta's traditional institutions; the city's military decline and rapid depopulation, especially after the defeat at Leuctra and the subsequent loss of helot-tilled land in Messenia, destroyed the mainstays of the Spartiate way of life. As the third century opened, the entire *diaita* was gradually abandoned as Sparta began to transform itself into a Hellenistic state with all the modern cultural conveniences. With this modernization policy's signal lack of success at recovering much of Sparta's former glory, the way opened for attempts at regaining military and political power through cultural revival. As regards education, King Cleomenes III had the greatest success, even though his aspirations to dominate Greece militarily came to nought. Under the guise of a revival, Cleomenes' culture minister Sphaerus remade the traditional coming-of-age rituals into the Spartan version of a contemporary Hellenistic ephebate. He dropped the first and last age groups of the Classical period, concentrating instead on the seven middle years from fourteen to twenty. These he divided into year classes, with names he devised on the basis of customary Spartan age designations. Sphaerus' impact on ephebic activity remains beyond our ken, except possibly for the ritual fight at Artemis' altar that used to mark the attainment of military age; he may have transformed this battle into a trial of endurance for those about to enter the most senior grade.

The *agōgē* of Cleomenes and Sphaerus was the foundation upon which Spartans reconstructed their traditional customs after seceding from the defeated Achaean League in 146 B.C. For the next five hundred years the *agōgē* seems to have functioned more or less continuously until its demise, probably in the later fourth century A.D. At first, only a few changes seem to have been made to the *agōgē* of the previous phase: the length of time spent within the system was further shortened with the elimination of the two youngest age grades, and some grades were given names with a more heavily Laconian emphasis than before. With a few adjustments, the *agōgē* survived as long as it did because it answered to the Spartans' need for a distinctive cultural identity and because, in its revived form, Spartan education corresponded so perfectly to the picture of the city that contemporaries carried around with them. Although we can perceive very few of the details of how this was accomplished, some few fragments of evidence hint at a gradual process of laconization throughout the final phase of the *agōgē*, shaping its institutions little by little to appear more unique, anachronistic, and Spartan than they had before.

Because the *agōgē* was central to Spartan identity, it had to be distinctly Spartan. Unlike Athens and other major cities that possessed a wealth of traditions in arts, philosophy, architecture, and the like, which they might draw on to assert their place and uniqueness, an accident of history had endowed the Spartans with only one — their famous way of life. Through the *agōgē* alone were they able to define themselves in contrast to other Greek cities and the Romans. From the other Greeks, they kept themselves somewhat aloof; to the Romans, they were linked by putative ties of kinship. Such adept employment of the past, as I have endeavored to show lies behind our picture of the *agōgē*, was not confined to Sparta. A stimulating recent study has revealed the processes behind an Ephesian festival by which the inhabitants of that city negotiated a place for themselves within the wider contexts of Roman power and the increasing homogenization of Greek culture in the second century A.D.[18] I suggest that the Spartan *agōgē* represents for us the epitome of this phenomenon.

This account must remain only an extremely tenuous outline, since evidence is so patchy, scattered, and obscure that virtually all subtlety and nuance have faded from our picture of traditional Spartan education. Still, enough remains to document what may justifiably be called one of the most successful and influential manipulations of the past in history. From a set of initiatory rituals and customs little different from those anywhere else in Greece, Spartans in the Hellenistic and Roman periods constructed a unique institution, the *agōgē*, through whose powerful re-enactments of an idealized cultural legacy they claimed for themselves a lasting place in Greek culture and projected an image of Sparta that has endured for almost two millennia.

APPENDIX 1
Testimonia on the Whipping Contest

1. Cic. *Tusc.* 2.34
   Spartae vero pueri ad aram sic verberibus accipiuntur, "ut multus e visceribus sanguis exeat," non numquam etiam, ut, cum ibi essem, audiebam, ad necem; quorum non modo nemo exclamavit umquam, sed ne ingemuit quidem.

   At Sparta, in fact, the boys at the altar are so received with whips, "that much blood flows out from their flesh," sometimes even, as I kept hearing when I was there, to the point of death; not only has none of them ever cried out, but none has even groaned.

2. Cic. *Tusc.* 2.46
   Tune, cum pueros Lacedaemone, adulescentis Olympiae, barbaros in harena videris excipientis gravissimas plagas et ferentis silentio, si te forte dolor aliquis pervellerit, exclamabis ut mulier, non constanter et sedate feres?

   And you, although you have seen boys at Sparta, youths at Olympia, and barbarians in the arena taking the harshest blows and bearing them silently, if by chance some pain should pinch you, will you cry out like a woman, and not endure it steadily and calmly?

3. Cic. *Tusc.* 5.77
   Pueri Spartiatae non ingemescunt verberum dolore laniati.

   Spartan boys do not groan when they have been cut up by the pain of the whips.

4. Hor. *Carm.* 1.7.10–11
   Me nec tam patiens Lacedaemon / ... percussit.

   Nor has Lacedaemon so long-suffering struck me.

5. Nic. Dam. *FGrHist.* 90 F103 (Z.11)
   οἱ δὲ παῖδες νομίμως περί τινα βωμὸν περιιόντες μαστιγοῦνται, ἕως ἂν ὀλίγοι λειφθέντες στεφανωθῶσιν.

   The boys are ritually whipped as they are going around an altar, until the few remaining receive crowns.

6. Hyg. *Fab.* 261
   [sc. Orestes] qui accepto oraculo carendi sororis causa, cum amico Pylade Colchos petierat, et cum occiso Thoante simulacrum sustulit, absconditum fasce lignorum ... et Ariciam detulit. Sed cum postea Romanis sacrorum

crudelitas displiceret, quanquam servi immolarentur, ad Laconas Diana translata est, ubi sacrificii consuetudo adolescentum verberibus servabatur, qui vocabantur Bomonicae, quia aris superpositi contendebant, qui plura posset verbera sustinere.

Upon obtaining an oracle because he had lost his sister, [Orestes] had sought Colchis with his friend Pylades and, following the killing of Thoas, made off with the image, hidden in a bundle of wood, . . . and brought it to Aricia. But since the cult's cruelty subsequently displeased the Romans, although slaves were sacrificed, Diana was transferred to the Spartans, where the custom of sacrifice was maintained in the whipping of the youths, who were called Bomonicae because they contended, placed above the altar, as to who could endure more blows.

7. Petron. *Sat.* 105
   Et ego quidem tres plagas Spartana nobilitate concoxi.

   And I for my part digested three blows with Spartan excellence.

8. Sen. *Prov.* 4.11
   Numquid tu invisos esse Lacedaemoniis liberos suos credis, quorum experiuntur indolem publice verberibus admotis? Ipsi illos patres adhortantur ut ictus flagellorum fortiter perferant, et laceros ac semianimes rogant perseverent vulnera praebere vulneribus.

   Or do you believe that the Spartans find their children hateful because they test their character publicly by applying whips? Their own fathers encourage them to endure the blows of the whips bravely and ask them, when they are mangled and fainting, to persist in submitting their wounds to further blows.

9. Stat. *Theb.* 4.231–33.
   Gaudent natorum fata parentes / hortanturque mori, deflet iamque omnis ephebum / turba, coronato contenta est funere mater.

   Parents rejoice in the fates of their offspring / and exhort them to die, and already the whole crowd of youths / is weeping, the mother is satisfied by a garlanded corpse.

10. Stat. *Theb.* 8.436–37
    dilecta genis morientis oberrant / Taygeta et pugnae laudataque verbera matri.

    Before the dying man's eyes float beloved / Taygetus and the fights and the lashes praised by his mother.

11. Musonius (Hense) pp. 52–53
    ὡς δὲ οὔτε αἰσχρὸν οὔτε ὑβριστικὸν ἔχουσιν οὐδέν, δηλοῦν Λακεδαιμονίων παῖδας δημοσίᾳ μαστιγουμένους καὶ ἐπ' αὐτῷ τούτῳ ἀγαλλομένους.

Because [lashes] are neither intrinsically shameful nor insulting, he points out that Spartan boys are whipped publicly and rejoice in this very thing.

12. Martial *Epig.* 7.80.10
vel non caesus adhuc matre iubente Lacon.

Or a Spartan, not yet whipped at his mother's behest.

13. Dio Chrys. *Or.* 25.3
ἐκείνου γὰρ κελεύσαντος ἔτι νῦν μαστιγοῦνται Λακεδαιμόνιοι καὶ θυραυλοῦσι καὶ γυμνητεύουσι καὶ ἄλλα πολλὰ καὶ χαλεπὰ δόξαντα ἂν ἑτέροις ἀνέχονται.

For at his command, even today Lacedaemonians are being whipped and living in the wild and going naked and enduring many other things others would find disagreeable.

14. Favorinus *De Exilio* (Barigazzi) 21 col. 20
[καί, ἐάν τις]/ μαστιγοῦσθαι κελεύῃ, μαστιγωσόμεθ[α ἐ]πὶ τῷ βω/μῷ τῶν Ἑλλήνων ὁρώντων μηδὲν ἐξ[ῶ]λες δ[οκοῦ]ν/τες, πιστεύοντες αὐτὸν εἰς τὸ κοινῇ συ[μ]έφρο[ν (*sic*) καὶ λ]υ/σιτελοῦν νομοθετῆσαι τάσδε τὰς πληγάς.

And, if someone should order us to be whipped, we'll be whipped at the altar with the Greeks looking on and know that it is nothing pernicious, trusting that he ordained these strokes for the advantage and profit of the community.

15. Epictetus 1.2.2
— "πληγαὶ οὐκ εἰσὶν ἀφόρητοι τῇ φύσει."
— "Τίνα τρόπον;"
— "Ὅρα πῶς· Λακεδαιμόνιοι μαστιγοῦνται μαθόντες ὅτι εὔλογόν ἐστιν."

— "Blows are not unbearable for the soul."
— "In what way?"
— "Look; Spartans who are whipped learn that it is reasonable."

16. Plut. *Lyc.* 18.2
καὶ τοῦτο μὲν οὐδ' ἀπὸ τῶν νῦν ἐφήβων ἄπιστόν ἐστιν, ὧν πολλοὺς ἐπὶ τοῦ βωμοῦ τῆς Ὀρθίας ἑωράκαμεν ἀποθνῄσκοντας ταῖς πληγαῖς.

This, too, can be believed of present-day ephebes, many of whom I have seen expiring from the blows at the altar of Orthia.

17. Plut. *Arist.* 17.10
ἔνιοι δέ φασι τῷ Παυσανίᾳ μικρὸν ἔξω τῆς παρατάξεως θύοντι καὶ κατευχομένῳ τῶν Λυδῶν τινας ἄφνω προσπεσόντας ἁρπάζειν καὶ διαρρίπτειν τὰ περὶ τὴν θυσίαν, τὸν δὲ Παυσανίαν καὶ τοὺς περὶ αὐτὸν οὐκ ἔχοντας ὅπλα ῥάβδοις καὶ μάστιξι παίειν· διὸ καὶ νῦν ἐκείνης τῆς ἐπιδρομῆς

μίμημα τὰς περὶ τὸν βωμὸν ἐν Σπάρτῃ πληγὰς τῶν ἐφήβων καὶ τὴν μετὰ ταῦτα τῶν Λυδῶν πομπὴν συντελεῖσθαι.

Some say that, as Pausanias was sacrificing and praying a short distance outside the barricade, some Lydians suddenly attacked, seizing and scattering the sacrificial equipment, and that Pausanias and his companions, having no weapons, struck them with staffs and whips. Therefore, even now, the blows of the ephebes around the altar at Sparta and the subsequent parade of the Lydians are performed in imitation of this assault.

18. [Plut.] *Inst. Lac.* 40.239C–D
Οἱ παῖδες παρ᾽ αὐτοῖς ξαινόμενοι μάστιξι δι᾽ ὅλης τῆς ἡμέρας ἐπὶ τοῦ βωμοῦ τῆς Ὀρθίας Ἀρτέμιδος μέχρι θανάτου πολλάκις διακαρτεροῦσιν ἱλαροὶ καὶ γαῦροι, ἁμιλλώμενοι περὶ νίκης πρὸς ἀλλήλους ὅστις αὐτῶν ἐπὶ πλέον τε καὶ μᾶλλον καρτερήσει τυπτόμενος· καὶ ὁ περιγενόμενος ἐν τοῖς μάλιστα ἐπίδοξός ἐστι. καλεῖται δὲ ἡ ἅμιλλα διαμαστίγωσις· γίνεται δὲ καθ᾽ ἕκαστον ἔτος.

Among them, the boys, lacerated by whips all day long at the altar of Artemis Orthia, often until death, bear it cheerfully and proudly, contending over victory with one another as to who of them will endure being beaten the most. And the one remaining wins extraordinary renown among them. The competition is called "The Flagellation"; it happens every year.

19. Lucian *Anach.* 38–39
ΣΟΛΩΝ· μάλιστα δὲ ἢν ὁρᾷς μαστιγουμένους αὐτοὺς ἐπὶ τῷ βωμῷ καὶ αἵματι ῥεομένους, πατέρας δὲ καὶ μητέρας παρεστώσας οὐχ ὅπως ἀνιωμένας ἐπὶ τοῖς γιγνομένοις ἀλλὰ καὶ ἀπειλούσας, εἰ μὴ ἀντέχοιεν πρὸς τὰς πληγάς, καὶ ἱκετευούσας ἐπὶ μήκιστον διαρκέσαι πρὸς τὸν πόνον καὶ ἐγκαρτερῆσαι τοῖς δεινοῖς. πολλοὶ γοῦν καὶ ἐναπέθανον τῷ ἀγῶνι μὴ ἀξιώσαντες ἀπαγορεῦσαι ζῶντες ἔτι ἐν ὀφθαλμοῖς τῶν οἰκείων μηδὲ εἶξαι τοῖς σώμασιν· ὧν καὶ τοὺς ἀνδριάντας ὄψει τιμωμένους δημοσίᾳ ὑπὸ τῆς Σπάρτης ἀνασταθέντας.
   Ὅταν τοίνυν ὁρᾷς κἀκεῖνα, μήτε μαίνεσθαι ὑπολάβῃς αὐτοὺς μήτε εἴπῃς, οὐδεμιᾶς ἕνεκα αἰτίας ἀναγκαίας ταλαιπωροῦσι, μήτε τυράννου βιαζομένου μήτε πολεμίων διατιθέντων. εἴποι γὰρ ἄν σοι καὶ ὑπὲρ ἐκείνων Λυκοῦργος ὁ νομοθέτης αὐτῶν πολλὰ τὰ εὔλογα καὶ ἃ συνιδὼν κολάζει αὐτούς, οὐκ ἐχθρὸς ὢν οὐδὲ ὑπὸ μίσους αὐτὸ δρῶν οὐδὲ τὴν νεολαίαν τῆς πόλεως εἰκῆ παραναλίσκων, ἀλλὰ καρτερικωτάτους καὶ παντὸς δεινοῦ κρείττονας ἀξιῶν εἶναι τοὺς σῴζειν μέλλοντας τὴν πατρίδα. καίτοι κἂν μὴ ὁ Λυκοῦργος εἴπῃ, ἐννοεῖς, οἶμαι, καὶ αὐτὸς ὡς οὐκ ἄν ποτε ληφθεὶς ὁ τοιοῦτος ἐν πολέμῳ ἀπόρρητόν τι ἐξείποι τῆς Σπάρτης αἰκιζομένων τῶν ἐχθρῶν, ἀλλὰ καταγελῶν αὐτῶν μαστιγοῖτο ἂν ἁμιλλώμενος πρὸς τὸν παίοντα, ὡς πρότερος ἀπαγορεύσειεν.
ΑΝΑΧΑΡΣΙΣ· Ὁ Λυκοῦργος δὲ καὶ αὐτός, ὦ Σόλων, ἐμαστιγοῦντο ἐφ᾽ ἡλικίας, ἢ ἐκπρόθεσμος ὢν ἤδη τοῦ ἀγῶνος ἀσφαλῶς τὰ τοιαῦτα ἐνεανιεύσατο;
ΣΟ· Πρεσβύτης ἤδη ὢν ἔγραψε τοὺς νόμους αὐτοῖς Κρήτηθεν ἀφικόμενος.

ἀποδεδημήκει δὲ παρὰ τοὺς Κρῆτας, ὅτι ἤκουεν εὐνομωτάτους εἶναι, Μίνωος
τοῦ Διὸς νομοθετήσαντος ἐν αὐτοῖς.

ΑΝ· Τί οὖν, ὦ Σόλων, οὐχὶ καὶ σὺ ἐμιμήσω Λυκοῦργον καὶ μαστιγοῖς τοὺς
νέους; καλὰ γὰρ καὶ ταῦτα καὶ ἄξια ὑμῶν ἐστιν.

ΣΟ· "Οτι ἡμῖν ἱκανά, ὦ 'Ανάχαρσι, ταῦτα τὰ γυμνάσια οἰκεῖα ὄντα· ζηλοῦν
δὲ τὰ ξενικὰ οὐ πάνυ ἀξιοῦμεν.

ΑΝ· Οὔκ; ἀλλὰ συνίης, οἶμαι, οἷόν τί ἐστι μαστιγοῦσθαι γυμνὸν ἄνω τὰς
χεῖρας ἐπαίροντα μηδενὸς ἕνεκα ὠφελίμου ἢ αὐτῷ ἑκάστῳ ἢ κοινῇ τῇ πόλει.
ὡς ἔγωγε ἤν ποτε ἐπιδημήσω τῇ Σπάρτῃ καθ' ὃν καιρὸν ταῦτα δρῶσι, δοκῶ
μοι τάχιστα καταλευσθήσεσθαι δημοσίᾳ πρὸς αὐτῶν, ἐπιγελῶν ἑκάστοις,
ὁπόταν ὁρῶ τυπτομένους καθάπερ κλέπτας ἢ λωποδύτας ἤ τι ἄλλο τοιοῦτον
ἐργασαμένους. ἀτεχνῶς γὰρ ἐλλεβόρου δεῖσθαί μοι δοκεῖ ἡ πόλις αὐτῶν
καταγέλαστα ὑφ' αὑτῆς πάσχουσα.

SOLON: Most of all, [don't laugh] if you see them being whipped at the altar
and running with blood, with their fathers and mothers standing by, not
only unmoved by what is happening but even threatening them if they don't
bear up against the blows and begging them to hold out still longer against
the affliction and endure the agonies. In fact, many have died in the
competition because they refused to give up before their relatives' eyes as
long as they still lived or even to succumb bodily. You will see their statues
which were erected at public expense by Sparta being honored.

So, when you see that, don't suppose they are mad or say that they are
putting up with hardship for no compelling reason, as no tyrant is forcing
them nor enemy laying down the law. For Lycurgus, their lawgiver, could
tell you the many good reasons he has adduced for chastising them; he is not
hostile to them and does not do this out of hatred, nor is he squandering the
city's youth in vain, but thinks that those who are destined to protect their
country should have supreme endurance and be above all terror. Yet, even if
Lycurgus does not say so, you yourself understand, I think, that if such a
man were taken prisoner in war he would never utter any Spartan secret
under torture by the enemy, but would laugh at them and take the whipping
in a spirit of competition with the flogger, to see who would yield first.

ANACHARSIS: Was Lycurgus himself whipped as a youth, Solon? Or did he
introduce his innovation at no risk to himself, when he was already over the
eligible age for the competition?

SO: He was already old when he drew up their laws after his return from
Crete. He had gone abroad to the Cretans because he heard that they had
the best laws, since Minos, son of Zeus, had been their lawgiver.

AN: So, Solon, why did you not imitate Lycurgus and whip your young men?
For this is a fine thing and worthy of you.

SO: Because our own gymnastic practices are sufficient for us, Anacharsis.
We don't think it right to look to foreign models.

AN: No? But you do understand, I think, what it is like to be whipped
naked, with hands raised up, with no benefit either for each individual or
for the city overall. Oh, if I ever visit Sparta during the time when they do

this, I think they will instantly stone me to death in public for laughing at them whenever I see them being beaten like bandits or thieves or others who do that sort of thing. I simply think their city needs psychiatric help because of the ridiculous things it's doing to itself.

20. Lucian *Demon.* 46 (Rabe)

καὶ μέντοι καὶ Λακεδαιμόνιόν τινα ἰδὼν τὸν αὑτοῦ οἰκέτην μαστιγοῦντα, "Παῦσαι," ἔφη, "ὁμότιμον σαυτοῦ τὸν δοῦλον ἀποφαίνων."

And also, when he saw a Spartan flogging his servant, he said, "Stop making your slave equal to yourself."

21. Schol. to Lucian *Demon.* 46

Λακεδαιμόνιον· ἐμάστιζον γὰρ ἑαυτοὺς Λάκωνες τελούμενοι καὶ εἰς τοῦτο αὐτὸν ἀποσκώπτει.

Spartan: Laconians used to whip themselves in an initiation ritual, and he is making fun of him because of this.

22. Paus. 3.16.9–11

τοῦτο δὲ οἱ Λιμνᾶται Σπαρτιατῶν καὶ Κυνοσουρεῖς καὶ ⟨οἱ⟩ ἐκ Μεσόας τε καὶ Πιτάνης θύοντες τῇ Ἀρτέμιδι ἐς διαφοράν, ἀπὸ δὲ αὐτῆς καὶ ἐς φθόνους καὶ ἐς φόνους προήχθησαν, ἀποθανόντων δὲ ἐπὶ τῷ βωμῷ πολλῶν νόσος ἔφθειρε τοὺς λοιπούς. καί σφισιν ἐπὶ τούτῳ γίνεται λόγιον αἵματι ἀνθρώπων τὸν βωμὸν αἱμάσσειν· θυομένου δὲ ὅντινα ὁ κλῆρος ἐπελάμβανε, Λυκοῦργος μετέβαλεν ἐς τὰς ἐπὶ τοῖς ἐφήβοις μάστιγας, ἐμπίπλαταί τε οὕτως ἀνθρώπων αἵματι ὁ βωμός. ἡ δὲ ἱέρεια τὸ ξόανον ἔχουσά σφισιν ἐφέστηκε· τὸ δέ ἐστιν ἄλλως μὲν κοῦφον ὑπὸ σμικρότητος, ἢν δὲ οἱ μαστιγοῦντές ποτε ὑποφειδόμενοι παίωσι κατὰ ἐφήβου κάλλος ἢ ἀξίωμα, τότε ἤδη τῇ γυναικὶ τὸ ξόανον γίνεται βαρὺ καὶ οὐκέτι εὔφορον, ἡ δὲ ἐν αἰτίᾳ τοὺς μαστιγοῦντας ποιεῖται καὶ πιέζεσθαι δι' αὐτούς φησιν.

On the other hand, the Spartan Limnatae and Cynosures, and those from Mesoa and Pitane, while sacrificing to Artemis, were drawn into hostilities and from there to homicide. Many were killed on the altar, and a plague wiped out the rest. After this, an oracle was conveyed to them to stain the altar with the blood of men. Though the victim was whomsoever the lottery chose, Lycurgus converted it into a flagellation for the youths, and thus the altar is satiated with the blood of men. The priestess stands beside them holding the sacred effigy; at other times it is light because of its smallness, but if the floggers should ever strike sparingly due to a youth's beauty or rank, then the effigy becomes heavy and no longer easy for the woman to carry. She, for her part, holds the floggers to blame and says that she is being oppressed because of them.

23. Paus. 8.23.1

(of Alea, near Stymphalos) καὶ ἐν Διονύσου τῇ ἑορτῇ κατὰ μάντευμα ἐκ

Δελφῶν μαστιγοῦνται ⟨αἱ⟩ γυναῖκες, καθὰ καὶ οἱ Σπαρτιατῶν ἔφηβοι παρὰ
τῇ Ὀρθίᾳ.

And in the festival of Dionysus, in accordance with an oracle from Delphi,
the women are whipped, just like the Spartan ephebes at the sanctuary of
Orthia.

24. Tert. *Apol.* 50.9
*Certe Laconum flagella sub oculis etiam hortantium propinquorum
acerbata tantum honorem tolerantiae domui conferunt, quantum sanguinis
fuderint.*

Certainly, the whips of the Spartans, made harsh beneath the eyes of
relatives who even give encouragement, grant the family as much honor
for endurance as they have caused blood to flow.

25. Tert. *Ad Mart.* 4.8
Nam quod hodie apud Lacedaemonas solemnitas maxima est,
διαμαστίγωσις, *id est, flagellatio, non latet. In quo sacro, ante aram
nobiles quique adolescentes flagellis affliguntur, astantibus parentibus et
propinquis, et uti perseverent adhortantibus. Ornamentum enim et gloria
deputatur maiore quidem titulo, si anima potius cesserit plagis, quam
corpus.*

For it is no secret that the most important ceremony among the Spartans
today is the *diamastigōsis*, "flagellation," that is. In this ritual, all the noble
youths are beaten with whips in front of an altar with their parents and
relatives standing by and encouraging them to persevere. For it is reckoned
an adornment and distinction of greater mark indeed, if the soul rather than
the body has yielded to the strokes.

26. Sex. Emp. *Pyr.* 3.208
τό τε ἀνθρωπείῳ μιαίνειν αἵματι βωμὸν θεοῦ παρ' ἡμῖν μὲν τοῖς πολλοῖς
ἄθεσμον, Λάκωνες δὲ ἐπὶ τοῦ βωμοῦ τῆς Ὀρθωσίας Ἀρτέμιδος μαστίζονται
πικρῶς ὑπὲρ τοῦ πολλὴν αἵματος ἐπὶ τοῦ βωμοῦ τῆς θεοῦ γενέσθαι ῥύσιν.

Staining a god's altar with human blood is unlawful for many of us, but
Laconians are whipped relentlessly at the altar of Orthosia Artemis for
there to be a plentiful stream of blood on the goddess's altar.

27. Alciphron *Ep.* 3.18.3 (Schepers)
καὶ δὴ μεχρὶ γέ τινος ἀντέστην γεννικῶς καὶ τὰς φορὰς τῶν πληγῶν
ὑπομένων καὶ τὰς ἐκστροφὰς τῶν δακτύλων ἀνεχόμενος, καὶ ἤμην οἷά τις
Σπαρτιάτης ἀνὴρ ἐπὶ τοῦ βωμοῦ τῆς Ὀρθίας τυπτόμενος. ἀλλ' οὐκ ἦν
Λακεδαίμων ἐν ᾗ ταῦτα ὑπέμενον, ἀλλ' Ἀθῆναι.

And for some time I resisted nobly, submitting to the force of the blows and
bearing patiently the dislocation of my fingers. I was like a Spartiate being

whipped at Orthia's altar, but it was not Lacedaemon where these things were happening to me but Athens.

28. Maxim. Tyr. 19.5E (90B) (Hobein)
ταῦτα δρῶντα ἐπαινῶ τὸν Ἀγησίλαον μᾶλλον, ἢ Τισσαφέρνην διώκοντα, ἢ Θηβαίων κρατοῦντα, ἢ τὰς μάστιγας καρτεροῦντα· ἐκεῖνα μὲν γὰρ ἦν τῆς τῶν σωμάτων τροφῆς καὶ παιδαγωγίας· ταῦτα δὲ ἔργα ψυχῆς τῷ ὄντι ἠσκημένης καὶ μεμαστιγωμένης.

I praise Agesilaus more for doing this than for pursuing Tissaphernes or for defeating the Thebans or for enduring the whips, for those deeds were due to physical sustenance and education, while these sprang from a soul truly trained and whipped.

29. Maxim. Tyr. 23.2D (102A) (Hobein)
τὸ δὲ καθαρῶς Σπαρτιατικόν, ἄφετον ἐκ γῆς ὂν καὶ ὄρθριον, καὶ πρὸς ἐλευθερίαν τετραμμένον, μαστιγούμενον καὶ τυπτόμενον.

The pure Spartiate ideal, freed early on from tilling the soil and turned toward freedom, whipped and beaten.

30. Maxim. Tyr. 32.10B (9A) (Hobein)
μάστιγες αὗται καὶ πληγαὶ Λακωνικαί, καὶ θῆραι, καὶ δρόμοι, καὶ δεῖπνα λιτά, καὶ στιβάδες εὐτελεῖς· ἀλλ' ὁρῶ καὶ τούτων τὰ τερπνά.

These are whips and Spartan blows, the hunts and races, the frugal feasts, and mean sleeping cots; but in these things, too, I see delights.

31. Maxim. Tyr. 34.9H (Hobein)
διὰ τοῦτο ἡ Σπάρτη ἐπὶ πλεῖστον ἐλεύθερα, ὅτι ἐν οὐδὲ εἰρήνη σχολὴν ἄγει· μάστιγες αὐταὶ καὶ πληγαὶ Λακωνικαί, καὶ ἔθη κακῶν ταῖς ἀρεταῖς ἀναμιγνύμενα.

Through this, Sparta is free in the highest degree, because not even in peace is she at leisure; the very whips and Spartan blows, even the custom of enduring hardships, are mixed with virtues.

32. Philostr. VA 6.20
Μετὰ ταῦτα ὁ Θεσπεσίων ὥσπερ μεθιστάμενος τουτουὶ τοῦ λόγου ἤρετο τὸν Ἀπολλώνιον περὶ τῆς Λακωνικῆς μάστιγος καὶ εἰ δημοσίᾳ οἱ Λακεδαιμόνιοι παίονται·
— "Τὰς ἐξ ἀνθρώπων γε," εἶπεν, "ὦ Θεσπεσίων, αὐτοὶ μάλιστα οἱ ἐλευθέριοί τε καὶ εὐδόκιμοι."
— "Τοὺς δὲ οἰκέτας ἀδικοῦντας τί," ἔφη, "ἐργάζονται;"
— "Οὐκέτ' ἀποκτείνουσιν," εἶπεν, "ὡς ξυνεχώρει ποτὲ ὁ Λυκοῦργος, ἀλλ' ἡ αὐτὴ καὶ ἐπ' ἐκείνους μάστιξ."
— "Ἡ δὲ Ἑλλὰς πῶς," ἔφη, "περὶ αὐτῶν γιγνώσκει;"

— "Ξυνίασιν," εἶπεν, "ὥσπερ ἐς τὰ Ὑακίνθια καὶ τὰς Γυμνοπαιδίας, θεασόμενοι ξὺν ἡδονῇ τε καὶ ὁρμῇ πάσῃ."

— "Εἶτ' οὐκ αἰσχύνονται," ἔφη, "οἱ χρηστοὶ Ἕλληνες ἢ τοὺς αὐτῶν ποτε ἄρξαντας ὁρῶντες μαστιγουμένους ἐς τὸ κοινόν, ἢ ἀρχθέντες ὑπ' ἀνθρώπων, οἳ μαστιγοῦνται δημοσίᾳ; σὺ δὲ πῶς οὐ διωρθώσω ταῦτα; φασὶ γάρ σε καὶ Λακεδαιμονίων ἐπιμεληθῆναι."

— "Ἅ γε," εἶπε, "δυνατὸν διορθοῦσθαι, ξυνεβούλευον μὲν ἐγώ, προθύμως δ' ἐκεῖνοι ἔπραττον, ἐλευθεριώτατοι μὲν γὰρ τῶν Ἑλλήνων εἰσί, μόνοι δ' ὑπήκοοι τοῦ εὖ ξυμβουλεύοντος, τὸ δὲ τῶν μαστίγων ἔθος τῇ Ἀρτέμιδι τῇ ἀπὸ Σκυθῶν δρᾶται χρησμῶν, φασιν, ἐξηγουμένων ταῦτα· θεοῖς δ' ἀντινομεῖν μανία, οἶμαι."

— "Οὐ σοφούς, Ἀπολλώνιε," ἔφη, "τοὺς τῶν Ἑλλήνων θεοὺς εἴρηκας, εἰ μαστίγων ἐγίγνοντο ξύμβουλοι τοῖς τὴν ἐλευθερίαν ἀσκοῦσιν."

— "Οὐ μαστίγων," εἶπεν, "ἀλλὰ τοῦ αἵματι ἀνθρώπων τὸν βωμὸν ῥαίνειν, ἐπειδὴ καὶ παρὰ Σκύθαις τούτων ἠξιοῦτο, σοφισάμενοι δὲ οἱ Λακεδαιμόνιοι τὸ ἀπαραίτητον τῆς θυσίας ἐπὶ τὸν τῆς καρτερίας ἀγῶνα ἥκουσιν, ἀφ' ἧς ἐστι μήτε ἀποθνήσκειν καὶ ἀπάρχεσθαι τῇ θεῷ τοῦ σφῶν αἵματος."

After this, Thespesion, as if to abandon this subject, asked Apollonius about the whipping at Sparta and whether Spartans were publicly beaten.

"As hard as men can, Thespesion," he said, "especially those who are noble and of good repute."

"But when their servants do something wrong, what do they do to them?" he asked.

"They don't kill them any more," he answered, "as Lycurgus once permitted, but it's the same whip for them, too."

"What does Greece think about this?"

"They assemble, as if for the Hyacinthia or the Gymnopaediae, to watch it with pleasure and all eagerness."

"Then," he said, "aren't the worthy Greeks embarrassed either at seeing those who once ruled them being flogged in front of everyone, or that they were once ruled by men who are publicly flogged? How it is you did not reform this practice? For they say that you took an interest in the Spartans too."

He replied, "What could be reformed, I advised them about and they eagerly carried out, for they are the freest of the Greeks, only submitting to one who gives sound advice. However, the custom of flogging is carried out in honor of Artemis from the Scythians, at the command, they say, of oracles, and I think it is madness to go against the gods."

"You are saying that the gods of the Greeks are ignorant, if they advised whipping for those training for freedom."

"Not whipping, but sprinkling the altar with human blood, since even the Scythians thought it worthy of these things. The Spartans modified the essential element of the ceremony and progressed to the endurance contest, from which there is no loss of life, while the goddess receives an offering of their blood."

33. Philostr. *Gymn.* 58 p. 293
    φασὶ δὲ αὐτοὶ Λακεδαιμόνιοι μηδὲ ἀγωνίας ἕνεκα γυμνάζεσθαι τὴν ἰδέαν
    ταύτην, ἀλλὰ καρτερίας μόνης, ὅπερ δὴ μαστιγουμένων ἐστίν, ἐπειδὴ νόμος
    αὐτοῖς ἐπὶ τοῦ βωμοῦ ξαίνεσθαι.

    They say that the Spartans themselves exercise in this style, not for the sake
    of competition, but only for endurance, which is a quality of those who are
    whipped, since the law is for them to be lacerated on the altar.

34. Libanius *Or.* 1.23
    τὴν Κόρινθον εἶδον οὐ φεύγων οὐδὲ διώκων, ἀλλὰ νῦν μὲν ἐφ' ἑορτὴν
    Λακωνικήν, τὰς μάστιγας, ἐπειγόμενος.

    I saw Corinth not as an attorney for the defense or the prosecution, but at
    one time when I was hurrying to the Whips, a Laconian festival.

35. Schol. to Libanius *Or.* 1.23
    οἱ Λακεδαιμόνιοι πρὸς καρτερίαν γυμναζόμενοι τὴν Ἄρτεμιν (*num* τῇ
    Ἀρτέμιδι?) ἑορτὴν ἐποίουν, ἐν ᾗ ἐμάστιζον ἀλλήλους, καὶ ἀνδρίαν τινὰ ἐκ
    τούτων ἐπαιδεύοντο, ἵνα ἀνδρικῶς ἔχοιεν περὶ τοὺς πολέμους.

    Training for endurance, the Spartans used to hold a festival for Artemis in
    which they whipped one another, and they learned some courage from this
    so that they would be brave in war.

36. Themist. *Or.* 21.250A
    Λακεδαιμονίους δὲ ἔγω πυνθάνομαι τά τε ἄλλα τὸν Λυκοῦργον αἰχύνειν
    καὶ ἐπὶ τὸν βωμὸν τῆς Ὀρθίας ὁμοίως μὲν δούλους, ὁμοίως δὲ ἐλευθέρους
    ἀνάγειν, τόν τε εἵλωτα, εἰ τύχοι, τόν τε Εὐρυπωντίδην ἢ Ἀγιάδην. ἢ τοῦτό
    γε ἴσως οὐκ ἀπὸ τρόπου· μαστίγων γὰρ τὸ ἀγώνισμα καὶ ὁ στέφανος.

    I know that the Spartans dishonor Lycurgus in other ways too, but
    especially in bringing to the altar of Orthia slaves and free men in the same
    way, either a helot, if it so chances, or a Eurypontid or Agiad. Well, perhaps
    at least this is not unreasonable; for the contest and the garland are of the
    whips.

37. Greg. Naz. *Or.* 4.70 (Bernardi)
    ὁ τοὺς Λακωνικοὺς ἐπαινῶν ἐφήβους ξαινομένους ταῖς μάστιξι καὶ τὸ
    ἐπιβώμιον αἷμα τέρπνον θεὰν ἁγνὴν καὶ παρθένον.

    [You] who praise the Laconian ephebes lacerated by the whips and the
    blood on the altar to delight a goddess, holy and virgin.

38. Greg. Naz. *Or.* 4.103 (Bernardi)
    καὶ τοῦτο εἶναι θεοῦ τιμήν τὰς εἰς αὐτὸν λοιδορίας; ἢ Ταύροις τὸ
    ξενοκτονεῖν ἢ Λάκωσι τὸ ἐπιβώμια ξαίνεσθαι;

And is this honoring a god, this abuse of him? Is the Taurians' killing of strangers? Or the Spartans' laceration at the altar?

39. Greg. Naz. *Or.* 39.4 (Moreschini)
οὐδὲ Ταύρων ξενοκτονίαι καὶ Λακωνικῶν ἐφήβων ἐπιβώμιον αἷμα, ξαινομένων ταῖς μάστιξι καὶ τοῦτο μόνον κακῶς ἀνδριζομένων, οἷς τιμᾶται θεά, καὶ ταῦτα παρθένος.

Nor the Taurians' killing of strangers and the Laconian ephebes' blood shed on the altar when they are torn by the whips and only in this way basely become men, with which practices a goddess is honored, and a virgin at that.

40. Greg. Naz. *Carm.* 2.2.7.272–73
καὶ σὺ, Λάκαινα τάλαινα, διασταδὸν, ἔνθα καὶ ἔνθα / τεμνομένων μάστιξι νέων ἐπιβώμιος ἀλκή.

And you, wretched courage of Spartan youths beside the altar being cut one by one with whips here and there.

41. Eunapius *VS* 485
ὁ δὲ ἀνθύπατος τὸ μὲν διωκόμενον μέρος ἐξελθεῖν κελεύσας, τοῦ δὲ διώκοντος τὸν διδάσκαλον μόνον, εἶτα ἀπολαβὼν τὸν Θεμιστοκλέα καὶ τοὺς Λάκωνας, τῶν ἐν Λακεδαίμονι μαστίγων ὑπέμνησε, προσθεὶς αὐτοῖς καὶ τῶν Ἀθήνῃσι.

After the proconsul had ordered the departure of all the accused and, of the accusers, the teacher alone, he then took Themistocles and the "Laconians" aside and caused them to remember the whips in Sparta, with some of the Athenian sort for good measure.

42. Synes. *Ep.* 41 (Garzya)
Ποῖοι Ταυροσκύθαι, τίνες Λακεδαιμόνιοι τοσούτῳ τῷ διὰ τῶν μαστίγων αἵματι τὴν παρ᾽ αὐτοῖς ἐτίμησαν Ἄρτεμιν;

What sort of Tauroscythians, what Spartans honored the Artemis in their midst with so much blood from their whips?

43. Simp. *In Epict.* c. 5 (Dübner)
Οἱ δὲ Λακεδαιμονίων νέοι, διὰ τὴν φιλοτιμίαν μόνην, τὴν μαστίγωσιν ἐκείνην τὴν φοβερὰν ὑπέμενον, ἄχρι θανάτου σχεδὸν τὴν καρτερίαν ἐπιδεικνύμενοι. καὶ δῆλον ὅτι εὐφόρως καὶ ἡδόμενοι· οὐ γὰρ ἂν ἑκόντες εἰς τοιοῦτον ἀγῶνα κατέβαινον.

The Spartans' young men submitted to that fearsome flogging because of their competitive spirit alone, displaying their endurance to the point of death. And it is clear that they did so easily and gladly, for they would not otherwise enter into such a contest willingly.

44. Simp. *In Epict.* c. 8 (Dübner)
[ὥστε], κἂν πρὸς ἀλγηδόνας [γυμνάζηταί τις], τὸν διαμαστιγώσεως ἀγῶνα τῶν ἐν Λακεδαίμονι νέων εὐγενῶν ζηλοῦν, καὶ τὰ πρὸς ἐκεῖνον τὸν ἀγῶνα γυμνάσια πάντα ἀλγεινὰ ὄντα.

[So that] if [someone trains] for suffering, he emulates the flagellation contest of well-born youths in Lacedaemon, and all the painful exercises associated with that contest.

45. Schol. to Pl. *Leg.* 633A (Greene)
τέταρτον· τὰς διαμαστιγώσεις, τὰς γυμνοπαιδίας, τὰ κρύπτια· ταῦτα γὰρ πρὸς ἀνδρείαν τείνει.

The fourth: the Flagellations, the Gymnopaediae, the *krupteia*; for these aim at courage.

46. Schol. to Pl. *Leg.* 633B (Greene)
Καρτερήσεις· τὰς διαμαστιγώσεις φησί. ἐγένοντο δ' αὗται πρὸς τῷ βωμῷ τῆς Ὀρθωσίας Ἀρτέμιδος, τῆς τὴν πολιτείαν ἀνορθούσης. παρειστήκει γὰρ ἡ ταύτης ἱέρεια φέρουσά τι ἐπὶ τῆς χειρὸς κεκρυμμένον, ὃ μέχρι τοῦ νῦν ἄγνωστόν ἐστι, καὶ εἰ μὲν ἧττον τοῦ δέοντος ἐμαστιγοῦτο· κινεῖν γὰρ τὰς χεῖρας οὐκ ἐτόλμα, ἔχων ταύτας ἐπὶ τῆς κεφαλῆς ὁ μαστιζόμενος· ἐβαρεῖτο ἐκείνη ὑπὸ τοῦ φερομένου, δεόντως δὲ τὴν δίκην εἰ ὑπεῖχεν, κούφως ἡ ἱέρεια διετίθετο.

Endurances: He means the Flagellations. They took place at the altar of Artemis Orthosia, who restored the constitution. Nearby stood her priestess carrying in her hand something hidden, which remains unknown until now. And if the person being flogged was whipped less than he should (for he was not allowed to move his hands, which he held on his head), she was weighed down by what she was holding, but if he suffered the proper punishment, the priestess felt a light weight.

47. Schol. to *Od.* 4.245 (Dindorf)
καλῶς οὖν Λακεδαιμόνιοι παιδεύουσι τὴν μαστίγωσιν τοὺς νέους καρτερεῖν τὰ δεινὰ ἐθίζοντες.

Well, therefore, did the Spartans teach their young men to endure flagellation, accustoming them to terrible things.

48. Ps. Nonn. *In Greg. Naz. Or.* 4 11 (Smith)
Ἐνδεκάτη ἐστὶν ἱστορία ἡ κατὰ τοὺς Λακωνικοὺς ἐφήβους. ἔστι δὲ αὕτη. Οἱ Λακεδαιμόνιοι βουλόμενοι καρτερικοὺς καὶ ἀνδρείους εἶναι τοὺς ἑαυτῶν πολίτας καὶ παῖδας, ἐγύμναζον ταῖς διαμαστιγώσεσι, καὶ τῷ ἐπὶ πλέον καρτεροῦντι ἆθλον ἐδίδοτο.

The eleventh *historia* concerns the Laconian ephebes. It is this:
The Lacedaemonians, who wanted their own citizens and children to be

hardy and courageous, trained them with the Flagellations, and a prize used to be given to the one who endured the most.

49. Ps. Nonn. *In Greg. Naz. Or. 4* 58 (Smith)
Πεντηκοστὴ ὀγδόη ἐστὶν ἱστορία τὸ τοὺς Λάκωνας ξαίνεσθαι παρὰ τοὺς βωμούς. ἔστι δὲ αὕτη ῥηθεῖσα μὲν καὶ ἤδη πρότερον, καὶ νῦν δὲ λέγεται. Οἱ Λακεδαιμόνιοι καρτερικοὺς τοὺς ἑαυτῶν παῖδας εἶναι ἐκδιδάσκοντες ταῖς διαμαστιγώσεσιν ἐχρῶντο, ἐκδιδάσκοντες αὐτοὺς ὑπομονητικῶς ἔχειν, καὶ τούτους ἔξαινον ταῖς πληγαῖς παρὰ τοῖς βωμοῖς, καὶ τῷ μὴ ὀλιγωρήσαντι ἀλλὰ γενναίως ἐνεγκόντι ἆθλον ἐδίδοσαν.

The fifty-eighth *historia* is about lacerating the Laconians beside the altars. The same subject has already been discussed previously, and is referred to at this point.

The Lacedaemonians, in teaching their own children to be hardy, used the Flagellations, teaching them to bear it patiently, and they lacerated them with lashes by the altars, and they gave a prize to the one who did not despise it but bore up nobly.

50. Ps. Nonn. *In Greg. Naz. Or. 39* 8 (Smith)
Ὀγδόη ἐστὶν ἱστορία τὸ τῶν Λακωνικῶν ἐφήβων ἐπιβώμιον αἷμα. ἔστι δὲ αὕτη.
Οἱ Λακεδαιμόνιοι πρὸς καρτερίαν γυμναζόμενοι ἑορτὴν ἐποίουν ἐν ᾗ ἐμάστιζον ἀλλήλους. καὶ ἀνδρείαν τινὰ ἐκ τούτου ἐπαιδεύοντο ἵνα καρτερικῶς ἔχοιεν περὶ τοὺς πολέμους. ἐτίμων δὲ οἱ Λάκωνες ἐν τῇ ἑορτῇ τῶν μαστιγῶν τὴν Ἄρτεμιν. ταύτην γὰρ λέγει παρθένον θεόν. καρτερικὴ γὰρ καὶ ὑπεράνω πάσης δειλίας καὶ ἐμπαθείας.

The eighth *historia* is about the Laconian ephebes' blood on the altar. It is this:

Training for endurance, the Spartans used to hold a festival in which they whipped one another. And from this they learned some courage so that they would be brave in war. The Laconians honored Artemis in the festival of the whips. For they call her a virgin goddess. For she is patient and above all cowardice and sentiment.

51. Hesych. s.v. φούαξιρ.
ἡ ἐπὶ τῆς χώρας σωμασκία τῶν μελλόντων μαστιγοῦσθαι.

Phouaxir: Training in the country of those about to be whipped.

52. Suda s.v. Λυκοῦργος.
τήν τε διαμαστίγωσιν, ἀρετῆς γυμνασίαν, ἀντὶ φόνου σκυθρωποῦ· ἔφηβος γὰρ πρότερον ἐθύετο τῇ Ἀρτέμιδι τῇ Ὀρθωσίᾳ.

Lycurgus: The Flagellation, an exercise in virtue, in place of gloomy murder; for previously, an ephebe used to be sacrificed to Artemis Orthosia.

APPENDIX 2
The Status of Amyclae

In the preceding chapters, I have often emphasized how much the later *agōgē* served as a treasure house of traditional culture for the Spartans of the Roman period. Modern scholars too have viewed the agogic inscriptions as essentially reliable evidence for Spartan society in the Archaic and Classical periods. However, an important consequence of the reevaluation of the evidence I have presented here is that many reconstructions of early Spartan history that are based almost entirely on this late evidence need to be reexamined.

The *ōbai*, the communities whose amalgamation formed Sparta, are a case in point. We have met them as the names of the teams of ballplayers in the *sphaireis* tournament. Although the inscriptions in which this term appears all come from the Roman *agōgē*, they have figured prominently in discussions of Sparta's formation and early constitutional structure. Orthodoxy on this aspect of Spartan history was established in the years between the two world wars.[1] Its essence is as follows: Sparta had originally consisted of four villages (*ōbai*) until it absorbed the nearby settlement of Amyclae, either peacefully or by conquest, early in the expansion of Spartan power over Laconia — perhaps as early as 750 B.C. Amyclae thus joined Sparta's other constituent communities as the fifth *ōba*. This fivefold constitutional structure was reflected in the five ephors and, most importantly, in the five *lochoi* of the early Spartan army. A sixth *ōba*, the Neopolitae, was added in the late third century B.C. to accommodate Cleomenes III's newly enfranchised Spartiates. The final change took place by the first century B.C., when Amyclae gained a form of semi-independence. From that time on, Sparta consisted, once again, of five *ōbai* — Mesoa, Limnae, Pitane, Cynooura, and the Neopolitae.[2]

The question of Amyclae's status is in fact intertwined with that of the *ōba* of the Neopolitae. Early in the third century A.D., the victorious *sphaireis* of the Neopolitae erected a stele bearing a relief.[3] The stone was unfortunately lost in a fire at the Sparta museum before Walter Kolbe, the editor of the Laconian fascicle of the corpus, had a chance to examine it. The inscription's first editor, however, left a precise description of the relief, here given in full: "Fragment of an inscription in Sparta (1847) in the house of the governor there. It is adorned above with a triangular frame in which there is a standing female figure in crude relief, frontally presented, with four arms; the upper arm on the right holds an olive sprig, opposite to which a snake rears up; the upper arm on the left holds a bow, the lower arm on the same side holds a shallow bowl. To the left of the figure sits a big ball, on the right behind the snake stands a sort of amphora."[4]

Although Ross mistakenly identified the relief's subject as a woman, others soon realized that it represented one of the oddest local variations of Apollo known, Apollo Tetracheir (Apollo Fourhands).[5] The scrappy extant testimonia indicate that Tetracheir was worshiped at Amyclae.[6] Although some have identified Tetracheir as a hybrid of Hyacinthus and Apollo worshiped together with

Apollo of the Amyclaeum, whose statue and throne so fascinate archaeologists, this god has attributes quite different from those Pausanias enumerates.[7] Since nothing, either in the testimonia for Tetracheir or in Pausanias' description of the Amyclaeum, supports that identification, I prefer to keep the two divinities separate and to locate Tetracheir in Amyclae town.[8] In any event, whatever the precise location of this unusual god's shrine, there is no reason to question his ties to Amyclae.

A *sphaireis* team erecting an inscription has a logical connection to the subject of its relief; consequently, the *sphaireis* of the Pitanatae mentioned previously adorned their victory stele with a relief of the Dioscuri. As the sanctuary of Castor and Pollux at Sparta was evidently in Pitane, these *sphaireis* naturally chose them as team patrons.[9] Parallels can be found with modern sports teams who advertise their origins by their names or with mascots and emblems. For instance, the lion symbolizes the United Kingdom to most of the world, but during World Cup competition only the English team wears this emblem; Scotland, Wales, and Northern Ireland each have their own. To other Greeks, then, the Dioscuri may well have been associated with Sparta as a whole, but in the matches between the young Spartan ballplayers they were the patrons of the Pitanatae. We should expect a similar correlation between the ball team of the Neopolitae and Apollo Tetracheir of Amyclae, and indeed there is. Thus, the Neopolitae were the inhabitants of Amyclae and not Cleomenes' sixth *ōba*, invented to hold the new Spartiates he had enfranchised. More than this is gained, though, since the stone shows that Amyclaean youths competed in one of the contests of the *agōgē* in the third century A.D. By this time the cult of Tetracheir seems to have been integrated into the *agōgē*, and the youthful Amyclaean god's priesthood was now held by a suitably aristocratic Spartan ephebe.[10] Consequently, Amyclaeans must have been Spartan citizens long after they are supposed to have separated from the city.

If Amyclae was not "quasi-independent" from Sparta in the Roman age, then the question of Amyclae's status in previous centuries needs reopening. That Amyclae had ever been part of Sparta before the Roman conquest rests solely on *IG* V.1 26, a decree dated to the end of the second century B.C. or the beginning of the first and emanating from the "*ōba* of the Amyclaeans." The text is as follows:[11]

Δογματογράφων Λυσινίκου τοῦ Σωτηρίδα, Νηκλέος
τοῦ ᾿Αριστοκράτεος, Πασικράτεος τοῦ Πασικλέος·
τὸ δοχθὲν ὑπὸ ᾿Αμυκλαιέων.
᾿Επεὶ κα[τ]ασταθέντες ἔφοροι εἰς τὸν ἐπὶ Νικέα ἐνιαυτὸν Πασιτέλης
5 Τετάρτου, Εὔθυμος Λυσικράτεος, Δαμιάδας Δαμιάδα ἀξίως
ἀνεστρέφησαν αὐτῶν τε καὶ τὰς ἐνχειρισθείσας αὐτοῖς πίσ-
τεως, ἐμ πᾶσιν ἀκερδῶς καὶ ἡμέρως τὸν ἐνίαυτον διεξα-
γαγόντες, δεδόχθαι τοῖς ᾿Αμυκλαιέοις ἐπαινέσαι ἐφόρους
τοὺς περὶ Πασιτέλη τῶ καλῶς τὰν ἀρχὰν διεξαγνηκέναι.
ποιούντω δὲ αὐτοῖς καὶ ἐπὶ τᾶι προστροπᾶι ἀεὶ μερίδα, ἕως

10   ἂν ζῶσι, ὅπως ἀε[ὶ] ἁ ὠβὰ μναμονεύουσ[α] τῶν γεγο⟨νό⟩των φι-
     [λ]ανθρώπων εἰς αὐτὰν ἀποδιδοῦσα φαίνηται τὰς καταξίους
     τιμάς. ἐγδόμεν δὲ τοὺς κατασταθέντας στάλαν λιθίναν,
     εἰς ἂν ἀναγραφήσεται τὸ δόγμα, καὶ στᾶσαι εἰς [τ]ὸ ἱερὸν τᾶς
     Ἀλεξάνδρας. τὰν δὲ εἰς ταύταν δαπάναν δότω ἁ ὠβὰ καὶ λόγον
15   ἐνεγκόντω περὶ τᾶς γεγενημένας δαπάνας τοὺς ἐπὶ ταῦτα
     κατασταθέντας. ἐπαινέσαι δὲ καὶ τὸν γραμματέα αὐτῶν
     Καλλικλῆ.

Dogmatographoi: Lysinicus son of Soteridas, Necles son of Aristocrates, Pasi-
crates son of Pasicles.

Decreed by the Amyclaeans that:

Whereas the ephors in office for the year under Niceas, Pasiteles son of Tetar-
tus, Euthymus son of Lysicrates, Damiadas son of Damiadas, conducted themselves in a manner worthy of themselves and of the pledge entrusted to them, in
all ways carrying out their year without thought of gain and in a civilized way,
it was decided by the Amyclaeans to praise the ephors around Pasiteles for
carrying out their office well. Let them always make a portion for them in the
Supplication, as long as they shall live, so that the *ōba*, in remembrance of the
benefits that came about for it, might appear to give back fitting honors. That
those appointed contract for a marble stele, onto which the decree will be
inscribed, and erect it in the sanctuary of Alexandra. Let the *ōba* pay the
expense for this, and let those appointed for this submit an account of the
expenses arising. And, moreover, to praise their secretary, Callicles.

This same inscription doubles, ironically, as evidence for Amyclae's later autonomy, and so we are faced with the anomalous situation of a single testimony
being used to support two apparently contradictory states — amalgamation into
Sparta and independence.[12] This methodological problem has been papered over
with the hypothesis that, while Amyclae had once been a part of Sparta, it had
gained a form of independence at an unknown date before the passage of *IG*
V.1 26.

In spite of never having been set out explicitly, this argument rests on two
features of the document — the Amyclaeans styling themselves as an *ōba*, and
their apparent independence of action. Amyclae's independence, or more accurately, autonomy can be seen in the array of public officials the *ōba* enjoyed: three
dogmatographoi (lines 1–2), three ephors (lines 4–5), and their secretary (lines
16–17). More important are the public funds, for whose supervision ("the *pistis*
entrusted to them") the ephors were praised, and which were to be used to pay for
the erection of the stele.[13] This situation contrasts with the only other evidence for
an *ōba*'s internal activity, a stone set up by the Cynooureis in honor of An-
tamenes, a water commissioner; on one side of the stone is a list of the subscribers
who paid for its erection.[14] Clearly, unlike the Amyclaeans, the *ōba* of the Cynooureis had no public treasury to draw on for such an expenditure and probably
lacked all but a minimal bureaucracy.

IG V.1 26 does indicate that Amyclae had a degree of autonomy from Sparta, but that autonomy was something less than the outright independence enjoyed by cities of the former perioeci. These cities had been detached from Spartan control upon the defeat of the "tyrant" Nabis in 195 B.C. and placed under the tutelage of the Achaean League until they became fully independent after 146. At some time during this period they formed themselves into a league, the League of Lacedaemonians or, as it became known later, the League of Free Laconians. Thanks to a list provided by Pausanias, we know that Amyclae, although separate from Sparta, was not a member of the league.[15]

Amyclae's ties to Sparta are indicated by the use of the name of Sparta's eponymous magistrate in the dating formula identifying the ephors praised in the decree (lines 4–5). Pasiteles, Euthymus, and Damiadas are called "the ephors in office for the year under Niceas." Although no office is indicated for Niceas, we can soon supply it through a process of elimination. Niceas was not among the officials to be praised, so he was not the eponymous ephor of Amyclae. The cities of the League of Lacedaemonians dated documents by the league's *stratēgos*; since Amyclae was not a member, Niceas cannot have been a *stratēgos*.[16] Within a Laconian context, the only possible official remaining is the Spartan *patronomos*, who had earlier replaced the ephor as eponymous magistrate.[17] Niceas, then, must have been the *patronomos* of Sparta, whose name also appeared on documents at Amyclae.[18] Amyclae was evidently a Spartan possession at this time, allowed a certain amount of internal autonomy but still dependent on the city in matters of substance.

Prevailing opinion, though it can be proved correct as regards Amyclae's status at the turn of the first century B.C., has a far weaker case regarding that community's earlier position. The only evidence, or "proof" as it has been called, that Amyclae had ever been a Spartan *ōba* is the word's appearance in the Amyclae decree.[19] Since the city's constituent communities were called *ōbai*, its appearance here is taken as a relic of Amyclae's previous status as a Spartan "ward." Attractive though this reasoning seems, it is fatally flawed by its dependence on the assumption that the word *ōba* was always used exclusively to denote a unit of the Spartan citizenry, and nothing else. In the mountain of literature on the *ōbai* of Sparta, this assumption has hardly ever been questioned, even though it lacks any basis in ancient evidence. No lexical citation, no gloss, no scholion, not even the Great Rhetra itself supports this limitation.

With the exception of the Great Rhetra (if we assume that Plutarch's version accurately reflects a genuine Archaic original), all the evidence for *ōbai* is found in sources from the Roman period. We have already seen that, in some inscriptions, *ōbai* are associated with teams of ballplayers, whose names were the same as those of the city's archaic constituent communities. These names were also given to Sparta's civic tribes: there are references to a "tribe of Cynooureis" and a "tribe of Limnaeis."[20] Evidently, in the Roman period, at least, there was no difference between a Spartan *ōba* and a Spartan civic tribe. The lexicographical sources, when read in this light, present a clear and consistent picture: an *ōba* could be a village (*kōmē*) or a civic tribe (*phulē*).[21] The villages whose amalgamation gave birth to the city of Sparta changed in the course of time into the equivalent of civic tribes, whose activities seem to have been confined mainly to the *agōgē* and athletics in general.[22] Nothing, however, compels us to believe that the word *ōba* had ever lost its original meaning. Like its synonym *kōmē*, *ōba* could be used for a unit of citizenry.[23] But, just as no one would assume that all appearances of the word *kōmē* have precise constitutional significance, so none should assume that the word *ōba* was used only for Sparta's constituent communities. Surely, it is much more likely that, although the word acquired a secondary technical meaning at Sparta, it was at bottom the Laconian for "village," as the lexicographers have been trying to tell us for centuries.[24]

The appearance of *ōba* in *IG* V.1 26 tells us nothing about Amyclae's earlier history. That Amyclae was an *ōba* simply means it was, as Pausanias characterized it, a village and not a fully fledged *polis* like the former perioecic communities who now formed the League of Lacedaemonians.[25]

If, as I have argued, all Spartan constituent communities were *ōbai*, but not all *ōbai* were constituent communities of Sparta, a nagging irritant disappears in the bargain. The *ōba* of the Arkaloi has received scant attention and less respect since the inscription in which it appears was published in 1951.[26] The reason is not hard to find: since all *ōbai* were supposed to have been parts of Sparta, the *ōba* of the Arkaloi simply could not exist and had to be explained away. Now that the existence of non-Spartan *ōbai* can be countenanced, the Arkaloi may be rescued from oblivion and placed back in their Laconian village.

Although *IG* V.1 26 constitutes the sole explicit testimony for Amyclae's status, other material has been pressed into service to bolster the view that Amyclae was part of Sparta. The most commonly cited is a passage in Xenophon's *Hellenika*, in which Agesilaus allowed Amyclaeans from all the Spartan army to go home to celebrate the Hyacinthia.[27] It received its relevance from the contention that perioeci and other non-Spartiates were brigaded into separate, distinct military units.[28] If Amyclaeans were spread throughout the army, the argument went, in the same units as Spartiates, they too must have been Spartiates. However, it has been convincingly argued that by the late fifth century perioeci served in the same units as Spartiates.[29] Thus, a distribution of Amyclaeans throughout the army signifies nothing about Amyclae's constitutional status.

The Hyacinthia was one of the most significant festivals in the Spartan calendar. That the Hyacinthia was celebrated at the Amyclaeum after a sacred procession from the city might be thought to indicate that Amyclae was part of Sparta.[30] On the contrary, all it shows is that the sanctuary of Apollo Amyclaeus was under Spartan control, as we would expect of such a prominent Laconian shrine. Political unity is not suggested by the procession linking the two places. Such processions out of a city to a notable sanctuary outside the walls, often a considerable distance away, were very common elements of civic festivals, but imply nothing more than political control of the outlying areas in question.[31]

In the eyes of modern scholars, Amyclae's most important role has probably been as the "fifth *ōba*," whose presence accounts for the five *lochoi* of the early Spartan army and the five-member colleges, such as the ephorate, which pepper the Spartan constitution.[32] Logical as this correlation may seem in the case of the ephorate, we simply know too little about Classical Sparta's constitution to assume that any magistracy was structured in this way. On this subject, it has been sensibly suggested that the existence of boards of five "no more proves a five-fold division of Sparta, than the nine archons or the Eleven prove a nine-fold or eleven-fold division for Athens."[33]

How many divisions, or *lochoi*, the early Spartan army had, and whether these divisions were raised according to *ōbai* has bedeviled students of Sparta since the fifth century B.C. Of course, if Amyclae was not part of Sparta in the Classical period, then either the *lochoi* were not connected with the number of *ōbai* or, if they were, the army had not five, but four "obal *lochoi*." Relevant to this is the notorious question of the "*lochos* of Pitane," whose existence would confirm the obal basis of the *lochoi*.[34] This consideration has caused a majority of scholars to side with Herodotus, even in the face of Thucydides' forceful denial that there had ever been such a unit. Apart from the passage in Herodotus, the link between *ōbai* and *lochoi* depends upon a list of five names for the Spartan *lochoi* preserved in two scholia and thought to derive ultimately from Aristotle's lost *Constitution of the Lacedaemonians*. In one, a note on a line from Aristophanes' *Lysistrata*, the names are Edolos, Sinis, Arimas, Ploas, and Messoages; in the other, on a section from book 4 of Thucydides, they are Aidolios, Sinis, Sarinas, Ploas, and Mesoates.[35] Modern writers have seized upon the last name as proof positive that *lochoi* were raised according to *ōbai*.[36] While the other four are considered to be nicknames or "fancy names," "Mesoates," as it appears in the Thucydides scholion, seems to clinch the argument since it is the adjectival form of Mesoa, one of the Spartan *ōbai*. A *lochos* called "Mesoan" is thought quite logically to consist of men from Mesoa. Moreover, if one *lochos* was raised from a single *ōba*, then the other four *lochoi* may reasonably be assumed to have been raised in the same manner.

We must ask, however, why the *lochos* of the Mesoatae alone had no nickname. Toynbee conjectured that it was punishment for Mesoan involvement in the plot of the Partheniae, an unconvincing suggestion, to say the least.[37] On the other hand, surely either all *lochoi* had nicknames or none did. The other names, while unusual, are not completely devoid of significance.[38] "Sinis" means "ravager" or "plunderer" and was used as the name of Theseus' murderous opponent on the Isthmus of Corinth, while "Sarinas" is clearly derived from the Laconian word for a palm branch, *sarir*.[39] In other words, "Sinis" and "Sarinas" are equivalent to such titles as *rapax* and *victrix* given to Roman legions. The remaining two names, "Aidolios" and "Ploas," are more reticent, though it is hard to avoid the impression that "Ploas" had a connection with the marines. In light of this, there is no reason why "Messoages" should not be the correct form, perhaps referring to the central unit of a Spartan battle formation.[40] "Mesoates," then, may just as likely have resulted from an educated misreading as "Messoages" from an ignorant one. Moreover, the chaos of the sources, where the number of *lochoi* ranges from four to seven, cannot furnish support for accepting one reading over another beyond satisfying the desire to match five *lochoi* with five *ōbai*.[41]

Finally, the canonical view of Amyclae's status begs questions of historical probability and has, moreover, led to internal contradiction. To take the second point first, a recent study has averred, on the basis of Pausanias' account of the whipping contest at the altar of Artemis Orthia, that the Amyclaeans did not participate in her cult.[42] Leaving aside the dubious authenticity of this evidence, we know from archaeology and epigraphy that ephebic activity in general and the contests of the *agōgē* in particular centered on the shrine of Orthia.[43] Plutarch states categorically that passage through the *agōgē* was mandatory for Spartan citizens.[44] If the Amyclaeans did not join in worshiping Orthia, then they could not enter the *agōgē* and, consequently, could not have become citizens.

The historical questions hinge on determining the circumstances for so drastic an action as the separation of Amyclae from Sparta, an action tantamount to the partial dismemberment of the city. While hypothesizing that such a separation did take place, scholars have been notably reticent about suggesting when it may have happened. Obviously, a time when Sparta suffered a severe reversal of fortune is needed, hardly difficult to find in the years from Leuctra to the first century B.C. But Epaminondas, first of all, did not concern himself with breaking up Sparta itself.[45] Although the catalog of defeats the Spartans suffered in the years following shows the dismal state of their military prowess, the city's integrity was never in doubt. Direct intervention in Sparta's internal affairs first came on the heels of Cleomenes III's defeat at Sellasia in 222. But the victorious Antigonus Doson, Polybius tells us, did no more than restore the "ancestral constitution" so battered by Cleomenes' reforms.[46] In 195, the Romans, after defeating the tyrant Nabis, took the maritime perioeci from Spartan hands and made them protectorates of Rome's ally, the Achaean League, while leaving Sparta itself alone.[47] Later, when the Spartans reluctantly joined the Achaean League in 192 they entered with all their laws and constitution intact.[48] Sparta reached the nadir of its fortunes in 188 when the Achaean general Philopoemen punished the city after an abortive rebellion by forcing the Spartan constitution into an Achaean framework and suspending the *agōgē*, without, however, any hint that he went so far as to split the city up.[49]

Wade-Gery was alone in tentatively suggesting that Amyclae separated as part of what he termed "the reorganization after 146 B.C."[50] Unfortunately he misunderstood Sparta's situation following the Achaean War: as the provider for Rome of a *casus belli* and a friendly noncombatant, the city was rewarded with reinstatement of the "Lycurgan constitution," regained full autonomy, and was free from tribute. This was scarcely the moment for the Romans to demand the removal of one *ōba*. Moreover, he mistakenly thought that Amyclae "got the same sort of independence as the towns of the perioikoi," since he erroneously believed that the perioecic towns still dated their documents by the Spartan eponymous magistrate, whereas they actually dated according to the *stratēgos* of the League of Lacedaemonians.[51]

The earliest extant evidence for Amyclae's status, the inscription *IG* V.1 26, shows it was semiautonomous in the late Hellenistic period, with no evidence that it had ever previously been a part of Sparta. All the earlier evidence is consistent with Amyclae being a Spartan possession, in Spartan territory, but not yet politically amalgamated with the city itself. On the other hand, the Tetracheir relief of the third century A.D. shows Amyclaean youths in the *agōgē*, so Amyclae must have become a part of Sparta at some time between the dates of the two inscriptions. A suitable historical context for this unification can be found in the late first century B.C. I suggest that Augustus allowed Sparta to incorporate Amyclae during the rule of the Spartan privateer C. Julius Eurycles, whose ships were virtually alone in mainland Greece in having fought on the right side at Actium.[52] Before his downfall, sometime between 7 and 2 B.C., Eurycles had succeeded in reestablishing Spartan control over the cities of Laconia.[53] The absorption of nearby Amyclae into Sparta would have fitted neatly into such an expansionist policy.

NOTES

ABBREVIATIONS

Besides the readily identifiable abbreviations of modern works, the following abbreviations appear in this book.

AAWW	*Anzeiger der Österreichischen Akademie der Wissenschaften in Wien, Philos.-Hist. Klasse*
AR	*Archaeological Reports*
AS	*Anatolian Studies*
BStudL	*Bollettino di Studi Latini*
CIG	*Corpus Inscriptionum Graecarum*
EA	*Epigraphica Anatolica*
FGH	C. Müller and T. Müller, *Fragmenta historicorum Graecorum,* 1868–78
FGrHist	F. Jacoby, *Die Fragmente der griechischen Historiker,* 1926–58
HTR	*Harvard Theological Review*
IEphesos	H. Engelmann, D. Knibbe, and R. Merkelbach, *Die Inschriften von Ephesos,* IGSK no. 14, 1980
IG	*Inscriptiones Graecae*
IGR	R. Cagnat, *Inscriptiones Graecae ad res Romanas pertinentes,* 1911–27
IIasos	W. Blümel, *Die Inschriften von Iasos,* IGSK no. 28.1, 1985
Ins. Magnesia	O. Kern, *Die Inschriften von Magnesia am Maeander,* 1900
Ins. Olympia	W. Dittenberger and K. Purgold, *Olympia,* vol. 5, *Die Inschriften,* 1896
Ins. Priene	F. Hiller von Gaertringen, *Inschriften von Priene,* 1906
Inscr. Cret.	M. Guarducci, ed., *Inscriptiones Creticae,* vol. 1, 1935
ISelge	J. Nollé and F. Schindler, *Die Inschriften von Selge,* IGSK no. 37, 1991
ISestos	J. Krauss, *Die Inschriften von Sestos und der thrakischen Chersones,* IGSK no. 19, 1980
ITralleis	F. B. Poljakov, *Die Inschriften von Tralleis und Nysa,* IGSK no. 36.1, 1989
OGIS	W. Dittenberger, *Orientis Graeci inscriptiones selectae,* 1903–5
QAL	*Quaderni di Archeologia della Libia*
RBPh	*Revue Belge de Philologie*
SEG	*Supplementum epigraphicum Graecum*
SIG³	W. Dittenberger, *Sylloge inscriptionum Graecarum,* 3rd ed., 1915–24
SVF	J. von Arnim, *Stoicorum veterum fragmenta,* 1904–24
ZDP	*Zeitschrift für deutsche Philologie*

CHAPTER ONE

1. Description of Sparta: Paus. 3.11.2–18.5. Pausanias worked from ca. A.D. 155 to ca. A.D. 180: see Habicht, *Pausanias' Guide*, pp. 9–11. On Roman Sparta in general, see now Cartledge and Spawforth, *Hellenistic and Roman Sparta*, pp. 93–211.

2. There are references to ephebic institutions and monuments in 15 of the 69 paragraphs devoted to Spartan antiquities.

3. Gymnopaediae choruses: Paus. 3.11.9. Persian Stoa: Paus. 3.11.3. On a possible Hadrianic restoration, see French, "Archaeology, 1989–90," p. 26; Waywell, "Excavations on the Acropolis," p. 14. Ballplayers: Paus. 3.14.6; Lucian *Anach.* 38; *IG* V.1 674–88. Ball playing a Spartan invention: Athen. *Deipnos.* 1.25 (14E).

4. On these contests (μῶα, κελοῖα, καθθηρατόριον, etc.), see Chapter 3.

5. Cic. *Flacc.* 63. Cicero in Sparta: *Tusc.* 2.34.

6. On the Achaean War, see Gruen, "Origins," pp. 46–49, and *Hellenistic World*, 2:514–28.

7. Ancient scholarship was equivocal as to Lycurgus' exact dates: Plut. *Lyc.* 1.1; [Pl.] *Minos* 318C; X. *Lac.* 10.8; Diod. 7.12.8; Paus. 5.4.5. Civil strife: Plut. *Lyc.* 2.5–6.

8. For a good overview of this period with extensive bibliography, see Cartledge and Spawforth, *Hellenistic and Roman Sparta*, pp. 74–79, 247–48.

9. Plb. 13.6.1–6, 16.13.1; Livy 34.26.12, 34.31.11.

10. Livy 34.35.3–11, 34.36.2, 35.13.2; Gruen, *Hellenistic World*, 2:450–55.

11. Plut. *Philop.* 15.3; Paus. 8.50.10.

12. Livy 35.35.6–19; Oliva, *Social Problems*, pp. 295–97.

13. Livy 35.37.1–3; Plut. *Philop.* 15.4–5; Shimron, *Late Sparta*, pp. 101–2. On the "leading men" as members of the Gerousia, see Aymard, *Les premiers rapports*, p. 319 n. 28.

14. On laws, see Aymard, *Les premiers rapports*, p. 320; Shimron, *Late Sparta*, p. 102. On accession treaties and internal autonomy, see Swoboda, "Studien," pp. 30–32.

15. Attack on Las: Livy 38.30.6–32. Treaty of 195: Livy 34.35.14. Senate decision: Livy 38.33.6–11.

16. Plut. *Philop.* 16.4; Paus. 8.51.3.

17. Plb. 21.32C.3, συμφέρον δὲ τὸ ταπεινῶσαι τὴν τῶν Λακεδαιμονίων πόλιν.

18. Livy 38.34.1–3; Paus. 8.51.3.

19. Livy 38.34.1–3, 9.

20. Paus. 8.51.3.

21. *IG* V.1 4 and 5. The offices are *sunarchiai*, *engdoter/ekdoter*, and *epidamiourgos*; on these, see Kennell, "Public Institutions," pp. 19–20.

22. The exceptions are Chrimes, *Ancient Sparta*, pp. 45–47, and Shimron, *Late Sparta*, p. 106. For the full bibliography on this question, see Cartledge and Spawforth, *Hellenistic and Roman Sparta*, p. 248 n. 31.

23. Kennell, "*IG* V 1,16," pp. 198–202.

24. 184 B.C.: Swoboda, *Die griechischen Volksbeschlüsse*, p. 141. 183 B.C.: Busolt and Swoboda, *Die griechische Staatskunde*, 1:734; Kolbe, *IG* V.1, p. xiii. 181 B.C.: Tarn, *Hellenistic Civilization*, p. 30. 179 B.C.: Chrimes, *Ancient Sparta*, pp. 46–48; Shimron, *Late Sparta*, pp. 117–18. 178 B.C.: Dawkins, in Dawkins and others, *Artemis Orthia*, p. 34. 183–178 B.C.: Oliva, *Social Problems*, p. 311 and n. 2. More circumspect is Touloumakos, "Der Einfluss Roms," p. 102 n. 2.

25. Livy 45.28.4, *non operum magnificentia, sed disciplina institutisque memorabilem.*

26. Tigerstedt, *Legend of Sparta*, 2:344 n. 130.

27. Plut. *Philop.* 16.9.

28. Paus. 8.51.3.

29. Plb. 23.4.1–5; Livy 39.48.2–4.

30. Plb. 23.4.11–16; Livy 39.48.4; Paus. 7.9.5. On Rome as arbiter, see Larsen, "Was Greece Free?," pp. 193–214.

31. Plb. 23.9.11, 23.17.5–18.2; Larsen, *Greek Federal States*, p. 455.

32. Plb. 24.9.11–14, 24.10.6–7.

33. On this period, see Gruen, *Hellenistic World*, 2:488–99, who stresses the Senate's unwillingness to delve into such problems (cf. *Hellenistic World*, 1:119–22).

34. Livy *Per.* 51; Paus. 7.11.4–14.7; Dio Cass. 21.72.1; Cartledge and Spawforth, *Hellenistic and Roman Sparta*, pp. 87–90.

35. Strabo 8.5.5; Paus. 7.16.6–7, 10.

36. Plb. 6.10–19.5; Posidonius, *FGrHist* 87 F59; Tigerstedt, *Legend of Sparta*, 2:95–160; Taïphakos, "Τὸ Σπαρτιάτικον Πολίτευμα," pp. 428–40.

37. 1 Maccabees 12.6–8; Katzoff, "Jonathan," pp. 485–89. Katzoff associates the letter with the *agōgē*'s revival, which he dates to 178 B.C.

38. On the later constitution, see Kennell, "Public Institutions."

39. Plut. *Cleom.* 11.4. On Sphaerus' and Stoicism's role in Cleomenes' program, see Ollier, "Le philosophe stoïcien," pp. 536–70; Erskine, *Hellenistic Stoa*, pp. 123–49.

40. Lycurgus: Plut. *Cleom.* 10.2–8, 18.2. On Cleomenes' reforms, see Oliva, *Social Problems*, pp. 230–68; Shimron, *Late Sparta*, pp. 29–52.

41. Plut. *Cleom.* 8–10; Paus. 2.9.1. On the *patronomos*, see Shimron, "Original Task," pp. 155–58; Kennell, "Spartan Patronomate," pp. 131–37.

42. Plut. *Lyc.* 18.2; Paus. 3.16.9–11. On the tetradrachms, see Grunauer-von Hoerschelmann, *Münzprägung*, pp. 7–16. Dawkins, in Dawkins and others, *Artemis Orthia*, p. 34, preferred 178 B.C. as the date of the temple's reconstruction, since he believed the Spartan constitution was restored at that time.

43. Plut. *Cleom.* 2.2–3; Sphaerus, *FGrHist* 585 T1; F1–2.

44. See the excellent summation by Erskine, *Hellenistic Stoa*, p. 137, on which this section depends.

45. Plut. *Cleom.* 18.4, ἁψάμενοι μόνον τῶν πατρίων ἐθῶν καὶ καταστάντες εἰς ἴχνος ἐκείνης τῆς ἀγωγῆς; Cartledge and Spawforth, *Hellenistic and Roman Sparta*, p. 54.

46. Plb. 2.65–69; Plut. *Cleom.* 27–28; Walbank, *Commentary on Polybius,* 1:272–87.

47. Plb. 2.70.1; Plut. *Cleom.* 30.1; Shimron, *Late Sparta,* pp. 53–63; Mendels, "Polybius," pp. 161–66. On the changed role of the *patronomos* after Sellasia, see Chapter 2, at note 96.

48. Agis and the *agōgē:* Plut. *Agis* 4.2. Agis' reign and reforms: Plut. *Agis* 6–21; Cartledge and Spawforth, *Hellenistic and Roman Sparta,* pp. 42–47.

49. Teles (Hense²) p. 28. On the date of the speech, see Wilamowitz, *Antigonos,* pp. 301–4. On the link with Agis' reforms, see Wilamowitz, *Antigonos,* p. 303 n. 16; Fuks, "Non-Phylarchean Tradition," pp. 118–21.

50. Mendels, "Sparta in Teles' περὶ φυγῆς," pp. 111–15.

51. Plut. *Agis* 4.2.

52. Plut. *Agis* 4.2, 7.1, 10.1, 14.3–4, 15.1, 19.6, 19.8, 21.5.

53. Plut. *Pyrrh.* 26.21; cf. *IG* V.1 569; Cartledge and Spawforth, *Hellenistic and Roman Sparta,* p. 33.

54. Plb. 1.32.1, Λακεδαιμόνιον, ἄνδρα τῆς Λακωνικῆς ἀγωγῆς μετεσχηκότα καὶ τριβὴν ἐν τοῖς πολεμικοῖς ἔχοντα σύμμετρον; Bradford, *Prosopography,* s.v. "Xanthippos." On Spartan mercenaries, see Launey, *Recherches,* pp. 113–18.

55. Walbank, *Historical Commentary,* 1:65, 89.

56. Cartledge and Spawforth, *Hellenistic and Roman Sparta,* pp. 41, 240 n. 9.

57. Ibid., pp. 34–37.

58. On the possible link between the sixth-century renovation of Orthia's sanctuary and Spartan education, see Chapter 6, at note 140. Libanius, *Or.* 1.23, saw the endurance contest in the early fourth century A.D.: see Chapter 4, at note 3.

59. Hdt. 9.85.1–2, Λακεδαιμόνιοι μὲν τριξὰς ἐποιήσαντο θήκας· ... ἐν μὲν δὴ ἑνὶ τῶν τάφων ἦσαν οἱ ἱρέες, ἐν δὲ τῷ ἑτέρῳ οἱ ἄλλοι Σπαρτιῆται, ἐν δὲ τῷ τρίτῳ οἱ εἵλωτες.

60. See Chapter 2.

61. The Budé text of Ph.-E. Legrand (1954) retains the mss. readings; the emendations are those of L. Valckenaer (1763).

62. Cf. Garland, "Religion and Power," pp. 77–81.

63. Willetts, "Herodotos IX 85, 1–2," pp. 272–77.

64. Λέξεις Ἡροδότου, s.v. εἰρήν, in Stein, *Herodoti historiae,* 2:465.

65. Thuc. 5.68.2, 5.74.3.

66. den Boer, *Laconian Studies,* pp. 294–98, who went on to argue from the problematic passage, Plut. *Lyc.* 27.3, that the names of the fallen in the first group had been inscribed on a grave marker. This is unnecessary; Herodotus could just as easily have obtained the names from an oral source. Compare his memorization of the 300 names of the heroes of Thermopylae: Hdt. 7.224.1.

67. E.g., Dumézil, *Idéologie,* esp. pp. 7–33.

68. X. *Lac.* 11.3; Arist. *Rhet.* 1.9 [1367A 28–31]; for a later parallel, see Kennell, "Women's Hair and the Law," pp. 526–36, esp. 531–36.

69. X. *Lac.* 11.3; Dumézil, *Idéologie,* pp. 26–27; Benveniste, *Le vocabulaire,* 2:279; Puhvel, *Comparative Mythology,* pp. 159–60.

70. Puhvel, *Comparative Mythology*, pp. 141–43; Fowler, "Separate Functions," pp. 193–202. Lycurgus' loss of an eye in the course of reforming Sparta (Plut. *Lyc.* 11.2) echoes Odin's loss of an eye in the pursuit of wisdom (Puhvel, *Comparative Mythology*, pp. 193–94) and is all the more reason to consider Lycurgus divine rather than mortal (Hdt. 1.65; Plut. *Lyc.* 31.4; Paus. 3.16.6; cf. Piccirilli, "Licurgo e Alcandro," pp. 1–10).

71. On the Indo-European attitude to slaves, see Benveniste, *Le vocabulaire*, 2:355–61. On the Messenian wars and the enslavement of the Messenians, see Cartledge, *Sparta and Lakonia*, pp. 116–19.

72. Paus. 3.2.7; Hellanicus, *FGrHist* 4 F188; Ephorus, *FGrHist* 70 F117.

73. Cartledge, *Sparta and Lakonia*, pp. 96–99, 347–56.

74. Critias in Diels and Kranz, *Fragmente der Vorsokratiker*[10] 88b F37; Tyrtaeus F5, 7; Thuc. 4.26.6, 7. On helots in general, see Lotze, *Μεταξὺ Ἐλευθέρων*, pp. 26–47.

75. Talbert, "Role of the Helots," pp. 22–40.

76. Antiochus, *FGrHist* 555 F13.

77. Chrimes, *Ancient Sparta*, pp. 276–77; Cartledge, *Sparta and Lakonia*, pp. 116–19.

78. The long-simmering debates over the work's date and unity need not concern us. For an overview, see Breitenbach, "Xenophon"; Nickel, *Xenophon*, pp. 60–62. On Xenophon's attitude to Sparta, see Tigerstedt, *Legend of Sparta*, 1:159–79.

79. D.L. 2.54. But see the cautionary remarks of Higgins, *Xenophon the Athenian*, p. 160 n. 46.

80. X. *Lac.* 2.5, 2.11.

81. X. *Lac.* 2.5, σῖτόν γε μὴν ἔταξε τοσοῦτον ἔχοντα συμβολεύειν τὸν εἴρενα: this is the generally accepted reading of a confused passage in the manuscripts, even though it requires the creation of an otherwise unattested verb, συμβολεύειν; 2.11, ἔθηκε τῆς ἴλης ἑκάστης τὸν τορώτατον τῶν εἰρένων ἄρχειν.

82. X. *Lac.* 2.2, ὁ δὲ Λυκοῦργος . . . ἄνδρα ἐπέστησε κρατεῖν αὐτῶν ἐξ ὧνπερ αἱ μέγισται ἀρχαὶ καθίστανται, ὃς δὴ καὶ παιδονόμος καλεῖται. τοῦτον δὲ κύριον ἐποίησε καὶ ἀθροίζειν τοὺς παῖδας καὶ ἐπισκοποῦντα, εἴ τις ῥᾳδιουργοίη, ἰσχυρῶς κολάζειν; 4.3, αἱροῦνται τοίνυν αὐτῶν οἱ ἔφοροι ἐκ τῶν ἀκμαζόντων τρεῖς ἄνδρας· οὗτοι δὲ ἱππαγρέται καλοῦνται. τούτων δ' ἕκαστος ἄνδρας ἑκατὸν καταλέγει.

83. X. *Lac.* 3.5, 4.3, 10.1. φιλίτιον is a variant of the more familiar φιδίτιον (common mess); cf. Plut. *Lyc.* 12.1.

84. X. *Lac.* 11.4–10. See the remarks of Ollier, *Xénophon: la république des Lacédémoniens*, pp. xxiii–xxv.

85. Plut. *Lyc.* 17.2, καὶ κατ' ἀγέλας αὐτοὶ προΐσταντο τῶν λεγομένων εἰρένων ἀεὶ τὸν σωφρονέστατον καὶ μαχιμώτατον. On the relationship between Xenophon's *ilē* and Plutarch's *agelē*, see Chapter 6, at note 24.

86. On this phenomenon, see Tigerstedt, *Legend of Sparta*, 2:13–94.

87. The fragments of Critias' *Politeia* are best consulted in Diels and Kranz, *Fragmente der Vorsokratiker*[10] 88 F32–37. Beginning the description at conception: Diels and Kranz, *Fragmente der Vorsokratiker*[10] 88 F32; X. *Lac.* 1.3.

88. Plut. *Lyc.* 1.2; 5.12; 6.4; 28.2, 7; 31.4; Tigerstedt, *Legend of Sparta*, 2:236–37.

89. The exception is his account of the *krupteia* preserved in Plut. *Lyc.* 28.2–6.

90. Arist. *Pol.* 8.1.4 (1337A), 8.4.1 (1338B); cf. 7.2.9 (1324B), 8.5.7 (1339A-B).

91. The fragments are collected in Rose, *Fragmenta* F532–45, 611.9–13; with English translations in Dilts, *Excerpta*, pp. 16–19; cf. Tigerstedt, *Legend of Sparta*, 1:280–87.

92. Rose, *Fragmenta* F611.13, τρέφουσι δὲ τὰ τέκνα ὥστε μηδέποτε πληροῦν, ἵνα ἐθίζωνται δύνασθαι πεινεῖν. ἐθίζουσι δὲ αὐτοὺς καὶ κλέπτειν, καὶ τὸν ἁλόντα κολάζουσι πληγαῖς, ἵν᾿ ἐκ τούτου πονεῖν καὶ ἀγρυπνεῖν δύνωνται ἐν τοῖς πολεμίοις. μελετῶσι δὲ εὐθὺς ἐκ παίδων βραχυλογεῖν, εἶτα ἐμμελῶς καὶ σκώπτειν καὶ σκώπτεσθαι.

93. Bloch, "Herakleides Lembos," p. 37; Dilts, *Excerpta*, p. 9.

94. Cf. X. *Lac.* 2.5–8. Aristotle's account may be related to Xenophon's, since the technical term "to keep night vigil" (ἀγρυπνεῖν) appears in both.

95. Bloch, "Herakleides Lembos," p. 33.

96. *Inst. Lac.* 1–42 (236F–240B).

97. Tigerstedt, *Legend of Sparta*, 1:285. Spartan sensitivity regarding the *agōgē*: *Apophth. Lac.* Anon. 54 (235B). The *agōgē*, if anything, was surely at the heart of what Thucydides (5.68.2) called "the secrecy surrounding the constitution" (τῆς πολιτείας τὸ κρυπτόν).

98. Tigerstedt, *Legend of Sparta*, 1:244–76; Ollier, *Le mirage spartiate*, 1:217–93.

99. For an example of Platonism's effect on Spartan historiography, see Schütrumpf, "The *Rhetra* of Epitadeus," pp. 441–57.

100. Martini, "Dikaiarchos (3)," 546–51; Wehrli, "Dikaiarchos"; Flashar, *Philosophie der Antike*, 13:535–39.

101. Suda, s.v. Δικαίαρχος, οὗτος ἔγραψε τὴν πολιτείαν Σπαρτιατῶν· καὶ νόμος ἐτέθη ἐν Λακεδαίμονι καθ᾿ ἕκαστον ἔτος ἀναγινώσκεσθαι τὸν λόγον εἰς τὸ τῶν ἐφόρων ἀρχεῖον, τοὺς δὲ τὴν ἡβητικὴν ἔχοντας ἡλικίαν ἀκροάσθαι. καὶ τοῦτο ἐκράτει μεχρὶ πολλοῦ.

102. Taïphakos, "Δικαιάρχου Τριπολίτικος," pp. 124–29, dates the official adoption of the text at Sparta to the fourth century B.C. and attempts to link it to constitutional struggles between the ephors and the kings. Cartledge and Spawforth, *Hellenistic and Roman Sparta*, p. 198, argue for a Hellenistic date, since the work would have had no relevance to the Roman-era constitution.

103. Kennell, "Where Was Sparta's Prytaneion?," pp. 421–22.

104. See Chapter 2, at note 4; Diller, "New Source," pp. 499–501.

105. The fragments are collected in Nauck, *Aristophanis Byzantii fragmenta*, pp. 87–127; Slater, *Aristophanis Byzantii fragmenta*, pp. 28–71. On Aristophanes' lexicon and its influence, see Tolkiehn, "Lexikographie," 2439–40.

106. Cohn, "Aristophanes (14)," 995; Sandys, *History*[3], pp. 126–31. On the Library at Alexandria, see the lively account by Canfora, *Vanished Library*.

107. *IG* V.1 1120, with the improved text of Bingen, "ΤΡΙΕΤΙΡΗΣ," pp. 105–7. See Chapter 6, at note 15.

108. Nachstädt, Sieveking, and Titchener, *Moralia*, pp. 65–167; Fuhrmann, *Plutarque: oeuvres morales*, pp. 132–33. Plutarch's note-taking habits: Plut. *De tranq.* 1 (464F); cf. Tigerstedt, *Legend of Sparta*, 2:232–34.

109. *Inst. Lac.* 42 (239E–240B).

110. Tigerstedt, *Legend of Sparta*, 2:91, 371 n. 422.

111. *Inst. Lac.* 42 (239E–240B), ἀπείρητο δ' αὐτοῖς ναύταις εἶναι καὶ ναυμαχεῖν· ὕστερον μέντοι ἐναυμάχησαν, καὶ τῆς θαλάττης κρατήσαντες πάλιν ἀπέστησαν, διαφθειρόμενα τὰ ἤθη τῶν πολιτῶν θεωροῦντες. ἀλλὰ πάλιν μετεβάλοντο καθάπερ ἐν τοῖς ἄλλοις πᾶσι . . . τοῖς μὲν οὖν Λυκούργου χρωμένη νόμοις ἡ πόλις καὶ τοῖς ὅρκοις ἐμμείνασα ἐπρώτευε τῆς Ἑλλάδος εὐνομίᾳ καὶ δόξῃ χρόνον ἐτῶν πεντακοσίων· κατ' ὀλίγον δὲ παραβαινομένων καὶ πλεονεξίας καὶ φιλοπλουτίας παρεισδυομένης, καὶ τὰ τῆς δυνάμεως ἠλαττοῦτο· καὶ οἱ σύμμαχοι διὰ ταῦτα δυσμενῶς εἶχον πρὸς αὐτούς . . . · ἕως οὗ παντάπασιν ὑπεριδόντες τὴν Λυκούργου νομοθεσίαν ὑπὸ τῶν ἰδίων πολιτῶν ἐτυραννεύθησαν μηδὲν ἔτι σῴζοντες τῆς πατρῴου ἀγωγῆς, καὶ παραπλήσιοι τοῖς ἄλλοις γενόμενοι τὴν πρόσθεν εὔκλειαν καὶ παρρησίαν ἀπέθεντο καὶ εἰς δουλείαν μετέστησαν, καὶ νῦν ὑπὸ Ῥωμαίοις καθάπερ οἱ ἄλλοι Ἕλληνες ἐγέγοντο.

112. Tigerstedt, *Legend of Sparta*, 2:370 nn. 418, 419.

113. Nachstädt, Sieveking, and Titchener, *Moralia*, p. 215; Fuhrmann, *Plutarque: Oeuvres morales*, 3:346–47 n. 1.

114. Tigerstedt, *Legend of Sparta*, 2:91–92, attributes it to the source's carelessness. Gomme, *Historical Commentary*, p. 18 n. 1, suggested that Plutarch may have arranged *apophthegmata* in the order he wanted to use them in the *Lives*. This is an attractive suggestion but does not account for the manner in which the *Institutiones* are disordered.

115. Conveniently listed in Tigerstedt, *Legend of Sparta*, 2:90.

116. On Laconian *apophthegmata* in particular, see Tigerstedt, *Legend of Sparta*, 2:16–30.

117. *Inst. Lac.* 42 (240B), καὶ νῦν . . . ἐγένοντο was originally καὶ νῦν . . . εἰσιν. *Inst. Lac.* 13 (237E) violates the sequence of tenses in having a subjunctive (ἵν' ἐθίζωνται) depend on a verb in the imperfect tense (γλίσχρον ἦν). Although this is possible in certain vivid constructions, one is not called for here; cf. Kühner, Blass, and Gerth, *Ausführliche Grammatik*³, 2:553.3. The other mistake occurs in *Inst. Lac.* 14 (238A) where two nouns and a participle that belong in the accusative appear in the nominative: Nachstädt, Sieveking, and Titchener, *Moralia*, p. 208 app. crit., "*neglegenter excerpta*"; Fuhrmann, *Plutarque: Oeuvres morales*, 3:238 n. 2.

118. *Inst. Lac.* 3 (237A), 12 (237D–E), 25 (238F), 26 (239A), 28 (239A), 40 (239C–D).

119. Plut. *Lyc.* 17–21.

120. On this question, the prudent will echo the "*non liquet*" of Tigerstedt, *Legend of Sparta*, 2:233–45.

121. Boy and fox: Plut. *Lyc.* 18.1. Endurance contest: Plut. *Lyc.* 18.2.

122. On the use of different tenses, see Wheeldon, " 'True Stories,' " pp. 45–46.

123. Some examples of these uses: Plut. *Lyc.* 1.1–18 (a survey of scholarship on Lycurgus); 4.4 (oral tradition about Lycurgus' sojourn on Crete); 12.11 (a definition of the Laconian word κεκαδδίσθαι); 12.1 (on the Spartan word φιδί-τιον; cf. *IG* V.1 128; *SEG* XI [1954], nos. 598–601, for the word's survival into Roman times); 13.1, 4 (on the word ῥήτρα; cf. *IG* V.1 20); 22.6 (a comment on the beneficial effects of ritual and music on Spartan soldiers).

124. Plut. *Lyc.* 17.3–18.2.

125. E.g., Plut. *Lyc.* 16.10 (*Inst. Lac.* 4 [237A]); Plut. *Lyc.* 16.12 (*Inst. Lac.* 5 [237B]); Plut. *Lyc.* 16.13–14 (*Inst. Lac.* 6 [237B]); Plut. *Lyc.* 17.7 (*Inst. Lac.* 13 [237E–F]); 18.1 (*Apophth. Lac.* Anon. 35 [234A–B]); 21.1–2 (*Inst. Lac.* 14 [237F–38A]).

126. Plut. *Lyc.* 17.6 (*Inst. Lac.* 12 [237D–E]).

127. Plut. *Lyc.* 17.3.

128. εἰρήν: *IG* V.1 279 (*Artemis Orthia*, no. 31). μελλείρην: 296 (*Artemis Orthia*, no. 41).

129. Plut. *Ages.* 19.10–11.

130. Plut. *Lyc.* 16.1–2.

131. Pliny *Ep.* 10.65.3.

132. Cameron, "ΘΡΕΠΤΟΣ," pp. 27–62, esp. 48–54.

133. Battle at the Platanistas grove: Paus. 3.14.8–10. Endurance contest: Paus. 3.16.7–11.

134. Paus. 3.16.9–10.

135. Hyg. *Fab.* 261; Plut. *Arist.* 17.10. For an examination of these origin stories, see Chapter 4, at note 41.

136. For testimonia on the whipping contest, see Appendix 1.

137. Jones, *Culture and Society*, pp. 6–23.

138. On Lucian's intent in this dialogue, see Kindstrand, *Anacharsis*, pp. 65–67.

139. Lucian *Anach.* 38–39.

140. Lucian *Anach.* 39 (the ephebes are naked, with their hands raised).

141. Platanistas: Lucian *Anach.* 38; Paus. 3.14.8–10. Statues: Lucian *Anach.* 38. On the title *bōmonikēs* (altar victor), see Chapter 4, at note 38.

142. Philos. *VA* 6.20; *IG* V.1 290 (*Artemis Orthia*, no. 37). This alone vitiates Chrimes' attempt (*Ancient Sparta*, pp. 134–36) to Platonize the endurance contest. On Philostratus, see Bowersock, *Greek Sophists*, pp. 1–16.

143. E.g., Hesych. s.v. κατὰ πρωτείρας. Phot. s.v. πρωτεῖραι; συνέφηβος.

144. Collected in *IG* V.1 and *SEG* XI (1954), nos. 456–884. Ephebic victory dedications were also treated by Woodward, in Dawkins and others, *Artemis Orthia*, pp. 287–377. The lengthiest discussions are in "Excavations at Sparta. The Inscriptions," *ABSA* 12 (1905–6) through to *ABSA* 15 (1909) and *ABSA* 26 (1923–25) through to *ABSA* 30 (1929–30). The excavator's final remarks are contained in Woodward, "Afterthoughts," pp. 209–59. The absence of large-scale excavation until recently had slowed the flow of inscriptions to barely a

trickle. Happily, the renewed British excavations on the acropolis and the joint British-Dutch survey of Laconia will help reverse this trend; see French, "Archaeology 1989–90," p. 22, and "Archaeology 1990–91," p. 28.

145. Fifth century: *IG* V.1 213, 1120. Fourth century: *IG* V.1 255 (*Artemis Orthia*, no. 1).

146. On invented tradition, see Hobsbawm and Ranger, *Invention*. On its applicability to Roman Sparta, see Cartledge and Spawforth, *Hellenistic and Roman Sparta*, pp. 190 and 264 n. 1.

CHAPTER TWO

1. Sickle dedications: *IG* V.1 255–356 (*Artemis Orthia*, nos. 1–135). Sickle as prize: *IG* V.1 264 (*Artemis Orthia*, no. 4). Endurance contest: *IG* V.1 290 (*Artemis Orthia*, no. 37), 652, 653, 653A (*Artemis Orthia*, no. 142), 653B (*Artemis Orthia*, no. 143); *Artemis Orthia*, no. 144. *Sphaireis* inscriptions: *IG* V.1 674–88.

2. On age grades generally, see Gulliver, "Age Differentiation," pp. 157–62. On the term's use relative to the *agōgē*, see Cartledge, *Agesilaos*, p. 25.

3. Plut. *Lyc.* 17.3. See subsequent discussion, at note 35.

4. Λέξεις Ἡροδότου, s.v. εἰρήν, in Stein, *Herodoti historiae*, 2:465, παρὰ Λακεδαιμονίοις ἐν τῷ πρώτῳ ἐνιαυτῷ ὁ παῖς ῥωβίδας καλεῖται, τῷ δευτέρῳ προμικιζόμενος [ms. προκομιζόμενος], τῷ τρίτῳ μικιζόμενος, τῷ τετάρτῳ πρόπαις, τῷ πέμπτῳ παῖς, τῷ ἕκτῳ μελείρην, ἐφηβεύει δὲ παρ' αὐτοῖς ὁ παῖς ἀπὸ ἐτῶν δεκατεσσάρων μέχρι καὶ εἴκοσιν.

5. Diller, "New Source," p. 499, εἰρήν, μελλείρην, παρὰ Λακεδαιμονίοις ὁ μέλλων εἰρὴν ἔσεσθαι. ἐφηβεύει δὲ παρ' Λακεδαιμονίοις ἐπ' ἐτῶν ΙΔ' μέχρι Κ'. καλεῖται δὲ τῷ μὲν πρώτῳ ἐνιαυτῷ ῥωβίδας, τῷ δὲ δευτέρῳ προμικιζόμενος [ms. προκομιζόμενος], τῷ τρίτῳ μικιζόμενος, τῷ Δ' πρόπαις, τῷ Ε' παῖς, τῷ ϛ' μελλείρην, τῷ Ζ' εἰρήν.

6. Bingen, "ΤΡΙΕΤΙΡΗΣ," pp. 105–7. The references to *eirenes* in Herodotus and Xenophon are modern conjectures: see Chapter 1, at note 59.

7. Tazelaar, "ΠΑΙΔΕΣ ΚΑΙ ΕΦΗΒΟΙ," pp. 127–53. In the following pages I focus on Tazelaar's article because it so nicely represents the traditional synchronic approach in the highest degree and has had an acknowledged influence on later works. Three studies of recent years have accepted his conclusions: Hodkinson, "Social Order," pp. 245–51; Cartledge, *Agesilaos*, p. 25; Kukofka, "παιδίσκοι," pp. 197–205.

8. Tazelaar, "ΠΑΙΔΕΣ ΚΑΙ ΕΦΗΒΟΙ," pp. 149, 152–53, is emphatic that Spartans became *eirenes* on the very day marking their twentieth birthday.

9. Ibid., p. 149.

10. *IG* V.1 279 (*Artemis Orthia*, no. 31).

11. Tazelaar, "ΠΑΙΔΕΣ ΚΑΙ ΕΦΗΒΟΙ," pp. 140, 147–48.

12. X. *Lac.* 3.1, ὅταν γε μὴν ἐκ παίδων εἰς τὸ μειρακιοῦσθαι ἐκβαίνωσι.

13. Hippocr. *Hebd.* 8.636 (Littré). For a discussion of the meanings of μειράκιον, see Roesch, *Études béotiennes*, pp. 320–21.

14. Plut. *Lyc.* 16.12, γενόμενοι δὲ δωδεκαετεῖς, ἄνευ χιτῶνος ἤδη διετέλουν, ἐν ἱμάτιον εἰς τὸν ἐνιαυτὸν λαμβάνοντες.

15. The phrase γενόμενοι δωδεκαετεῖς appears by itself, out of context, as one of the "most important indications as to age" in Tazelaar, "ΠΑΙΔΕΣ ΚΑΙ ΕΦΗ-ΒΟΙ," pp. 127–28.

16. Tazelaar, "ΠΑΙΔΕΣ ΚΑΙ ΕΦΗΒΟΙ," p. 147: "It remains to be seen, however, if elsewhere in Greece fourteen-year-old boys and older ones were no longer superintended, which would be the case according to Xenophon. Moreover, no change at all takes place in the training of the Spartan boys at that age: this change took place two years earlier, as I have expounded before."

17. Cobet, *Novae lectiones*, p. 728.

18. [Plut.] *De lib. ed.* 16 (12A), πολλάκις γὰρ κατεμεμψάμην τοὺς μοχθηρῶν ἐθῶν γεγονότας εἰσηγητάς, οἵτινες τοῖς μὲν παισὶ παιδαγωγοὺς καὶ διδασκάλους ἐπέστησαν, τὴν δὲ τῶν μειρακίων ὁρμὴν ἄφετον εἴασαν νέμεσθαι, δέον αὖ τοὐναντίον πλείω ποιεῖσθαι τούτων εὐλάβειαν καὶ φυλακὴν ἢ τῶν παίδων: see Pl. *La.* 2.179D.

19. Plut. *Lyc.* 16.11.

20. See Chapter 1, at note 108.

21. *Inst. Lac.* 5 (237B).

22. Plut. *Lyc.* 16.12.

23. E.g., *Ins. Priene*, no. 112, lines 57–59, [συ]λλογισάμενος δὲ τὸ πρὸς ὥραν [τεθ]ησόμενον / [ἄ]λειμμα τῆς τε ἰδίας οὐκ ἄξιον ἔσεσ[θ]αι κρίσεως / καὶ πολλοὺς διακλείσειν τῆς φιλανθρωπίας; no. 113, lines 54–56, πρὸς τὴν τοῦ ἀκρατίσ/ματος φιλανθρωπίαν τὴ[ν π]ρώτην τ[ῆς ἀρχῆς ἡμέρ]αν κοινοποιησάμενος; *SEG* XIII (1956), no. 258 (Gytheum), lines 38–39, βουλόμαι δὲ καὶ τοὺς δούλους τῆς τοῦ [ἀλείμματος φι/λανθρωπ]ίας μετέχει⟨ν⟩.

24. As discussed in Chapter 1, at note 93.

25. X. *Lac.* 2.4, καὶ ἀντί γε τοῦ ἱματίοις διαθρύπτεσθαι ἐνόμισεν ἑνὶ ἱματίῳ δι' ἔτους προσεθίζεσθαι.

26. E.g., X. *Lac.* 1.3–4 (the rearing of girls), 1.5–6 (marriage customs), 2.1–2 (slaves or free men as instructors, children with or without shoes).

27. X. *Lac.* 2.1, σώματα δὲ ἱματίων μεταβολαῖς διαθρύπτουσι.

28. For instance, a ἱμάτιον χείμαστρον was a thicker version worn in the winter, according to Pollux 7.61: see Amelung, " Ἱμάτιον."

29. A possible reason may be found in the association between Sparta and philosophers, since a *himation* without a *chitōn* was considered virtually the philosophers' uniform; D. Chr. *Or.* 72.2; Bremmer, "Symbols of Marginality," pp. 206–7. There is, admittedly, a slim possibility that ephebes in the *agōgē* resurrected by the Stoic philosopher Sphaerus were required to wear quasi-philosophical attire; on Stoicism and the Hellenistic *agōgē*, see Chapter 5.

30. X. *Lac.* 2.4–8, 12–14; *Inst. Lac.* 5 (237B), 7 (237B–C).

31. For Plutarch's consultation of Xenophon, cf. X. *Lac.* 2.8 and Plut. *Lyc.* 1.5.

32. Puberty: Hesych. ἄνηβος; schol. to Theocr. 8.3. Pederasty: *Anth. Pal.* (Strato) 12.4; Buffière, *Éros adolescent*, pp. 609–11. Athletics: Paus. 6.2.10;

Klee, *Zur Geschichte der gymnischen Agone*, pp. 48–56; Ebert, "ΠΑΙΔΕΣ ΠΥΘΙ-ΚΟΙ," pp. 152–56.

33. Delvaux, "Retour aux sources," pp. 27–48, esp. 40; Pelling, "Truth and Fiction," pp. 19–52, esp. 35–43.

34. Hodkinson, "Social Order," pp. 249–51, follows Tazelaar in accepting Cobet's emendation and suggests that the Spartan term for those just entering adulthood was παιδίσκοι. On this term, see Chapter 6, at note 3.

Cobet, *Novae lectiones*, p. 728, rejected the passage εἰς τὸ μειρακιοῦσθαι because the word μειρακιοῦσθαι "*non est probae et antiquae notae vocabulum*" and because ἐκβαίνειν did not fit well with the preposition εἰς. Although the first word does only appear in late writers such as Philo (1.531) and Aelian (*VH* 12.1), Xenophon's own words in the *Cyropaedia* (1.2.8) refute the second objection: ⟨οἱ παῖδες⟩ ἐκ τούτου δὲ εἰς τοὺς ἐφήβους ἐξέρχονται.

35. Plut. *Lyc.* 17.3.

36. Tazelaar, "ΠΑΙΔΕΣ ΚΑΙ ΕΦΗΒΟΙ," pp. 128–29.

37. Plut. *Lac.* 17.4, οὗτος οὖν ὁ εἰρήν, εἴκοσιν ἔτη γεγονώς.

38. Plut. *Lyc.* 17.3; Tazelaar, "ΠΑΙΔΕΣ ΚΑΙ ΕΦΗΒΟΙ," p. 140.

39. Tazelaar, "ΠΑΙΔΕΣ ΚΑΙ ΕΦΗΒΟΙ," p. 137.

40. E.g., *Plutarch's Lives* (tr. Perrin), 1.B:259, "those who had been for two years out of the class of boys." The "class of children" is an age category used in athletic festivals: see Chapter 3, at note 91. Cf. Tazelaar, "ΠΑΙΔΕΣ ΚΑΙ ΕΦΗΒΟΙ," p. 137.

41. Teles (Hense[2]) p. 50, ἐξ ἐφήβων ἐστί; Lucian *JTr.* 26, πρόπαλαι μὲν ἐξ ἐφήβων γεγόνως; Pollux 1.59, ἐπὶ διέτες δὲ ἡβάσκων ὁ ἐξ ἐφήβων δύο ἔτη; Philostr. *Her.* 147.9, ὅτ' ἀνὴρ ἐκ παίδων ἔνικα πάλην; *IG* II/III[2] 956, line 64, [τῆι λαμπά]δι τοὺς ἐφήβους οἱ ἐξ ἐφήβων; *IG* VII 212 (Aegosthena), [τ]οίδε ἐξ ἐφήβων; cf. *IG* VII 215–18, 220, 222; *IG* XII.3 330 (Thera), line 138, γενομένος ἐκ τῶν ἐφήβων.

42. Pollux 1.57.

43. Plutarch's usage conforms exactly to the principles noted by Smyth, *Greek Grammar*, 1585, who says that the accusative is used with an ordinal number to mark how much time has elapsed since something happened. In this construction, the calculation includes the current day or year; cf. Kühner, Blass, and Gerth, *Ausführliche Grammatik*[3], 2.1:314–15. This is not noticed by MacDowell, *Spartan Law*, p. 162: "There seems to be no parallel for this form of expression."

44. Misconstruing this passage, Tazelaar ("ΠΑΙΔΕΣ ΚΑΙ ΕΦΗΒΟΙ," pp. 138, 148) regards the supposed hiatus between the *melleiren* and *eirēn* grades as caused by the conflict between years reckoned as divisions of calendrical time and years as calculated from a fixed date within the calendar year. Underlying this is an assumption that the end of the *melleironeia* did not coincide with the end of the Spartan civic year. Some cities did not coordinate their educational and civic years: e.g., Hellenistic Miletus (Ziebarth, *Schulwesen*, pp. 16–17), Beroea (*SEG* XXVII [1977], no. 261A, lines 34–35: see Sontheimer, "Peritios"), and Roman Athens (Pélékidis, *Histoire de l'éphébie*, p. 217 n. 1; on the pre-Hadrianic period, see Graindor, *Chronologie des archontes athéniens*, pp. 15–16). But at other places the two sorts of year ran concurrently; e.g., Sestos (*ISestos*, no. 1, line 1

and p. 43); Iasos (*IIasos* I, no. 99, line 3); and Teos (*SIG*³, no. 578, lines 8–10). Evidence indicates that officials in charge of the contests of the *agōgē* entered and left office on the same dates as other civic magistrates: e.g., *SEG* XI (1954), nos. 605, 609, 611, all lists of *biduoi* dated by eponymous magistrate, the *patronomos*, whose main duties were to preside over the various agogic ceremonies: see subsequent discussion, at note 96.

45. Tazelaar, "ΠΑΙΔΕΣ ΚΑΙ ΕΦΗΒΟΙ," p. 148; followed implicitly by Hodkinson, "Social Order," p. 242.

46. In dismissing attempts to establish continuity between the two age grades, Tazelaar, "ΠΑΙΔΕΣ ΚΑΙ ΕΦΗΒΟΙ," p. 137, says, "If, however, this continuity is taken for granted . . . , the indication of length of time especially added is not acknowledged adequately, for without the words δεύτερον ἤδη ἔτος Plutarch might have said as clearly that a boy becomes an *eiren* as soon as he ceases to be a *melleiren*." Plutarch made precisely this point, but has been misunderstood by modern scholars, e.g., Kukofka, "παιδίσκοι," p. 197.

47. See the discussion in Tazelaar, "ΠΑΙΔΕΣ ΚΑΙ ΕΦΗΒΟΙ," pp. 128–34.

48. For an example of the word's ambiguity and the confusion it may cause, see Bowersock, "Zur Geschichte," p. 283.

49. Pl. *Lg.* 4.721B, ἐπειδὰν ἐτῶν ᾖ τις τριάκοντα, μέχρι ἐτῶν πέντε καὶ τριάκοντα.

50. Pl. *Lg.* 4.721D, μηδὲ γαμῶν ἔτη τριάκοντα γεγονὼς καὶ πέντε.

51. Pl. *Lg.* 8.833D, ταῖς δὲ τριακαιδεκέτεσι μέχρι γάμου.

52. Pl. *Lg.* 6.771C, ἡμεῖς δὲ οὖν νῦν φαμεν ὀρθότατα προῃρῆσθαι τὸν τῶν πεντακισχιλίων καὶ τετταράκοντα ἀριθμόν, ὃς πάσας τὰς διανομὰς ἔχει μέχρι τῶν δώδεκα ἀπὸ μιᾶς ἀρξάμενος πλὴν ἐνδεκάδος. If Plato had used μέχρι exclusively, he would have been claiming that the highest number by which 5,040 was divisible was 10: see Pl. *Lg.* 5.738A.

53. Pl. *Lg.* 7.793E, τριετεῖ δὲ δὴ καὶ τετραετεῖ καὶ πενταετεῖ ἔτι ἑξετεῖ ἤθει ψυχῆς παιδιῶν δέον ἂν εἴη; 7.794A, ἀπὸ τριετοῦς μέχρι τῶν ἓξ ἐτῶν; 7.794C, μέτα δὲ τὸν ἑξέτη καὶ τὴν ἑξέτιν.

54. Arist. *Pol.* 7.133B; [Pl.] *Ax.* 366D; Marrou, *Histoire de l'éducation*, p. 16. In the real world, however, this applied only to boys.

55. See Stalley, *Introduction to Plato's Laws*, p. 132; Morrow, *Plato's Cretan City*, p. 329; Piérart, *Platon et la cité*, p. 363.

56. Tazelaar, "ΠΑΙΔΕΣ ΚΑΙ ΕΦΗΒΟΙ," p. 129 and n. 5. Plato's usage here conforms to Tazelaar's principles for expressing age: e.g., Pl. *Lg.* 7.793E, τὴν [τοῦ] τριετῆ γεγονότος ἡλικίαν.

57. While not completely novel, this scheme does accord with all the relevant evidence. Some earlier studies of this question: Marrou, "Les classes d'âge"; Billheimer, "Age-Classes"; Michell, *Sparta*, pp. 165–203; den Boer, *Laconian Studies*, pp. 233–38; MacDowell, *Spartan Law*, pp. 159–67. Largely outdated: Gilbert, *Staatsalterthümer*, 1:69–71; Nilsson, "Die Grundlagen des spartanischen Lebens."

58. Cf. the treatment of age grades in Cartledge and Spawforth, *Hellenistic and Roman Sparta*, p. 203.

59. Hesych. s.v. βουᾶ· ἀγέλη παίδων, Λάκωνες.

60. Hesych. s.v. βουαγόρ· ἀγελάρχης, ὁ τῆς ἀγέλης ἄρχων; e.g., *IG* V.1 223 (*Artemis Orthia*, no. 33); 288 (*Artemis Orthia*, no. 45); 294 (*Artemis Orthia*, no. 52); 306 (*Artemis Orthia*, no. 59).

61. Cartledge and Spawforth, *Hellenistic and Roman Sparta*, pp. 203–4.

62. The post of *bouagos* was probably instituted as part of the Hellenistic *agōgē*, on which see Chapter 5. On the evocation of the past in the later *agōgē*, see Chapter 4.

63. Chrimes, *Ancient Sparta*, pp. 131–33; Woodward, "Some Notes," pp. 191–99.

64. Lucian *Anach.* 38.

65. Woodward, in Dawkins and others, *Artemis Orthia*, pp. 285–86; *IG* V.1 674–88.

66. Paus. 3.14.6, ᾧ θύουσιν οἱ σφαιρεῖς· οἱ δέ εἰσιν ⟨οἱ⟩ ἐκ τῶν ἐφήβων ἐς ἄνδρας ἀρχόμενοι συντελεῖν. On the meaning of συντελεῖν, see Isoc. 12.212.

67. On ἐκ τῶν ἐφήβων, see previous discussion, at note 41; Forbes, *NEOI*, pp. 18, 59–60.

68. Paus. 3.11.2.

69. Lucian *Anach.* 38.

70. The *sphaireis* inscriptions' dating formula proves the game was only held once a year: e.g., *IG* V.1 676; cf. *SEG* XI (1954), no. 493, lines 2–3.

71. Ziebarth, *Schulwesen*, pp. 18–19; Marrou, *Histoire de l'éducation*, pp. 226–27; Nilsson, *Die hellenistische Schule*, pp. 47–48. For an example of a list of victors in an ἀπόδειξις, see Keil, "Das Unterrichtswesen," p. 332.

72. νικάσαντες τὰς ὠβάς; e.g., *IG* V.1 674, 675.

73. Limnaeis: *IG* V.1 676, 682, 686. Cynooureis: *IG* V.1 681, 684. Pitanatae: *IG* V.1 675, 685. Neopolitae: *IG* V.1 [677], 683. Mesoatae: Paus. 3.16.9.

On the ancient *ōbai*, see Ehrenberg, "Spartiaten und Lakedaimonier," pp. 28–29; "Obai," 1696. The *ōba* of the Neopolitae is usually thought to have been created by Cleomenes III to hold his newly enfranchised citizens: e.g., Busolt and Swoboda, *Griechische Staatskunde*, 2:645 n. 3. But see Appendix 2.

74. E.g., Jones, *Public Organization*, pp. 119, 121.

75. *IG* V.1 480 (a gymnasiarch is honored ἀπὸ φυλῆς Κονοουρέων), 566 (honors for a σφαιρέα Κονοουρέα), 663 (a dedication by a Λακεδαιμόν[ι]ος Πιτανάτης, victor in the youths' wrestling): see *SEG* XI (1954), no. 493.

76. *IG* V.1 32A, 32B; *SEG* XI (1954), no. 493. On the *diabetēs*, see subsequent discussion, at note 115.

77. Chrimes, *Ancient Sparta*, pp. 163–68.

78. *IG* V.1 26, a late Hellenistic decree from the *ōba* of the Amyclaeans, is a different case: see Appendix 2. The mutilated lost inscription, *IG* V.1 688, contains a variation on the *sphaireis* victory formula — [τὰν] ὠβᾶν ἔνικα — for which reason Kolbe correctly classed it with the other *sphaireis* dedications. I believe it commemorates a victory in a lesser intraobal version of the ball tournament.

79. Paus. 3.16.9.

80. See Chapter 4, at note 68.

81. X. *Lac.* 2.10.

82. *IG* V.1 286 (*Artemis Orthia*, no. 46).

83. *Bouagoi* coeval with *sunephēboi*: Marrou, *Histoire de l'éducation*, p. 54; Woodward, review of Chrimes, *Ancient Sparta*, p. 618. Older: Kahrstedt, *Griechisches Staatsrecht*, 1:343; Chrimes, *Ancient Sparta*, p. 96; Brelich, *Paides*, p. 115 n. 8; Calame, *Les choeurs des jeunes filles*, p. 375.

84. Cartledge and Spawforth, *Hellenistic and Roman Sparta*, p. 204; Spawforth, "Sparta and the Family of Herodes Atticus," p. 209.

85. Plut. *Lyc.* 17.4, οὗτος οὖν ὁ εἰρήν, εἴκοσιν ἔτη γεγονώς, ἄρχει τε τῶν ὑποτεταγμένων ἐν ταῖς μάχαις καὶ κατ' οἶκον ὑπηρέταις χρῆται πρὸς τὸ δεῖπνον. ἐπιτάσσει δὲ τοῖς μὲν ἄδροις ξύλα φέρειν, τοῖς δὲ μικροτέροις λάχανα.

86. Paus. 3.16.11.

87. ἄδρος clearly signifies "big" in this passage (see *Thes. Gr. Ling.* I s.v. ἄδρος), but its root meaning of "full-grown, ripe" also comes into play.

88. On Plutarch's statement in the previous paragraph, to the effect that the members of each *agelē* "used to appoint" (προΐσταντο) the best *eirēn* as their leader (*Lyc.* 17.2), see Chapter 5, at note 66. On the *paidonomoi*, see Chapter 6, at note 27.

89. Base: *IG* V.1 564, Μᾶρ(κον) Αὐρ(ήλιον) Δάμαρχον/ Παρδαλᾶ, πρέσβυν/ τῆς Λιμναέων φυ/λῆς, ἀνδρείας χάριν. *Sphaireis*: e.g., *IG* V.1 676, σφαιρεῖς Λιμναέων οἱ νικ[ά]/σαντες τάς ὠ[βά]ς, ὧν πρέ[σ(βυς)]/ Ἐπάγαθος Σωκράτους. Courage (ἀνδρεία) was a virtue characteristic of Spartan ephebes, e.g., *IG* V.1 566, 652, 653: see Chapter 5, at note 99.

90. See *IG* V.1 686, where a *presbus* of the *sphaireis* was also a *bouagos*.

91. *IG* V.1 653A.

92. *IG* V.1 653A, 653B; *SEG* XI (1954), no. 536, βουαγὸς καὶ συνέφηβοι at the bottom of the catalog.

93. Oliver, "Athenian Lists of Ephebic Teams," pp. 66–74; Cartledge and Spawforth, *Hellenistic and Roman Sparta*, p. 204.

94. Cartledge and Spawforth, *Hellenistic and Roman Sparta*, p. 167.

95. X. *Cyr.* 1.2.15.

96. On the composition of this magistracy, see Kennell, "Spartan Patronomate."

97. διά τε τὴν περὶ τὰ Λυκούργεια ἔθη προστασίαν, e.g.: *IG* V.1 543, 544. Λυκούργεια ἔθη: *IG* V.1 500, 527, 554, 569; *SEG* XI (1954), no. 791: see Plut. *Pyrrh.* 26.21.

98. The gymnasiarchy and patronomate are the only Spartan offices known to have been held simultaneously: *IG* V.1 481, 535, 539; *SEG* XI (1954), no. 803. Elsewhere, the gymnasiarchy was often held in conjunction with another office: Öhler, "Γυμνασίαρχος," 1994.

99. Robert, *Études anatoliennes*, p. 38; *Documents de l'Asie Mineure*, p. 83 n. 7: see *IG* V.1 20, lines 5–6.

100. *IG* V.1 560, τῆς τε κατὰ τὴν γυμνασιαρχίαν λαμ/πρ[ότ]ητος καὶ τῆς τῶν Λυκουργείων [ἐ]θῶν προστασίας . . . ἕνεκεν; 505, γυνασιαρχοῦντα ἀξίως

τῆς πόλεως εὐνοίας/ χάριν·/ οἱ συνάρχοντες τῆς πατρονομίας/ προσεδέξαντο τὸ ἀνάλωμα.

101. Substitute *patronomoi* (πατρονομοῦντες ὑπὲρ τὸν δεῖνα): *IG* V.1 275 (*Artemis Orthia*, no. 30), 280 (*Artemis Orthia*, no. 29), 291 (*Artemis Orthia*, no. 47), 295 (*Artemis Orthia*, no. 48); *SEG* XI (1954), no. 631 (agogic), 542 (non-agogic). *Epimelētai*: *IG* V.1 311, 312, 542, 683 (agogic/gymnastic), 541 (non-agogic). On this type of *epimelētēs*, see Robert, "Recherches épigraphiques," pp. 294–96 (*OMS*, 2:810–12).

102. Agogic texts: *IG* V.1 311 (*Artemis Orthia*, no. 66), [ἐπὶ πα]τρονόμω σεῶ Λυκούργω/ [τὸ δ'], ἐπιμελωμένω τᾶρ πατρον-/[ομίαρ] Π(οπλίω) Μεμ(μίω) Πρα-τολά[ω]: see *IG* V.1 312 (*Artemis Orthia*, no. 68), 541, 542, 683; Kourinou-Pikoulas, "Ἐπιγραφές," pp. 96–97, no. 5. Nonagogic texts: *IG* V.1 130 (*SEG* XXXIV [1984], no. 311) [ἄρξας τὴν τῶν ἀγορα]/νόμων ἀρχήν· ο[ἱ ἐπὶ πατρο-νό]/μου θεοῦ Λυκούρ[γου τὸ . σύναρ]/χοι; *IG* V.1 45; *SEG* XI (1954), no. 496. The same is true of inscriptions from the year of Timomenes: his substitute appears in *IG* V.1 295 (*Artemis Orthia*, no. 48), a sickle dedication, but not in a list of *gerontes*, *IG* V.1 109 (*SEG* XI [1954], no. 588).

103. Only one substitute *patronomos* is known to have appeared in a non-agogic text, P. Memmius Sidectas, mentioned as the stand-in for L. Volusenus Aristocrates in a list of *nomophulakes* (*SEG* XI [1954], no. 542). He appears in the dating formula above a list of *biduoi* for that year, but not in a catalog of *gerontes* (*SEG* XI [1954], nos. 569, 631).

104. *IG* V.1 18B, lines 3–4, εἰ δέ τις ἀντιλέγοι τῶν ζημιωθέντων, κρινοῦσιν ὀμόσαντε[ς ἐν/ ἱερ]ῷ οἱ πεπατρονομηκότες. On the Leonidea, see Cartledge and Spawforth, *Hellenistic and Roman Sparta*, pp. 192–93.

105. *IG* V.1 137. The first (incomplete) list lacks a heading but the number of secretaries attached to it is consistent with the patronomate rather than with the Gerousia: see Kennell, "Public Institutions," p. 97; Cartledge and Spawforth, *Hellenistic and Roman Sparta*, pp. 201–2; *pace* Bradford, *Prosopography*, s.v. Apollonidas (2).

106. Paus. 3.11.2.

107. See Cartledge and Spawforth, *Hellenistic and Roman Sparta*, p. 202, where the patronomate's liturgical character is stressed.

108. Collignon, *Quid de collegiis*, p. 43; Forbes, *Physical Education*, p. 207.

109. *IG* V.1 136–40, 556; *SEG* XI (1954), nos. 605–11, 617 [631?]. One list of *biduoi* contains only five names (*SEG* XI [1954] no. 611). However, from the arrangement of names on the stone it seems that the last name was simply omitted either deliberately or by accident, for the fourth and fifth names are inscribed on the same line, leaving sufficient space on the block for one more name.

110. See Cartledge and Spawforth, *Hellenistic and Roman Sparta*, pp. 201 (*biduoi*), 144–46 (*sunarchia*); Kennell, "Synarchia."

111. *SEG* XI (1954), no. 610.

112. *IG* V.1 137. On the *boulē*, see Kennell, "*IG* V 1,16."

113. *SEG* XI (1954), no. 610, βίδυοι ἐπ[ὶ ----], /ἐφ' ὧν παντ.....γει..... ο----/βησαν Διονυσίδες δεκαδύο; Paus. 3.13.7.

114. Cartledge and Spawforth, *Hellenistic and Roman Sparta*, pp. 205–6, where other evidence for girls' contests is considered. Scanlon, "*Virgineum gymnasium,*" pp. 185–216, goes far beyond what the evidence can support.

115. *Diabetai* appear as the last element in the dating formula of *sphaireis* dedications. Forbes, *Physical Education*, p. 39, rendered διαβέτης as "annual officer," evidently associating it with ἔτος. Tod and Wace, *Catalogue*, p. 15, on the other hand, thought it was connected with ἔτης, "clansman," which is probably correct.

116. διαβέτης αὐτεπάγγελτος: IG V.1 677, 679, 680, [687]; Szanto, "Διαβέτης." On volunteering for liturgies, see Jones, *Greek City*, p. 184.

117. *IG* V.1 32B, lines 3–7, καὶ ὑπὲρ/ τὸν [ὑ]ὸν Δαμονεί/κη διαβέτης Λι/-μναέων. The phenomenon was not unknown elsewhere: e.g., *IGR* III 648, lines 10–15; Balland, *Xanthos*, 2:232–33; Robert and Robert, *La Carie*, 2:110–11; cf. Lib. *Or.* 14.6.

118. *SEG* XI (1954), no. 493, lines 2–3, [δια]βέτης ἐπὶ Ἑρμογένους, ἐφ' οὗ/ ἐνίκησαν Κονοουρεῖς δι' ἐτῶν τεσ⟨σ⟩εράκοντα. On the interpretation of this last phrase, see Woodward, "Excavations at Sparta, 1924–1925. 3 – The Inscriptions," p. 181.

119. Teachers: *IG* V.1 500, [οἱ διδ]άσκαλοι ἀμ[φὶ τὰ/ Λυκούργει]α ἔθη; 542, [οἱ ἐ]πὶ τὰ ἔ[θη]. Drill instructors: *IG* V.1 542; Lucian *Salt.* 10. Trainers: *IG* V.1 542, 543, 569. On *hoplomachoi*, see Grasberger, *Erziehung und Unterricht*, 3:139; Wheeler, "*Hoplomachoi,*" pp. 1–20.

120. On athletics in Greek education, see Nilsson, *Die hellenistische Schule*, p. 43. On Sparta's curriculum, see Cartledge and Spawforth, *Hellenistic and Roman Sparta*, pp. 204–5.

121. Cartledge and Spawforth, *Hellenistic and Roman Sparta*, pp. 176–84.

122. Delorme, *Gymnasion*, pp. 421–80.

123. Paus. 3.14.2–14; cf. *IG* V.1 20A, line 3; *SEG* XI (1954), no. 492, lines 10–12.

124. Forbes, *NEOI*, pp. 1–20.

125. *IG* V.1 159, lines 33–43; Forbes, *NEOI*, pp. 61–62.

126. Gauthier and Hatzopoulos, *La loi gymnasiarchique*, pp. 51–52, adduce evidence for thirty years old as a common upper limit for *neoi*. Forbes, *NEOI*, p. 2, on the other hand, held there was no upper limit.

127. *IG* V.1 32A, 33, 34 (*SEG* XI [1954], no. 486), 247, 479, 541, 568; *SEG* XI (1954), nos. 492, 783; Hesych. s.v. ἵππαρχος· ὁ τῶν νεῶν ἐπιμελητὴς παρὰ Λάκωσιν. Cartledge and Spawforth, *Hellenistic and Roman Sparta*, pp. 211–12, assign the hipparch to the *agōgē*.

128. *IG* V.1 479, 541.

129. E.g., *IGR* IV 915 (Cibyra), lines 5–7, ἐχαρίσατο δὲ τῇ πόλει καὶ εἰς τὴν μετὰ ταῦτα γυμνασι/αρχίαν τὴν αἰώνιον μυριάδας δραχμῶν Ῥοδίων τεσ/σαράκοντα, ὡς γυμνασιαρχεῖσθαι ἐκ τῶν τόκων; Robert, "Recherches épigraphiques," pp. 294–95 (*OMS*, 2:810–11); Jones, *Greek City*, pp. 226, 353 n. 30.

130. Forbes, *NEOI*, pp. 21–33. Processions: *SIG*³ 589 (Magnesia), line 38; *SEG* XI (1954), no. 923 (Gytheum).

131. *IG* V.1 37 (*bis*) (*SEG* XI [1954], no. 481), 44 (*SEG* XI [1954], no. 486).

132. Thuc. 5.66.3; X. *Lac.* 11.4.

133. Herodian 4.8.3; Cartledge and Spawforth, *Hellenistic and Roman Sparta*, pp. 118–19. On *neoi* in imperial campaigns, see Jones, "Levy at Thespiae," pp. 45–48; *SEG* XXXIX (1989), no. 456.

CHAPTER THREE

1. Foreign visitors are attested as early as the Classical period: Hdt. 6.67.3; X. *Mem.* 1.2.61; Cic. *Tusc.* 2.14.34; Plut. *Cim.* 10.6; *Ages.* 29.3; *De tranq.* 20 (477C); Lucian *Anach.* 38; Philos. *VA* 20.

2. For an example of this, see the notice of a Hellenistic ephebic law from Amphipolis in Lazarides, " Ἀνασκαφές," p. 37 no. 13.

3. See Chapter 1, at note 100.

4. Dawkins, in Dawkins and others, *Artemis Orthia*, p. 34; Grunauer-von Hoerschelmann, *Münzprägung*, pp. 14–16.

5. On the sanctuary's history, see Dawkins, in Dawkins and others, *Artemis Orthia*, pp. 1–51.

6. μῶα, κελοῖα, and καθθηρατόριον: *Artemis Orthia*, pp. 285–353, nos. 1–135. κυναγέτας: *Artemis Orthia*, nos. 11, 16, 18, 84. εὐβάλκης: *Artemis Orthia*, nos. 16, 18, 84. δέρος: *Artemis Orthia*, no. 16.

7. The contests are usually grouped together as the παιδικὸς ἄγων, a modern name coined in 1904 by Tod, "Παιδικὸς Ἄγων," pp. 50–56. In the publication of inscriptions from the first season's excavation, they were called, correctly, "the boys' contests": Tillyard, "Artemisium," pp. 353–55.

8. Ar. *Lys.* 1297, μῶά μόλε μόλε Λάκαινα; Hesych. s.v. μῶά· ὠδὴ ποιά: see Woodward, in Dawkins and others, *Artemis Orthia*, p. 288.

9. *Artemis Orthia*, no. 4, εὔστομον εὐτροχάλου/ γλώσσης τόδ' ἄεθλον ἀείρας.

10. Chantraine, *Dictionnaire*, 2:511, s.v. κελοῖα, pessimistically states, "ni le sens exact ni l'étymologie ne sont connus."

11. E.g., κελεύω, κέλομαι, κέλαδος, κελαδέω, κελαρύζω. Pokorny, *Wörterbuch*, 1:548, s.v. 6 *kel-*.

12. E.g., κέλομαι, κέλης, κελήτιον; Lat. *celer* is cognate. Chantraine, *Dictionnaire*, 2:513, s.v. κέλλω; Pokorny, *Wörterbuch*, 1:548, s.v. 5 *kel-*.

13. It is well recognized that ὅμαδος/ὁμαδέω and κέλαδος/κελαδέω are analogous formations: Buck and Peterson, *Reverse Index*, p. 436; Chantraine, *Dictionnaire*, 2:511, s.v. κέλαδος; p. 796, s.v. ὅμαδος; pp. 799–800, s.v. ὅμος.

If *keloia* is an adjective, it would support the restoration [τὰ κελ]οῖα κρατή-σα[ς] for *Artemis Orthia*, no. 8.

14. Schol. to Hom. *Il.* 16.183 (Erbse), κελαδεινῆς δὲ διὰ τὰς ἐν ταῖς θήραις ἐκβοήσεις; *An. Bachm.* 1:275, κελαδεινή· κυνηγός. θόρυβον κατὰ τὰς ἄγρας ποι-οῦσα.

15. X. *Cyn.* 6.20, ἐὰν μὲν ἐν τῷ ἴχνει ὦσι, προσστάντα ἐγκελεύειν, τοὔνομα μεταβάλλοντα ἑκάστης τῆς κυνός, ὁπασαχῇ οἷόν τ' ἂν ᾖ τοὺς τόνους τῆς φωνῆς ποιούμενον, ὀξύ, βαρύ, μικρόν, μέγα.

16. Liban. *Or.* 200.23.

17. See also Woodward, in Dawkins and others, *Artemis Orthia,* p. 288; Chrimes, *Ancient Sparta,* p. 120.

18. Although it is tempting to see a connection with κελοῖα and the καλα-οίδια/καλαβοίδια, hymns in honor of Artemis Dereatis (Hesych. s.v.), they cannot be etymologically related.

19. Baunack, "κασσηρατόριν," p. 295; Woodward, in Dawkins and others, *Artemis Orthia,* p. 288; Chrimes, *Ancient Sparta,* p. 124; Chantraine, *Études,* pp. 73–74 n. 2.

20. Hom. *Il.* 9.544, πολλέων ἐκ πολίων θηρήτορας ἄνδρας ἀγείρας. The word occurs only here.

21. Buck and Peterson, *Reverse Index,* p. 46. On κατα-/καθ- see Buck, *Greek Dialects,* pp. 81–82.

22. Woodward, in Dawkins and others, *Artemis Orthia,* pp. 288–89; *pace* Chrimes, *Ancient Sparta,* pp. 126–27.

23. See Cartledge and Spawforth, *Hellenistic and Roman Sparta,* pp. 190–211.

24. Pleket, "*Collegium iuvenum,*" pp. 291–94. Hunting traditionally had the imprimatur of Lycurgus: X. *Lac.* 4.7; David, "Hunting."

25. Chrimes, *Ancient Sparta,* pp. 126–27. Woodward, in Dawkins and others, *Artemis Orthia,* p. 289, argued for the identification of the εὐβάλκης with the endurance contest. For the names of various dances, see Poll. 4.99–106.

26. *Artemis Orthia,* nos. 2, 10.

27. Bourguet, *Le dialecte laconien,* p. 48.

28. Chantraine, *Études,* pp. 92–95.

29. *Artemis Orthia,* no. 1, from the fifth century B.C., does not mention the name of any contest. On contests dating from the Roman phase, see Cartledge and Spawforth, *Hellenistic and Roman Sparta,* pp. 204–5.

30. Cartledge and Spawforth, *Hellenistic and Roman Sparta,* p. 205. On the festival of Artemis associated with the endurance contest, see Chapter 4, at note 32. There is no reason to think that this festival had anything to do with the boys' contests.

31. Multiple victories: *Artemis Orthia,* nos. 11, 16, 52, 55, 57, 67–70, 85, 91, 107, 108. The order is reversed in *Artemis Orthia,* no. 70, a text comprising two noncontiguous pairs of fragments.

32. *Bouagoi* as dedicants: *Artemis Orthia,* nos. 33, 36, [42], 45–46, 49–54, [58], 59–61, 64, 67–68, 71–72, [73], 74–75, [85], 88, [99].

33. For a discussion of this earlier view, see Woodward, in Dawkins and others, *Artemis Orthia,* p. 287.

34. *Artemis Orthia,* nos. 44, 45. Aristocrates was *sunephēbos* of Eurycles; on this term, see Chapter 2, at note 84.

35. Contest only: *Artemis Orthia,* nos. 2, 6–8, 25A and B, 41, 46, 50, 53, 55, 57, 59, 60–62, 65, 67–71, [85], [87], 91, 94, 107, 108. Contest and age grade: *Artemis Orthia,* nos. 31 (πρατοπαμπαίδων, ἀτροπαμπαίδων, εἰρένων), 44 (μικιχι-ζομένων), [49?] (μικιχιζομένων), [63?] (μικιχιζομένων), 87 (πρατοπαμπαίδων).

Contest and τὸ παιδικόν: *Artemis Orthia*, nos. 4, 10–23, 26–30, 32–36, 39–40, 43, 45, [47], 48, 51–52, [84?], 88–90, 92, [95], 96, 98 [99], 105, [109]–[111], [131]; Kourinou-Pikoulas, " Ἐπιγραφές," pp. 96–97, no. 5. Woodward's text of *Artemis Orthia*, no. 49, lines 4–5, βοαγὸς νικήσας κελοῖαν(?)/ μικιχιζόμε[νος κτλ.], is unparalleled; for μικιχιζόμε[νος] read μικιχιζομέ[νων].

36. Woodward, in Dawkins and others, *Artemis Orthia*, p. 287, who, however, believed that contests between all age grades were the only sort to exist. Chrimes, *Ancient Sparta*, p. 92, took the opposite position, arguing that τὸ παιδικόν was merely the generic name for all contests among members of single age grades.

37. Mie, "Über διὰ πάντων," pp. 6–9; Robert, "Deux concours," p. 21 (*OMS*, 5:662); Wörrle, *Stadt*, pp. 229–30.

38. *Artemis Orthia*, no. 8 [Αὐτὸ]ς δ' ἐκ πάν[τ]ων συν/[εφήβων ε]ἷλον [ἄ]εθλον.

39. Paus. 3.14.8, 3.20.2, 3.20.8; Lucian *Anach.* 38; Cic. *Tusc.* 5.27.77.

40. Paus. 3.14.9.

41. Paus. 3.14.10.

42. Paus. 3.20.8.

43. Paus. 3.14.8, καὶ χωρίον Πλατανιστᾶς ἐστιν ἀπὸ τῶν δένδρων, αἳ δὴ ὑψηλαὶ καὶ συνεχεῖς περὶ αὐτὸ αἱ πλάτανοι πεφύκασιν. αὐτὸ δὲ τὸ χωρίον, ἔνθα τοῖς ἐφήβοις μάχεσθαι καθέστηκε, κύκλῳ μὲν εὔριπος περιέχει κατὰ ταὐτὰ καὶ εἰ νῆσον θάλασσα, ἔφοδοι δὲ ἐπὶ γεφυρῶν εἰσι. γεφυρῶν δὲ ἐφ' ἑκατέρᾳ τῇ μέν ἐστιν ἄγαλμα Ἡρακλέους, τῇ δὲ εἰκὼν Λυκούργου.

44. Lucian *Anach.* 38, ὕδατι περιγεγραμμένον.

45. Paus. 3.14.10, μάχονται δὲ καὶ ἐν χερσὶ καὶ ἐμπηδῶντες λάξ, δάκνουσί τε καὶ τοὺς ὀφθαλμοὺς ἀντορύσσουσιν. ἀνὴρ μὲν δὴ πρὸς ἄνδρα τὸν εἰρημένον τρόπον μάχεται· ἀθρόοι δὲ ἐμπίπτουσι βιαίως καὶ ἐς τὸ ὕδωρ ὠθοῦσιν ἀλλήλους; Lucian *Anach.* 38.

46. Cic. *Tusc.* 5.27.77.

47. Lucian *Anach.* 38.

48. Lucian *Salt.* 10–11. That Lucian is describing the aftermath of the Platanistas battle is evident from the words at the beginning of his account here, ὅταν γὰρ ἀκροχειρισάμενοι καὶ παίσαντες ἀλλήλους καὶ παισθέντες ἐν τῷ μέρει παύσωνται, which complement those at the end of his description of the battle in the *Anacharsis*, τὸ γὰρ ἀπὸ τούτου εἰρήνη λοιπὸν καὶ οὐδεὶς ἂν ἔτι παίσειε.

49. Cartledge and Spawforth, *Hellenistic and Roman Sparta*, pp. 129–30.

50. Theater: Paus. 3.14.1. *Dromos*: Paus. 3.14.6–7. Platanistas: Paus. 3.14.8.

51. Stibbe, "Beobachtungen," p. 82.

52. Ibid.; Armstrong, Cavanagh, and Shipley, "Crossing the River," pp. 306–7.

53. This is the tentative solution proposed by Armstrong, Cavanagh, and Shipley, "Crossing the River," p. 307.

54. Delorme, *Gymnasion*, pp. 332–36.

55. Such invented or fictive portraits, as they are called, of long-dead historical personages are attested as early as the fifth century B.C.: Richter, *Portraits*, 1:5. However, a sculpture of Lycurgus at Sparta can hardly be any earlier than the

portraits of other Greek sages such as Solon and Periander, which Richter, *Portraits*, 1:81–91, assigns to the fourth century B.C., and was very probably erected much later.

56. On the pairing of Heracles and Lycurgus at Sparta, see now the statue base of Octavia Agis, to be published by A. J. Spawforth with other new inscriptions from the University of London's excavations at Sparta in *ABSA* 89 (1994).

57. Torelli, in Musti and Torelli, *Pausania*, pp. 217–18. However, his attempt ("Da Sparta," p. 230 n. 46) to associate construction of the amphitheater at Artemis Orthia with this building cannot stand. Inscriptions from the mid-third century A.D. were built into the amphitheater's foundations: see Dawkins, in Dawkins and others, *Artemis Orthia*, p. 34. The excavation of the complex is described briefly in Wace, "Laconia. II—Excavations, 1906," pp. 407–14. Cartledge and Spawforth, *Hellenistic and Roman Sparta*, p. 130, identified it as the gymnasium built by the wealthy Eurycles Herculanus because of several herms of Heracles found nearby. These have recently been tentatively assigned to the city theater: see Palagia, "Seven Pilasters," pp. 122–29.

58. Torelli, "Da Sparta," pp. 225–33. For this identification, first proposed by Sebastiani, see Winnefeld, *Die Villa*, pp. 60–61; Ueblacker, *Das Teatro Marittimo*, p. 52.

59. SHA *Hadr.* 26.5, *Tiburtinam villam mire exaedificavit, ita ut in ea et provinciarum et locorum celeberrima nomina inscriberet, velut Lycium, Academian, Prytanium, Canopum, Picilen, Tempe vocaret.*

60. Paus. 3.11.2.

61. Plut. *Lyc.* 17.4, οὗτος οὖν ὁ εἰρήν . . . ἄρχει τε τῶν ὑποτεταγμένων ἐν ταῖς μάχαις; on *eirenes* and ephebic tribes, see Chapter 2, at note 85. Sources explicitly on the Platanistas are less helpful: e.g., Cic. *Tusc.* 5.77 (*greges*); Paus. 3.14.8 (μοῖρα, τάξιν); Lucian *Anach.* 38 (φάλαγγα, σύνταγμα).

62. On the tribes in the Roman period, see Appendix 2.

63. *IG* V.1 677, 679, 680, 687.

64. *IG* V.1 679, διαβέτεος/ [δὲ αὐτεπαγ]γέλτω καὶ ἀ[ρι/στίνδου]; 680, ἀριστίν/δου δὲ καὶ διαβέτεος αὐτε/παγγέλτου; *SEG* XI (1954), no. 501, Γάιος Ἰούλιος Ἀρίων, ἀριστίνδης, σύνδικος/ ἐπὶ τὰ ἔθη.

65. As Woodward, "Sparta, 1926. Inscriptions," p. 234, pointed out.

66. Hesych. s.v. ἀριστίνδης· ὁ ἐκ τῶν ἀρίστων ἐκλελεγμένος. Ἀριστίνδης is Musurus' emendation of ἀριστήδης. In his edition, Latte, p. 245 (cf. p. XVII n. 1), condemned the form ἀριστίνδης as *spurius nominativus ab Hesychio fictus.*

67. *IG* V.1 680, 681, 682, 685.

68. On the evidence for Spartan tribes in the Roman period, see Appendix 2. On the significance of ἀνέφεδροι, see Woodward, Review, p. 621, arguing against Chrimes' contention, *Ancient Sparta*, pp. 163–68, that there were only four ephebic tribes.

69. Lucian *Anach.* 38.

70. Poll. 9.107, ἔξεστι δὲ καὶ σφαιρομαχίαν εἰπεῖν τὴν ἐπίσκυρον τῆς σφαίρας παιδιάν; Eustath. on *Od.* 9.376, καὶ ἐπεχωρίαζέ φασι Λακεδαιμονίοις ἀγὼν τὰ σφαιρομάχια. Spartan invention: Athen. *Deipnos.* 1.25 (14D–E), ὀρχήσεις δ' εἰσὶ

παρ' Ὁμήρῳ μέν τινες τῶν κυβιστητήων, αἱ δὲ διὰ τῆς σφαίρας· ἧς τὴν εὕρεσιν . . .
ἀνατίθησιν . . . Ἵππασος δὲ Λακεδαιμονίοις ταύτην τε καὶ τὰ γυμνάσια πρώτοις.
The connection was first made by Woodward, "Some Notes," p. 199, who confused Pausanias' account of the Platanistas battle with the *sphaireis* tournament.

71. Poll. 9.104, ἦν δὲ τῆς ἐν σφαίρᾳ παιδιᾶς ὀνόματα ἐπίσκυρος, φαινίνδα,
ἀπόρραξις, οὐρανία. καὶ ἡ μὲν ἐπίσκυρος καὶ ἐφηβικὴ καὶ ἐπίκοινος ἐπίκλην ἔχει·
παίζεται δὲ κατὰ πλῆθος διαστάντων ἴσων πρὸς ἴσους, εἶτα μέσην γραμμὴν λατύ-
πῃ ἑλκυσάντων, ἣν σκῦρον καλοῦσιν ἐφ' ἣν καταθέντες τὴν σφαῖραν, ἑτέρας δύο
γραμμὰς κατόπιν ἑκατέρας τῆς τάξεως καταγράψαντες, ὑπὲρ τοὺς ἑτέρους οἱ προ-
ανελόμενοι ῥίπτουσιν, οἷς ἔργον ἦν ἐπιδράξασθαί τε τῆς σφαίρας φερομένης καὶ
ἀντιβαλεῖν, ἕως ἂν οἱ ἕτεροι τοὺς ἑτέρους ὑπὲρ τὴν κατόπιν γραμμὴν ἀπώσωνται.

72. *SEG* XI (1954), no. 493: see Chapter 2, at note 118.

73. For more on rites of passage at Sparta, see Chapter 4, at note 16, and
Chapter 6, at note 48.

74. On rites of passage and ephebes, see Jeanmaire, *Couroi*; Vidal-Naquet, *Le
chasseur noir*.

75. Paus. 3.14.9, 20.8. On the Platanistas, see the earlier discussion, at note
39.

76. Palagia, "Seven Pilasters," pp. 122–29.

77. *SEG* XI (1954), nos. 773, 810. The third base is unpublished: see Spawforth, "Notes," p. 275. On the phrase "near Lycurgus" (παρὰ τῷ Λυκούργῳ), see
now Charneux, "Du côté," pp. 211–12.

78. On assemblies meeting in theaters, see Kolb, *Agora*, pp. 88–99, esp. 88 n.
9. As a consequence of this, many theaters were also places of display for important documents: see, e.g., Reynolds, *Aphrodisias and Rome*, pp. 36–37; Heberdey, Niemann, and Wilberg, *Das Theater*, pp. 96–203 (Ephesus); Kolb, *Agora*, p.
90 n. 14.

Sparta's assembly also met at a building called the Skias: Paus. 3.12.10, ⟨ἡ⟩
καλουμένη Σκιάς, ἔνθα καὶ νῦν ἔτι ἐκκλησιάζουσιν. Following the consensus,
Seiler, *Tholos*, p. 35 n. 123, suggests Pausanias means that the so-called Little
Assembly met here, since the Skias could not have accommodated the full assembly. This is anachronistic, as there is no evidence for the continued existence of the
Little Assembly down into Roman times and every likelihood that it had been
replaced, probably by the *boulē*: see Kennell, "*IG* V 1,16," pp. 201–2. Kolb,
Agora, p. 111, identifies the Skias as the *theatron* of Classical Sparta and the site
of the celebration of the Gymnopaediae.

79. Pélékidis, *Histoire de l'éphébie*, pp. 217–19, 256.

80. *IG* V.1 674, while not preserved in its entirety, still has the top and bottom
of the catalog and only lacks the first letters of the six names after that of the
presbus, which does not affect the calculation since each line contains only one
name. The next-best preserved catalog, in *IG* V.1 676, which has lost its lower
portion, preserves thirteen names.

81. Forbes, *Physical Education*, pp. 173–76; *IG* II/III² 2048, lines 14–16,
ἐγένον/το ἔφηβοι διακό/σιοι καὶ δύο.

82. E.g., *IG* V.1 543, 544, 560.

83. Collignon, *Quid de collegiis*, p. 32; Kleijwegt, *Youth*, pp. 91–92.

84. *Artemis Orthia*, nos. 45, 46, 50, 52–54, 58, 59, [63], 64, 67–69, 71. They range in date from A.D. 134/5 (no. 45) to shortly after A.D. 220 (no. 67).

85. Woodward, in Dawkins and others, *Artemis Orthia*, p. 287.

86. *Artemis Orthia*, no. 48.

87. See previous discussion, at note 35.

88. Spawforth, "Herodes Atticus," p. 204.

89. E.g., the gymnasiarchal law of Beroea provides for an ἀπόδειξις of children to be held by the *paidotribai* every four months: *SEG* XXVII (1977), no. 261B, lines 24–26: see Ziebarth, *Schulwesen*, pp. 136–47; Gauthier and Hatzopoulos, *La loi gymnasiarchique*, pp. 75–76.

90. On these festivals and agonistic spectacles in Sparta generally, see Cartledge and Spawforth, *Hellenistic and Roman Sparta*, pp. 184–89.

91. Eligibility for the Leonidea: Paus. 3.14.1.

92. E.g., *IG* V.1 19 (Leonidea), line 6 (παῖς), line 8 (ἀγένειος, ἀνήρ). On the subdivisions of the boys' class at the Leonidea into παῖδες καθαροί and παῖδες κρίσεως τῆς Ἀγησιλάου, see Robert, "Inscriptions grecques," pp. 239–44.

93. *IG* V.1 663, Γά(ιος) Ἀβίδιος Ἀγαθάνγε/λος, νικήσας ἀγε/νείων πάλην ἐπὶ/ ἀγωνοθέτου τῶν/ μεγάλων Εὐρυκλε[ί]/ων Γαί(ου) Ἰου(λίου) Ἀντιπά/τρου τοῦ Λυσικρά/τους, Λακεδαιμόν[ι]/ος Πιτανάτης.

94. *Artemis Orthia*, no. 41, lines 8–14, καὶ ἀπὸ μ/ικιχιζομένων/ μέχρι μελλειρο/νείας τοὺ⟨ς⟩ Γααό/χους καὶ Ἀσάνεα/ τὴν τῶν παίδων/ παλήν.

95. Frisch, "Klassifikation," pp. 179–85; *IG* IV 206, lines 3–4, παῖς παλαιστής, ἀσι/ονείκης, ἐτῶν ιη'; cf. *Iasos* I, no. 110, lines 3–8, ἐφη/βαρχήσαντα λαμπρῶς/ καὶ στεφανωθέντα παῖ/δας κιθαρῳδοὺς τὸν ἐν/ Ἐφέσῳ κοινὸν τῆς Ἀσί/ας ἱερὸν ἀγῶνα.

96. There is more evidence for the age categories in festivals open to non-Spartans. Urania: *IG* V.1 659, 667. Euryclea: *IG* V.1 666. For more on foreign victors, see Cartledge and Spawforth, *Hellenistic and Roman Sparta*, pp. 232–33.

97. *IG* V.1 209, line 20, Φιλωνίδας Φιλωνίδα Καρνεονείκας; 586; 587, lines 4–6, τοῦ σεμνο/τάτου ἀγῶνος τῶν Ὑακινθί/ων; cf. 455; Lactantius Placidus on Stat. *Theb.* 4.223; Philos. *VS* 2.12.

98. Sosibius, *FGrHist* 595 F3; Jacoby, *FGrHist*, 3b.1:637–38; Hellanicus, *FGrHist* 4 F85–86. Note also the shadowy citharoedus Periclitus, a victor in the Carnea, who is supposed to have lived in the eighth century: [Plut.] *De mus.* 6 (1133D).

99. Burkert, *Griechische Religion*, pp. 354–58.

100. On the dedication, see Skias, "Ἀνακοινώσεις," p. 34 no. 8, who dated it by letter forms. His transcription can be restored [---]ς τῷ Ἀπέλλ[ωνι]/[---]ν μ' ἀνέθηκε/ [ἀπὸ] νίκας. The version of *SEG* I (1923), no. 87, is unreliable. On Polycrates, see *FGrHist* 588 F1; Jacoby, *FGrHist*, 3b.1:624–25.

101. Antiochus, *FGrHist* 555 F13, τοῖς Ὑακινθίοις ἐν τῷ Ἀμυκλαίῳ συντελουμένου τοῦ ἀγῶνος.

102. Mellink, *Hyakinthos*, pp. 22–23.

103. Choral music is implied by *SEG* I (1923), no. 88, a dedication from the Amyclaeum honoring a διδάσκαλος; Cartledge and Spawforth, *Hellenistic and Roman Sparta*, p. 194. Discus: de Ridder, *Catalogue*, no. 530. The inscription is discussed by Mellink, *Hyakinthos*, p. 23.

104. This has not stopped anyone from attempting a solution. For a short précis of relevant scholarship, see now Pettersson, *Cults*, pp. 12–14, 44–45, 59–60, the most recent attempt at using the evidence synchronically.

105. Polycrates, *FGrHist* 588 F1; X. *Ages.* 2.17.

106. For the ancient testimonia on the Hyacinthia, see Wide, *Kulte*, pp. 285–93.

107. On this problem, see the extensive treatment by Roesch, *Études*, pp. 323–46.

108. Reisch, "Chor," 2381–82, 2393.

109. X. *Lac.* 9.5; *Ages.* 2.17; *Apophth. Lac.* 208D.

110. On the age grades of the later *agōgē*, see Chapter 2.

111. Wörrle, *Stadt*, p. 10, lines 65–66, ὁμοίως αἱρεῖσθαι ὑπ' αὐτοῦ ἀγελάρχας β' ἐκ τῶν εὐγενεστά[των]/ παίδων, οἵτινες ἐπιλέξουσι ἀνὰ παῖδας κ', [οὓς ἂν α]ὑτοὶ δοκιμάσωσι, τοὺς ἀσκήσοντας δρόμον ὥστε λαμπαδοδρομεῖν; and pp. 220–22.

112. Athen. *Deipnos.* 4.141F.

113. Ehrenberg, "Spartiaten," pp. 24–25.

114. *Anecdota Graeca* (Bekker), 1:305.

115. Burkert, *Griechische Religion*, pp. 355–57.

116. See Chapter 2, at note 126.

117. *IG* V.1 650, 651.

118. His role in the preservation of the epigraphic record at Sparta has long been controversial: see Dodwell, *Tour*, 2:405–6; Robert, "Deux inscriptions," p. 153 n. 1; Spawforth, "*Fourmontiana*," pp. 139–45. Indeed, there is a danger that the *staphulodromoi* inscriptions are themselves forgeries because the name Aristandros (*IG* V.1 651) also ominously occurs in the abbé's counterfeit Amyclaean decree (*IG* V.1 515). I thank Antony Spawforth for drawing this to my attention.

119. See previous discussion, at note 93.

120. Forbes, *NEOI*, pp. 18–19; on *neoi* at Sparta, see Chapter 2, at note 124.

121. Hesych. s.v. σταφυλοδρόμοι· τινὲς τῶν Καρνεατῶν, παρορμῶντες τοὺς ἐπὶ τρύγῃ· καρνεᾶται· οἱ ἄγαμοι· κεκληρωμένοι δὲ ἐπὶ τὴν Καρνείου λειτουργίαν. πέντε δὲ ἀφ' ἑκάστης . . . ἐπὶ τετραετίαν ἐλειτούργουν.

122. Hesych. s.v. ἔφηβοι; X. *Eph.* 1.2.2, where ἔφηβοι are equated with πάρθενοι.

123. Plut. *Ages.* 29.2. As usual, inquiries into the Gymnopaediae have used the evidence synchronically: see Jeanmaire, *Couroi*, pp. 531–40; Brelich, *Paides*, pp. 139–40, 171–73, 187–91; Pettersson, *Cults*, pp. 42–56.

124. Paus. 3.11.9, ἐν ταύταις οὖν [sc., ταῖς γυμνοπαιδίαις] οἱ ἔφηβοι χοροὺς ἱστᾶσι τῷ Ἀπόλλωνι: see also *Anecdota Graeca* (Bekker), 1:32, 234; *Etymologicum Magnum* s.v. γυμνοπαιδία.

125. Bölte, "Festen," pp. 126–27, reconstructed an elaborate scheme for a five-day celebration with three choruses every day for each of the "*obai*" of the Classical period. On *obai* and their number in the Classical period, see Appendix 2.

126. Χορός: Paus. 3.11.9. θέατρον: Hdt. 6.67.3; Plut. *Ages.* 29.2. On the theater, see Woodward, "Sparta, 1927. Theatre," pp. 3–36.

127. Sosibius, *FGrHist* 595 F5, χοροὶ δὲ εἰσὶν τὸ μὲν †πρόσω παίδων ... τὸ δ' ἐξ ἀρίστου† ἀνδρῶν, γυμνῶν ὀρχουμένων καὶ ᾀδόντων Θαλητᾶ καὶ Ἀλκμᾶνος ᾄσματα καὶ τοὺς Διονυσοδότου τοῦ Λάκωνος παιᾶνας. No accurate translation of the fragment is possible at present without making what I consider unfounded assumptions about the identity of these choruses with the *trichoria*. For instance, Wyttenbach in the eighteenth century restored the text, ὁ μὲν πρόσω παίδων, ⟨ὁ δ' ἐκ δεξιοῦ γερόντων⟩, ὁ δ' ἐξ ἀριστέρου ἀνδρῶν. On the *trichoria*, see my subsequent discussion.

128. Plut. *Lyc.* 21.3, τριῶν γὰρ χορῶν κατὰ τὰς τρεῖς ἡλικίας συνισταμένων ἐν ταῖς ἑορταῖς, ὁ μὲν τῶν γερόντων ἀρχόμενος ᾖδεν· " Ἀμμές ποκ' ἦμες ἄλκιμοι νεανίαι," ὁ δὲ τῶν ἀκμαζόντων ἀμειβόμενος ἔλεγεν· " Ἀμμες δέ γ' εἰμές· αἱ δὲ λῇς, πεῖραν λαβέ," ὁ δὲ τρίτος ὁ τῶν παίδων· " Ἀμμες δέ γ' ἐσσόμεθα πολλῷ κάρρονες." *Inst. Lac.* 15 (238A–B); Poll. 4.107.

129. Compare the fragment of Sosibius, *FGrHist* 595 F8, Ἀμὲς ποτ' ἦμες· Λακωνική ἐστιν αὕτη, μέμνηται δὲ αὐτῆς Σωσίβιος ἐν τῷ Περὶ Ἐθῶν, καί φησιν ὅτι οἱ πρεσβύτεροι [Λακεδαμόνιοι] χορεύοντες τοῦτο ἔλεγον, "ἀμὲς ποκ' ἦμες." Plutarch's much fuller version (*Lyc.* 21.3) depends on *Inst. Lac.* 15, which it follows almost word for word. Both it and the Sosibian version reproduce the Laconian dialect of the old men's song accurately, and the *Institutions*' styling the chorus of adult men οἱ ἀκμάζοντες echoes authentic Spartan usage as reported by Xenophon in his *Constitution of the Lacedaemonians* 4.3. See also Jacoby, *FGrHist*, 3b.1:649.

130. The verb he uses is the imperfect ᾖδεν. On the significance of the tenses Plutarch uses in the *Lycurgus*, see Chapter 1.

131. X. *HG.* 6.4.16, γυμνοπαιδιῶν τε οὔσης τῆς τελευταίας καὶ τοῦ ἀνδρικοῦ χοροῦ ἔνδον ὄντος; Plut. *Ages.* 29.3.

132. A change in the celebration of the Gymnopaediae was cautiously offered as a possibility by Hiller von Gaertringen, "Gymnopaidien," 2088.

CHAPTER FOUR

1. Dawkins, in Dawkins and others, *Artemis Orthia*, p. 34.

2. Ibid. On Sparta in the third century A.D. and later, see Cartledge and Spawforth, *Hellenistic and Roman Sparta*, pp. 120–26.

3. References in this form are to the testimonia collected in Appendix 1.

4. On Christian use of pagan exempla, see Carlson, "Pagan Examples," p. 98. On Tertullian's use of them, see Barnes, *Tertullian*, pp. 217–19.

5. On the epigraphical remains, see Dawkins, in Dawkins and others, *Artemis Orthia*, pp. 35–36.

6. A date in May or June may be inferred from Libanius, *Or.* 14.8, where he says that, upon his return through Corinth from Sparta (after viewing "the whips" [T34]), he first saw his friend Aristophanes paraded around (παραπεμ-πόμενον) in the full regalia of a *duovir*, to the acclamations of the crowd. He watched, "marveling that one so young should be obtaining high office from the city" (μακαρίζων δὲ τῷ τηλικοῦτον ὄντα κτᾶσθαι τὴν παρὰ τῆς πόλεως τιμήν). Libanius witnessed Aristophanes' *acclamatio populi* and so must have been at Corinth during the duoviral elections, which were probably still held in July, as they had been in the first century A.D.: West, *Corinth*, 8.2:31; Liebenam, *Städteverwaltung*, p. 273 and n. 2. Therefore, the endurance contest must have taken place not long before.

For the force of παραπεμπόμενον, from παραπέμπω and related to παραπόμπη (*prosecutio*), words customarily used of official escorts for emperors in their travels, see Halfmann, *Itinera principum*, pp. 78–81.

7. Paus. 3.16.9.

8. I take the φουάξιρ as a development of the earlier *krupteia*, on which see now Lévy, "La kryptie," pp. 251–52.

9. *Artemis Orthia*, p. 37 and no. 141.

10. On the total number of ephebes in the *agōgē* in any one year, see Chapter 3, at note 80.

11. Dawkins, in Dawkins and others, *Artemis Orthia*, p. 37.

12. These measurements have been calculated from *Artemis Orthia*, pl. 1: "Sanctuary of Artemis Orthia, Sparta 1910."

13. This may account for *bouagoi* or their families paying for statues to altar victors: see n. 39.

14. On Lucian at Sparta, see Chapter 1, at note 137; on Philostratus, see Cartledge and Spawforth, *Hellenistic and Roman Sparta*, p. 209.

15. *LSJ* s.v. ἀποθνῄσκω. The anonymous emendation ἐναποθνῄσκοντας, adopted by Ziegler (1973) and by Manfredini and Piccirilli (1980), would vitiate this interpretation.

16. Frazer, *Pausanias' Guide*, 4:341–43. On initiation rituals, see van Gennep, *Les rites*.

17. Turner, "Betwixt and Between," pp. 339–40; van Gennep, *Les rites*.

18. On "mitigation" as it relates to the endurance contest, see the cogent summary in Hughes, *Human Sacrifice*, pp. 79–81, 228. On the interpretation of this and the other mythic accounts of the contest's beginnings, see my subsequent discussion, at note 41.

19. Brelich, *Paides*, p. 80 n. 83.

20. Turner, "Betwixt and Between," p. 342.

21. On the contest as initiatory rite, see the references in Hughes, *Human Sacrifice*, p. 228. These works and the many other anthropologically influenced studies of the *agōgē*'s rituals are without exception synchronic and ahistorical in their approach to the evidence: e.g., Vernant, "Entre la honte," pp. 269–300.

22. Burkert, *Griechische Religion*, p. 393.

23. *Pueri*/παῖδες: T1–3, T5, T8 (*liberi*), T11, T18, T48–49. *Adulescentes*/

ἔφηβοι: T6, T9, T16–17, T22–23, T25, T37, T39, T48, T50, T52. Νεοί: T19, T40, T43–44, T47. Ἄνδρες: T27.

24. See Chapter 2, at note 5.

25. *IG* V.1 493, παῖδες ἀνίκατοι, σθεναροί, κρατεροὶ συνέφηβοι.

26. Plut. *Lyc.* 17.3: see Chapter 2, at note 44.

27. On the ball tournament, see Chapter 3, at note 67. On the *sphaireis* dedications, see Chapter 2, at note 65.

28. Wernicke, "Artemis," 1346; Burkert, *Griechische Religion*, pp. 236–37.

29. See Chapter 2, at note 64.

30. For *eirenes* competing in the boys' contests, see *Artemis Orthia*, no. 31.

31. This transition did not of course depend on the endurance contest occurring precisely at the end of the ephebic year.

32. Liban. *Or.* 5.23, δηλοῖ δὲ ἡ τῶν Λακεδαιμονίων πόλις· μάλιστα δὴ δοκοῦσα φροντίσαι ⟨τῶν⟩ πολεμικῶν μάλιστα δὴ φαίνεται φροντίσασα τῶν περὶ θήραν. νόμος γοῦν αὐτοῖς ἐν τῇ Ἀρτέμιδος ἑορτῇ τὸν ἥκοντα ἐπὶ τὸ δεῖπνον οὐ τεθηρευκότα δοκεῖν τε ἀδικεῖν καὶ διδόναι δίκην. ἡ δὲ δίκη, ἀμφορέα τις ὕδατος κομίσας καταχεῖ τῆς τοῦ παιδὸς κεφαλῆς, ἢν παῖς οὗτος ᾖ, ἀνδρὸς δὲ τῆς χειρὸς ὁ δάκτυλος τοῦτο ὑπομενεῖ, καὶ ἔστιν ἐν Λακεδαίμονι τοῦτο τὸ ὕδωρ ἀτιμία. Since Libanius went to Sparta specifically to see the endurance contest, there can be no doubt that this festival was associated with it.

33. Parker, *Miasma*, p. 113 n. 37.

34. Burkert, *Griechische Religion*, p. 102.

35. Athen. *Deipnos.* 1.31 (18A).

36. Plut. *Lyc.* 12.4.

37. Vidal-Naquet, *Le chasseur noir*, esp. pp. 169–72.

38. E.g., *IG* V.1 554.

39. Bases: *Artemis Orthia*, nos. 142–44: see T19. All were erected by the city, at the expense of either the victor's *bouagoi* (142), the mother of the victor's *bouagos* (143), or the victor's brother (144). *IG* V.1 653, a second base for the victor of *Artemis Orthia*, no. 142, not found in Orthia's sanctuary, was erected at public expense; why this victor should warrant such an honor is unknown.

On erecting public statues at private expense, see Robert, "Inscriptions grecques," pp. 230–34; *ISestos*, no. 1, lines 102–4; *SEG* XXXV (1985), no. 744, lines 49–51; Wörrle, *Stadt und Fest*, p. 10, lines 66–68.

40. See Chapter 6, at note 69.

41. Inscribed dedications from the early sixth century have been found at the site: see Woodward, in Dawkins and others, *Artemis Orthia*, pp. 367–71 (cf. pp. 187–88). For a revision of the dates, see Boardman, "Artemis Orthia and Chronology," pp. 1–7.

42. *Inst. Lac.* 40 (239 C–D) (T18). On this redating of the *Institutions*, see Chapter 1, at note 113.

43. X. *Lac.* 2.9, καὶ ὡς πλείστους δὴ ἁρπάσαι τυροὺς παρ' Ὀρθίας καλὸν θεὶς μαστιγοῦν τούτους ἄλλοις ἐπέταξε, τοῦτο δὴ δηλῶσαι καὶ ἐν τούτῳ βουλόμενος, ὅτι ἔστιν ὀλίγον χρόνον ἀλγήσαντα πολὺν χρόνον εὐδοκιμοῦντα εὐφραίνεσθαι.

44. Pl. *Lg.* 1. 633B, ἐν ἁρπαγαῖς τισιν διὰ πολλῶν πληγῶν; Plut. *Arist.* 17.10 (T17).

45. Cf. Paus. 3.16.10–11.

46. Tigerstedt, *Legend of Sparta*, 2:453 n. 49.

47. Suggested by Cartledge and Spawforth, *Hellenistic and Roman Sparta*, p. 207. The place of the endurance contest in Sphaerus' program is discussed in Chapter 5.

48. Cf. Starr, *Essays*, pp. 107–10.

49. Wade-Gery, *Essays*, p. 75 n. 2. Followed by Kiechle, *Lakonien*, p. 151; Oliva, *Sparta*, p. 81; Cartledge, *Sparta and Lakonia*, p. 107.

50. On the date of Amyclae's political amalgamation with Sparta, see Appendix 2.

51. Carter, "Masks of Ortheia," p. 381.

52. E.g., Wade-Gery, *Essays*, p. 75 n. 2, "It was before Lycurgus."

53. E.g., Cartledge, "Early Lakedaimon," p. 55, who calls it an "antiquarian mythological detail preserved by 'Baedeker' Pausanias."

54. On the *Fabulae*'s author and his disputed identity, see Desmedt, "Fabulae Hygini" (1970), pp. 26–35; and "Fabulae Hygini" (1973), pp. 26–34. Contra, Rose, *Hygini Fabulae*, p. xii.

55. Tigerstedt, *Legend of Sparta*, 2:95–160.

56. Polyb. 6.10–19.5.

57. Tigerstedt, *Legend of Sparta*, 2:109. For a modern-day rehearsal of the same arguments, see Perotti, "Roma e Sparta," pp. 74–79.

58. Cicero *Rep.* 2.2.

59. Posidonius, *FGrHist* 87 F 59.

60. D.H. 2.49.4; cf. Plut. *Num.* 1.5.

61. Prop. 3.14.1–4, 21–24. The concluding couplet makes explicit Propertius' intent to satirize the hunt for parallels between Sparta and Rome (33–34), *quod si iura fores pugnasque imitata Laconum, / carior hoc esses tu mihi, Roma, bono.*

62. Servius on *Aen.* 8.638; Hyginus F9 (Peter); Ovid *Fasti* 1.260, 3.230; Tigerstedt, *Legend of Sparta*, 2:99, 141.

63. Flacelière, "Quelques passages," p. 400.

64. Cartledge and Spawforth, *Hellenistic and Roman Sparta*, pp. 191–93.

65. Paus. 3.14.1.

66. Robertson, "A Point of Precedence," pp. 88–102.

67. The catalogs of the different magistracies, considered as a single set, barely outnumber the sickle dedications.

68. On Lycurgus at the Platanistas battle and the ball tournament, see Chapter 3, at notes 45 and 78. Lycurgus' altar: Paus. 3.16.6; Dickins, "The Great Altar," pp. 295–302. Stibbe, "Beobachtungen," p. 87, identifies the remains as those of Lycurgus' temple.

69. The full title occurs first in an inscription from the joint reign of Marcus Aurelius and Lucius Verus (*IG* V.1 500). A σύνδικος/ἐπὶ τὰ ἔθη is attested early in the second century (*IG* V.1 65).

70. πάτριος ἀγωγή: *Apophth. Lac.* Anon. 54 (235B); *Inst. Lac.* 11 (237D);

Agis 4.2. Λακωνικὰ ἔθη: Plut. *Pyrrh.* 26.21. On the use of ancient Laconian in the *agōgē*, see subsequent discussion, at note 100.

71. For a modern etiological myth with an equally dubious claim to veracity, see Siskind, "Invention of Thanksgiving," pp. 169–74.

72. On present-day engagement with the past, see Lowenthal, *Past*. On civic elites and the past, see Bowie, "Greeks and Their Past," pp. 166–209; Rogers, *Sacred Identity*, pp. 136–51. On traveling historians, see Chaniotis, *Historie*, pp. 369–72. On "nationalist" scholarship, see Robert, "Documents I–IV," pp. 120–32; Chaniotis, *Historie*, p. 322 E28.

73. On the Amphictyonic Council, see Cartledge and Spawforth, *Hellenistic and Roman Sparta*, p. 112. On the Panhellenion, see Spawforth and Walker, "World of the Panhellenion I–II." A new inscription has clarified some of the questions of the Panhellenion's early development: see Wörrle, "Neue Inschriftenfunde," pp. 337–49.

74. Spawforth and Walker, "World of the Panhellenion I," pp. 82–94.

75. Ibid., pp. 81–82; Graindor, *Athènes*, pp. 102–11.

76. Woodward, "Sparta and Asia Minor," pp. 868–83, with the cautionary comments of Robert and Robert, *La Carie*, 2:88; Robert, "Documents XXIII–XXVIII," pp. 562–67; Spawforth and Walker, "World of the Panhellenion II," pp. 95–96; Strubbe, "Gründer," p. 264.

77. On coinage: Imhoof-Blumer, *Münzen*, 2:355 no. 2, Ἀμβλαδέων Λα-κεδαιμονί(ων). On city walls: *ISelge*, no. 6, ὁ δῆμος ὁ Λακεδαιμονίων/ [ἐτείμησεν] τὸν δῆμον τὸν Σελγέ[ων]. On official nomenclature: *IGR* I 418, ἡ Κιβυρατῶν πόλις ἄποικος Λ[ακεδαιμονίων καὶ]/ συγγενὶς Ἀθηναίων.

78. E.g., *IGR* IV 915c, lines 5–7 (Cibyra); *Ins. Magnesia*, no. 113, lines 115–16.

79. Coulton, "Oinoanda," pp. 76–88. See Hall, "Diogenes," pp. 160–63.

80. *IGR* III 500.I, lines 1–10.

81. *ITralleis* I, no. 141, lines 8–10, νικήσαντα/ τὸν ἱερὸν ἀγῶνα τῶν Σπαρ/τιατῶν; no. 142, lines 1–3, νικήσαντα τ[ὸν]/ ἱερὸν τὸν Σπαρτιάτη[ν]/ ἀγῶνα (both dated f.IIp – in.IIIp). On relations with Sparta, see Woodward and Robert, "Decrees," pp. 71–72.

82. E.g., it appears in the list of local Trallean festivals in Ruge, "Tralleis (2)," 2119–22.

83. Robert, "La titulature de Nicée," pp. 22–33.

84. Spawforth, "Severan Statue Group," pp. 327–32.

85. In calling the Spartans of his day "Spartiates," Pausanias follows his models Herodotus and Thucydides; cf. Strid, *Über Sprache*, pp. 99, 103.

86. Reynolds, "Hadrian," pp. 111–21.

87. The fragment contains references to ἀγωγὰν καὶ σοφ[ίαν], παιδείαν, and παρὰ Λακεδαιμονίων: Reynolds, "Hadrian," pp. 118–19; Cartledge and Spawforth, *Hellenistic and Roman Sparta*, p. 113.

88. [Λα]κωνικὴ/ σωφροσύνη καὶ ἄσκη[σις]: Reynolds, "Hadrian," p. 113, lines 42–43; Robert, "Inscriptions grecques," p. 235; Spawforth and Walker, "World of the Panhellenion II," p. 97.

89. On the Cyrenean ephebate, see Luni, "Documenti," pp. 223–84.

90. *SEG* XX (1964), no. 741; Luni, "Documenti," pp. 246–49, no. 15; *SEG* XX (1964), no. 742; Luni, "Documenti," pp. 254–55, no. 19.

91. The process is easily traced. E.g., the ephebic leaders called τριακατιάρχαι in the earlier inscriptions (e.g., *SEG* XX [1964], nos. 739, 741) become ἐφή-βαρχοι τριακατιάρχαι (e.g., *SEG* XX [1964], no. 742) in the second century and end up as ἐφήβαρχοι (*SEG* IX [1944], no. 128) in the third. Other positions, such as that of ἀπορυτιάζων, simply disappear.

On an inscription attesting to an ephebic reform in the late second century A.D., see Mohamed and Reynolds, "Some New Inscriptions," pp. 116–17.

92. Tigerstedt, *Legend of Sparta*, 1:237–41.

93. Cartledge and Spawforth, *Hellenistic and Roman Sparta*, pp. 180–82, 207–11.

94. Ibid., p. 113. Philos. *VS* 2.1 (564), κριτιάζουσα ἠχώ.

95. See Chapter 2, at note 96.

96. Woodward, "Afterthoughts," pp. 257–59; Cartledge and Spawforth, *Hellenistic and Roman Sparta*, pp. 113–14.

97. On Charax, see now Andrei, *A. Claudius Charax*.

98. Paus. 2.9.1; Shimron, "Original Task," pp. 155–58.

99. Kennell, *Public Institutions*, pp. 101–5.

100. Mommsen, *Römische Geschichte*, 258; Woodward, "Sparta, 1908. Inscriptions," p. 117; Ehrenberg, "Sparta (Geschichte)," 1451–52; Chrimes, *Ancient Sparta*, pp. 85, 160–61; Tigerstedt, *Legend of Sparta*, 2:163.

101. Kennell, "Public Institutions," pp. 74–248; Cartledge and Spawforth, *Hellenistic and Roman Sparta*, pp. 143–76.

102. *IG* V.1 139, βίδυ(οι) ἐπὶ Κλ[αυδ(ίω) Ἀρι]/στοβούλω; *SEG* XI (1954), nos. 499, συναγορανό/μος Αἰλίω/ Ἀλκανδρίδα; 500, συνπατρονόμος θεῶ Λυκουργῶ.

103. *Sphaireis*: *IG* V.1 679. Sickle dedications: *Artemis Orthia*, nos. 31, 39, 43, 45, 46, 50, 52–71, 73, 75–76, 84–85, 87, 92, 94, 99, 102, 105, 109, 111, 113–14. *Bōmonikai*: *Artemis Orthia*, no. 142.

104. The latest sickle dedication (*IG* V.1 314 [*Artemis Orthia*, no. 71]) uses *koinē* forms throughout, with only one archaizing form. For the date, see Spawforth, "Notes," p. 285.

105. Buck, *Greek Dialects*, pp. 56–57; Bourguet, *Le dialecte laconien*, p. 6.

106. E.g., *IG* V.1 213.

107. On Aristophanes' later influence, see Tolkiehn, "Lexikographie," 2440. On the section dealing with Laconian, cf. Hesych. s.v. Πουστάκους. ὡς Ἀριστοφάνης φησὶν ἐν ἐξηγήσει Λακωνικῶν. See also Chapter 1, at note 103.

108. Bourguet, *Le dialecte laconien*, pp. 25–28; Buck, *Greek Dialects*, pp. 272–73; Zgusta, "Die Rolle des Griechischen," p. 124; Cassio, "Continuità," p. 145.

109. Pernot, *Introduction*.

110. By "doricizing *koinē*," I refer to the appearance of a very few Doric elements, usually alpha in place of eta, in texts otherwise written in ordinary *koinē*. On Doric *koinē*, see Buck, *Greek Dialects*, pp. 173–80.

111. On the possible survival of Doric in remote parts of the Peloponnese, see Zgusta, "Die Rolle des Griechischen," p. 123.

112. *IG* V.1 296 (*Artemis Orthia*, no. 41); Chrimes, *Ancient Sparta*, p. 465.

113. Bourguet, *Le dialecte laconien*, p. 25, points to these solecisms and inconsistencies as signs of a living language, not one resuscitated by academics. He was, however, unaware of the distribution of the archaizing inscriptions in the epigraphy of Roman Sparta.

114. Bourguet, *Le dialecte laconien*, p. 26.

115. *IG* V.1 294 (*Artemis Orthia*, no. 52).

116. *IG* V.1 309 (*Artemis Orthia*, no. 62).

117. The tendency is extremely common in papyri: see Gignac, *Grammar*, 1:25–29. For an epigraphical example, see Dagron and Feissel, *Inscriptions de Cilicie*, p. 31, no. 11, lines 8 and 23 (Γερόντις, Γυμνάσις).

118. *Artemis Orthia*, nos. 43, 85. The process of transformation was as follows, Πόπλιος — Πόπλῖος — Πόπλῖς — Πόπλῖρ — Πόπληρ; Ἀριστοτέλεος (Buck, *Greek Dialects*, p. 177) — Ἀριστοτέλιος — Ἀριστοτέλῖς — Ἀριστοτέλῖρ — Ἀριστοτέληρ. See also Bourguet, *Le dialecte laconien*, p. 128.

119. *Artemis Orthia*, nos. 67, 69. See also Bourguet, *Le dialecte laconien*, pp. 131–32; Gignac, *Grammar*, 1:82.

120. Κασσηρατόριν: *Artemis Orthia*, nos. 52–53, 55, 57, 59, 61, 67–71, 85, 94. Βο(υ)αγόρ: *Artemis Orthia*, nos. 46, 50–54, 60, 61, 64, 68–69, 72, 75. On this change, see Gignac, *Grammar*, 1:213.

121. *Artemis Orthia*, nos. 69 (cf. *IG* V.1 649), 66 (cf. *IG* V.1 1317).

122. *Artemis Orthia*, no. 142.

123. E.g., ἀτιμάσδη for ἀτιμάζει; ἐττάν for εἰς τήν; μέμψατται for μέμψασθαι. See Wilamowitz-Möllendorf, *Timotheos*, pp. 70–71.

124. See Chapter 2, at note 5.

125. See Chapter 1, at note 38.

126. On πρατο-/πρωτο- and ἀτρο-/ἑτερο-, see Buck, *Greek Dialects*, pp. 94, 272.

127. *IG* VII, 1764 (Lebadia [Roesch, *Études*, p. 322 n. 70]), line 13, πάμπαιδας; 2871 (Lebadia [Roesch]), line 21, πάμπαιδας; *IG* XII.9, 952 (Chalcis) col. 1, παῖδας πάμπαιδας.

128. Bourguet, *Le dialecte laconien*, p. 104. On the significance of -ιζομενος, see Jannaris, *Historical Grammar*, p. 301.

129. Bowie, "The Greeks and Their Past," pp. 170–72.

130. Apsines *Rh.* 1 (468); Philos. *VS* 1.82 (522), 1.25 (542), 2.5 (573); Kennedy, "Sophists," pp. 17–18, 20.

131. Cf. Oudet, "Images d'Athènes," pp. 101–7.

132. Vermeule, *Greek Sculpture*, pp. 1–25. For an example of archaism in architecture, see Spawforth and Walker, "World of the Panhellenion II," pp. 100–101.

133. Plut. *Per.* 17.1–3. A connection was first seen by Oliver, *Marcus Aurelius*, pp. 94, 132.

134. Paus. 3.11.3; Waywell, "Excavations," p. 14.

135. Cartledge and Spawforth, *Hellenistic and Roman Sparta*, pp. 115, 118–19.

136. Herodian 4.8.1–3; Millar, *Cassius Dio*, p. 151.

137. Hdt. 9.53; Thuc. 1.20; Cartledge and Spawforth, *Hellenistic and Roman Sparta*, p. 118.

138. Plut. *Alex.* 16.18.

139. This sophistic bias even imposes itself on current research. A new book on the Second Sophistic mentions Lycurgus but once and Sparta not at all: Anderson, *Second Sophistic*, p. 109.

140. Cf. Elsner, "Pausanias," p. 5.

141. Philos. *VS* 1.25 (585); Apsines *Rh.* 1 (469).

142. Apsines *Rh.* 1 (498).

143. Philos. *VS* 1.16 (501); Paus. 11.32.10.

144. Cf. Anderson, *Second Sophistic*, pp. 101–32.

145. For instance, in his notice on the succession of world empires, Ampelius (*Lib. Mem.* 10.1) places the Lacedaemonians' empire immediately before that of the Athenians.

146. The germ of the story is Hdt. 1.82.

147. Ehrenberg, "Othryadas," 1871–72.

148. Lucian *Rh. Pr.* 18; cf. Aristid. *Rh.* 1.6.

149. Paus. 3.11.10.

150. Plut. *Lyc.* 6.7.

151. Cartledge, *Sparta and Lakonia*, p. 134; Marasco, "La leggende di Polidoro," pp. 115–27.

152. Paus. 3.3.2, καὶ κατὰ γνώμην Λακεδαιμονίων μάλιστα ὄντα τῷ δήμῳ — οὔτε γὰρ ἔργον βίαιον οὔτε ὑβριστὴν λόγον παρείχετο εἰς οὐδένα, ἐν δὲ ταῖς κρίσεσι τὰ δίκαια ἐφύλασσεν οὐκ ἄνευ φιλανθρωπίας.

153. Cf. Apsines *Rh.* 5 (510).

154. Philos. *VS* 1.24 (528).

155. Philos. *VS* 1.20 (514), 2.9 (583). Aphthonius (*Prog.* 13 [109]) set it during Xerxes' invasion of Greece.

CHAPTER FIVE

1. Ollier, "Le philosophe stoïcien," pp. 547–62.

2. *SVF* 1 (Sph.) F630 = Athen. *Deipnos.* 4.19 (141C).

3. *SVF* 1 (Sph.) F622 = Plut. *Cleom.* 2.3.

4. *SVF* 1 (Z.) F1 = D.L. 7.2.

5. *SVF* 1 (Z.) F1, F41 = D.L. 7.2. Sandbach, *Stoics*, p. 24, accepts that it was early; Erskine, *Hellenistic Stoa*, pp. 9–15, argues that it is a mature work.

6. Erskine, *Hellenistic Stoa*, pp. 18–20.

7. *SVF* 1 (Z.) F259 = D.L. 7.32, ἔνιοι μέντοι, ἐξ ὧν εἰσιν οἱ περὶ Κάσσιον τὸν σκεπτικόν, ἐν πολλοῖς κατηγοροῦντες τοῦ Ζήνωνος, πρῶτον μὲν τὴν ἐγκύκλιον παιδείαν ἄχρηστον ἀποφαίνειν λέγοντα ἐν ἀρχῇ τῆς Πολιτείας. Diogenes' source

is late and avowedly hostile to Zeno but the information it contains on the contents of his *Republic* is essentially sound, since the existence of other points for which Zeno was criticized by the same authors (alienation of wise men from friends and family; sharing of wives; and banning of temples, lawcourts, gymnasia, and coinage) is corroborated by other sources (*SVF* 1 [Z.] F264–66, 269).

8. Pire, *Stoïcisme*, p. 22.

9. Marrou, *Saint Augustin*, pp. 210–35, esp. 214.

10. Marrou, *Histoire de l'éducation*, pp. 266–67. On the curriculum in the third century B.C., see Marrou, *Saint Augustin*, p. 216.

11. Epicur. F163 (Usener), παιδείαν δὲ πᾶσαν, μακάριε, φεῦγε τἀκάτιον ἀράμενος.

12. *SVF* 1 (Z.) F41 = D.L. 7.4; Pire, *Stoïcisme*, p. 23.

13. *SVF* 1 (Z.) F247–50, esp. F250, Ζήνων ἐν ταῖς διατριβαῖς φησι περὶ παίδων ἀγωγῆς κτλ. X. *Lac.* 2.13; *Inst. Lac.* 7 (237 B–C); cf. Plut. *Lyc.* 18.8–9. Schofield, *Stoic Idea*, pp. 35–42.

14. *SVF* 1 (Z.) F261 = Plut. *Lyc.* 31.2; *De stoic.* 3 (1033F).

15. Schofield, *Stoic Idea*, pp. 22–56; Ollier, "Le philosophe stoïcien," p. 548.

16. Persaeus: *SVF* 1 (P.) F435 = D.L. 7.36. Herillus: *SVF* 1 (H.) F409 = D.L. 7.165.

17. *SVF* 1 (Z.) F1 = D.L. 7.1.

18. *SVF* 1 (P.) F442 = Paus. 2.8.4. Since Erskine views the early Stoics as essentially anti-Macedonian, he brands Persaeus as a "renegade": *Hellenistic Stoa*, pp. 75–102, esp. p. 97 n. 27.

19. *SVF* 1 (P.) F435 = D.L. 7.36; Ollier, "Le philosophe stoïcien," p. 556.

20. Ollier, "Le philosophe stoïcien," p. 543.

21. *SVF* 1 (Sph.) F622 = Plut. *Cleom.* 2.3, ὁ δὲ Σφαῖρος ἐν τοῖς πρώτοις ἐγεγόνει τῶν Ζήνωνος τοῦ Κιτιέως μαθητῶν; *SVF* 1 (Sph.) F628 = Cic. *Tusc.* 4.53, *Sphaeri, hominis in primis bene definientis, ut putant Stoici.*

22. *SVF* 1 (Sph.) F620 = D.L. 7.177.

23. Several anecdotes link Sphaerus with a Ptolemy of Egypt: *SVF* 1 (Sph.) F621 = D.L. 7.185; *SVF* 1 (Sph.) F624 = Athen. *Deipnos.* 8.50 (354E); *SVF* 1 (Sph.) F625 = D.L. 7.177. According to the last in the series, he was Ptolemy Philopator. This would render unhistorical the first anecdote, which describes a summons from Ptolemy to Cleanthes either to attend the king himself or to send a substitute, because Philopator ascended the Egyptian throne in 222 or 221, well after Cleanthes' death in 232 B.C.

24. *SVF* 1 (Sph.) F27 = Plut. *De stoic.* 2 (1033B).

25. *SVF* 1 (Sph.) F622 = Plut. *Cleom.* 2.2.

26. Chrysippus became scholarch soon after Cleanthes' death in 232 B.C.: von Arnim, "Chrysippos (14)," 2505. Cleomenes' coup took place in 227 B.C.: Cartledge and Spawforth, *Hellenistic and Roman Sparta*, p. 50.

27. *SVF* 2 (Chr.) F6 = D.L. 7.183.

28. *SVF* 2 (Chr.) F16 = D.L. 7.198, πρὸς τὸ Ἀρκεσιλάου μεθόδιον πρὸς Σφαῖρον α΄.

29. *SVF* 3 (Chr.) F738 = D.L. 7.129, εὐχρηστεῖν δὲ καὶ τὰ ἐγκύκλια μαθήματα φησὶν ὁ Χρύσιππος.

30. On Sphaerus as a Zenonian, see Schofield, *Stoic Idea*, p. 42.

31. See Chapter 2, at note 4.

32. See Chapter 1, at note 108.

33. The average word-count of *Institutions* 1–17 is 46.3, that of *Institutions* 18–41 is only 25.6. The first seventeen contain a total of 805 words, but the next twenty-four (18–41) only 576. I exclude *Inst. Lac.* 42 because it was written by the epitomator himself and therefore does not reflect his habits of excerption: see Chapter 1, at note 112.

34. Simpleminded: *Inst. Lac.* 33, where it is claimed that the Spartans prohibited comedy and tragedy because they could not endure the breaking of laws even in pretense. Obscure: *Inst. Lac.* 38, "They reprimanded the youth from the gymnasium [τὸν ἐκ τοῦ γυμνασίου νεανίσκον] for knowing the road to Pylaea." I doubt that anyone but a Spartan would have understood the reference to "the road to Pylaea" or have been absolutely sure who "they" were.

35. *Inst. Lac.* 21 (238E) (*agōgē* and citizenship), 30 (239A) (display of drunken helots to children), 40 (239C–D) (endurance contest).

36. On this point, see Chapter 1.

37. *Inst. Lac.* 13 (237F), νομίζοντες . . . τὰς γὰρ ἰσχνὰς καὶ διακένους ἕξεις ὑπακούειν πρὸς τὴν διάρθρωσιν, τὰς δὲ πολυτρόφους διὰ βάρος ἀντιβαίνειν.

38. X. *Lac.* 2.5, καὶ εἰς μῆκος δ' ἂν τὴν ῥαδινὰ τὰ σώματα ποιοῦσαν τροφὴν μᾶλλον συλλαμβάνειν ἡγήσατο ἢ τὴν διαπλατύνουσαν τῷ σίτῳ.

39. E.g., Hp. *Aff.* 12.9; *Vict.* 2.59.1, 3.81.29; Gal. on Hp. *Acut.* 2.10 (528, 531, 532); on Hp. *Medic.* 2.9 (750); *De plac. Hp. et Pl.* 8.4.5 (675); *De alim. fac.* 1.10.2 (504); *De bonis mal. suc.* 12.4 (810); *De prag.* 6.13 (634), 8.20 (647).

40. Gal. *Def. med.* 95 (372), ἕξις ἐστὶ πνεῦμα συνέχον καὶ συγκρατοῦν τὰ μέρη. Stoic definition: Long, "Soul and Body," p. 41; Hahm, *Origins*, p. 164. Cf. *SVF* 2 (Chr.) F458 = Philo *Leg. alleg.* 2.22; *SVF* 2 (Chr.) F449 = Plut. *De stoic.* 43 (1053F).

41. Cf. Ast, *Lexicon Platonicum*, s.v. ἕξις .

42. *Inst. Lac.* 4 (237A), γράμματα ἕνεκα τῆς χρείας ἐμάνθανον· τῶν δ' ἄλλων παιδευμάτων ξενηλασίαν ἐποιοῦντο, οὐ μᾶλλον ἀνθρώπων ἢ λόγων. Χρεία is usually misconstrued as "necessity," obscuring its precise significance here. Fuhrmann's version in his Budé edition, *Plutarque: Oeuvres morales*, 3:235, is typical: "Leur étude des lettres se bornait au stricte necessaire." Cf. Perrin, *Plutarch's Lives*, 1:257.

43. Sandbach, *Stoics*, pp. 28–32.

44. *SVF* 3 (Chr.) F126 = D.L. 7.105, τὴν δὲ εἶναι μέσην τινα δύναμιν ἢ χρείαν συμβαλλομένην πρὸς τὸν κατὰ φύσιν βίον.

45. *SVF* 3 (Chr.) F135 = D.L. 7.107, ἔτι τῶν προηγμένων τὰ μὲν δι' αὐτὰ προῆκται, τὰ δὲ δι' ἕτερα, . . . δι' αὐτὰ μὲν, ὅτι κατὰ φύσιν ἐστί, δι' ἕτερα δέ, ὅτι περιποιεῖ χρείας οὐκ ὀλίγας .

46. *SVF* 1 (Z.) F309 = D.L. 7.22, μὴ τὰς φωνὰς καὶ τὰς λέξεις δεῖν ἀπομνη-

μονεύειν, ἀλλὰ περὶ τὴν διάθεσιν τῆς χρείας τὸν νοῦν ἀσχολεῖσθαι, μὴ ὥσπερ ἔψησίν τινα ἢ σκευασίαν ἀναλαμβάνοντας.

47. Pire, *Stoïcisme*, pp. 23–24; cf. *SVF* 1 (Z.) F50 = Plut. *De stoic.* 8 (1034F). Zeno's division of philosophy: D.L. 7.39; *SVF* 1 (Z.) F46 = D.L. 7.40.

48. *Inst. Lac.* 14 (238A), κέντρον δ' εἶχε ταῦτα ἐγερτικὸν θυμοῦ καὶ φρονήματος καὶ παραστατικὸν ὁρμῆς ἐνθουσιώδους καὶ πρακτικῆς.

49. *Inst. Lac.* 16 (238B), καὶ οἱ ἐμβατήριοι δὲ ῥυθμοὶ παρορμητικοὶ ἦσαν πρὸς ἀνδρείαν καὶ θαρραλεότητα καὶ ὑπερφρόνησιν θανάτου.

50. On this sequence, see the full discussion in Inwood, *Ethics*, pp. 18–101.

51. *SVF* 3 (Diog.) F68 = Phld. *Mus.* p. 15, (ἔχειν) φύσει τὸ μέλος κ(ινητικό)ν τι καὶ παραστα(τικὸ)ν πρὸς τὰς πράξεις.

52. *Inst. Lac.* 11 (237D); on the use of *agōgē*, see my subsequent discussion.

53. Dionysius: περὶ ἀρχαίων βασιλέων; περὶ βαρβαρικῶν ἐθῶν (*SVF* 1 [Dion.] F422 = D.L. 7.166). Persaeus: περὶ βασιλείας; πολιτεία Λακωνική (*SVF* 1 [P.] F435 = D.L. 7.36). Cleanthes: ἀρχαιολογία; πολιτικός; περὶ νόμων; περὶ βασιλείας (*SVF* 1 [C.] F481). Herillus' work, νομοθέτης, was probably of this type as well (*SVF* 1 [H.] F409 = D.L. 7.165).

54. *SVF* 1 (P.) F454 = Athen. *Deipnos.* 4.18 (140E); *SVF* 1 (Sph.) F630 = Athen. *Deipnos.* 4.19 (141C); cf. *SVF* 1 (P.) F455 = Athen. *Deipnos.* 4.17 (140B).

55. On the epitomator's identity, see Chapter 1, at note 113.

56. *Inst. Lac.* 6 (237B), ἐκάθευδον δὲ οἱ νέοι ὁμοῦ κατ' ἴλην καὶ κατ' ἀγέλην ἐπὶ στιβάδων.

57. Hesych. s.v. βουαγόρ; βοῦα. See Chapter 2, at note 60.

58. X. *Lac.* 2.11.

59. Plut. *Lyc.* 17.2.

60. Plut. *Lyc.* 16.7, 16.8, 16.13, 17.2; *Ages.* 2.1. There is at least one other anachronism in the *Agesilaus*: cf. *Ages.* 1.1, on which see subsequent discussion, at note 109.

61. Hesych. s.v. ἀγέλας, βουαγόρ, βοῦα.

62. *Inscr. Cret.* I, p. 84 (Dreros) 1A, lines 10–11, τάδε ὤμοσαν/ ἀγελάοι; p. 90 (Eltynia) 2, line 6, ἦν ἀγ[έ]λα[ι]; *CIG* 2892 (Miletus), line 8, νέων ἀ[γ]έ[λ]ας; *CIG* 3326 (Smyrna), αἰθέων [ἄ]λικος ἐξ ἀγέλας; *SEG* XXXV (1985), no. 1165, (Kula [Lydia]) ἐξ ἀγέλης πέ/δων (= παίδων); Varinlioğlu, "Inschriften von Stratonikeia," pp. 79–82, 1, line 13, [ἀγ]έλην τῶν παίδων; Robert, "Sur des inscriptions de Chios I–III," p. 519 (*OMS* I:487), line 13, [μ]ετὰ τῆς ἀγέλης τῶν π[αίδων]; Heberdey, "Gymnische und andere Agone," p. 197 (Termessus), νείκησ[α πάλη?]/ παίδων ἐξ ἀγέλης.

63. Torch race: Wörrle, *Stadt und Fest*, p. 10, lines 65–66; p. 221 (Oenoanda); Balland, *Xanthos*, pp. 41–42; *CIG* 2892 (Miletus), line 8, νέων ἀ[γ]έ[λ]ας ἔδρακεν ἄγεμονα. *Agelarchēs*: *IGR* III 648 (Idebessus); *SEG* XXXVIII (1988), no. 1482 (Xanthus), line 5; Pékary, "Inschriftenfunde," p. 128, no. 15 (Miletus). Definition: Hesych. s.v. βουαγόρ· ἀγελάρχης, ὁ τῆς ἀγέλης ἄρχων παῖς. Λάκωνες.

64. Plut. *Lyc.* 3.2 (πρόδικοι), 6.1 (ῥήτρα), 12.1 (φιδίτια), 12.11 (κεκαδδίσθαι), 23.1 (οὐλαμός).

65. Cf. Nilsson, "Grundlagen," p. 312.

66. *An. Bachm.* 1:261, ἵλας· ἀγέλας. ἢ τάξεις.

67. Plut. *Lyc.* 16.8, ἄρχοντα δ᾽ αὐτοῖς παρίσταντο τῆς ἀγέλης τὸν τῷ φρονεῖν διαφέροντα καὶ θυμοειδέστατον ἐν τῷ μάχεσθαι.

68. Plut. *Lyc.* 17.2, καὶ κατ᾽ ἀγέλας αὐτοὶ προΐσταντο τῶν λεγομένων εἰρένων ἀεὶ τὸν σωφρονέστατον καὶ μαχιμώτατον.

69. Plut. *Lyc.* 17.4: see Chapter 2, at note 85.

70. See Chapter 2, Table 1.

71. On the Classical system, see Chapter 6.

72. Klee, *Geschichte des gymnischen Agone*, pp. 43–51.

73. Chios: *SIG³*, no. 959, lines 11–14, ἐφήβων νεωτέρων . . . μέσων . . . πρεσβυτέρων. Teos: *CIG* 3088, col. A, line 1, [πρεσβυτέρας ἡλικίας]; line 4, μέσης ἡλικίας; col. B, line 1, νεωτέρας [ἡλικίας]. Heraclea Pontica: Pargoire, "Inscriptions," p. 493 II, line 8, ἐφήβων νεωτέρων. Halicarnassus: Hula and Szanto, "Bericht," p. 29, no. 2, νικήσας ἐφήβους νεωτέρου[ς].

74. Athens: *IG* II/III² 956, line 76, [παῖδας] στάδιον τῆς πρώτης ἡλικίας; line 78, [παῖδας στ]άδιον τῆς δευτέρας ἡλικίας; line 80, [π]αῖ{ι}δας [σ]τάδ[ιον]. E.g., *IEphesos* IV, no. 1101.

75. Lebadea: *IG* VII 1764, line 13, πάμπαιδας; line 21, πάμπαιδας; cf. Roesch, *Études*, p. 322 n. 70. Chalcis: *IG* XII.9 952 col. 1, παῖδας πάμπαιδας.

76. Samos: *SIG³*, no. 1061. Athens: *IG* II/III² 2986, 2991, 2991A. Cf. Pélékidis, *Histoire de l'éphébie*, p. 209.

77. Eustath. *Il.* 2 p. 962, 20, ὁ δὲ μετ᾽ αὐτὸν ⟨i.e., παῖδα⟩, πάλλαξ καὶ βουπαῖς καὶ ἀντίπαις καὶ μελλέφηβος; Poland, *Geschichte des griechischen Vereinswesens*, p. 97.

78. Nilsson, *Die hellenistische Schule*, p. 41.

79. Collignon, *Quid de collegiis epheborum*, pp. 31–32, 69; Ziebarth, *Schulwesen*, p. 145.

80. Nilsson, *Die hellenistische Schule*, p. 41; Hp. *Hebd.* p. 9.

81. Plutarch's contention (*Lyc.* 16.7) that boys entered the *agōgē* at age seven belongs with the Classical phase; cf. X. *Lac.* 1.2.

82. *Inst. Lac.* 14 (237F), ἐσπούδαζον δὲ καὶ περὶ τὰ μέλη καὶ τὰς ᾠδὰς οὐδενὸς ἧττον.

83. On the position of music in Hellenistic Greek education, see Nilsson, *Die hellenistische Schule*, p. 45.

84. Classical (early fourth century B.C.): *Artemis Orthia*, no. 1. Roman (late second century B.C.): *Artemis Orthia*, no. 2, e.g.

85. The earliest evidence for ball games in the Roman period is *IG* V.1 674; Woodward, "Some Notes," p. 193. On the *sphaireis* game in the Classical period: X. *Lac.* 9.5; see Chapter 6, at note 95.

86. Pl. *Lg.* 1.633B–C; Cic. *Tusc.* 5.27.77. On the antiquity of the contests of the Roman *agōgē*, see Chapter 3, at note 26, and Cartledge and Spawforth, *Hellenistic and Roman Sparta*, pp. 206–7.

87. See Chapter 4, at note 71.

88. Cic. *Tusc.* 2.34 = T1.

89. *Inst. Lac.* 40 (239C–D) = T18.

90. On the ritual in Xenophon, see Chapter 4, at note 43, and Chapter 6, at note 69.

91. E.g., Cartledge and Spawforth, *Hellenistic and Roman Sparta*, p. 207.

92. *IG* V.1 653a (*Artemis Orthia*, no. 142).

93. D.L. 6.15.

94. E.g., *SVF* 3 (Chr.) F264 = Stob. *Ecl.* 2.60.9.

95. *SVF* 1 (Sph.) F628 = Cic. *Tusc.* 4.53, *Fortitudo est igitur "adfectio animi legi summae in perpetiendis rebus obtemperans," vel "conservatio stabilis iudici in eis rebus quae formidolosae videntur subeundis et repellendis," vel "scientia rerum formidolosarum contrariumque aut omnino neglegendarum conservans earum stabile iudicium."*

96. *SVF* 3 (Chr.) F274 = Sext. Emp. *Adv. Math.* 9.153.

97. *SVF* 1 (Sph.) F628 = Cic. *Tusc.* 4.53; Dyroff, *Ethik*, pp. 79–80.

98. Cf. Dyroff, *Ethik*, p. 79.

99. X. *Lac.* 2.2–11.

100. E.g., Lucian *Anach.* 24; *Ins. Olympia*, no. 55; Robert, "Inscriptions d'Aphrodisias," pp. 429–30.

101. *ISestos*, no. 1 (*OGIS*, no. 339), lines 71–72, ἐξ ὧν αἱ τῶν νεωτέρων ψυχαὶ πρὸς ἀνδρείαν ἁμιλλώμεν/αι καλῶς ἄγονται τοῖς ἤθεσιν πρὸς ἀρετήν.

102. Ephebes honored for ἀνδρεία: *IG* V.1 472, 564–66, 660(?). *Bōmonikai*: *IG* V.1 652, 653, 653B (*Artemis Orthia*, no. 143).

103. Pl. *Lg.* 1.633B. The "thefts" are an allusion to the cheese-stealing contest at the altar of Artemis: see Chapter 6, at note 69. On the *krupteia*, see Lévy, "La kryptie," pp. 245–52. On the Gymnopaediae, see Chapter 3, at note 124.

104. Tigerstedt, *Legend of Sparta*, 2:26–27.

105. *Apophth. Lac.* Anon. 54 (235B), ἵνα μὴ ἀπαίδευτοι γένωνται, τῆς πατρίου ἀγωγῆς ἀτευκτήσαντες· οὐδὲ πολῖται γὰρ ἂν εἴησαν.

106. Teles (Hense²) p. 28; on this speech, see Chapter 1, at note 49.

107. See Chapter 1, at note 40.

108. Plut. *Agis* 4.2, καὶ λέγειν ὡς οὐδὲν δέοιτο τῆς βασιλείας, εἰ μὴ δι' αὐτὴν ἀναλήψοιτο τοὺς νόμους καὶ τὴν πάτριον ἀγωγήν; *Cleom.* 16.3 (πάτριον σχῆμα); 16.6 (πάτριον πολιτείαν); 18.4 (πατρίων ἐθῶν). Cf. Phylarchus, *FGrHist* 81 F44.

109. πάτριος ἀγωγή: *Apophth. Lac.* Anon. 54 (235B); *Inst. Lac.* 11 (237D), 42 (240B); Plut. *Agis* 4.2. Λυκουργεῖος ἀγωγή: Plut. *Phil.* 16.8; Hesych. s.v. ἄφορτος. Λακωνικὴ ἀγωγή: Polyb. 1.32.1. ἀγωγή: *Inst. Lac.* 21 (238E); Sosibius, *FGrHist* 595 F4; Polyb. 24.7.1; Plut. *Cleom.* 11.3, 18.4, 37.14; *Lyc.* 22.1; *Phoc.* 20.4; *Ages.* 1.1, 3.3.

CHAPTER SIX

1. Recent exceptions are Hodkinson, "Social Order," pp. 245–51, and Powell, *Athens and Sparta*, p. 230, who calls it "detailed and believable."

2. X. *Cyr.* 1.2.8, 1.2.9.

3. X. *Lac.* 2.1–4.7.

4. X. *HG* 5.4.32, παῖς τε ὢν καὶ παιδίσκος καὶ ἡβῶν.

5. Thuc. 4.132; Schwarz, "Damonon," pp. 177–78; *IG* V.1 213, line 39; cf. *Apophth. Lac.* 215B.

6. Phot. s.v. συνέφηβος; Ar. *Lys.* 983, 1248; Hesych. s.v. κυρσανίας; cf. σκυρθάλια.

7. X. *Lac.* 2.1, ἐπειδὰν τάχιστα αὐτοῖς οἱ παῖδες τὰ λεγόμενα συνιῶσιν, εὐθὺς μὲν ἐπ᾽ αὐτοῖς παιδαγωγοὺς θεράποντας ἐφιστᾶσιν. On school age, see Marrou, *Histoire de l'éducation*, p. 161.

8. Plut. *Lyc.* 16.7.

9. On this age for *paidiskoi* (= *meirakia*), see Chapter 1, at note 12. Cf. Hesych. s.v. παιδίσκοι· οἱ ἐκ παίδων εἰς ἄνδρας μεταβαίνοντες.

10. X. *Lac.* 4.6. On this point, see subsequent discussion, at note 31.

11. X. *HG* 5.4.13; Plut. *Lyc.* 26.1.

12. X. *Lac.* 1.6 (marriage); 4.7 (political office); 11.3 (hair), misinterpreted by Plutarch, *Lyc.* 22.2; Plut. *Lyc.* 25.1 (economic, political activity). Xenophon's use of ἀκμάζων: Teles (Hense²) p. 50; Poll. 2.11, εἶτα ἀνὴρ τὴν μάχιμον ἡλικίαν ἔχων, τὴν στρατεύσιμον ἡλικίαν ἔχων, τῶν ἐκ καταλόγων, ἀκμάζων, σφρίγων.

13. Cf. Rhodes, *Boule*, p. 1.

14. Teles (Hense²) p. 50, ἐξ ἐφήβων ἐστὶ καὶ ἤδη εἴκοσι ἐτῶν· ἔτι φοβεῖται καὶ παρατηρεῖ καὶ γυμνασίαρχον καὶ στρατηγόν. παρακοιτεῖν εἴ που δεῖ, οὗτοι παρακοιτοῦσι· φυλάττειν καὶ ἀγρυπνεῖν, οὗτοι φυλάττουσιν· εἰς τὰ πλοῖα ἐμβαίνειν, οὗτοι ἐμβαίνουσιν. ἀνὴρ γέγονε καὶ ἀκμάζει· στρατεύεται καὶ πρεσβεύει ὑπὲρ τῆς πόλεως, πολιτεύεται, στρατηγεῖ, χορηγεῖ, ἀγωνοθετεῖ.

15. *IG* V.1 1120; better text in Bingen, "ΤΡΙΕΤΙΡΗΣ," p. 106, line 5, τριετίρες ἐόν.

16. *IG* V.1 1386; Bingen, "ΤΡΙΕΤΙΡΗΣ," p. 106.

17. Hesych. s.v. κατὰ πρωτείρας; Phot. s.v. προτεῖραι.

18. See Chapter 5, at note 72.

19. Hom. *Il.* 8.518, παῖδας πρωθήβας; *Od.* 8.262–63, κοῦροι/πρωθήβας; Poll. 2.9, τὸ γὰρ πρωθήβης ποιητικόν; cf. Luc. *DMort* 15(5).2, πρωθήβης γενόμενος.

20. Hesych. s.v. κατὰ πρωτείρας· ἡλικίας ὄνομα οἱ πρωτεῖρες παρὰ Λακεδαιμονίοις; Phot. s.v. προτεῖραι· οἱ περὶ εἴκοσι ἔτη παρὰ Λάκωσι.

21. Call. F487 (Pfeiffer), ἀλλ᾽ ἀντὶ βρεφέων πολιὸν νέον εἴρενα μέσσον.

22. Unaware of the epigraphical evidence, Forbes, "Medial Intervocalic -ρσ-," pp. 252–53, postulated that the original form of εἰρήν was *ἤρην. She is followed by Cotter, "Etymology," pp. 31–34.

23. Cf. Hesych. s.v. εἰρήν.

24. X. *Lac.* 2.11.

25. X. *Lac.* 2.11, τὸν τορώτατον τῶν ἀρρένων. On this reading, see Chapter 1, at note 80. On the number of *ōbai* in the Classical period, see Appendix 2.

26. X. *Lac.* 2.10.

27. X. *Lac.* 2.2; cf. 4.7.

28. X. *Lac.* 2.2; Lebessi, "Flagellation," pp. 118, 121–22, erroneously identifies the *mastigophoroi* with the youths who defended the altar in the cheese-stealing ritual. On this ritual, see subsequent discussion, at note 61.

29. Glotz, "Hellanodikai," pp. 60–64, esp. p. 63; Saglio, "Agonothetes II," p. 150.

30. On the lack of public education in the Classical period, see Ziebarth, *Schulwesen*, pp. 30–34; Marrou, *Histoire de l'éducation*, p. 163. Education in Classical Athens was a private affair, although schools were regulated by law: Golden, *Children*, p. 62. Sparta: Arist. *Pol.* 8.1.4 (1337A), ἐπαινέσειε δ' ἄν τις κατὰ τοῦτο Λακεδαιμονίους· καὶ γὰρ πλείστην ποιοῦνται σπουδὴν περὶ τοὺς παῖδας καὶ κοινῇ ταύτην.

31. X. *Lac.* 4.6.

32. Agatharchidas, *FGrHist* 86 F10.

33. X. *Lac.* 4.3. For more on the *hippeis*, see subsequent discussion, at note 80.

34. Ael. *VH* 3.10.

35. On this magistracy, see Chapter 2, at note 108. Striano, "Laconien βιδεος," pp. 40–47, argues that it derives from Myc. *wid-wos-jo*.

36. X. *Lac.* 2.5, σῖτόν γε μὴν ἔταξε τοσοῦτον ἔχοντα συμβολεύειν τὸν ἄρρενα, ὡς ὑπὸ πλησμονῆς μὲν μήποτε βαρύνεσθαι, τοῦ δὲ ἐνδεεστέρως διάγειν μή ἀπείρως ἔχειν. On the reading ἄρρενα instead of εἴρενα, see Chapter 1, at note 80. On the clause ὡς . . . βαρύνεσθαι, almost always mistranslated, see Smyth, *Greek Grammar*, 2267.

37. X. *Lac.* 2.7.

38. *Apophth. Lac.* Anon. 35 (234A–B), ἕτερον παιδάριον, ἐπεὶ παρῆν ὁ καιρός, ἐν ᾧ κλέπτειν νενόμιστο τοὺς ἐλευθέρους παῖδας ὅ τί τις δύναιτο καὶ μὴ λαθεῖν αἰσχρὸν ἦν, ὡς οἱ σὺν αὐτῷ παῖδες ζῶν ἔκλεψαν ἀλωπέκιον καὶ ἔδοσαν αὐτῷ φυλάττειν, παραγενομένων τῶν ἀπολωλεκότων ἐπὶ ζήτησιν, ἔτυχε μὲν ὑποβαλὼν τὸ ἀλωπέκιον ὑπὸ τὸ αὐτοῦ ἱμάτιον, ἀγριαίνοντος δὲ τοῦ θηρίου καὶ τὴν πλευρὰν αὐτοῦ κατεσθίοντος μέχρι τῶν σπλάγχνων ἠρέμει, ἵνα μὴ γένηται καταφανής. ὡς δ' ὕστερον ἐκείνων ἀπελθόντων ἐθεάσαντο τὸ γεγονὸς οἱ παῖδες καὶ ἐμέμφοντο, λέγοντες ἄμεινον εἶναι φανερὸν ποιῆσαι τὸ ἀλωπέκιον ἢ μέχρι θανάτου κρύπτειν, "Οὐ μὲν οὖν," εἶπεν, "ἀλλὰ κρεῖττον ταῖς ἀληδόσι μὴ ἐνδόντα τελευτᾶν ἢ περίφωρον γενόμενον διὰ μαλακίαν τὸ ζῆν αἰσχρῶς περιποιήσασθαι."

39. den Boer, *Laconian Studies*, p. 270.

40. Paus. 3.16.9; Hesych. s.v. φούαξιρ, φουάδδει. Cf. Vernant, *Mortals*, p. 241.

41. Hesych. s.v. πλαγιάδδοντερ; Ar. *Pax* 1067–68, ἀλωπεκιδεῦσι πέπεισθε; *Lys.* 1270, αἱμυλᾶν ἀλωπέκων παυαΐμεθα.

42. On the Spartan origins of many apophthegmata, see Tigerstedt, *Legend of Sparta*, 2:28.

43. E.g., Roussel, *Sparte*, p. 46; Jones, *Sparta*, p. 35; Forrest, *History of Sparta*, p. 54; Parker, "Spartan Religion," p. 148.

44. E.g., Plut. *QG* 55 (303D); Athen. *Deipnos.* 14.44–45 (639B–40A). Michell, *Sparta*, pp. 177–79, makes some similar points.

45. X. *Lac.* 2.9.

46. X. *Lac.* 2.3.

47. Frazer, *Golden Bough*, 3:310–13. Andania: *IG* V.1 1390, line 15, Εἱματισμοῦ. οἱ τελούμενοι τὰ μυστήρια ἀνυπόδετοι ἔστωσαν; Lycosura: *IG* V.2 514,

lines 1–7, μὴ ἐξέστω/ παρέρπην ἔχοντας ἐν τὸ ἱερὸν τᾶς/ Δεσποίνας . . . μηδὲ ὑπο/δήματα.

48. Burkert, *Griechische Religion*, pp. 367–68.

49. On the initiatory character of the Athenian ephebate, see Jeanmaire, *Couroi*, pp. 308–21; Vidal-Naquet, *Le chasseur noir*, pp. 151–75.

50. *Inst. Lac.* 6 (237B). The detail, from Sphaerus' study of the Spartan constitution, is consistent with ephebic traditions of the Classical period.

51. Burkert, *Griechische Religion*, pp. 174–76.

52. X. *Lac.* 2.12–14.

53. Sergent, *L'homosexualité*, pp. 11–71.

54. Compare the description of Cleonymus, beloved of Agesilaus' son Archidamus, X. *HG* 5.4.25: ἡλικίαν τε ἔχων τὴν ἄρτι ἐκ παίδων, καὶ ἅμα κάλλιστός τε καὶ εὐδοκιμώτατος τῶν ἡλίκων.

55. X. *Lac.* 3.1–5, esp. 3.2.

56. X. *Lac.* 3.5. In Plutarch's time (*Lyc.* 18.3), this custom was subsumed under the *agōgē*, with the *eirēn* asking questions of the younger ephebes.

57. X. *Lac.* 3.4.

58. On this subject, see Boring, *Literacy*.

59. Arist. *Pol.* 8.4.2 (1338B).

60. Marrou, *Histoire de l'éducation*, pp. 31–44.

61. X. *Lac.* 2.9: see previous discussion, at note 1.

62. Plut. *Arist.* 17.1 (T17): see Chapter 4, at note 43.

63. *IG* V.1 255 (*Artemis Orthia*, no. 1), ϝωρθείαι τάδ' Ἀρ[ή]ξιππος/ νικῶν ἀνέσηκε/ ἐν συνόδοις πα[ί]δων πᾶhιν hορῆν φανερά.

64. See previous discussion, at note 24.

65. See Chapter 2, at note 44.

66. See Chapter 4, at note 26.

67. Vernant, *Mortals*, pp. 198–99.

68. On the identification of Artemis with Orthia, see subsequent discussion, at note 126.

69. Pl. *Lg.* 1.633B–C.

70. Wyss, *Die Milch*, pp. 58–61; Sokolowski, *Lois sacrées*, nos. 62 (line 12), 89 (line 15), 135 (lines 72 and 79); Alcm. F17.

71. Plut. *QG* 55 (303D); Hdt. 3.48.2–3. The classic modern study is Rose, "Greek Rites," pp. 1–5, whose explanations are now completely obsolete.

72. Cf. Sokolowski, *Lois sacrées*, no. 50 A, lines 8–9, [ἐὰν δέ τι]ς παρὰ ταῦτα πράξη ἢ βιάσηται ἔστω κ[ατ' αὐτοῦ/ ἔνδειξι]ς πρὸς τὴν βουλὴν; no. 55, line 8, ἐὰν δέ τις βιάσηται, ἀπρόσδεκτος/ ἡ θυσία παρὰ τοῦ θεοῦ; no. 178, lines 7–9, ἐὰν δέ/ [τ]ις βιαζόμενος πίνηι, ἀποτίν/[ε]ν πέντε δραχμάς.

73. On sacrifice as an act of killing, see Burkert, *Homo Necans*, pp. 8–20.

74. Burkert, *Griechische Religion*, pp. 101–5.

75. On this point, see Vernant, *Mortals*, pp. 235–36. This incongruity was a commonplace in accounts of the endurance contest: Mus. (Hense) 523 (T11); Luc. *Demon.* 46.9 (T20); Philos. *VA* 6.20 (T30).

76. Burkert, *Griechische Religion*, pp. 351–52, 390–94. For an interesting,

albeit flawed, attempt to find this ritual's origin in Bronze Age self-flagellation, see Lebessi, "Flagellation," pp. 99–123.

77. X. *Lac.* 4.1–7.

78. X. *Lac.* 4.6.

79. Cartledge, *Agesilaos*, pp. 204–5. Both he and Lazenby, *Spartan Army*, p. 12, agree that the *hippeis* were drawn from men between twenty and thirty years of age.

80. Ephorus, *FGrHist* 70 F149, p. 87. On the reason for this, see the subsequent discussion, at note 173.

81. Cartledge, *Sparta and Lakonia*, p. 294; Lazenby, *Spartan Army*, pp. 7–8.

82. X. *HG* 3.3.4–11, esp. 3.3.8–9; Cartledge, *Sparta and Lakonia*, p. 275.

83. Hdt. 1.67.5.

84. Arist. *Pol.* 2.9.32 (1271A).

85. Arist. *Pol.* 2.9.31 (1271A); Dosiades, *FGrHist* 458 F2.

86. Plut. *Lyc.* 12.9; Hodkinson, "Social Order," p. 253.

87. I take the number of members of a *phidition* from Plut. *Lyc.* 12.3. A much larger number (300) can be derived from *Agis* 8.4, but it is probably not valid for the Classical period.

88. Hesych. s.v. †διαφοιγοιμόρ.

89. Xenophon, *Lac.* 5.5, stresses the value of the older men's experience in the education of young men in the *phiditia*.

90. Dicaearchus, *FGH*, 2:242 F23 (= Athen. *Deipnos.* 4.19 141A–C) and Plutarch, *Lyc.* 12.3, give two slightly different versions of their shopping list. For more on this subject, see Figueira, "Mess Contributions," pp. 87–109.

91. X. *Lac.* 5.3. Athenaeus, 4.17–19 (140C–141F), brings together a large collection of ancient scholarship on Spartan eating habits.

92. Molpis, *FGrHist* 590 F2. Xenophon, *Lac.* 4.7, characterizes hunting as the main occupation of those above the age of *hēbōn*.

93. X. *Lac.* 2.2: see previous discussion, at note 28.

94. Jeanmaire, *Couroi*, p. 526. On these festivals, see Chapter 3, at note 97.

95. X. *Lac.* 9.5, πολλάκις δ' ὁ τοιοῦτος καὶ διαιρουμένων τοὺς ἀντισφαιριοῦν-τας ἀχώριστος περιγίγνεται.

96. X. *Lac.* 5.1: οἵαν δὲ καὶ πᾶσι δίαιταν κατεσκεύασε, νῦν πειράσομαι διη-γεῖσθαι.

97. Pl. *Lg.* 1.633B–C; schol. to Pl. *Lg.* 1.633B.

98. Lévy, "La kryptie," pp. 245–52.

99. Plut. *Lac.* 28.1–7; Lévy, "La kryptie," p. 250.

100. Cartledge, "Politics," p. 22; Plut. *Lyc.* 25.1. On the specialized Spartan vocabulary for such relationships, see Cartledge, "Politics," p. 31 n. 18.

101. X. *Lac.* 1.6, πρὸς δὲ τούτοις καὶ ἀποπαύσας τοῦ ὁπότε βούλοιντο ἕκαστοι γυναῖκα ἄγεσθαι ἔταξεν ἐν ἀκμαῖς τῶν σωμάτων τοὺς γάμους ποιεῖσθαι, καὶ τοῦτο συμφέρον τῇ εὐγονίᾳ νομίζων.

102. X. *Lac.* 2.2, 4.3, 4.7. On *akmazontes*, see previous discussion, at note 12.

103. *Apophth. Lac.* 227E–F; Plut. *Lyc.* 15.2–3. This practice may have been the inspiration for Plato's setting the age of marriage in his city at between thirty

and thirty-five (*Lg.* 4.721B–D), with penalties for those who remained unmarried after that point.

104. X. *Lac.* 1.5; *Apophth. Lac.* 228A; Plut. *Lyc.* 15.4–10. For a completely different interpretation of these sources, see Hodkinson, "Social Order," p. 242.

105. Teles (Hense²) p. 28; Plutarch *Ages.* 1.2.4.

106. X. *An.* 4.8.25. On sickles, see subsequent discussion, at note 180.

107. Parker, *Miasma,* pp. 104–43.

108. On boys' mess contributions, see X. *Lac.* 2.5 and my earlier discussion, at note 36. Adult contributions: Arist. *Pol.* 2.9.32 (1271A), ὅρος δὲ τῆς πολιτείας οὗτός ἐστιν αὐτοῖς ὁ πάτριος, τὸν μὴ δυνάμενον τοῦτο τὸ τέλος φέρειν μὴ μετέχειν αὐτῆς.

109. X. *Lac.* 3.3.

110. The term appears only in X. *HG* 3.3.6; Cartledge, *Sparta and Lakonia,* pp. 313–15.

111. X. *HG* 3.3.5.

112. Bizos, *Xénophon: Cyropédie,* 1:xiii; Carlier, "L'idée de monarchie," pp. 141–43, rightly draws attention to the differences.

113. X. *Cyr.* 1.2.15, ἀλλ' ἔξεστι πᾶσι Πέρσαις πέμπειν τοὺς ἑαυτῶν παῖδας εἰς τὰ κοινὰ τῆς δικαιοσύνης διδασκαλεῖα. ἀλλ' οἱ μὲν δυνάμενοι τρέφειν τοὺς παῖδας ἀργοῦντας πέμπουσιν, οἱ δὲ μὴ δυνάμενοι οὐ πέμπουσιν. οἳ δ' ἂν παιδευθῶσι παρὰ τοῖς δημοσίοις διδασκάλοις, ἔξεστιν αὐτοῖς ἐν τοῖς ἐφήβοις νεανισκεύεσθαι, τοῖς δὲ μὴ διαπαιδευθεῖσιν οὕτως οὐκ ἔξεστιν. οἳ δ' ἂν αὖ ἐν τοῖς ἐφήβοις διατελέσωσι τὰ νόμιμα ποιοῦντες, ἔξεστι τούτοις εἰς τοὺς τελείους ἄνδρας συναλίζεσθαι καὶ ἀρχῶν καῖ τιμῶν μετέχειν, οἳ δ' ἂν μὴ διαγένωνται ἐν τοῖς ἐφήβοις οὐκ ἔρχονται εἰς τοὺς τελείους.

114. For a new view of the problems of Spartan land tenure, see Hodkinson, "Land Tenure," pp. 378–406, who argues that the system of inalienable equal lots of land (*klēroi*) thought to obtain in Archaic and Classical Sparta was an invention of Hellenistic propaganda (pp. 383–86). See also Schütrumpf, "The *Rhetra* of Epitadeus," pp. 441–57.

115. Finley, *Use and Abuse,* pp. 170–71; Oliva, *Sparta,* pp. 174–79.

116. Arist. *Pol.* 2.4.17–19 (1270A); Cartledge, *Sparta and Lakonia,* pp. 307–16; Lazenby, *Spartan Army,* p. 17.

117. X. *HG* 5.3.9; Ehrenberg, "Τρόφιμοι," 675–76. For a similar usage in the Roman period, see Jones, "Τρόφιμος," pp. 194–97.

118. Phylarchus, *FGrHist* 81 F43. There are also a number of other testimonia (e.g., schol. to Ar. *Pl.* 279; Hesych. s.v. μόθακες, μόθωνες), of doubtful value because of the degree to which they interpret the Spartan institution in terms of societal conventions of the Hellenistic and Roman periods. The clearest way through this maze of evidence is shown by Cartledge, *Agesilaos,* p. 28. See also Lazenby, *Spartan Army,* pp. 19–21.

119. Phylarchus, *FGrHist* 81 F43.

120. On *kasens,* see Chapter 2, at note 94.

121. Plut. *Cleom.* 8.1.

122. Plut. *Ages.* 1.4.

123. Jalabert, "Syntrophoi," p. 1590. Chrimes, *Ancient Sparta*, p. 222, completely misinterprets this passage.

124. E.g., Marrou, *Histoire de l'éducation*, pp. 45–60; Michell, *Sparta*, pp. 164–65; Oliva, *Sparta*, p. 29. On the other hand, Lazenby, *Spartan Army*, p. 17, appreciates its religious and social significance.

125. Cartledge, *Agesilaos*, p. 25.

126. Cartledge, *Sparta and Lakonia*, p. 358; Carter, "Masks of Ortheia," pp. 374–75.

127. *IG* V.1 277 (*Artemis Orthia*, no. 25).

128. Grunauer-von Hoerschelmann, *Münzprägung*, table 1, group 3.

129. Ibid., pp. 13–16.

130. On the date of the *Laconian Institutions*, see Chapter 1, at note 108.

131. Pipili, *Laconian Iconography*, p. 44. Wace, in Dawkins and others, *Artemis Orthia*, p. 283, came to the same conclusion, drawing attention to a increase in dedications of lead deer in the sixth century and a concomitant reduction in the number of lion figurines, which he considered to be sacred to Orthia.

132. A bracingly skeptical account of this process is given by Finley, *Use and Abuse*, pp. 161–77. See also Cartledge, *Sparta and Lakonia*, pp. 154–57.

133. The excavators (Dawkins and others, *Artemis Orthia*, p. 17) dated the renovation, which included laying down a layer of archaeologically significant sand over the site, to 600 B.C. Some years ago, Boardman, "Artemis Orthia," pp. 1–7, successfully argued for 576–60 B.C., while there have been recent hints that the pendulum might swing back to a date closer to the beginning of the century: see Carter, "Masks of Ortheia," p. 374. On the limitations of the excavators' chronology, particularly regarding the "pre-sand" strata, see Cartledge, *Sparta and Lakonia*, pp. 357–61.

134. The precise number of figurines found is 100,773: Wace, in Dawkins and others, *Artemis Orthia*, pp. 251–52. Of these, 16,561 date from before the site was refurbished, 15,390 were dedicated after 500 B.C., and 68,822 come from the sixth century. On decline, see Bosanquet, "Excavations at Sparta, 1906," p. 310; Cartledge, *Sparta and Lakonia*, p. 359.

135. Dickins, in Dawkins and others, *Artemis Orthia*, pp. 164–66.

136. Wace, in Dawkins and others, *Artemis Orthia*, p. 283.

137. Pipili, *Laconian Iconography*, p. 79.

138. Dickins, in Dawkins and others, *Artemis Orthia*, pp. 163–86; Vernant, *Mortals*, pp. 226–27.

139. Jeanmaire, *Couroi*, pp. 520–21.

140. Vernant, *Mortals*, p. 225. That some, at least, of the customs associated with Spartan warrior initiation were even older is suggested by two bone figurines from prerenovation layers: a nude boy with short hair and a nude man with waist-length hair (Dawkins and others, *Artemis Orthia*, p. 240, pl. CLXX, 1 and 5). Dawkins's identification of the boy as a *bōmonikēs* is anachronistic; the striations on his back and the hole piercing his head from side to side show that the carving was worn as an amulet.

141. Huxley, *Early Sparta*, pp. 63–65. Rolley, "Problème," pp. 125–40, surveys Laconian art in the sixth century.

142. Cartledge, *Sparta and Lakonia*, pp. 136–48.

143. Vernant, *Mortals*, pp. 195–206.

144. Sanders, "Dioskouroi Reliefs," pp. 205–10, who bases her argument upon a comparison of the hoplite virtues praised by Tyrtaeus and the behavior of Castor and Pollux in myth. A much stronger case can be made, as will become apparent.

145. Tod and Wace, *Catalogue*, pp. 113–18; Sanders, "Dioskouroi Reliefs," pp. 206–8; Grunauer-von Hoerschelmann, *Münzprägung*, p. 20, group 7.

146. Pi. N. 52–54, εὐρυχόρου ταμίαι Σπάρτας ἀγώνων/ μοῖραν Ἑρμᾷ καὶ σὺν Ἡρα/κλεῖ διέποντι θάλειαν. Pindar elsewhere alludes to their athletic qualities: O. 3.34–38; I. 1.19–24.

147. Paus. 3.14.7, 3.13.6. On the *dromos*, see Chapter 3, at note 49.

148. Paus. 3.14.9, 3.20.2. On the Platanistas, see Chapter 3, at note 39.

149. X. *Cyn.* 3.1. The other was thought to have come from a highly unlikely cross between a dog and a fox, hence its name, rather suggestive in the context of Spartan ephebes, Vulpine (ἀλωπεκίς).

150. Pl. *Lg.* 7.796B; schol. to Pi. *P.* 5.128; cf. Luc. *Salt.* 10; Theogn. 1.1087.

151. Burkert, *Griechische Religion*, p. 325; Plut. *Lyc.* 22.4; [Plut.] *De mus.* 26.

152. Diod. 6.6.

153. Carlier, "La vie politique," p. 76 n. 42.

154. Hdt. 7.75.2.

155. Kiechle, *Lakonien*, pp. 21–22. Fellow citizens: X. *HG* 6.3.6.

156. Stob. 4.1.138, a fragment from a work spuriously ascribed to the early fourth-century Pythagorean Archytas of Tarentum; Wellman, "Archytas (3)," 601; cf. Hesych. s.v. εἰρήν.

157. *IG* V.1 457, [τοὶ] κόροι Θιοκλῆ Ναμ[----ἀνέθηκαν---].

158. Wace, "A Spartan Hero Relief," p. 219.

159. Tod and Wace, *Catalogue*, pp. 102–13; Stibbe, "Dionysos," pp. 1–44.

160. Wide, *Lakonische Kulte*, p. 357.

161. Theocles relief: Dressel and Milchhoeffer, "Die antike Kunstwerke," pp. 314–15, no. 15; Tod and Wace, *Catalogue*, p. 104, fig. 4; Blümel, *Griechische Skulpturen*, p. 13, A13 and pl. 25. On single standing figures, see Stibbe, "Dionysos," pp. 41–42, group C.

162. On the *hippeis* as infantrymen, see previous discussion, at note 80.

163. E.g., Stibbe, *Vasenmaler*, p. 138, pl. 75, 1; "Dionysos," p. 43, a15, a16. The hoplite type for bronze statuettes may have originated in Laconia: see Jost, "Statuettes," pp. 358–63; Rolley, "Problème," p. 130.

164. Schröder, "Archaïsche Skulpturen," pp. 44–46; Stibbe, "Dionysos," p. 41, C.2.

165. Bethe, "Dioskuren," 1091–92; Alcm. 2 (Page), πώλων ὠκεών δματῆρες, ἱππόται σοφοί.

166. For the iconography of the Dioscuri, see Hermary, "Dioskouroi."

167. Burkert, *Griechische Religion*, p. 44; on other Indo-European aspects of Spartan life, see Chapter 1, at note 67.

168. Theocr. 22.23–24, ὦ ἄμφω θνητοῖσι βοηθόοι, ὦ φίλοι ἄμφω,/ ἱππῆες κιθαρισταὶ ἀεθλητῆρες ἀοιδοί.

169. On Spartan *piloi*, see Lazenby, *Spartan Army*, p. 46. For the Dioscuri with *chlamudes* and spears, see Tod and Wace, *Catalogue*, nos. 356, 575; Pipili, *Laconian Iconography*, pp. 54–58; Hermary, "Dioskouroi," p. 569, nos. 2–4.

170. Paus. 4.27.1; cf. Polyaen. 2.31.3.

171. Tod and Wace, *Catalogue*, p. 158, no. 201.

172. In fact, Wagner, "Dioskuren," pp. 226, 238, followed by Burkert, *Griechische Religion*, p. 325, sees the Dioscuri as divinized reflections of young warriors.

173. Thuc. 5.72.4.

174. Jeanmaire, *Couroi*, pp. 307, 310; Vidal-Naquet, *Le chasseur noir*, p. 160.

175. Engelmann, "Helena II," 1932–34.

176. Dawkins and others, *Artemis Orthia*, p. 157. This equine association is itself sufficient to call into question the thesis of Carter, "Masks of Ortheia," pp. 374–78 (accepted by Morris, *Daidalos*, pp. 135–36) that Orthia was originally a purely Phoenician deity.

177. Droop, in Dawkins and others, *Artemis Orthia*, pp. 87, fig. 59(l); 89, fig. 60(n); Stibbe, *Vasenmaler*, no. 205.

178. Stibbe, *Vasenmaler*, nos. 306, 307; Pipili, *Laconian Iconography*, pp. 76–77.

179. Pipili, *Laconian Iconography*, p. 76.

180. Vernant, *Mortals*, pp. 229–35. The custom of Spartan ephebes carrying sickles sometimes had dire consequences: X. *An.* 4.8.25; *Apophth. Lac.* Anon. 34 (233F–234A): see previous discussion, at note 106.

181. Ar. *Pax* 872–76; Lloyd-Jones, "Artemis and Iphigeneia," pp. 87–102.

182. On the divinity of Lycurgus and a possible foundation myth for Spartan warrior initiation, see Piccirilli, "Licurgo e Alcandro," pp. 1–10.

CONCLUSION

1. As he himself admits: X. *Lac.* 15.1–7.

2. Jeanmaire, *Couroi*.

3. Ibid., p. 164.

4. Cf. Cartledge, *Agesilaos*, pp. 24–25, following Finley, *Use and Abuse*, pp. 116–17.

5. Cartledge, *Agesilaos*, p. 25.

6. Jeanmaire, *Couroi*, pp. 160–61.

7. Curtin, *Precolonial*, p. 43; Ranger, "Invention," pp. 249–50; Iliffe, *Modern History*, pp. 323–24; Willis, "Makings," pp. 199–204.

8. Ranger, "Invention," pp. 247–48.

9. Oliver, *African Experience*, pp. 147–48; Curtin, *Precolonial*, p. 43; Iliffe, *Modern History*, p. 323; cf. Geschiere, "Chiefs and Colonial Rule," pp. 151–75.

10. Iliffe, *Modern History*, p. 323.

11. Ranger and Kimambo, *Historical Study*, pp. 2–3.

12. Ambler, "Renovation," p. 140.

13. Cf. Cohn, "History and Anthropology," p. 218.

14. Baxter and Almagor, *Age*, p. 1.

15. Keiser, *Vice Lords*, p. 15.

16. Arist. *Pol.* 8.1.4 (1337A).

17. As early as 1921, Roussel (review of Brenot, *Recherches*) criticized this assumption.

18. Rogers, *Sacred Identity*, esp. pp. 136–49.

APPENDIX TWO

1. Ehrenberg, "Spartiaten," pp. 28–29; "Sparta (Geschichte)," 1437; "Obai," 1696.

2. Michell, *Sparta*, pp. 97–99; Jones, *Sparta*, pp. 31–32; Jones, *Public Organization*, pp. 119, 121. Sealey, *History*, pp. 67–68, well represents the *communis opinio*, "The city of Sparta arose from the union of four neighboring villages, Pitana, Mesoa, Limnae, and Conooura, and from an early stage it included the town of Amyclae." For Parker, "Some Dates," p. 45, Amyclae's early annexation is "undoubted."

The single dissenter is Lazenby, *Spartan Army*, pp. 51–52, who argues against Amyclae's "obal" status.

3. *IG* V.1 675.

4. Ross, "Epigraphische Nachlese," pp. 128–29.

5. Furtwängler, "Apollon," 449; Höfer, "Tetracheir," 398–99; Kruse, "Tetracheir," 1070; Ziehen, "Sparta (Kulte)," 1461; Mellink, *Hyakinthos*, p. 22 n. 4.

6. *Artemis Orthia*, no. 6; Liban. *Or.* 11.204; Hesych. s.v. κυνακίας; Sosibius, *FGrHist* 595 F25; Diogenian. 2.5. Cf. Wide, *Kulte*, p. 95.

7. Farnell, *Cults*, 4:127.

8. Greve, "Hyakinthos," 2763–64; Mellink, *Hyakinthos*, p. 22 n. 4; Jacoby, *FGrHist*, 3b.3:378 n. 217. On Apollo of the Amyclaeum, see Paus. 3.18.9–19.5; Lambrinudakis, "Apollon," p. 196.

9. Paus. 3.14.6. On the location of Pitane, see now Cartledge and Spawforth, *Hellenistic and Roman Sparta*, pp. 131–32 and 214–15.

10. *IG* V.1 259 (*Artemis Orthia*, no. 6). On the god's youth, see Hesych. s.v. κουρίδιον. For a similar ephebic priesthood, see Robert, "Le dieu Fulvus," pp. 37–42.

11. *IG* V.1 515, another inscription referring to Amyclae, has been shown to be a forgery by Spawforth, "*Fourmontiana*," pp. 139–45.

12. Cartledge, *Sparta and Lakonia*, p. 107, "An inscription of Roman date . . . proves that Amyclae became one of the 'obes' of Sparta"; Parker, "Some Dates," p. 45 n. 2, "Amyclae was in fact a Spartan obe: *IG* V 1.26." Chrimes, *Ancient*

Sparta, p. 166, "It is clear that Amyklai enjoyed some kind of municipal organization which was conceded by Sparta."

13. On πίστις, see Panagopoulos, "Vocabulaire et mentalité," p. 225; Migeotte, *L'emprunt public*, p. 26.

14. Peek, "Artemis Eulakia," pp. 295–302. Side A: τοὶ Κονοϝουρέες ἀνέσηκαν Ἀνταμένην/ τᾶι Εὐλακίαι ϝυδραγὸν γενόμενον κτλ. Side B: τοίδε ϝυγέδωκαν ἐς τὰν κασκευάν κτλ.

IG V.1 27, often cited as evidence for an *ōba*'s internal structure (most recently by Jones, *Public Organization*, p. 122) is too fragmentary to be of much use; the *ōba*'s name is missing and key passages, most notably the anomalous reference to *sitēsis* in the *ōba*'s prytaneum (lines 19–20), have been restored.

15. Paus. 3.21.7. On the league's history, see Cartledge and Spawforth, *Hellenistic and Roman Sparta*, pp. 77, 90, 100–101.

16. On dating by *stratēgoi*, see subsequent discussion, at note 51.

17. The creation of the patronomate by Cleomenes III: Paus. 2.9.1. Eponymous *patronomoi*: e.g., *IG* V.1 32b; *SEG* XI (1954), no. 495. On the number of *patronomoi*, see Kennell, "Spartan Patronomate," pp. 131–37.

18. A *patronomos* also appears at Cardamyle, a Messenian town given to Sparta by Augustus: *IG* V.1 1333; Paus. 3.26.7.

19. Cartledge, *Sparta and Lakonia*, p. 107.

20. *IG* V.1 480, 564. I assume that these names, which appear in ephebic contexts, are also those of Sparta's civic tribes.

21. Hesych. s.v. ὤας· τὰς κώμας καὶ τὰς διφθέρας οὕτω φασί. ὠβαί· τόποι μεγαλομερεῖς. ὠβάτας· τοὺς φυλέτας. οὐαί· φυλαί. Πιτανάτης στρατός· ἔστι δὲ ἡ Πιτάνη φυλή. Κυνόσουρα· φυλὴ Λακωνική. Steph. Byz. s.v. Μεσσόα. τόπος Λακωνικῆς. Στράβων ὀγδόη. ἔστι καὶ φυλὴ Λακωνική.

22. Jones, *Public Organization*, p. 123.

23. On *kōmē* as a unit of citizenry, see Jones, *Public Organization*, pp. 114–15 (Argos), 248–49 (Lindos).

24. As recognized by Hammond, *CAH*[2] 3.1:740–41.

25. Paus. 3.19.6.

26. Beattie, "*Lex Sacra*," pp. 46–58; cf. Jones, *Public Organization*, p. 128 n. 4.

27. X. *HG* 4.5.11, οἱ Ἀμυκλαῖοι ἀεί ποτε ἀπέρχονται εἰς τὰ Ὑακίνθια ἐπὶ τὸν παιᾶνα, ἐάν τε στρατοπεδευόμενοι τυγχάνωσιν ἐάν τε ἄλλως πως ἀποδημοῦντες. καὶ τότε δὴ τοὺς ἐκ πάσης τῆς στρατιᾶς Ἀμυκλαίους κατέλιπε Ἀγεσίλαος ἐν Λεχαίῳ.

28. Ehrenberg, "Spartiaten," pp. 28–29; Chrimes, *Ancient Sparta*, p. 318; Toynbee, *Some Problems*, pp. 365–68; Cartledge, *Sparta and Lakonia*, p. 286.

29. Cartledge, *Sparta and Lakonia*, pp. 255–56.

30. Hyacinthia procession: Polycrates, *FGrHist* 588 F1; Wide, *Kulte*, pp. 285–93.

31. Nilsson, "Die Prozessionstypen," pp. 309–39.

32. Jones, *Sparta*, p. 32; Michell, *Sparta*, p. 98.

33. Lazenby, *Spartan Army*, p. 52.

34. Hdt. 9.53; Thuc. 1.20.4.

35. Schol. to Ar. *Lys.* 452–54 (Dübner), τέτταρες λόχοι· ἀργότερον τὰ Λακώ-νων ἔοικεν ἐξειργάσθαι ὁ ποιητής. λόχοι γὰρ οὐκ εἰσὶ τέτταρες ἐν Λακεδαιμονίᾳ, ἀλλὰ ε', Ἔδωλος, Σίνις, Ἀρίμας, Πλοάς, Μεσσοάγης. Schol. to Thuc. 4.8.9 (Hude), λόχων· λόχοι Λακεδαιμονίων πέντε, Αἰδώλιος, Σίνις, Σαρίνας, Πλόας, Μεσοάτης. Cf. Rose, *Fragmenta*, F541.

36. E.g., Toynbee, "Growth of Sparta," pp. 256–57; Andrewes, *Greek Tyrants*, p. 71; Wade-Gery, *Essays*, p. 77; Kiechle, *Lakonien*, p. 147 n. 4; Cartledge, *Agesilaos*, p. 431.

37. Toynbee, "Growth of Sparta," p. 257 n. 44.

38. They are neither "odd and generally meaningless names" (Lazenby, *Spartan Army*, p. 52) nor "unintelligible to us" (Andrewes, *Greek Tyrants*, p. 71).

39. *LSJ* s.v. σίνις; Chantraine, *Dictionaire étymologique*, 4.1:1005; Hesych. s.v. σαρίρ· κλάδος φοίνικος. For the formation, see Buck and Peterson, *Reverse Index*, p. 427, 7 μυρίς/μυρ(ρ)ίνης, κεντρίς/κεντρίνης, κεγχρίς/κεγχρίνης.

40. For similar interpretations, see Chrimes, *Ancient Sparta*, pp. 316, 392, and Lazenby, *Spartan Army*, p. 52, who argue the names may refer to the files of an *enomotia*.

41. See the passages in Rose, *Fragmenta*, F541.

42. Cartledge, *Sparta and Lakonia*, p. 106; cf. Parker, "Some Dates," p. 45.

43. Woodward, in Dawkins and others, *Artemis Orthia*, pp. 206–358.

44. Plut. *Ages.* 1.2.4.

45. X. *Ages.* 2.25; Plut. *Ages.* 31.1–35.4; Cartledge, *Agesilaos*, pp. 234–36.

46. Polyb. 2.70.1; Shimron, *Late Sparta*, p. 57.

47. Livy, 35.13.2; Cartledge and Spawforth, *Hellenistic and Roman Sparta*, p. 77.

48. Livy, 35.37.1–3; Plut. *Phil.* 15.4; Aymard, *Les premiers rapports*, p. 320.

49. Livy 38.34.1–3; Paus. 8.51.3. The Spartan ambassadors to Rome later had many complaints about the Achaeans, but this does not seem to have been one of them: Polyb. 22.12.3; Livy 39.33.6. On Philopoemen and the Spartan constitution, see Kennell, "*IG* V 1,16," pp. 201–2.

50. Wade-Gery, *Essays*, p. 75.

51. Ibid., pp. 75–76. Dating by *stratēgos* of the league: e.g., *IG* V.1 1110 (Geronthrae), lines 12–13; 1145 (Gytheum), line 45. Geronthrae as a member of the League of Lacedaemonians/Eleutherolaconian League: Paus. 3.21.7.

52. Plut. *Ant.* 67.3–4.

53. On the date and circumstances of Eurycles' disgrace, see Bowersock, "Eurycles," pp. 111–18; "Augustus and the East," pp. 169–88.

BIBLIOGRAPHY

Ambler, C. H. "The Renovation of Custom in Colonial Kenya: The 1932 Generation Succession Ceremonies in Embu." *Journal of African History* (1989): 139–56.

Amelung, W. "Ἱμάτιον." *RE* 8.2 (1913): 1609–13.

Anderson, G. *The Second Sophistic: A Cultural Phenomenon in the Roman Empire*. London and New York, 1993.

Andrei, O. *A. Claudius Charax di Pergamo: Interessi antiquari e antichità cittadine nell'età degli Antonini*. Opuscula Philologa, no. 5. Bologna, 1984.

Andrewes, A. *The Greek Tyrants*. New York, 1963.

Armstrong, P., W. G. Cavanagh, and G. Shipley. "Crossing the River: Observations on Routes and Bridges in Laconia from the Archaic to Byzantine Periods." *ABSA* 87 (1992): 293–310.

Ast, F. *Lexicon Platonicum*. 2nd ed. 3 vols. Berlin, 1908.

Aymard, A. *Les premiers rapports de Rome et de la Confédération achaienne (198–189 avant J.-C.)*. Bibliothèque des universités du Midi, fasc. 22. Bordeaux, 1938.

Bachmann, L., ed. *Anecdota Graeca*. 2 vols. Leipzig, 1828 (repr. 1965).

Balland, A. *Fouilles de Xanthos*. Vol. 2, *Inscriptions d'époque impériale du Létôon*. Paris, 1981.

Barnes, T. D. *Tertullian: A Historical and Literary Study*. Oxford, 1971.

Baunack, J. "Ueber das lakonische Wort κασσηρατόριν und die θηρομαχία bei den Griechen." *RhM*, n.s., 38 (1883): 293–300.

Baxter, P. T. W., and U. Almagor. *Age, Generation and Time: Some Features of East African Age Organisations*. London, 1978.

Beattie, A. J. "An Early Laconian *Lex Sacra*." *CQ*, n.s., 1 (1951): 46–58.

Bekker, I., ed. *Anecdota Graeca*. 3 vols. Berlin, 1814–21.

Benveniste, E. *Le vocabulaire des institutions indo-européens*. 2 vols. Paris, 1969.

Bethe, E. "Dioskuren." *RE* 5.1 (1903): 1087–1123.

Billheimer, A. "Age-Classes in Spartan Education." *TAPhA* 78 (1947): 99–104.

Bingen, J. "ΤΡΙΕΤΙΡΗΣ (*IG* V 1, 1120)." *AC* 27 (1958): 105–7.

Bizos, M. *Xénophon: Cyropédie*. 3 vols. Paris, 1971–78.

Bloch, H. "Herakleides Lembos and His *Epitome* of Aristotle's *Politeiai*." *TAPhA* 71 (1940): 27–39.

Blümel, C. *Katalog der Staatliche Museen zu Berlin: Sammlung antiker Skulpturen*. Vol. 2.1, *Griechische Skulpturen des sechsten und fünften Jahrhunderts v. Chr*, pt. 1. Berlin and Leipzig, 1940.

Blümel, W., ed. *Die Inschriften von Iasos*. Vol. 1. Inschriften griechischer Städte aus Kleinasien, no. 28.1. Berlin, 1985.

———. *Die Inschriften von Mylasa*. 2 vols. Inschriften griechischer Städte aus Kleinasien, nos. 34–35. Bonn, 1987–88.

Boardman, J. "Artemis Orthia and Chronology." *ABSA* 58 (1963): 1–7.

Bölte, F. "Zu lakonischen Festen." *RhM* 78 (1929): 124–43.

Boring, T. A. *Literacy in Ancient Sparta. Mnemosyne* Supplement no. 54. Leiden, 1979.

Bosanquet, R. C. "Excavations at Sparta, 1906. 5.—The Sanctuary of Artemis Orthia." *ABSA* 12 (1905–6): 303–17.

Bourguet, É. *Le dialecte laconien.* Collection linguistique de la société de linguistique de Paris, no. 23. Paris, 1927.

Bowersock, G. W. "Augustus and the East: The Problem of the Succession." In *Caesar Augustus: Seven Aspects,* edited by F. Millar and E. Segal, pp. 169–88. Oxford, 1984.

———. "Eurycles of Sparta." *JRS* 51 (1961): 111–18.

———. *Greek Sophists in the Roman Empire.* Oxford, 1969.

———. "Zur Geschichte des römischen Thessaliens." *RhM,* n.s., 108 (1965): 277–89.

Bowie, E. L. "The Greeks and Their Past in the Second Sophistic." In *Studies in Ancient Society,* edited by M. I. Finley, pp. 166–209. London, 1974.

Bradford, A. S. *A Prosopography of Lacedaemonians from the Death of Alexander the Great, 323 BC, to the Sack of Sparta by Alaric, AD 396.* Vestigia Beiträge zur alten Geschichte, vol. 27. Munich, 1977.

Breitenbach, H. R. "Xenophon." *RE* 9A.2 (1967): 1567–2052.

Brelich, A. *Paides e Parthenoi.* Vol. 1. Incunabula Graeca, vol. 36. Rome, 1969.

Bremmer, J. N. "Symbols of Marginality from Early Pythagoras to Late Antique Monks." *G&R,* n.s., 39 (1992): 205–14.

Buck, C. D. *The Greek Dialects.* 2nd ed. Chicago, 1955.

Buck, C. D., and W. Peterson. *A Reverse Index of Greek Nouns and Adjectives.* Chicago, 1939.

Buffière, F. *Éros adolescent: La pédérastie dans la Grèce antique.* Paris, 1980.

Burkert, W. *Griechische Religion der archaischen und klassischen Epochen.* Die Religionen der Menschheit, vol. 15. Stuttgart, 1977.

———. *Homo Necans: Interpretationen altgriechischer Opferriten und Mythen.* Religionsgeschichtliche Versuche und Vorarbeiten, vol. 32. Berlin and New York, 1972.

Busolt, G., and H. Swoboda. *Die griechische Staatskunde.* 2 vols. Handbuch der Altertumswissenschaft, no. 4.1.1. Munich, 1920–26.

Calame, C. *Les choeurs des jeunes filles en Grèce archaïque.* Vol. 1, *Morphologie, fonction religieuse et sociale.* Vol. 2, *Alcman.* Rome, 1977.

Cameron, A. "ΘΡΕΠΤΟΣ and Related Terms in the Inscriptions of Asia Minor." In *Anatolian Studies Presented to William Hepburn Buckler,* edited by W. M. Calder and J. Keil, pp. 27–62. Manchester, 1939.

Canfora, L. *The Vanished Library: A Wonder of the Ancient World.* Translated by M. Ryle. Hellenistic Culture and Society, no. 7. Berkeley, 1989.

Carlier, P. "L'idée de monarchie impériale dans la *Cyropédie* de Xénophon." *Ktèma* 3 (1978): 133–63.

———. "La vie politique à Sparte sous le règne de Cléomène Ier. Essai d'interprétation." *Ktèma* 2 (1977): 65–84.

Carlson, M. L. "Pagan Examples of Fortitude in the Latin Apologists." *CPh* 43 (1948): 93–104.

Carter, J. B. "The Masks of Ortheia." *AJA* 91 (1987): 355–83.

Cartledge, P. *Agesilaos and the Crisis of Sparta*. Baltimore, 1987.

———. "Early Lakedaimon: The Making of a Conquest-State." In *ΦΙΛΟΛΑΚΩΝ: Lakonian Studies in Honour of Hector Catling*, edited by J. M. Sanders, pp. 49–55. London, 1992.

———. "The Politics of Spartan Pederasty." *PCPhS*, n.s., 27 (1981): 17–36.

———. *Sparta and Lakonia: A Regional History, 1300–362 BC*. London, 1979.

Cartledge, P., and A. Spawforth. *Hellenistic and Roman Sparta: A Tale of Two Cities*. London, 1989.

Cassio, A. C. "Continuità e riprese arcaizzanti nell'uso epigrafico dei dialetti greci: Il caso dell'eolico d'Asia." *AION*(ling) 8 (1986): 131–46.

Chaniotis, A. *Historie und Historiker in den griechischen Inschriften*. Heidelberger althistorische Beiträge und epigraphische Studien, vol. 4. Stuttgart, 1988.

Chantraine, P. *Dictionnaire étymologique de la langue grecque*. 4 vols. Paris, 1968–80.

———. *Études sur le vocabulaire grecque*. Études et commentaires, vol. 24. Paris, 1956.

Charneux, P. "Du côté du chez Héra." *BCH* 111 (1987): 207–23.

Chrimes, K. M. T. *Ancient Sparta: A Re-examination of the Evidence*. Manchester, 1949.

Cobet, C. G. *Novae lectiones quibus continentur observationes criticae in scriptores Graecos*. Leiden, 1858.

Cohn, B. S. "History and Anthropology: The State of Play." *Comparative Studies in Sociology and History* 22 (1980): 198–221.

Cohn, L. "Aristophanes (14)." *RE* 2.1 (1896): 994–1005.

Collignon, M. *Quid de collegiis epheborum apud Graecos, excepta Attica, ex titulis epigraphicis commentari liceat*. Paris, 1877.

Cotter, J. "The Etymology and Earliest Significance of εἴρων." *Glotta* 70 (1992): 31–34.

Coulton, J. J. "Oinoanda: The Agora." *AS* 36 (1986): 61–90.

Curtin, P. D. *Precolonial African History*. AHA Pamphlets, no. 501. Washington, D.C., 1974.

Dagron, G., and D. Feissel. *Inscriptions de Cilicie*. Travaux et mémoires de recherche d'histoire et civilisation de Byzance. Collège de France. Monographies, no. 4. Paris, 1987.

David, E. "Hunting in Spartan Society and Consciousness." *EMC/CV* 37 (1993): 393–414.

Dawkins, R. M., and others. *The Sanctuary of Artemis Orthia at Sparta*. Society for the Promotion of Hellenic Studies Supplementary Papers, no. 5. London, 1929.

de Ridder, A. *Catalogue des bronzes de la Société archéologique d'Athènes*. Paris, 1894.

Delorme, J. *Gymnasion: Étude sur les monuments consacrés à l'éducation en Grèce (des origines à l'empire romain)*. BEFAR, fasc. 196. Paris, 1960.

Delvaux, G. "Retour aux sources de Plutarque." *EC* 56 (1988): 27–48.

den Boer, W. *Laconian Studies*. Amsterdam, 1954.

Desmedt, C. "Fabulae Hygini." *BStudL* 3 (1973): 26–34.

———. "Fabulae Hygini." *RBPh* 48 (1970): 26–35.

Dickins, G. "Excavations at Sparta, 1906. 4. — The Great Altar near the Eurotas." *ABSA* 12 (1905–6): 295–302.

Diels, H., and W. Kranz. *Die Fragmente der Vorsokratiker*. 10th ed. Berlin, 1960.

Diller, A. "A New Source on the Spartan *Ephebia*." *AJPh* 62 (1941): 499–501.

Dilts, M. R., ed. and trans. *Heraclidis Lembi excerpta politiarum*. *GRBS* Monographs, no. 5. Durham, 1971.

Dittenberger, W., ed. *Orientis Graeci inscriptiones selectae*. 2 vols. Leipzig, 1903–5.

———. *Sylloge inscriptionum Graecarum*. 3rd ed. 4 vols. Leipzig, 1915–24.

Dittenberger, W., and K. Purgold. *Olympia: Die Ergebnisse der von dem deutschen Reich veranstalten Ausgrabung*. Vol. 5, *Die Inschriften*. Berlin, 1896.

Dodwell, E. *A Classical and Topographical Tour through Greece, during the years 1801, 1805, and 1806*. 2 vols. London, 1819.

Dressel, H., and A. Milchhoeffer. "Die antiken Kunstwerke aus Sparta und Umgebung." *MDAI(A)* 2 (1877): 293–474.

Dumézil, G. *L'idéologie tripartie des Indo-Européens*. Collection Latomus, no. 31. Brussels, 1958.

Dyroff, A. *Die Ethik der alten Stoa*. Berliner Studien für classische Philologie und Archaeologie, n.s., no. 2.2–4. Berlin, 1897.

Ebert, J. "ΠΑΙΔΕΣ ΠΥΘΙΚΟΙ." *Philologus* 109 (1965): 152–56.

Ehrenberg, V. "Obai." *RE* 17.2 (1937): 1693–1704.

———. "Othryadas." *RE* 18.2 (1942): 1871–72.

———. "Sparta (Geschichte)." *RE* 3A.2 (1929): 1373–1453.

———. "Spartiaten und Lakedaimonier." *Hermes* 59 (1924): 23–72.

———. "Τρόφιμοι." *RE* 7A.1 (1939): 675–76.

Elsner, J. "Pausanias: A Greek Pilgrim in the Roman World." *P&P* 135 (1992): 3–29.

Engelmann, H., D. Knibbe, and R. Merkelbach. *Die Inschriften von Ephesos*. Vol. 4. Inschriften griechischer Städte aus Kleinasien, no. 14. Bonn, 1980.

Engelmann, R. "Helena II." In *Ausführliches Lexikon der griechischen und römischen Mythologie*, edited by W. H. Roscher. Vol. 1.2 (1886–90), 1928–78.

Erbse, H., ed. *Scholia Graeca in Homeri Iliadem (Scholia Vetera)*. 7 vols. Berlin, 1969–88.

Erskine, A. *The Hellenistic Stoa*. Ithaca, 1990.

Farnell, L. R. *The Cults of the Greek States*. 5 vols. Oxford, 1896–1909.

Figueira, T. J. "Mess Contributions and Subsistence at Sparta." *TAPhA* 114 (1984): 87–109.

Finley, M. I. *The Use and Abuse of History*. New York, 1975.

Flacelière, R. "Sur quelques passages des *Vies* de Plutarque. II: Lycurgue—Numa." *REG* 61 (1948): 391–429.

Flashar, H., ed. *Ältere Akademie—Aristoteles—Peripatos*. Die Philosophie der Antike, vol. 3. Basel and Stuttgart, 1983.

Forbes, C. A. *Greek Physical Education*. New York, 1929.

———. *NEOI: A Contribution to the Study of Greek Associations*. Middletown, Conn., 1933.

Forbes, K. "Medial Intervocalic -ρσ-, -λσ- in Greek." *Glotta* 36 (1958): 235–72.

Forrest, W. G. *A History of Sparta, 950–192 B.C.* London, 1968.

Fowler, D. "The Separate Functions of the Indo-European Divine Twins." In *Myth and Law among the Indo-Europeans*, edited by J. Puhvel, pp. 193–202. Berkeley, 1970.

Frazer, J. G. *The Golden Bough: A Study in Magic and Religion*. 3rd ed. 13 vols. London, 1913 (repr. 1980).

———. *Pausanias' Description of Greece*. 6 vols. London and New York, 1898.

French, E., ed. "Archaeology in Greece 1989–90: Lakonia." *AR* 36 (1989–90): 21–26.

———. "Archaeology in Greece 1990–91: Lakonia." *AR* 37 (1990–91): 27–28.

Frisch, B. "Die Klassifikation der παῖδες bei den griechischen Agonen." *ZPE* 75 (1980): 179–85.

Fuhrmann, F. *Plutarque: Oeuvres morales*. Vol. 3, *Apophtegmes de rois et de généraux. Apophtegmes Laconiens*. Paris, 1988.

Fuks, A., "Non-Phylarchean Tradition of the Programme of Agis IV." *CQ*, n.s., 12 (1962): 118–21.

Furtwängler, A. "Apollon." In *Ausführliches Lexikon der griechischen und römischen Mythologie*, edited by W. H. Roscher. Vol. 1.1 (1884–86), 422–68.

Garland, R. "Religion and Power in Classical Athens." In *Pagan Priests: Religion and Power in the Ancient World*, edited by M. Beard and J. North, pp. 77–81. London, 1990.

Gauthier, P., and M. B. Hatzopoulos. *La loi gymnasiarchique de Beroia*. Μελετήματα, no. 16. Athens, 1993.

Geschiere, P. "Chiefs and Colonial Rule in Cameroon: Inventing Chieftancy, French and British Style." *Africa* 63 (1993): 151–75.

Gignac, F. T. *A Grammar of the Greek Papyri of the Roman and Byzantine Periods*. Vol. 1, *Phonology*. Vol. 2, *Morphology*. Testi e documenti per lo studio dell'antichità, no. 55. Milan, 1976–81.

Gilbert, G. *Handbuch der griechischen Staatsalterthümer*. Vol. 1. Leipzig, 1881.

Glotz, G. "Hellanodikai." In *Dictionnaire des antiquités grecques et romains*, edited by C. Daremberg and E. Saglio. Vol. 3.1 (1900), 60–64.

Golden, M. *Children and Childhood in Classical Athens*. Baltimore and London, 1990.

Gomme, A. W. *A Historical Commentary on Thucydides*. Vol. 1. Oxford, 1950.

Graf, F. *Nordionische Kulte: Religionsgeschichtliche und epigraphische*

Untersuchungen zu den Kulten von Chios, Erythrai, Klazomenai und Phokaia. Bibliotheca Helvetica Romana, no. 21. Rome, 1985.

Graindor, P. *Athènes sous Hadrien*. Cairo, 1934 (repr. 1973).

——. *Chronologie des archontes athéniens sous l'empire*. Brussels, 1922.

Grasberger, L. *Erziehung und Unterricht in klassischen Altertum*. Part 1, *Die leibliche Erziehung bei den Griechen und Römern*. Part 2, *Der musische Unterricht oder die Elementarschule bei den Griechen und Römern*. Part 3, *Die Ephebenbildung oder die musische und militärische Ausbildung der griechischen und römischen Jünglinge*. Würzburg, 1864–81 (repr. 1971).

Greve, D. "Hyakinthos." In *Ausführliches Lexikon der griechischen und römischen Mythologie*, edited by W. H. Roscher. Vol. 1.2 (1886–90), 2759–66.

Gruen, E. S. *The Hellenistic World and the Coming of Rome*. 2 vols. Berkeley, 1984.

——. "The Origins of the Achaean War." *JHS* 96 (1976): 46–69.

Grunauer-von Hoerschelmann, S. *Die Münzprägung der Lakedaimonier*. Antike Münzen und Geschnittene Steine, vol. 7. Berlin, 1978.

Guarducci, M., ed. *Inscriptiones creticae opere et consilio Friderici Halbherr collectae*. Vol. 1, *Tituli Cretae mediae praeter Gortynios*. Rome, 1935.

Gulliver, P. H. "Age Differentiation." In *International Encyclopedia of the Social Sciences*. Vol. 1 (1968): 157–62.

Habicht, C. *Pausanias' Guide to Ancient Greece*. Berkeley, 1985.

Hahm, D. E. *The Origins of Stoic Cosmology*. Columbus, Ohio, 1977.

Halfmann, H. *Itinera principum: Geschichte und Typologie der Kaiserreisen in römischen Reich*. Heidelberger althistorische Beiträge und epigraphische Studien, vol. 2. Stuttgart, 1986.

Hall, A. S. "Who Was Diogenes of Oenoanda?" *JHS* 99 (1979): 160–63.

Hammond, N. G. L. "The Peloponnese." *CAH²* 3.1 (1982): 696–744.

Heberdey, R. "Gymnische und andere Agone in Termessus Pisidiae." In *Anatolian Studies Presented to Sir William Mitchell Ramsay*, edited by W. H. Buckler and W. M. Calder, pp. 195–206. Manchester, 1923.

Heberdey, R., G. Niemann, and W. Wilberg. *Das Theater in Ephesos*. Forschungen in Ephesos, vol. 2. Vienna, 1912.

Hermary, A. "Dioskouroi." *LIMC* 3.1:567–93.

Higgins, W. E. *Xenophon the Athenian*. Albany, N.Y., 1977.

Hiller von Gaertringen, F. "Gymnopaidien." *RE* 7.2 (1912): 2087–89.

——, ed. *Inschriften von Priene*. Berlin, 1906.

Hobsbawm, E., and T. Ranger, eds. *The Invention of Tradition*. Cambridge, 1983.

Hodkinson, S. "Land Tenure and Inheritance in Classical Sparta." *CQ*, n.s., 36 (1986): 378–406.

——. "Social Order and the Conflict of Values in Classical Sparta." *Chiron* 13 (1983): 239–81.

Höfer, O. "Tetracheir." In *Ausführliches Lexikon der griechischen und römischen Mythologie*, edited by W. H. Roscher. Vol. 5 (1916–24), 398–99.

Hughes, D. D. *Human Sacrifice in Ancient Greece*. London and New York, 1991.

Hula, E., and E. Szanto. "Bericht über eine Reise in Karien." *SAWW* 132 (1895): 1–36.

Huxley, G. L. *Early Sparta*. London, 1962.

Iliffe, J. *A Modern History of Tanganyika*. African Studies series, no. 25. Cambridge, 1979.

Imhoof-Blumer, F. *Kleinasiatische Münzen*. Vol. 2. Sonderschriften des Österreichischen archäologischen Institutes in Wien, vol. 3. Vienna, 1902.

Inwood, B. *Ethics and Human Action in Early Stoicism*. Oxford, 1985.

Jacoby, F. *Die Fragmente der griechischen Historiker*. 18 vols. Berlin and Leiden, 1926–58.

Jalabert, L. "Syntrophoi." In *Dictionnaire des antiquités grecques et romains*, edited by C. Daremberg and E. Saglio. Vol. 4.2 (1877), 1590.

Jannaris, A. N. *An Historical Greek Grammar*. London, 1897.

Jeanmaire, H. *Couroi et courètes: Essai sur l'éducation spartiate et sur les rites d'adolescence dans l'antiquité hellénique*. Lille, 1939 (repr. 1975).

Jones, A. H. M. *The Greek City from Alexander to Justinian*. Oxford, 1940 (repr. 1970).

——. *Sparta*. Oxford, 1967.

Jones, C. P. *Culture and Society in Lucian*. Cambridge, Mass., 1986.

——. "The Levy at Thespiae under Marcus Aurelius." *GRBS* 12 (1971): 45–48.

——. "Τρόφιμος in an Inscription of Erythrai." *Glotta* 67 (1989): 194–97.

Jones, N. F. *Public Organization in Ancient Greece: A Documentary Study*. Philadelphia, 1987.

Jost, M. "Statuettes de bronze archaïques provenant de Lykosoura." *BCH* 99 (1975): 339–64.

Kahrstedt, U. *Griechisches Staatsrecht*. Vol. 1, *Sparta und seine Symmachie*. Göttingen, 1922.

Katzoff, R. "Jonathan and Late Sparta." *AJPh* 106 (1985): 485–89.

Keil, J. "Das Unterrichtswesen im antiken Ephesus." *AAWW* 88 (1951): 331–36.

Keiser, R L. *The Vice Lords: Warriors of the Streets*. New York, 1969.

Kennedy, G. "The Sophists as Declaimers." In *Approaches to the Second Sophistic*, edited by G. W. Bowersock, pp. 17–22. University Park, Pa., 1974.

Kennell, N. M. "*IG* V 1,16 and the Gerousia of Roman Sparta." *Hesperia* 61 (1992): 193–202.

——. "The Public Institutions of Roman Sparta." Diss. Toronto, 1985.

——. "The Size of the Spartan Patronomate." *ZPE* 85 (1991): 131–37.

——. "The Spartan Synarchia." *Phoenix* 46 (1992): 342–51.

——. "Where Was Sparta's Prytaneion?" *AJA* 91 (1987): 421–22.

Kennell, S. "Women's Hair and the Law: Two Cases from Late Antiquity." *Klio* 73 (1991): 526–36.

Kern, O., ed. *Die Inschriften von Magnesia am Maeander*. Berlin, 1900.

Kiechle, F. *Lakonien und Sparta*. Vestigia Beiträge zur alten Geschichte, no. 5. Munich, 1963.

Kindstrand, J. F. *Anacharsis: The Legend and the Apophthegmata*. Acta Universitatis Upsaliensis: Studia Graeca Upsaliensia, no. 16. Uppsala, 1981.

Klee, T. *Zur Geschichte der gymnischen Agone an griechischen Festen*. Leipzig and Berlin, 1918.

Kleijwegt, M. *Ancient Youth: The Ambiguity of Youth and the Absence of Adolescence in Greco-Roman Society*. Dutch Monographs on Ancient History and Archaeology, vol. 8. Amsterdam, 1991.

Kolb, F. *Agora und Theater: Volks- und Festversammlung*. DAI Archäologische Forschungen, no. 9. Berlin, 1981.

Kolbe, W. *Inscriptiones Graecae*. Vol. V.1, *Inscriptiones Laconiae et Messeniae*. Berlin, 1913.

Kourinou-Pikoulas, E. " Ἐπιγραφὲς ἀπὸ τὴ Σπάρτη II." *HOPOΣ* 8–9 (1990–91): 93–98.

Krauss, J., ed. *Die Inschriften von Sestos und der thrakischen Chersones*. Inschriften griechischer Städte aus Kleinasien, no. 19. Bonn, 1980.

Kruse, B. gr. "Tetracheir." *RE* 5A.1 (1934): 1070.

Kühner, R., F. Blass, and B. Gerth. *Ausführliche Grammatik der griechischen Sprache*. 3rd ed. 4 vols. Hanover and Leipzig, 1890–1904.

Kukofka, D.-A. "Die παιδίσκοι im System der spartanischen Altersklassen." *Philologus* 137 (1993): 197–205.

Lambrinudakis, W. "Apollon." *LIMC* 2.1 (1984): 183–327.

Larsen, J. A. O. *Greek Federal States*. Oxford, 1968.

——. "Was Greece Free between 196 and 146 B.C.?" *CPh* 30 (1935): 193–214.

Launey, M. *Recherches sur les armées hellénistiques*. Vol. 1. BEFAR, fasc. 169. Paris, 1949.

Lazarides, K. " Ἀνασκαφὲς καὶ ἔρευνες στὴν Ἀμφίπολη." *ΠΑΑ* 140 (1984; pub. 1988): 33–39.

Lazenby, J. F. *The Spartan Army*. Warminster, 1985.

Lebessi, A. "Flagellation ou autoflagellation: Données iconographiques pour une tentative d'interprétation." *BCH* 115 (1991): 99–123.

Lécrivain, C. "Ephoroi." In *Dictionnaire des antiquités grecques et romains*, edited by C. Daremberg and E. Saglio. Vol. 2.1 (1892), 650–54.

Lévy, E. "La kryptie et ses contradictions." *Ktèma* 13 (1988): 245–52.

Liebenam, W. *Städteverwaltung im römischen Kaiserreiche*. Leipzig, 1900.

Lloyd-Jones, H. "Artemis and Iphigeneia." *JHS* 103 (1983): 87–102.

Long, A. A. "Soul and Body in Stoicism." *Phronesis* 27 (1982): 34–57.

Lotze, D. *Μεταξὺ Ἐλευθέρων καὶ Δούλων: Studien zur rechtsstellung unfreier Landbevölkerungen in Griechenland bis zum 4. Jahrhundert v. Chr.* Deutsche Akademie der Wissenschaften zu Berlin: Schriften der Sektion für Altertumswissenschaft, no. 17. Berlin, 1959.

Lowenthal, D. *The Past Is a Foreign Country*. Cambridge, 1985.

Luni, M. "Documenti per la storia della istituzione ginnasiale e dell'attività atletica in Cirenaica, in rapporto a quelle della Grecia." *QAL* 8 (1976): 223–84.

MacDowell, D. M. *Spartan Law*. Scottish Classical Studies, vol. 1. Edinburgh, 1986.

Mallory, J. P. *In Search of the Indo-Europeans*. London, 1989.

Marasco, G. "La leggende di Polidoro e la ridistribuzione de terre di Licurgo nella propaganda spartana di III secolo." *Prometheus* 4 (1978): 115–27.

Marrou, H.-I. *Histoire de l'éducation dans l'antiquité*. 6th ed. Paris, 1965.

———. "Les classes d'âge de la jeunesse spartiate." *REA* 48 (1946): 216–30.

———. *Saint Augustin et la fin de la culture antique*. BEFAR, fasc. 145. Paris, 1938.

Martini, E. "Dikaiarchos (3)." *RE* 5.1 (1903): 546–63.

Mellink, M. J. *Hyakinthos*. Utrecht, 1943.

Mendels, D. "Polybius, Cleomenes III and Sparta's 'Patrios Politeia.'" *PP* 33 (1978): 161–66.

———. "Sparta in Teles' περὶ φυγῆς." *Eranos* 77 (1979): 111–15.

Michell, H. *Sparta*. Cambridge, 1952.

Mie, F. "Über διὰ πάντων und ὁ ἐπινίκιος in agonistischen Inschriften." *MDAI(A)* 34 (1909): 1–22.

Migeotte, L. *L'emprunt public dans les cités grecques*. Quebec and Paris, 1984.

Millar, F. *A Study of Cassius Dio*. Oxford, 1964.

Mohamed, F. A., and J. Reynolds. "Some New Inscriptions from Cyrenaica." In *L'Africa romana: Atti del IX convegno di studio su "L'Africa romana,"* vol. 9, edited by A. Mastino, pp. 114–22. Sassari, 1992.

Mommsen, T. *Römische Geschichte*. 5th ed. Vol. 5, *Die Provinzen von Caesar bis Diocletian*. N.p., 1904 (repr. 1976).

Morris, S. P. *Daidalos and the Origins of Early Greek Art*. Princeton, 1992.

Morrow, G. R. *Plato's Cretan City: A Historical Interpretation of the Laws*. Princeton, 1960.

Müller, C., and T. Müller. *Fragmenta Historicorum Graecorum*. 5 vols. Paris, 1868–78.

Musti, D., and M. Torelli. *Pausania: Guida della Grecia. Libro III: La Laconia*. Milan, 1991.

Nachstädt, W., W. Sieveking, and J. B. Titchener. *Plutarchi moralia*. Vol. 2. Leipzig, 1935.

Nauck, A. *Aristophanis Byzantii grammatici Alexandrini fragmenta*. Halle, 1848 (repr. 1963).

Nickel, R. *Xenophon*. Erträge der Forschung, vol. 111. Darmstadt, 1979.

Nilsson, M. P. *Die hellenistische Schule*. Munich, 1955.

———. "Die Grundlagen des spartanischen Lebens." *Klio* 12 (1912): 308–40.

———. "Die Prozessionstypen im griechischen Kult." *JDAI* 31 (1916): 309–39 (*Opuscula Selecta*, 1:166–213).

Nollé, J., and F. Schindler, eds. *Die Inschriften von Selge*. Inschriften griechischer Städte aus Kleinasien, no. 37. Bonn, 1991.

Öhler, J. "Γυμνασίαρχος." *RE* 7.2 (1912): 1969–2004.

Oliva, P. *Sparta and Her Social Problems*. Amsterdam and Prague, 1971.

Oliver, J. H. "Athenian Lists of Ephebic Teams." *AE* (1971): 66–74.

———. *Marcus Aurelius: Aspects of Civic and Cultural Policy in the East*. Hesperia Supplement, no. 13. Princeton, 1970.

Oliver, R. *The African Experience*. London, 1991.

Ollier, F. *Le mirage spartiate*. Vol. 1, *Étude sur l'idéalisation de Sparte dans l'antiquité grecque de l'origine jusqu'aux cyniques*. Vol. 2, *Étude sur l'idéalisation de Sparte dans l'antiquité grecque du début de l'école cynique jusqu'à la fin de la cité*. Paris, 1933–43 (repr. 1973).

———. "Le philosophe stoïcien Sphairos et l'oeuvre réformatrice des rois de Sparte Agis IV et Cléomène III." *REG* 49 (1936): 536–70.

———. *Xénophon: La république des Lacédémoniens*. Annales de l'université de Lyon. Nouvelle série. II: Droit, Lettres, fasc. 47. Lyon and Paris, 1934 (repr. 1979).

Oudet, E. "Images d'Athènes dans les romans grecs." In *Le monde du roman grec*, edited by M.-F. Baslez, P. Hoffmann, and M. Trédé, pp. 101–7. Études de litterature ancienne, vol. 4. Paris, 1992.

Palagia, O. "Seven Pilasters of Hercules from Sparta." In *The Greek Renaissance in the Roman Empire*, edited by S. Walker and A. Cameron, pp. 122–29. Bulletin of the Institute of Classical Studies Supplement, no. 55. London, 1989.

Panagopoulos, C. "Vocabulaire et mentalité dans les Moralia de Plutarque." *DHA* 3 (1977): 197–235.

Pargoire, J. "Inscriptions d'Héraclée du Pont." *BCH* 22 (1898): 492–96.

Parker, R. *Miasma: Pollution and Purification in Early Greek Religion*. Oxford, 1983.

———. "Spartan Religion." In *Classical Sparta: Techniques behind Her Success*, edited by A. Powell, pp. 142–72. London, 1989.

Parker, V. "Some Dates in Early Spartan History." *Klio* 75 (1993): 45–60.

Peek, W. "Artemis Eulakia." In *Mélanges helléniques offerts à Georges Daux*, pp. 295–302. Paris, 1974.

Pekáry, T. "Inschriftenfunde aus Milet 1959." *MDAI(I)* 15 (1965): 118–34.

Pélékidis, C. *Histoire de l'éphébie attique des origines à 31 avant Jésus-Christ*. Paris, 1962.

Pelling, C. B. R. "Truth and Fiction in Plutarch's Lives." In *Antonine Literature*, edited by D. A. Russell, pp. 19–52. Oxford, 1990.

Pernot, H. *Introduction à l'étude du dialecte tsakonien*. Collection de l'institute néo-hellénique de l'université de Paris, no. 2. Paris, 1934.

Perotti, P. A. "Roma e Sparta." *Vichiana* 3 (1992): 74–79.

Perrin, B. *Plutarch's Lives*. Vol. 1. Cambridge, Mass., and London, 1948.

Pettersson, M. *Cults of Apollo at Sparta: The Hyakinthia, the Gymnopaidiai, and the Karneia*. Skrifter Utgivna av Svenska Institutet i Athen, 8°, no. 12. Stockholm, 1992.

Piccirilli, "Licurgo e Alcandro: Monoftalmia e origine dell'*Agoge* spartana." *Historia* 30 (1981): 1–10.

Piérart, M. *Platon et la cité grecque: Théorie et réalité dans la constitutions des "Lois."* Académie royale de Belgique: Mémoires de la classe des lettres, vol. 62.3. Brussels, 1974.

Pipili, M. *Laconian Iconography of the Sixth Century B.C.* Oxford University Committee for Archaeology Monographs, no. 12. Oxford, 1987.

Pire, G. *Stoïcisme et pédagogie de Zénon à Marc-Aurèle. De Sénèque à Montaigne et à J.-J. Rousseau.* Liége and Paris, 1958.

Pleket, H. W. "*Collegium iuvenum Nemesiorum*: A Note on Ancient Youth-Organisations." *Mnemosyne* 22 (1969): 281–98.

Pokorny, J. *Indogermanisches etymologisches Wörterbuch.* 2 vols. Bern and Munich, 1959–69.

Poland, F. *Geschichte des griechischen Vereinswesens.* Leipzig, 1909.

Poljakov, F. B., ed. *Die Inschriften von Tralleis und Nysa.* Pt. 1, *Die Inschriften von Tralleis.* Inschriften griechischer Städte aus Kleinasien, no. 36.1. Bonn, 1989.

Powell, A. *Athens and Sparta: Constructing Greek Political and Social History from 478 B.C.* London, 1988.

Puhvel, J. *Comparative Mythology.* Baltimore, 1987.

Ranger, T. "The Invention of Tradition in Colonial Africa." In *The Invention of Tradition*, edited by E. Hobsbawm and T. Ranger, pp. 211–62. Cambridge, 1983.

Ranger, T., and I. Kimambo. *The Historical Study of African Religion.* Berkeley, 1972.

Reisch, E. "Chor." *RE* 3.2 (1899): 2373–2404.

Reynolds, J. M. *Aphrodisias and Rome.* Society for the Promotion of Roman Studies Monographs, no. 1. London, 1982.

———. "Hadrian, Antoninus Pius and the Cyrenaican Cities." *JRS* 68 (1978): 111–21.

Rhodes, P. J. *The Athenian Boule.* Oxford, 1972.

Richter, G. M. *The Portraits of the Greeks.* 3 vols. London, 1965.

Robert, L. "Deux concours grecs à Rome." *CRAI* (1970): 6–27 (*OMS* 5:647–68).

———. "Deux inscriptions de l'époque impériale en Attique." *AJPh* 100 (1979): 153–65.

———. "Le dieu Fulvus à Thessalonique." In *Hellenica.* Vols. 2–3, pp. 37–42. Paris, 1946.

———. "Documents d'Asie Mineure. I–IV." *BCH* 101 (1977): 43–132.

———. "Documents d'Asie Mineure. XXIII–XXVIII." *BCH* 107 (1983): 497–599.

———. *Documents de l'Asie Mineure méridionale.* Geneva and Paris, 1966.

———. *Études anatoliennes.* Paris, 1937.

———. "Inscriptions d'Aphrodisias." *AC* 35 (1966): 397–432 (*OMS* 5:1–56).

———. "Inscriptions grecques d'Asie Mineure." In *Anatolian Studies Presented to A. M. Buckler*, edited by W. M. Calder and J. Keil, pp. 227–48. Manchester, 1939.

———. "Recherches épigraphiques. IV–IX." *REA* 62 (1960): 276–361 (*OMS* 2:792–877).

———. "Sur des inscriptions de Chios. I–III." *BCH* 57 (1933): 505–43 (*OMS* 1:473–511).

———. "La titulature de Nicée et de Nicomédie: La gloire et la haine." *HSPh* 81 (1977): 1–39.

Robert, J., and L. Robert. *La Carie: Histoire et géographie historique*. Vol. 2, *Le plateau de Tabai et ses environs*. Paris, 1954.

———. "Bulletin épigraphique." *REG* 81 (1968): 420–549.

Robertson, N. "A Point of Precedence at Plataia: The Dispute between Athens and Sparta over Leading the Procession." *Hesperia* 55 (1986): 88–102.

Roesch, P. *Études béotiennes*. Paris, 1982.

Rogers, G. M. *The Sacred Identity of Ephesos: Foundation Myths of a Roman City*. London, 1991.

Rolley, C. "Le problème de l'art laconien." *Ktèma* 2 (1977): 125–40.

Rose, H. J. "Greek Rites of Stealing." *HTR* 34 (1941): 1–5.

———. *Hygini Fabulae*. Leiden, 1934.

Rose, V. *Aristotelis qui ferebantur librorum fragmenta*. Leipzig, 1886.

Ross, L. "Epigraphische Nachlese." *RhM* 8 (1853): 122–29.

Roussel, P. Review of *Recherches sur l'éphébie attique*, by A. Brenot. *REG* 34 (1921): 459–60.

———. *Sparte*. Paris, 1960.

Ruge, W. "Tralleis (2)." *RE* 6A.2 (1937): 2093–2128.

Saglio, E. "Agonothetes II." In *Dictionnaire des antiquités grecques et romains*, edited by C. Daremberg and E. Saglio. Vol. 1.1 (1877), 1–50.

Sandbach, F. H. *The Stoics*. New York, 1975.

Sanders, J. M. "The Early Lakonian Dioskouroi Reliefs." In *ΦΙΛΟΛΑΚΩΝ: Lakonian Studies in Honour of Hector Catling*, edited by J. M. Sanders, pp. 205–10. London, 1992.

Sandys, J. E. *A History of Classical Scholarship*. 3rd ed. Vol. 1. New York, 1964.

Scanlon, T. F. "*Virgineum gymnasium*: Spartan Females and Early Greek Athletics." In *The Archaeology of the Olympics: The Olympics and Other Festivals in Antiquity*, edited by W. J. Raschke, pp. 185–216. Madison, 1988.

Schofield, M. *The Stoic Idea of the City*. Cambridge, 1991.

Schröder, B. "Archaïsche Skulpturen aus Lakonien und der Maina." *MDAI(A)* 29 (1904): 21–49.

Schütrumpf, E. "The *Rhetra* of Epitadeus: A Platonist's Fiction." *GRBS* 28 (1987): 441–57.

Schwarz, G. S. "I.G. V¹ 213: The Damonon Stele — A New Restoration for Line 39." *ZPE* 22 (1976): 177–78.

Sealey, R. *A History of the Greek City States, ca. 700–338 B.C.* Berkeley, 1976.

Seiler, F. *Die griechische Tholos: Untersuchungen zur Entwicklung, Typologie und Funktion kunstmäßiger Rundbauten*. Mainz, 1986.

Sergent, B. *L'homosexualité dans la mythologie grecque*. Paris, 1984.

Shimron, B. "The Original Task of the Spartan Patronomoi: A Suggestion." *Eranos* 63 (1965): 155–58.

———. *Late Sparta: The Spartan Revolution 243–146 BC.* Buffalo, 1972.

Siskind, J. "The Invention of Thanksgiving: A Ritual of American Nationality." *Critique of Anthropology* 12 (1992): 167–91.

Skias, A. " Ἀνακοινώσεις." *AE* (1919): 31–48.

Slater, W. J. *Aristophanis Byzantii fragmenta.* Berlin, 1986.

Smyth, H. W. *Greek Grammar.* Revised by G. M. Messing. Cambridge, Mass., 1956.

Sokolowski, F. *Lois sacrées des cités grecques.* École Française d'Athènes, travaux et mémoires, no. 18. Paris, 1969.

Sontheimer, W. "Peritios." *RE* 19.1 (1937): 861.

Souris, G. A. "A New List of the Gerousia of Roman Sparta." *ZPE* 41 (1981): 171–74.

Spawforth, A. J. S. "*Fourmontiana*: IG.V.1. 515: Another Forgery 'From Amyklai.'" *ABSA* 71 (1976): 139–45.

———. "Notes on the Third Century AD in Spartan Epigraphy." *ABSA* 79 (1987): 263–88.

———. "A Severan Statue-Group and an Olympic Festival at Sparta." *ABSA* 81 (1986): 313–32.

———. "Sparta and the Family of Herodes Atticus: A Reconsideration of the Evidence." *ABSA* 75 (1980): 203–20.

Spawforth, A. J. S., and S. Walker. "The World of the Panhellenion I: Athens and Eleusis." *JRS* 75 (1985): 78–104.

———. "The World of the Panhellenion II: Three Dorian Cities." *JRS* 76 (1986): 88–105.

Stalley, R. F. *An Introduction to Plato's Laws.* Oxford, 1983.

Starr, C. G. *Essays on Ancient History.* Edited by A. Ferrill and T. Kelly. Leiden, 1979.

Stein, H., ed. *Herodoti historiae.* Vol. 2. Berlin, 1871.

Stibbe, C. M. "Beobachtungen zur Topographie des antiken Sparta." *BABesch* 64 (1989): 61–99.

———. "Dionysos in Sparta." *BABesch* 66 (1991): 1–44.

———. *Lakonische Vasenmaler des sechsten Jahrhunderts v. Chr.* 2 vols. Studies in Ancient Civilization, n.s., vol. 1. Amsterdam and London, 1972.

Striano, A. "Laconien βιδεος, βιδυ(ι)ος." *Glotta* 68 (1990): 40–47.

Strid, O. *Über Sprache und Stil des Periegeten Pausanias.* Studia Upsaliensia, no. 9. Uppsala, 1976.

Strubbe, J. H. "Gründer kleinasiatischer Städte: Fiktion und Realität." *Ancient Society* 15–17 (1984–86): 253–304.

Swoboda, H. *Die griechischen Volksbeschlüsse: Epigraphische Untersuchungen.* Leipzig, 1890.

———. "Studien zu den griechischen Bünden II." *Klio* 12 (1912): 17–50.

Szanto, E. "Διαβέτης." *RE* 5.1 (1903): 302.

Taïphakos, I. "Δικαιάρχου Τριπολίτικος." *Πελοποννησιακά* 11 (1975): 124–29.

——. "Τὸ Σπαρτιάτικον Πολιτεῦμα εἰς τὴν Ῥωμαίκην Πολιτικὴν Σκέψιν."
    Ἑλλήνικος Λόγος 1 (1973): 428–40.
Talbert, R. J. A. "The Role of the Helots in the Class Struggle at Sparta."
    Historia 38 (1989): 22–40.
Tarn, W. W. Hellenistic Civilisation. 3rd ed. London, 1952.
Tazelaar, C. M. "ΠΑΙΔΕΣ ΚΑΙ ΕΦΗΒΟΙ: Some Notes on the Spartan Stages of
    Youth." Mnemosyne 20 (1967): 127–53.
Tigerstedt, E. N. The Legend of Sparta in Classical Antiquity. 2 vols. Stockholm
    and Uppsala, 1965–74.
Tillyard, H. J. W. "Excavations at Sparta, 1906. 9. — Inscriptions from the
    Artemisium." ABSA 12 (1905–6): 351–93.
Tod, M. N. "The Παιδικὸς Ἀγών at the Festival of Artemis Orthia at Sparta."
    MDAI(A) 29 (1904): 50–56.
Tod, M. N., and A. J. B. Wace. A Catalogue of the Sparta Museum. Oxford, 1906.
Tolkiehn, J. "Lexikographie." RE 12.2 (1925): 2432–82.
Torelli, M. "Da Sparta a Villa Adriana: Le terme dell'Arapissa, il ginnasio del
    Platanistas e il Teatro Marittimo." In Stips Votiva: Papers Presented to C. M.
    Stibbe, edited by M. Gnade, pp. 225–33. Amsterdam, 1991.
Touloumakos, J. "Der Einfluss Roms auf die Staatsform der griechischen
    Stadtstaaten des Festlandes und der Inseln im ersten und zweiten Jhdrt. vor
    Chr." Diss. Göttingen, 1967.
Toynbee, A. J. "The Growth of Sparta." JHS 33 (1913): 246–75.
——. Some Problems of Greek History. London, 1969.
Turner, V. W. "Betwixt and Between: The Liminal Period in rites de passage." In
    Reader in Comparative Religion: An Anthropological Approach, 3rd ed.,
    edited by W. A. Lessa and E. Z. Vogt, pp. 338–47. New York, 1972.
Ueblacker, M. Das Teatro Marittimo in der Villa Hadriana. DAI(R)
    Sonderschriften, no. 5. Mainz, 1985.
van Gennep, A. Les rites de passage. Paris, 1909.
Varinlioğlu, E. "Inschriften von Stratonikeia in Karien." EA 12 (1988): 79–128.
Vermeule, C. C. Greek Sculpture and Roman Taste: The Purpose and Setting of
    Graeco-Roman Art in Italy and the Greek Imperial East. Jerome Lectures,
    12th series. Ann Arbor, 1977.
Vernant, J.-P. "Entre la honte et la gloire: L'identité du jeune spartiate." Μῆτις 2
    (1987): 269–300.
——. Mortals and Immortals: Collected Essays. Edited by F. I. Zeitlin.
    Princeton, 1991.
Vidal-Naquet, P. Le chasseur noir: Formes de pensée et formes de société dans le
    monde grec. Paris, 1981.
von Arnim, J. "Chrysippos (14)." RE 3.2 (1899): 2502–9.
——. Stoicorum veterum fragmenta. 4 vols. Leipzig, 1905–24.
Wace, A. J. B. "Laconia. II — Excavations at Sparta, 1906. 11. — The Roman
    Baths (Arapissa)." ABSA 12 (1905–6): 407–14.
——. "A Spartan Hero Relief." AE (1937): 217–20.
Wade-Gery, H. T. Essays in Greek History. Oxford, 1958.

Wagner, N. "Dioskuren, Jungmannschaften und Doppelkönigtum." *ZDP* 79 (1960): 1–17, 225–47.

Walbank, F. W. *A Historical Commentary on Polybius.* Vol. 1. Oxford, 1957.

Waywell, G. "Excavations on the Acropolis of Ancient Sparta." *Classical Association News* 3 (1990): 14.

Wehrli, F. "Dikaiarchos." *RE* Suppl. 11 (1968): 526–34.

Wellmann, E. "Archytas (3)." *RE* 2.1 (1895): 600–602.

Wernicke, K. "Artemis (2)." *RE* 2.1 (1895): 1336–1440.

West, A. B. *Corinth: Results of the Excavations Conducted by the American School of Classical Studies.* Vol. 8.2, *Latin Inscriptions: 1896–1926.* Cambridge, Mass., 1931.

Wheeldon, M. J. " 'True Stories': The Reception of Historiography in Antiquity." In *History as Text: The Writing of Ancient History,* edited by A. Cameron, pp. 36–63. London, 1989.

Wheeler, E. L. "The *Hoplomachoi* and Vegetius' Spartan Drillmasters." *Chiron* 13 (1983): 1–20.

Wide, S. *Lakonische Kulte.* Leipzig, 1893.

Wilamowitz-Moellendorff, U. von. *Antigonos von Karystos.* Berlin, 1881.

———. *Timotheos: Die Perser.* Leipzig, 1903.

Willetts, R. F. "Herodotos IX 85, 1–2." *Mnemosyne* 33 (1980): 272–77.

Willis, J. "The Makings of a Tribe: Bondei Identities and Histories." *Journal of African History* 33 (1992): 191–208.

Winnefeld, H. *Die Villa des Hadrian bei Tivoli.* JDAI Ergänzungshefte, no. 3. Berlin, 1895.

Woodward, A. M. "Excavations at Sparta, 1908. 5.—Inscriptions." *ABSA* 14 (1907–8): 74–141.

———. "Excavations at Sparta, 1924–1925. 3.—The Inscriptions." *ABSA* 26 (1923–25): 159–239.

———. "Excavations at Sparta, 1926. 2.—The Theatre, 3.—The Inscriptions." *ABSA* 27 (1925–26): 175–209, 210–54.

———. "Excavations at Sparta, 1927. 2.—The Theatre." *ABSA* 28 (1926–27): 3–36.

———. "*Inscriptiones Graecae,* V.1: Some Afterthoughts." *ABSA* 43 (1948): 209–59.

———. Review of *Ancient Sparta,* by K. M. T. Chrimes. *Historia* 1 (1950): 616–34.

———. "Some Notes on the Spartan Σφαιρεῖς." *ABSA* 46 (1951): 191–99.

———. "Sparta and Asia Minor under the Roman Empire." In *Studies Presented to David Moore Robinson,* vol. 2, edited by G. E. Mylonas and D. Raymond, pp. 868–83. St. Louis, 1953.

Woodward, A. M., and L. Robert. "Excavations at Sparta, 1924–1928. Part II. Four Hellenistic Decrees." *ABSA* 29 (1927–28): 57–74.

Wörrle, M. "Neue Inschriftenfunde aus Aizanoi I." *Chiron* 22 (1992): 337–76.

———. *Stadt und Fest im kaiserzeitlichen Kleinasien.* Vestigia Beiträge zur alten Geschichte, no. 39. Munich, 1988.

Wyss, K. *Die Milch im Kultus der Griechen und Römer*. Religionsgeschichtliche
Versuche und Vorarbeiten, vol. 15.2. Giessen, 1914.

Zgusta, L. "Die Rolle des Griechischen im römischen Kaiserreich." In *Die
Sprachen im römischen Reich der Kaiserzeit*, edited by G. Neumann and J.
Untermann, pp. 121–46. Beihefte der Bonner Jahrbücher, no. 40. Cologne,
1980.

Ziebarth, E. *Aus dem griechischen Schulwesen: Eudemos von Milet und
Verwandtes*. 2nd ed. Leipzig and Berlin, 1914 (repr. 1971).

Ziehen, L. "Sparta (Kulte)." *RE* 3A.2 (1929): 1453–1525.

INDEX

Achaean League, 7–9, 168
Achilles, 56, 62
Aemilius Paullus, 10
Africa, 143, 144–45
Agathoergoi, 130
Age, 35–36, 37
Age categories, 64–65, 68, 93, 109
Age grades, 29, 63. See also Agōgē: phases of; names of specific age grades
Agelarchēs, 108
Agelē, 107–9. See also Boua
Agis IV, 12–13, 114
Agōgē: as tourist attraction, 5, 49; study of, 7, 31–32; as "Laconian customs," 13, 83; phases of, 13–14, 135; as "Lycurgan customs," 44, 46, 83; rites of passage and, 61, 74; as ephebate, 76; as source for Archaic period, 80; as patrios agōgē, 83, 114; as name for Spartan education, 113–14; foundation of, 146. See also Archaism; Hunting
Agōgē (Classical phase), 116–42; end of, 12–13; age categories in, 31, 117; administration of, 120–21; contests of, 126, 131. See also Cheese-stealing ritual; Hebōntes; Paides; Paidiskoi
Agōgē (Hellenistic phase), 107–14; end of, 9, 102; duration of, 12; age grades in, 29–30, 38–39, 109; and Roman phase, 98; curriculum of, 110; contests of, 110–11. See also Cleomenes III; Sphaerus of Borysthenes; names of specific age grades
Agōgē (Roman phase), 43–97; beginning of, 9–11; age grades in, 38–39; egalitarianism in, 42; administration of, 43–48; reorganization of, 64; Spartan identity and, 69, 82–83, 95, 131; foreigners in, 86; Hellenistic phase and, 98. See also Archaism; Laconian dialect; names of specific age grades
Agōn dia pantōn, 55
Agora (at Sparta), 68
Akmazontes, 68, 118, 132
Alcman, 68
Alexander the Great, 94–95
Alopecus, 71, 122
Amblada, 84
Amyclae: as ōba, 162–69; inhabitants of, in agōgē, 163, 168, 169; officials of, 164; Sparta and, 165, 166, 168, 169
Andania, 123
Antigonus Doson, 12, 168
Apodeixeis, 40, 64
Apollo, 64–65, 162–63. See also Carnea; Gymnopaediae; Hyacinthia
Apothetae, 25
Archaism, 69, 83–84; at Sparta, 43, 46, 49, 69, 87–94; Classical Greece and, 94–95. See also Laconian dialect
Aristindēs, 60
Aristophanes of Byzantium, 20, 29, 89
Aristotle, 17–18, 121, 125
Arkaloi (ōba of), 166
Artemis, 52, 76, 127–28, 135; identification with Orthia, 136
Artemis Orthia, 11, 50, 54, 76, 111; priestess of, 42, 73, 75; cult image of, 71, 75, 80, 122; "Laconian rider" and, 142. See also Archaism; Cheese-stealing ritual; Endurance contest; Sickles
Artemis Orthia, sanctuary of: location of, 6, 50, 61, 62; altar at, 50, 70, 71, 72–73; seating complex at, 61, 62; earliest evidence for worship at, 79; renovation of, 136, 146. See also

Archaism; Cheese-stealing ritual;
Endurance contest; Sickles
Athens: ephebes at, 63, 110, 123, 141,
146; Panhellenion at, 84; archonship at, 87; Thesea at, 109; age of
full citizenship at, 118; Thesmophoria at, 124; *arktoi* at, 142
Athletic festivals. *See* Commodea; Euryclea; Hyacinthia; Leonidea;
Urania
Athletics, 46, 110

Ball games, 59–63; Spartan invention
of, 6; described by Lucian, 39; as
apodeixis, 40; byes in, 60; identification of, 60–61; in Hellenistic period, 110–11; in Classical period,
131
Ballplayers (*sphaireis*), 29, 43, 87, 89;
status of, 38–40, 42, 59; teams of,
40, 63; team leaders of 42–43
Biduoi, 39, 58, 59, 60, 121; duties of,
45–46
Bōmonikēs, 26, 77–78, 80, 87, 89
Boua, 38, 41, 55, 85; *phulē* and, 42–
43; in ball games, 42–43, 59–60;
leader of, 43; size of, 63; *agelē* and,
108, 109. See also *Agelē*; *Ilē*; *Ōba*
Bouagos, 38, 67, 91, 108, 109; age of,
41–42; in ball games, 42–43; in
boys' contests, 55
Boulē: Spartan, 45
Boys' contests: *mōa*, 51, 53, 54, 110–
11; *keloia*, 51–52, 53, 54, 55; *kaththēratorion*, 52–53, 54, 55; *deros*,
53, 54; *eubalkēs*, 53, 54; *kunagetas*,
53–54; order of, 54–55; victories *to
paidikon* in, 55, 63, 64. *See also*
Laconian dialect

Callimachus, 119
Caracalla, 94–95
Carnea, 65, 66–67, 131
Castor. *See* Dioscuri
Cato the Elder, 81

Charax, A. Claudius, 86
Cheese-stealing ritual, 79, 82, 111,
123, 126–29
Chios, 109
Chlamus (cloak), 141
Choruses. *See* Gymnopaediae: cho-
ruses at; Hyacinthia: choruses at
Chreia (utility), 105
Chrysippus, 101, 102
Cibyra, 84
Cicero, 6, 70, 86; on battle at
Platanistas, 56; on endurance con-
test, 70, 73, 111; on Stoic definition
of courage, 112
Cinadon, 129–30
Cleanthes, 101, 102
Cleomenes III, 11–12, 79, 101, 114,
168; *patronomos* and, 11, 87; Neo-
politae and, 162, 163. *See also*
Sphaerus of Borysthenes
Clothing: of ephebes, 32–34, 121, 123
Commodea, 64, 85
Common messes: in reforms of
Cleomenes III, 11, 12; in Classical
period, 77, 125, 130–31; in Stoic
texts, 99, 107
Crates the Cynic, 99, 112
Critias, 17, 86, 95
Cynicism, 99, 100
Cynooureis, 40, 46, 58, 60; endurance
contest and, 72, 74; as constituent
community of Sparta, 164
Cyrene, 85–86

Damonon, 117
Demetrius of Scepsis, 66
Deros. See Boys' contests: *deros*
Diabetēs, 46, 60
Diaita, 116, 147
Diana of Nemi, 80–81. *See also* En-
durance contest: foundation myths
of
Dicaearchus, 19
Dionysius of Halicarnassus, 81
Dionysus: "daughters of," 45–46

Dioscuri, 138–42, 163; Indo-European elements of, 15, 141; as patrons of Sparta, 138–39; *hippeis* as, 141–42; Artemis Orthia and, 142. See also *Hippeis*

Dogmatographoi, 164

Dromos, 56, 138

Eirenes, 20, 24; in Roman period, 29, 64, 75–76, 78; in Hellenistic period, 31, 39, 109; age of, 35–37, 42; in ball games, 42–43; in Classical period, 118–19. See also Ballplayers; Endurance contest; *Hēbōntes*

Ek paidōn, 36

Eleutheria games, 82

Endurance contest (*ho tēs karterias agōn*), 6, 23, 26, 71–78; date held, 71; participants in, 72, 75–76; death in, 73–74; as rite of passage, 74–75, 77; foundation myths of, 74–75, 78–83; earliest evidence for, 79, 111; in Hellenistic period, 111–13

Enkuklios paideia, 101, 105

Enyalius, 56, 138

Epaikla, 130

Epaminondas, 168

Ephebate, 61, 76, 110, 112–13; at Athens, 63, 146; at Thuria, 118–19

Ephēbos, 36, 68, 75–76, 119. See also Age categories; *Sunephēbos*

Ephoreia: as cultural center, 19

Ephors, 11, 12, 19, 81, 121; at Amyclae, 164

Epimeletai. See *Patronomos*: deputies of

Equals, 130, 133

Erastēs, 121, 125, 126, 132. See also Pederasty

Erōmenos, 125. See also Pederasty

"Eternal" magistracy, 47

Eubalkēs. See Boys' contests: *eubalkēs*

Euryclea, 64

Eurycles, C. Julius, 169

Euryclids, 82

Ex ephēbōn, 36, 39, 118

Food: contribution of, 16, 17–18, 104, 122, 134; theft of, 18, 24, 71, 123; gathering of, 23, 42. See also Cheese-stealing ritual; Common messes

Foxes, 122. See also *Phouaxir*

Galen, 104

Geronthrae, 89, 118

Gerousia, 8, 11, 45, 81, 117

Girls: in *agōgē*, 45–46

Gregory Nazienzus, 71

Gymnasiarch, 44

Gymnasium, 47, 57

Gymnopaediae, 6, 49, 65, 69, 113; choruses at, 67–69, 131; bachelors barred from, 132

Gytheum, 89

Hadrian, 84, 85–86

Hatropampaides, 29, 31, 39, 93

Hēbōntes, 117–18, 121, 129–32. See also *Eirenes*

Heilōtai. See Helots

Helen, 139, 141, 142

Hellanicus, 65

Helots, 7, 15–16

Heracles: *sphaireis* and, 39, 43, 62; statue of, at Platanistas, 56, 57; herms of, at theater, 62; Dioscuri and, 138

Herillus (Stoic philosopher), 101

Hermes, 138

Herodes Atticus, 86

Herodotus, 14–16, 95

Herodotus, gloss on: age grades in, 20, 32, 35, 36, 102; and Aristophanes of Byzantium, 29; and Plutarch's *Lycurgus*, 38. See also *names of specific age grades*

Hesychius, 26, 89; *aristindēs* in, 60; *staphulodromoi* in, 67; *agelē* in, 108; *prōtirai* in, 119

Hieronikai, 85
Hippagretai, 121, 129
Hipparchēs, 47
Hippeis, 121, 129. See also *Koroi*
Homoioi. See Equals
Homosexuality. *See* Pederasty
Horace, 71
Hormē (impulse), 106
Hunting, 52–54, 76–77
Hupomeiones. See Inferiors
Hyacinthia, 49, 131, 166; choruses at, 65–66
Hyginus, 25, 80–81

Ilē, 107, 108, 120, 121, 126
Inferiors, 133
Inscriptions: as evidence for *agōgē*, 20, 27, 28; as evidence for boys' contests, 51–55; as evidence for endurance contest, 71; Laconian dialect in, 87–89. *See also* Laconian dialect
Iphigeneia, 80
Irenes, 14, 119, 120. See also *Eirenes*

Jonathan (high priest of Maccabees), 11

Karteria (endurance), 112, 113
Kasen, 43, 67
Kaththēratorion. See Boys' contests: *kaththēratorion*
Keloia. See Boys' contests: *keloia*
Koroi, 139–42
Krupteia, 113, 131–32
Kunagetas. See Boys' contests: *kunagetas*
Kursanioi, 117

Laconian dialect, 87–92, 93; in inscriptions, 87–89; characteristics of, 90; *koinē* and, 91–92; as official language of *agōgē*, 92
Laconian Institutions, 21–23; description of *agōgē* in, 18; as source for Plutarch, 21, 22, 24, 33–34; date

compiled, 22; sources of, 22, 102–7; Stoic elements in, 104–6; education in, 106; Artemis Orthia in, 136
League of Free Laconians (League of Lacedaemonians), 89, 165, 168
Leonidas, 94, 96
Leonidea, 45, 64, 82
Libanius, 70, 77, 86, 195 (n. 6)
Limnae (district of Sparta), 50, 61
Limnaeis, 40, 58, 60, 72, 74
Literacy, 125
Livy, 10
Lochagos, 47–48
Lochos, 47–48, 166–67; "of Pitane," 48, 95, 167
Lucian, 56, 60, 73, 96; *Anacharsis* of, 25–26, 39
Lycosura, 123
Lycurgus, 6, 22, 96, 101, 124; as founder of endurance contest, 25, 40, 75, 82, 83; as founder of ephebic contests, 49; statue of, at Platanistas, 56, 57, 62; statue of, in theater, 62; title "new Lycurgus" and, 62; as totemic figure, 78, 80; in Herillus' *The Lawgiver*, 101
Lydians, parade of, 75, 81, 129. *See also* Cheese-stealing ritual; Endurance contest
Lysander, 95, 96, 134

Marcus Aurelius, 94
Marriage, 132
Masks, 136–37
Mastigophoroi, 120, 131
Meirakion, 32–33, 35
Melleirenes, 24; in Roman period, 29, 35–37, 64; in Hellenistic period, 39, 109, 110; status of, 76, 126, 127. *See also* Age grades
Mellephēboi, 110
Mesoatae, 40, 60; Platanistas battle and, 58, 60; endurance contest and, 72, 74; names of *lochoi* and, 167. See also *Lochos*

Mikizomenoi, 29, 31, 93, 109. *See also* Age grades

Mikkichizomenoi, 29, 31, 55, 63–64; form of, 91, 93; status of, 127. *See also* Age grades

Mōa. See Boys' contests: *mōa*

Mothax, 134

Music, 17, 65–66, 106, 110, 138. *See also* Boys' contests: *keloia*; Boys' contests: *mōa*

Nabis, 7–8, 165

Neaniskarchēs. See Neoi

Neaniskoi, 66. *See also Neoi*

Neoi, 47, 48, 66–67

Neopolitae, 40, 58, 60, 72, 162

Nomophulakes, 43

Ōba: as ball team, 40, 41, 42–43, 59–60; as constituent community, 40, 80, 120, 165–66

Oenoanda, 66, 85

Orestes, 80

Orthia. *See* Artemis Orthia

Othryadas, 95–96

Ovid, 81

Paides: as age grade, 31, 39, 93, 109; in endurance contest, 75–76; as age category, 93, 109; in Classical period, 126–27, 132. *See also* Age categories; Age grades

Paidikos agōn. See Boys' contests

Paidiskoi, 117, 125–29; in cheese-stealing ritual, 126

Paidonomos, 117, 120–21, 126, 131, 132

Pallēkes, 110

Pampaides, 93, 109

Panhellenion, 84, 90

Partheniae, 167

Parthians, 94

Patronomos: Cleomenes III and, 11, 87; in dating formula, 29; deputies of, 44; duties of, 44–45; former,

and Leonidea, 45; foreigners as, 86–87; at Amyclae, 165

Pausanias, 81, 82

Pausanias (periegete): on *agōgē*, 6, 20, 25; on restoration of constitution, 10; on endurance contest, 25, 73, 80; on ballplayers, 39; on *ōbai*, 40, 60, 80; on Platanistas, 56–57; on public seal, 96; on false Dioscuri, 141

Pederasty, 35, 100, 124

Perioeci (*perioikoi*), 7–8, 165

Persaeus (Stoic philosopher), 99, 101, 107

Persian Stoa, 6

Phidition/Philition. See Common messes

Philopoemen, 8–9, 101

Philostratus, 26, 73

Phoebeum, 56, 62

Phoenicians, 80

Photius, 26

Phouaxir, 71, 74

Phulē: as civic tribe, 40, 41; as ephebic division, 40–41, 42, 43, 58, 67. *See also Agelē*

Phylarchus, 114

Piloi, 141

Pitanatae, 40, 58, 60, 64, 163; endurance contest and, 72, 74

Plataea, 14, 15, 81, 82

Platanistas: battle of ephebes at, 25, 45, 55–59; *biduoi* and, 45, 58; location of, 56–57, 62; *euripos* of, 57; Hadrian's villa and, 57; in Hellenistic period, 111; Dioscuri and, 138

Plato, 19; *Laws*, 37–38, 79, 82, 111, 128

Plutarch: on Agis IV, 13; on origin of endurance contest, 25, 79, 81–82; on Cleomenes III, 134–35

Plutarch, *Life of Lycurgus*: age grades in, 17, 31, 32–36; description of *agōgē* in, 20, 23–25; sources of, 23; importance to study of *agōgē*, 32;

Laconian Constitution of Xenophon and, 34–35; description of *trichoria* in, 68–69; description of endurance contest in, 73, 82; *agelai* in, 107–9

Pollux (deity). *See* Dioscuri

Pollux (lexicographer), 61

Polybius, 9, 13, 81, 168

Polydorus, 96

Posidonius, 81

Pratopampaides, 31, 39, 93. *See also* Age grades

Presbus (captain of ball team), 42–43, 58

Priesthood, 14

Promikizomenoi, 29, 31, 32, 93, 109

Propaides, 31, 39, 93, 109

Propertius, 81

Pratopampaides, 29, 31

Prōteirai/Prōteirenes, 118, 119

Pyrrhus, 13

Rhōbidas: in Hellenistic period, 29, 31, 37, 109; age of, 32–35; abandonment of, 93; *paidiskos* and, 117. *See also Paidiskoi*

Rites of passage, 61, 75. *See also* Endurance contest

Rome, 8, 10–11

Sabines, 81

Selge, 84

Sestos, 113

Sickles: dedications of, 6, 70, 83, 89; as prizes, 28, 55; used in murder, 133

Sideunai, 117. *See also Paidiskoi*

Solon, 26

Sosibius, 65, 68, 69

Sparta: as *civitas libera*, 7, 10; later constitution of, 9–11; Rome's debt to, 81; "colonies" of, 84–85; cultural influence of, 84–86; visitors to, 86; in declamations, 95; in sixth century, 137

Spartiatai: contest of, 85

Sphaerus of Borysthenes: Cleomenes III and, 11, 12, 99, 101, 102; books on Spartan constitution of, 98, 99; Zeno and, 99, 101, 102; as inventor of *agōgē*, 101–2, 114; as source for *Laconian Institutions*, 102–7, 108; age grades and, 109, 118, 120, 127; endurance contest and, 111; Stoic definitions of, 112

Sphaireis. See Ballplayers

Staphulodromoi, 66–67, 131

Stibades, 124

Stoicism: early teachings of, 99; views of, on *aretē*, 100; views of, on Sparta, 100–101; elements of, in *Laconian Institutions*, 104–6; elements of, in endurance contest, 112, 113. *See also* Herillus; Persaeus; Sphaerus of Borysthenes; Zeno of Citium

Strabo, scholion of: age grades in, 20, 29, 31, 32; Aristophanes of Byzantium and, 29; date of, 29; ages of *melleirenes/eirenes* in, 35–37; Plutarch's *Lycurgus* and, 38; Hellenistic *agōgē* and, 102. *See also Ephēbos*

Stratēgos (of League of Free Laconians), 165, 168

Street gangs, 146

Sumpatronomoi, 44

Sunarchia, 45

Sunarchoi, 44

Sunephēbos, 41, 43, 63, 67, 75

Sungeneia, 84

Suntrophoi, 134–35

Synnada, 84

Teles the Cynic, 12, 114, 118

Teos, 109

Terpander, 65

Tertullian, 71

Thales, 68

Theater: as site of ball games, 6, 39,

61–62, 76; location of, 56, 59, 61–
62; herms of Heracles in, 62; in-
scriptions in, 62; statue of Lycurgus
in, 62; precursor of, 68
Theatron, 68
Thermopylae, 82
Theseus, 141–42
Threptoi, 25
Thucydides, 14, 95
Thyreatis, 94
Timotheus (fifth-century poet), 92
Tralles, 85
Trichoria, 68–69
Trietirēs, 31, 118–19. See also *Eirenes*
Tritirenes/Triteirenes, 118, 119. See
also *Eirenes*
Trophimoi, 134

Urania, 64

Water: at festival of Artemis, 76–77

Xanthippus, 13
Xenophon: on hunting, 52; *Hellenica*,
69, 133, 167; *Cyropaedia*, 101,
117, 133
Xenophon, *Laconian Constitution*:
date of, 6, 16; on Spartan education, 18, 34, 112, 116–18, 120–26;
Plutarch's *Life of Lycurgus* and, 34;
on cheese-stealing ritual, 78, 82; on
youths' diet, 104, 122; on youths'
teams, 107; on *hippeis*, 129; on *hēbōntes*, 129, 132; on failure in Spartan education, 133; nostalgia of,
135. *See also* Cheese-stealing ritual;
Hēbōntes; *Hippeis*; *Paides*;
Paidiskoi

Zeno of Citium, 99–100, 101, 105–6,
112
Zōmos (black broth), 130